# VEDANTA
# FOR THE
# WESTERN WORLD

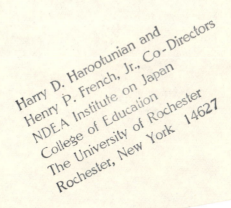

# *VEDANTA*

## FOR THE

# WESTERN WORLD

*Edited, and with an Introduction,*

*by*

*Christopher Isherwood*

THE VIKING PRESS
NEW YORK

# CONTENTS

# Contents

# Contents

# VEDANTA
## FOR THE
## WESTERN WORLD

# INTRODUCTION

FIRST OF ALL, WHAT IS VEDANTA?

Vedanta is the philosophy of the Vedas, those Indian scriptures which are the most ancient religious writings now known to the world. More generally speaking, the term "Vedanta" covers not only the Vedas themselves but the whole body of literature which explains, elaborates and comments upon their teaching, right down to the present day. The Bhagavad-Gita and the works of Shankara belong to Vedanta: so do many of the articles in this volume.

Vedanta is often, but less correctly, called "Hinduism"; a foreign word. The inhabitants of India were described by the Persians as Hindus, because they lived on the other side of the River Sindhu (the Indus). The Persians, apparently, could not manage the sound of the letter S.

In India today, as elsewhere, there are hundreds of sects. Vedanta Philosophy is the basis of them all. Indeed, in its simplest form, it may be regarded as a statement of the Philosophia Perennis, the least common denominator of all religious belief, which is defined by Aldous Huxley in his article, "The Minimum Working Hypothesis."

Reduced to its elements, Vedanta Philosophy consists of three propositions. First, that Man's real nature is divine. Second, that the aim of human life is to realize this divine nature. Third, that all religions are essentially in agreement. We shall examine each of these in turn.

"Man's real nature is divine": what does this actually mean? Vedanta asserts that the universe which is perceived by our senses is only an appearance. It is not what it seems. Here, the modern scientist will, of course, agree. Who would ever suppose, in looking at a flower, a rock and a waterfall,

1

that each was merely a different arrangement of identical units? The universe is other than its outward aspect. Moreover, this outward aspect is subject to perpetual change. The hills, said Tennyson, are shadows.

Vedanta goes on to assert that, beneath this appearance, this flux, there is an essential, unchanging Reality, which it calls Brahman, the Godhead. Brahman is Existence itself, Consciousness itself. Brahman is also said to be that almost indefinable quality which is called in the Sanskrit language "Ananda," and in the Christian Bible . . . "the peace of God, which passeth all understanding . . ." "Ananda" may be translated not only as "peace" but also as "bliss"; since this absolute peace, when it is known beneath all flux, appearance and unrest, must give the only permanent kind of happiness.

At the mention of Brahman, the scientist will become sceptical. And rightly so; for none of his apparatus is capable of detecting the existence of this fundamental Reality. Vedanta will reply that this proves nothing, either way. The scientist cannot possibly detect Brahman, because scientific analysis depends, necessarily, upon the evidence of the five senses, and Brahman is beyond all sense-perception. Why, it will be asked, should we believe with Vedanta instead of doubting with the scientist? But the answer to this question must be delayed for a moment, until we begin to consider the nature of the mystical experience.

Let us assume, in the meanwhile, that Brahman does exist. If there is indeed an essential Reality, a Godhead, in the universe, then it follows that this Reality must be omnipresent. It must be within each one of us; within every creature and object. It does not matter exactly what we mean by "within": that is a point for theologians to argue. Let us say simply, at the risk of offending the exponents of semantics, that Brahman is our real, essential nature. When speaking of Brahman-within-the-creature, Vedanta uses, for convenience, another term, "the Atman." The Atman, in Christian terminology, is God Immanent; Brahman is God Transcendent. Atman and Brahman are one.

And now, with the second of the Vedanta propositions, we come to most of our difficulties. The aim of human life, we are told, is to realize the Atman, our essential nature, and hence our identity with the one, underlying Reality.

Why? How? Who says so? How does he know?

In the first place, why? The answer to this question is by no means evident to the majority of people alive on earth today. Human life has many apparent aims: we can find them stated in the headlines and advertisements of any newspaper. Win the war. Win the peace. Get your man. Get a home. Get a better job. Become beautiful. Become strong. Become educated. Such are our objectives. And millions strive for them, with the greatest courage and devotion, year after year.

To seek to realize my essential nature is to admit that I am dissatisfied with my nature as it is at present. It is to admit that I am dissatisfied with the kind of life I am leading now. But am I, honestly? Oh yes, we admit our faults. We admit that the political and economic condition of the world leaves much to be desired. But we are optimistic. We believe in patching up and muddling through. We are prepared to take the rough with the smooth. We have our moments of triumph, we enjoy periods of vivid happiness; and for these we are ready to pay, if we must, with spells of disappointment, boredom, regret. On the whole, the majority of us are content. The great mass of normally healthy, well-adjusted men and women, absorbed in their families and their jobs, will protest: "Leave us alone. We are well enough off as we are."

"Are you? We doubt it," say Buddha, Jesus, Shankara, Shakespeare and Tolstoy. And they proceed to point out, in their different languages and figures of speech, that death brings an end to all desire, that worldly wealth is a house built upon the sand, that the beautiful body is a decaying bag of filth, that ambition will be pricked like an inflated bladder, that our bustling activity resembles the antics of patients in a madhouse. Their words depress us: for the truth is obvious, if we consider it. But we do not wish to consider it. There is no time, we say. We are in the midst of whatever we are doing. Action is begetting action. To pause, to philosophize, seems feeble, cowardly, and even downright wicked. So we dismiss our prophets as pessimists, and their teaching as other worldly defeatism. We hurry away with a sigh, resolved to have our fun while we can, or, at any rate, to get on with the next job.

But suppose I really am dissatisfied with my life and myself. Suppose I have actually attained some of the world's advertised objectives, and found beyond them an emptiness, a teasing question which I cannot answer. I am confronted with Life's subtlest riddle: the riddle of human boredom. In my desperation, I am ready to assume, provisionally, that this Atman, this essential nature, does exist within me, and does offer me a lasting strength, wisdom, peace and happiness. How am I to realize this nature? How am I to enjoy it?

The answer is given, unanimously, by all the teachers and prophets. It is very disconcerting:

"By ceasing to be yourself."

"What do you mean? That's nonsense. How can I stop being myself? I'm Christopher Isherwood, or I'm nothing."

"You are the Atman."

"Then why do I think I'm myself?"

"Because of your ignorance. Christopher Isherwood is only an appearance, a part of the apparent universe. He is a constellation of desires and impulses. He reflects his environment. He repeats what he has been taught. He mimics the social behaviour of his community. He copies gestures like a monkey and intonations like a parrot. All his actions are conditioned by those around him, however eccentric and individual he may seem to be. He is subject to suggestion, climate, disease and the influence of drugs. He is changing all the time. He has no essential reality."

"How did this ignorance start? What caused it?"

Here, the prophets will give slightly different answers. Buddha will refuse to discuss the question at all, saying that it is not important. When the house is burning, does it matter if the man who fired it had red hair? It is only necessary that we should realize that the house *is* burning. Or, to put it more mildly, that we should be dissatisfied with our present condition and ready to do something about it.

Christian theology will speak of Original Sin, and postulate a fall of Man from consciousness of his divine nature. Vedanta does not accept this idea. It conceives of a universe coexistent with Brahman, equally beginningless and endless. Even if this universe should apparently be destroyed, it will only have gone back into a kind of seed-state, a phase of potentiality, from which, in due time, it will re-emerge. Vedanta teaches that the stuff of this universe is an effect or power of Brahman. It stands to Brahman in the same relation as heat to fire. They are inseparable. Yet Brahman does not intervene in the world's affairs. The question "why does God permit evil?" is, to a Vedantist, as meaningless as "why does God permit good?" The fire burns one man and warms another, and is neither kind nor cruel.

An inhuman philosophy? Certainly. Brahman is not human. We must beware of thinking about the Reality in relative terms. It is not simply a giant person. It has nothing to do with our shifting standards of good and evil, pleasure, unhappiness, right and wrong.

"Very well: we'll forget about the cause of my ignorance. Now how do I stop being Christopher Isherwood?"

"By ceasing to believe that you are. What is this belief? Egotism, nothing else: an egotism which is asserted and reinforced by hundreds of your daily actions. Every time you desire, or fear, or hate; every time you boast or indulge your vanity; every time you struggle to get something for yourself, you are really asserting: 'I am a separate, unique individual. I stand apart from everything else in this universe.' But you don't, you know. The scientist will agree with me that you don't. Every living creature and every object are interrelated, biologically, psychologically, physically, politically, economically. They are all of a piece."

"So I merely have to stop believing I'm an individual?"

"It isn't so easy. First, you must start acting as though you had ceased to believe it. Try to overcome this possessive attitude toward your actions. Stop taking credit for your successes. Stop bemoaning your failures, and making excuses for them. Stop worrying so much about results. Just do the best you can. Work for the work's sake. Think of your body, if you like, as an instrument."

"Whose instrument?"

"The instrument of the Atman."

"Why should I work for the Atman? It doesn't need my help."

"There is no question of helping the Atman. All work done in this spirit is symbolic, like ritual. It becomes a form of worship."

"How dull that sounds! Where's the inducement? What's the motive?"

"Love."

"You mean, I should love the Atman? How can I?"

"You love Christopher Isherwood, don't you?"

"Yes, I suppose so. Most of the time. When I don't hate him."

"Then you ought to love your real Self much more. The Atman is perfect. Christopher Isherwood isn't."

"But I know him. I've never seen the Atman. I'm not even sure it exists."

"Try to feel that it exists. Think about it. Pray to it. Meditate on it. Know that you are it."

"You mean, hypnotize myself?"

"If it's nothing but auto-hypnosis, you'll soon find out. Hypnosis wouldn't give you any lasting results. It wouldn't give you the peace and understanding you are looking for. It wouldn't transform your character. Neither would alcohol, for that matter, or any other drug. I'm only asking you to try it. This is a matter for personal experiment."

"All right. What else am I to do?"

"Judge every thought and every action from this standpoint: 'Does it make me freer, less egotistic, more aware of the Reality; or does it attach me more tightly to the illusion of individual separateness?' You'll find, in practice, that certain thoughts and actions obstruct your progress. Give them up. Other thoughts and actions will assist your progress. Cultivate them."

"Tell me some."

"Chastity, truthfulness, charity toward others."

"Chastity? I'm to give up sex?"

"You'll find you have to, sooner or later."

"Why? It's not wrong."

"I never said it was. But what does it lead to? Attachment to this world of appearance. An added conviction that you are Christopher Isherwood, not the Atman."

"Oh, you just hate the world, that's all!"

"It's you who hate the world, in your heart of hearts. You are bound to hate it, because you know only its appearance, and its appearance seems to end in death. But I see the Reality within the appearance. I see the world within Reality. And I love it as I love the Reality itself."

"I must say, all this sounds very selfish. I'm to spend the rest of my life trying to know my real nature. Thinking about myself, in fact. What about my neighbours? Am I to forget them altogether? What about social service? What about my duty to the community?"

"As soon as you start thinking and acting in the way I have shown you, your life will be nothing but social service. You will be more available to your neighbours than ever before, because you will be less egotistic. You will do your duty to the community far better, because your motives will be less mixed with vanity and the desire for power and self-advertisement. You think you love some of your neighbours now. You cannot dream how you will love them all, when you begin to see the Reality within each human being, and to understand his absolute identity with yourself. What is it that your neighbour needs most? Isn't it just that reassurance, that knowledge and peace which are the objects of your search? How can you transmit them to others, until you have won them for yourself? By helping yourself, you are helping mankind. By helping mankind, you are helping yourself. That's the law of all spiritual progress."

"Provided, of course, that the Reality exists."

"The Reality does exist."

"How do you know?"

"Because I have experienced it."

"Why should I believe you?"

"Because you can experience it for yourself."

There we have it, our greatest difficulty. There the scientist cannot help us. He only shrugs his shoulders and says "perhaps." The prophet tells us that he has seen God, and we have each of us to make up our minds whether to believe him or not. (I have discussed this question more fully in my article: "Hypothesis and Belief.")

In order to be able to decide if the prophet is telling the truth or lying, we shall have to investigate the mystical experience for ourselves. This can be done in two ways: from the outside, by studying the biographies and writings of the saints; and from the inside, by following the instructions they have given us. To follow these instructions is to lead what Christians call "the unitive life." In Sanskrit, the word for this unitive life is "Yoga," from which is derived our English word "yoke," i.e., union. Yoga is the technique of union with the Atman. The various stages of Yoga are outlined in several of Swami Prabhavananda's articles.

However we may choose to explain it, the historical fact remains that thousands of men and women, belonging to every century, country and social class, have attempted, with apparent success, to follow this unitive way of life. According to the evidence of their contemporaries, they have undergone that slow, strange transformation, that inner process of readjustment, which ends in what is called sainthood. Hundreds of them, Christian, Vedantist, Buddhist, Taoist, Sufi and Jew, have left records of their experience; and these records show remarkable similarity. Remarkable, because the saints themselves are so very different. Some are devotional in the extreme: they worship the Reality in human form, a Krishna, a Rama, a Christ, with ecstasies of love. Some meditate on the impersonal Brahman, with the seeming coldness of pure discrimination, bowing before no altar or image. Some have visions. Some have powers over material nature, and can heal the sick. Some live in caves or cells: some in crowded cities. Some are great orators: some refuse to utter a word. Some are laughed at and believed to be mad: some are respected for their qualities of clear judgment and sanity. Some are martyred.

It is upon the nature of the final mystical experience that all agree. What is this experience? It seems that when the ego-sense has, through constant self-discipline, grown very weak, there comes a moment (it may be the moment of death) at which the presence of the essential nature is no longer concealed. The saint becomes aware that the Atman actually does exist. Further, he experiences the nature of the Atman as his own nature. He knows he is nothing but Reality. This

is what Christian writers call "the mystic union" and Vedantists "samadhi."

We have been told that the Reality is beyond sense-perception. How, then, can it be experienced? This is a very difficult question. Perhaps it cannot be answered in words.
Samadhi is said to be a fourth kind of consciousness: it is beyond the states of waking, dreaming and dreamless sleep.
Those who have witnessed it as an external phenomenon
report that the experiencer appeared to have fallen into a
kind of trance. The hair of the head and body stood erect.
The half-closed eyes became fixed. Sometimes there was an
astonishing loss of weight, or even levitation of the body
from the ground. But these are mere symptoms, and tell us
nothing. There is only one way to find out what samadhi is
like: you must have it yourself.

Vedanta's third proposition, that all religions are essentially in agreement, needs less discussion. But it is psychologically very important. Being a philosophy rather than a creed,
Vedanta is not sectarian and therefore not exclusive. It appeals, as it were, over the heads of the sectarians and dogma-
ists, to the practising mystics of all religions. Also, by classifying the sects themselves as different paths of Yoga leading
to the same goal, it seeks to establish a sort of religious syn-
thesis. Tolerance is, in any case, natural to the Indian temperament. But, unfortunately, it cannot be claimed that this
unifying effort has, so far, been very successful. Vedanta may
accept Christ as the Son of God: it may acknowledge Allah.
But Christians and Mohammedans persist in regarding their
respective religions as the only true faith. Christian and Sufi
mystics have been compelled, by the very nature of their
mystical experience, to take a more liberal attitude. In consequence, they have often been suspected of heresy and sometimes actually condemned by their co-religionists.

Nor does the Vedantist, in expressing his reverence for
Allah and Christ, mean quite what orthodox Mohammedans
and Christians would like him to mean. Vedanta, as I have
said already, offers a philosophical basis to all sects. It can do
this precisely because it is fundamentally monistic; because
it teaches that there is one Reality and nothing else. "Thou
art That." The creature is the Atman: the Atman is Brah-

man. The creature, in his ignorance, may think that he worships the creator. Very well: let him think that. It is a necessary stage in spiritual progress. The ultimate truth cannot be apprehended all at once. The Atman must be personified at first, if it is to be loved and realized; otherwise it will remain a mere intellectual abstraction. The true monist never disdains dualism. But it is very hard for the rigid dualist to accept monism. St. Ignatius Loyola was dismayed when the vision of his beloved Jesus faded into the impersonal, all-embracing Reality.

The Indian mind, because it is fundamentally monistic, has no difficulty in believing that the one impersonal Brahman may have an infinite number of personal aspects. As many, indeed, as there are worshippers; since an aspect is literally a view, and each traveller may see a different angle of a mountain. These aspects are represented in Indian art, sculpture and literature with such a wealth of form and attribute that the Western foreigner, whose religious mentality is dualistic, is apt to mistake them for gods and goddesses in the pagan sense, and to exclaim indignantly that this is polytheism. Hence, much misunderstanding arises.

According to Vedanta, the Reality may also take human form and enter the world, from time to time. Why it should do this is a mystery which no amount of philosophical analysis can solve. It is the paradox which we call Grace, expressed in its most startling terms. The Reality is manifested, occasionally, amidst the temporal phenomena. Brahman *does,* after all, sometimes intervene. As Sri Krishna says in the Gita:

> *"In every age I come back*
> *To deliver the holy,*
> *To destroy the sin of the sinner,*
> *To establish righteousness."*

The Vedantist calls such incarnations of the Reality "avatars." He recognizes Rama, Krishna, Buddha and Christ as avatars, along with several others, and believes that there will be many more. But the Christian, convinced of the uniqueness of Christ as a spiritual phenomenon, can hardly be expected to subscribe to this belief.

What follows samadhi? What happens to the few who attain it, and to the hundreds of millions who don't?

This brings us to the hypothesis of Karma and Reincarnation. I use the word "hypothesis" deliberately, because I am writing for Western and, I hope, intelligently sceptical readers. It is my business to describe, not to dogmatize. Here is one explanation of the known facts of our human experience. You can accept or reject it. But, unless you understand its main propositions, the literature of Vedanta will scarcely be intelligible to you.

Philosophically, Karma and Reincarnation are inseparable. Nevertheless, they have been separated, by the leaders of the many esoteric cults in Europe and America which have brought Indian thought into such discredit, and made the word "Yoga" synonymous with dishonest mystery-mongering and the exploitation of the superstitious. We have all met the lady who likes to believe that she has lived through previous births as Marie Antoinette, Cleopatra, or a priestess in an Egyptian temple. The character chosen is invariably glamorous, beautiful, distinguished, tragic. No cultist would ever admit to a former existence as an ordinary housewife, a small tradesman, or a cook. Here, the idea of Reincarnation, unconditioned by Karma, floats in a romantic, meaningless void. It is a convenient daydream for the escapist.

"Karma" means action, work, a deed. Not only physical action, conscious or reflex, but also mental action, conscious or subconscious. Karma is everything that we think or do. Philosophically speaking, Karma also means the Law of Causation: a law which is said to operate in the physical, mental and moral spheres of our lives.

I do an action; I think a thought. The Vedantist tells me that this action and this thought, even though they be apparently over and done with, will inevitably, sooner or later, produce some effect. This effect may be pleasant, unpleasant, or a mixture of both. It may be long delayed. I may never notice it. I may have altogether forgotten the action or the thought which caused it. Nevertheless, it will be produced.

Furthermore, every action and every thought makes an impression upon the mind. This impression may be slight at first; but, if the same action or thought is repeated, it will deepen into a kind of groove, down which our future behaviour will easily tend to run. These mental grooves we call our tendencies. Their existence makes it possible to predict fairly accurately just how each of us will behave in any given situation. In other words, the sum of our karmas represents our character. As fresh karmas are added and previous karmas exhausted or neutralized, our character changes.

So much is self-evident. But now comes the question: where does Karma begin? Are we all born equal? Do we all start life with the same chances of failure or success? Why Shakespeare? Why the mongolian idiot? Why the ordinary man in the street? Is there any justice at all?

There seem to be three possible answers to this problem. The first is the simplest: "No, there is no justice. Heredity and the accident of environment account entirely for your condition at birth. No doubt, you can improve your situation to some extent, along the lines of your inherited capacities and with the help of a good education. But there is a limit. Shakespeare was very lucky. The idiot is extremely unfortunate."

The second answer is more or less as follows: "Certainly, there is inequality, but there is justice, also. Life is a handicap race. To whom much was given, from him much will be expected. Shakespeare had better make good use of his talent. As for the idiot, as for cripples and the poor, let them be patient. After this life, there will be another, in which each will be judged, punished and rewarded according to his deserts."

This answer rightly infuriates the socialist, who exclaims: "What hypocrisy! What religious opium! Clean up your slums, establish prenatal clinics, provide free education, share the profits of industry. Never mind your promise of justice in heaven. Let's have justice here on earth."

The third answer is the one given by Vedanta. It is more complex, but also more logical than the second, more optimistic than the first. "I quite agree," says the Vedantist, "that existence continues after death. I agree that our actions in this life will condition the circumstances of that existence, since the Law of Karma will not cease to operate. I don't know why you limit yourselves to two lives. I foresee thousands. Lives on this earth, and lives elsewhere. I believe that an accumulation of very good karma will cause the individual to be reborn in what may be described as "heaven," and that very bad karma will place him in a sort of "hell." Only, my heaven and my hell have a time-limit, like life in the world. When the good or bad karma is exhausted, the individual will be reborn here on earth. I say this because I believe that human life has a peculiarity: it is the only condition in which one can create fresh karma. Elsewhere one merely enjoys or suffers the karmic effects of one's earthly actions. The socialist may disapprove of my attitude, but I thoroughly approve of his activity. I do not believe that it can produce any permanent material improvement in this world; but it is spiritually constructive, and that is all that finally matters. Right action is the language of spiritual progress.

"You claim that this particular birth was your beginning. I don't see why. Philosophically, your position is awkward, because it compels you to believe that the condition of the idiot and the genius of Shakespeare are due to the justice or injustice of some external Power. God is supposed to bind one man and free another, and then tell them both to make the best of it. Why blame God? Why not say that the idiot is an idiot because of his past actions in previous lives? It may sound brutal, but it is much more consistent. Don't misunderstand me: I am not denying heredity. I believe that heredity operates. But I also believe that the sum of our karmas compels us to be born into a certain kind of family, under certain physical and economic conditions. You may ask: 'Who would choose to be an idiot?' I reply: 'Who would choose to be a cocaine-addict?' Our thoughts and actions, apparently so harmless, create these appalling tendencies; and the tendencies are finally too strong for us."

The Vedantist has finished, and we can begin to heckle him.

"If we had past lives, why can't we remember them?"

"Can you remember exactly what you did this time yesterday? Can you remember what it felt like to be sitting on your mother's lap at the age of eighteen months? As a matter of fact, there is a Yoga technique of concentration which is supposed to enable you to recall your previous existences.

I'm not asking you to believe this. You would have to try it for yourself, and it would be a stupid waste of time. If you want a working hypothesis which sounds scientific, can't you simply assume that we suffer a kind of amnesia? After all, birth is a terrible shock."

"How do you account for the fact that Karma ever started at all?"

"I can't. I only say, as I have said already, that the phenomenal universe is beginningless and endless, coexistent with the Reality. The Law of Karma was always in operation. It always will be."

"Then we just go up and down, getting better, getting worse, for ever?"

"Certainly not. The individual can escape from Karma at any given moment, as soon as he realizes that he is the Atman. The Atman is not subject to reincarnation. It stands beyond Karma. It is only the individual ego which passes from life to life. Every individual will realize this, sooner or later. He must. The Atman within him will draw him to itself."

"And then?"

"When samadhi has been attained, the Law of Karma ceases to operate. No new karmas can be created. The liberated saint may live on in his human body for a while, just as a wheel goes on revolving after its motive power has stopped. But he will never be reborn, either in this world, or in any other karmic sphere. He will remain in the Atman. As an individual, he will have ceased to exist."

"What happens when everybody has attained samadhi? Won't the supply of individuals run out? Won't the universe disappear?"

"No. The ego-sense, which is the basis of individuality, will continue to work its way upward, through inanimate matter, through plant-life, through the lower animals, into human form and consciousness. . . . But how can we discuss these things? We stumble over our own words. The universe is an illusion. Our essential nature is Reality. We are never separated from it for an instant. The concept of Karma is only valuable insofar as it reminds us of the extraordinary importance of our every thought and action, and of our immense responsibility toward each other. . . . We have talked enough. Now do something. Start to practice Yoga. Try to realize the Atman. All your questions will ultimately be answered. All your doubts will gradually disappear."

During the late middle years of the nineteenth century, there lived, in a temple garden at Dakshineswar, a few miles outside Calcutta, the man who is, perhaps, Vedanta's greatest human exemplar. His name was Sri Ramakrishna.

He had come to the city as a sixteen-year-old boy, to join his elder brother, who was a priest. When the two of them moved out to Dakshineswar, Ramakrishna himself took up priestly duties in the Kali temple. Kali symbolizes Reality as the Mother of the universe, Giver of life and of death. Because of her dual aspect, she is the most misunderstood figure in Indian mythology. "How can you ask us," exclaims the foreigner, "to accept a Mother who is also a Destroyer? What a horrible parody of motherhood! Look at her; distributing boons with one hand while the other holds a sword!" Yet Kali embodies a profound spiritual truth. She teaches us to look beneath the appearances of Life. We must not cling to what seems beautiful and pleasant; we must not shrink from what seems ugly and horrible. The same Brahman underlies all experience. When we have learned to regard death and disaster as our Mother, we shall have conquered every fear.

Ramakrishna understood this. His intense devotion soon began to attract the attention of those who met him. The formidable stone image of the goddess was to him a living presence. He talked and joked with her, adored and reproached her with the freedom of perfect innocence and the candid faith which makes blasphemy a meaningless word. Kali was his own Mother, he was her Son. Why would she not reveal herself to him? "Oh Mother," he wept, "another day has passed and I have not seen you!"

His ardor was rewarded by a vision. But he was not satisfied. Desiring perpetual awareness of Kali's presence, he entered upon a period of severe austerities, passing weeks and months in almost unbroken meditation. Religious fervour is not considered unhealthy or abnormal in India, even by the layman, but Ramakrishna's ecstasies were so extreme that fears were expressed for his sanity. He particularly scandalised the temple attendants by giving some consecrated food to a cat. Why not? Mother was in everything. After a while, he ceased to officiate as a priest. But he remained at Dakshineswar until the last year of his life.

Gradually, his fame spread. Two celebrated pundits visited him, discussed his visions and subjected them to elaborate theological analysis. At length, both the great scholars solemnly declared that, in their opinion, the young man was an avatar, an incarnation of the ultimate Reality. Ramakrishna received this staggering announcement with childlike indifference and a certain sly humour. "Just fancy," he remarked: "Well, I'm glad it's not a disease. . . . But, believe me, I know nothing about it."

The dualist's approach to God may correspond, in type, to any one of our earthly relationships: it may be that of the servant, the child, the parent, the husband, the lover or the friend. As the years passed, Ramakrishna explored them all. It is easy enough to write these words, but almost impossible to imagine, even faintly, what such an undertaking would involve. Here is a complete sublimation of Life, in every aspect: a transposition, as it were, of the entire human experience into another key. Perhaps the nature of Ramakrishna's achievement can best be hinted at if we compare it with that of Shakespeare or Tolstoy in the sphere of art. Beside these masters, the intuition of lesser writers seems partial and restricted; it can only function along certain narrow lines. The essence of spiritual, as of artistic greatness is in its universality. The minor saint knows one way of worship only. Ramakrishna's genius embraced the whole of mystical realization.

Nothing now remained but the supreme monistic experience, the union with impersonal Reality. In 1864, a monk named Totapuri came to Dakshineswar, to instruct Ramakrishna in this highest truth, the Brahman which is beyond all forms and aspects. The lesson was a hard one, even for such a pupil. Again and again, as he tried to meditate, the figure of his adored Kali rose before him, creating the illusion of duality. At last, Totapuri picked up a piece of glass from the ground, stuck it between Ramakrishna's eyebrows and told him to fix his mind on that point. "When Mother appeared," Ramakrishna said later, "I drew the sword of discrimination and cut her in half." For three days, he remained absorbed in samadhi.

To most mystics, samadhi comes as the crowning attainment of a lifetime: for Ramakrishna, it was only the beginning of a new phase of experience. Established in the knowledge of Reality, he was now able to regard the entire phenomenal universe *sub specie aeternitatis,* seeing in all matter and circumstance the play of the divine Power. He loved the world, as only the illumined saint can love it. Kali, Shiva, Rama and Krishna, the personal aspects and incarnations of the impersonal Brahman, were still his constant companions. He did not deny duality; but now he knew it in its true relation to the unity of the Absolute. He lived always on the threshold of transcendental consciousness, and the least word or hint was sufficient to raise his mind into oneness with the Eternal. An English boy watching a balloon happened to cross his legs in the attitude of the young Krishna; a lecturer with a telescope talked of the heavenly bodies; the sight of a lion at the zoo suggested the traditional mount of the Divine Mother—and Ramakrishna was in samadhi at once. It was necessary to accompany him everywhere, or he might have fallen to the ground and been injured. Once, in an unguarded moment of ecstasy, he did fall and dislocated a bone in his arm.

His appetite for spiritual experience in all its forms was insatiable. "Cake tastes nice," he used to say, "whichever way you eat it." In 1866, we find him practising the disciplines of Islam, dressing as a Mussulman, and repeating the name of Allah, under the direction of a Mohammedan teacher. Eight years later, he became fascinated by the personality of Jesus. The Bible was read aloud to him. He went into ecstasy before a painting of the Madonna and Child. One day, while he was walking in the temple garden, the figure of Christ approached him, embraced him, and was merged into his own body.

At the age of twenty-three, Ramakrishna had been betrothed, to please his Mother and in conformity with ancient Indian custom, to Saradamani, a little girl of five. In 1872, Saradamani, now eighteen years old, came to join her husband at Dakshineswar. The idea of a sexual union was utterly repugnant to Ramakrishna's nature; and Sarada, herself a saint in the making, gladly agreed to their monastic relationship. When the day came round for the worship of Kali, Ramakrishna did homage to his wife as an embodiment of the Divine Mother. (This incident is described in Amiya Corbin's story.) Sarada outlived her husband by many years. She became the spiritual Mother of the Ramakrishna Order.

During the last ten years of Ramakrishna's life, a number of disciples began to gather round him. Some of these were famous men, such as Girish Ghosh, Bengal's most distinguished dramatist, and Keshab Sen, the religious leader and social reformer. Others were schoolboys in their teens: the future monks who were to preach his message throughout India, and to carry it overseas. There were also many women.

In 1882, the circle of visitors to Dakshineswar was joined by Mahendranath Gupta, headmaster of a Calcutta highschool. To Mahendranath's devotion and unusually retentive memory we owe a record which is almost unique in the literature of religious biography. From the day of his first visit, Mahendranath (or "M," as he modestly signed himself) began to write down everything which was said and done in his presence by Ramakrishna and his disciples. The result is a very large volume, known in English as "The Gospel of Sri Ramakrishna." Its most recent, and only complete, translation is by Swami Nikhilananda, of the Ramakrishna Center in New York. I have referred to it extensively in writing these notes.

As we read M's book, we can begin to form some mental picture of a saint's daily life. It is certainly very strange; and, in this particular case, doubly remote from our experience. Firstly, because, as ordinary unregenerate human beings, our own behaviour has an entirely different frame of reference; secondly, because the cultural background itself is alien and complex.

The Dakshineswar temple garden was, of course, a stronghold of tradition and religious orthodoxy. Yet its northern wall was bounded, symbolically enough, by a powder magazine belonging to the British Government; and the nearby city of Calcutta was the center of Western influence in India. Nearly all Ramakrishna's followers were men who had come into some contact with European ideas. Keshab advocated the abolition of the caste-system and of child-marriage; and he had been to England, where he was the guest of Queen Victoria. Even M would quote English philosophers and expound the latest discoveries of modern science.

Amidst these ideological contrasts sat Ramakrishna: the living embodiment of a wisdom that transcended and reconciled them all. Mother is everywhere. What else, on this earth, do we need to know? In the presence of his smiling certainty, the scholar and the reformer became silent; their own doubts and anxieties ceased. One is reminded of another great prophet who lived as a member of a subject race within a vast imperial system; but the parallel is misleading. Nobody ever asked Ramakrishna to head a nationalist movement, or to decide whether it is right to pay tribute to Caesar. His life was happier than that of the Galilean. Its very significance is in its quietness, its utter lack of external drama. Calcutta was at his doorstep; yet there were probably not a dozen Englishmen who were even aware of his existence.

Ramakrishna could scarcely read or write. But he knew the Scriptures by heart and quoted them continually, with the comments of his own unique experience. His talk was a blend of sublime subtlety and homely illustration. He spoke with a slight stammer, in a country dialect, sometimes using coarse, vivid words with the innocent frankness of a peasant. Most of his parables are based upon the everyday circumstances of village life and the folklore of the people. A man of faith is compared to well-boiled sugar; a monk to a snake, which seldom stays long in one place and has no hole of its own. Greed and lust are likened to moisture in wood; they must be dried out by the flame of discrimination before the fire will burn. We are to walk through the world like the girl who carries five water-pots on her head, never losing her balance.

The few existing photographs of Ramakrishna show us a slender, bearded man of medium height. They were taken while he was in samadhi; the lips are parted and the eyes half closed. In one picture he stands supported by a devotee, with the right arm raised and two fingers of the left hand rigidly extended; an attitude which somehow suggests the concentration of an intense, mysterious delight. The figure has an eager poise, a childlike unselfconsciousness. There is no trace of egotism here; no hint of a desire to dominate, to fascinate, to create an impression. What attracts us is precisely that absence of demand, that joyful openness, in a face which seems to promise the love that makes no reservations, and is without pathos or fear.

He was always smiling, laughing, crying aloud in his joy. Those who visited him felt as if they had arrived at a party which never stopped. A really happy party has no sense of past or future: life at Dakshineswar was lived in a perpetual present tense. The awareness of God's presence was always here and now. Sometimes there would be animated discussion. Sometimes musicians came, and Ramakrishna sang and danced, or clowned to amuse the boys. Often, he passed into samadhi, and the little room was filled with ecstasy and silence.

The experience of samadhi is, literally, a death to the things of this world. It is said that the body of an ordinary human being could not survive it for more than a few weeks. Ramakrishna had entered samadhi daily for many years. In the process, his whole physical organism had been transformed: it was extraordinarily sensitive and delicate. One night, in 1885, he had a hemorrhage of the throat. The doctor diagnosed cancer.

That autumn, he was moved into Calcutta, for better nursing. Despite his weakness and terrible pain, he continued to teach his disciples, to laugh, to joke and to sing. One of his attendants has even expressed a belief that Ramakrishna was not suffering at all. The eyes of the saint regarded the wasting body with a kind of calm, secret amusement, as though this horrible disease were only a masquerade.

His disciples begged him to pray that he might recover; for their sake, if not for his own. At last, Ramakrishna agreed to do so. A little later, he told them: "I said to Her: 'Mother, I can't swallow food because of my pain. Make me able to eat a little.' But she pointed to you and said: 'What? Aren't you eating enough through all those mouths?' I was ashamed. I couldn't say another word."

Toward the end, his chief concern was for the future of

his young disciples. Two he had especially loved. One of them, later to be known as Swami Brahmananda, he regarded as his own spiritual son. The other, Naren (afterwards Swami Vivekananda), he had trained to be the bearer of his message to the world.

One day, while Ramakrishna lay in the last stage of his illness, Naren was in a downstair room, meditating. Suddenly, he lost consciousness, and went into samadhi. At first, the experience terrified him. Coming to himself, he cried "Where is my body?" Another of the boys saw him, and ran upstairs in a fright to tell Ramakrishna. "Let him stay that way for a while," said the Master, calmly. "He has worried me long enough."

Much later, Naren himself came into Ramakrishna's room. He was full of delight and peace. "Now Mother has shown you everything," said Ramakrishna. "But I shall keep the key. When you have done Mother's work, you will find the treasure again."

On August 15th, 1886, Ramakrishna uttered the name of Kali three times, in a clear ringing voice, and passed into the final samadhi. At noon, next day, the doctor found that life had left his body. There is a photograph, taken that same evening, in which we see the mourners grouped around the corpse before its removal to the cremation-ground. The young faces are all sombre and meditative, but there is no sign of frantic grief or despair. The disciples were worthy of their Master. Their faith seems never to have left them, even at this supreme moment of loss. Not long after, they resolved unanimously to enter the monastic life. And thus the group was formed which afterwards became the Ramakrishna Order.

The boys had little money and few friends. Their first monastery was a tumbledown old house, midway between Calcutta and Dakshineswar, with nests of cobras under the floor, which could be rented cheaply because it was supposed to be haunted. Here they lived, and often starved, in meditation and ecstasy. M, who went to visit them, marvelled at their joy. So vivid was their awareness of Ramakrishna's presence that they could even joke about him. M records how, one evening, Vivekananda mimicked the Master going into samadhi, while his brother-monks roared with laughter.

Vivekananda and Brahmananda (or "Swamiji" and "Maharaj," as they were more familiarly called) were the group's natural leaders. The two had been friends from early boyhood; both were now twenty-three years old. Handsome and athletic, Vivekananda was the embodiment of physical and intellectual energy; impulsive, ardent, sceptical, impatient of all hypocrisy, conservatism or sloth. His faith had not come to him easily. He had questioned Ramakrishna at every step, and would accept nothing on trust, without the test of personal experience. Well-read in western philosophy and science, and inspired by the reformist doctrines of Keshab Sen, he brought to his religious life that most valuable quality, intelligent doubt. If he had never visited Dakshineswar, he might well have become one of India's foremost national leaders.

Brahmananda is a more mysterious figure. Few knew him intimately, and those few confessed to the inadequacy of their knowledge. He was a very great mystic and saint. His wisdom and his love seemed superhuman. His brother-disciples did not hesitate to compare him to Ramakrishna himself. "Whatever Maharaj tells you," said one of them, "comes directly from God." Brahmananda was elected head of the Ramakrishna Order in 1902, and held that office until the end of his life, in 1922. I refer the reader to the excellent biographical essay by his disciple, Swami Prabhavananda, in "The Eternal Companion."

For seven years, the young monks wandered all over India, visiting shrines and places of pilgrimage, passing months of meditation in lonely huts, preaching, begging. Sometimes, they were royally entertained by wealthy devotees. More often, they shared the rice and the hard bread of the very poor. These experiences were especially valuable to Vivekananda. They gave him a standard of comparison, a true picture of India's hunger and wisdom, her economic misery and deep spiritual culture, which he carried with him on his journey to the West.

In 1893, a Parliament of Religions was to be held at the World's Columbian Exposition in Chicago. Vivekananda was anxious to attend it, and his disciples and friends raised the money for the passage. What followed was a typically Indian comedy of errors. He arrived much too early in the United States. His funds ran out. He lost the address of his Chicago hosts, did not know how to use the telephone or the directory, and spent the night sleeping in a box in the freight-yards. Next morning, after much walking, he found himself in a fashionable residential district, without a cent in his pocket. There seemed no point in going any further. He sat down on the sidewalk and resigned himself to the will of God. Presently, a door opened, and a well-dressed lady came out. "Sir," she asked, "are you a delegate to the Parliament of Religions?" A few minutes later, he was sitting down to breakfast, with all his difficulties solved.

The other delegates to the Parliament were prominent men, admirably representative of their respective creeds. Vivekananda, like his Master, was unknown. For this very reason, his magnificent presence created much speculation among the audience. When he rose to speak, his first words, "Sisters and Brothers of America," released one of those mysterious discharges of enthusiasm which seem to be due to an exactly right conjunction of subject, speaker and occasion. People rose from their seats and cheered for several minutes. Vivekananda's speech was short, and not one of his best; but, as an introduction, it was most effective. Henceforward, he was one of the Parliament's outstanding personalities. The newspapers took him up. Invitations to lecture began to come in from all over the country. It was clear that he would have to remain in the United States for some time.

In those days, a foreign lecturer touring America found himself in a position midway between that of a campaigning politician and a circus performer. He had to face the rough-and-tumble of indiscreet publicity, well-meant but merciless curiosity, reckless slander, crude hospitality, endless noise and hurry and fuss. Vivekananda was surprisingly well-equipped for all these trials. He was outspoken, quick at repartee, dynamic, witty and courageous. Above all, he was a true monk; and only a monk could have preserved his inner calm amidst such a tumult. On one occasion, a party of cowboys fired pistols around his head during a lecture, for a joke. Vivekananda went on imperturbably. He said what he had to say, whether the audience liked it or not. "In New York," he used to remark, "I have emptied entire halls."

His main theme was the universality of religious truth, a dangerous topic in communities which still clung to a rigid Christian fundamentalism. To such listeners, the doctrine of the Atman must have sounded like the most appalling blasphemy: "Look at the ocean and not at the wave; see no difference between ant and angel. Every worm is the brother of the Nazarene. . . . Obey the Scriptures until you are strong enough to do without them. . . . Every man in Christian countries has a huge cathedral on his head, and on top of that a book. . . . The range of idols is from wood and stone to Jesus and Buddha. . . ." Vivekananda is preeminently the prophet of self-reliance, of courage, of individual enquiry and effort. His favourite story was of the lion who imagined himself to be a sheep, until another lion showed him his reflection in a pool. "You are lions, you are pure, infinite and perfect souls. The might of the universe is within you. . . . After long searches here and there, at last you come back, completing the circle from where you started, and find that He, for whom you have been weeping and praying in churches and temples, on whom you were looking as the mystery of all mysteries shrouded in the clouds, is nearest of the near, your own Self, the reality of your life."

Vivekananda really loved America: that was part of his greatness. As few men, before or since, he stood between East and West impartially, admiring the virtues and condemning the defects of both. To Americans and Englishmen, he preached India's religious tolerance, her freedom of spiritual investigation, her ideal of total dedication to the search for God. To Indians, he spoke severely of their sloth, their timid conservatism in manners and customs, and held up for their imitation the efficiency of the American and the Englishman's energy and tenacity. "You have not the capacity to manufacture a needle and you dare to criticize the English! Fools! sit at their feet and learn their arts and industries. . . . Without the necessary preparation, what's the use of just shouting in Congress?" With himself, he was equally ruthless. Some friends once unkindly tricked him into eating beef. When he discovered that he had done so, his involuntary disgust was so extreme that he vomited. "But I must overcome this ridiculous prejudice," he exclaimed, a few moments later. And he asked for a second helping.

In 1897, after two visits to England, he returned to India, where he witnessed the founding of the Ramakrishna Order, with its headquarters in Calcutta, and the establishment of several other monasteries. His progress through the country was triumphal; and his achievements in the West, real as they were, were wildly exaggerated by the enthusiasm of his Indian disciples. Yet, amidst all this adulation, Vivekananda never lost his emotional balance. Again and again, he paid homage to Brahmananda, whose spirituality was the inner strength of the movement and the inspiration of its growth. The relation between these two men, the ardent missionary and the calm, taciturn mystic remained deep and beautiful throughout their lives.

In 1899, Vivekananda returned to America. His second visit was less spectacular than his first; it was concerned chiefly with the development of small groups and the training of devotees in different parts of the country. But it made great demands upon his already failing strength. He came back to India by way of England and Europe at the end of 1900, sick and exhausted. His mood, too, had changed. He was weary of talk, of letter-writing, of the endless problems of organization. He was weary of activity. He longed for the Himalayas, and the peace of meditation. Through much struggle, he had learned resignation and acceptance. He was happier, perhaps, than at any other period of his life. Already, before leaving America, he had written to a friend: "I am glad I was born, glad I suffered so, glad I did make big blunders, glad to enter peace. Whether this body will fall and release me or I enter into freedom in the body, the old man is gone, gone for ever, never to come back again! Behind my work was ambition, behind my love was personality, behind my purity was fear, behind my guidance the thirst for power. Now they are vanishing and I drift. . . ."

His departure from this life, on July 4th, 1902, had all the marks of a premeditated act. For some months, he had been quietly releasing himself from his various responsibilities and making final arrangements. His health gave no particular cause for alarm. He had been ill, and now seemed better. He ate his midday meal with relish, talked philosophy with his brother swamis, and went for a walk. In the evening, he sat down to meditate, giving instructions that he was not to be disturbed. Presently, he passed into samadhi, and the heart stopped beating. It all happened so quietly that nobody could believe this was the end. For hours, they tried to rouse him. But his Mother's work was done. And Ramakrishna had set him free at last.

I have already suggested that Vivekananda had two messages to deliver; one to the East, the other to the West. In the United States and in England, he preached the universality of religious truth, attacked materialism, and advocated spiritual experiment, as against dogma and tradition. In India, on the other hand, we find that he preferred to stress the ideal of social service. To each, he tried to give what was most lacking.

Side by side with the Ramakrishna Order, he established the Ramakrishna Mission, an institution which has grown steadily throughout the four decades of this century. There are now nearly a hundred centers in different parts of India, devoted either to the contemplative life, or to social service, or to a combination of both. The Mission has its own hospitals, dispensaries, high-schools, industrial and agricultural schools, libraries and publishing-houses. In 1941, it opened a college which is affiliated with the University of Calcutta. It has been consistently active in famine, flood and epidemic relief. During the great Bengal famine of 1943–44, it took the lead in organizing emergency food supplies.

Vivekananda founded the first American Vedanta Society in New York City. Four direct disciples of Ramakrishna came from India to carry on his work. From that time onward, the Order has met an increasing demand for teachers. Each one of them has come to this country upon the invitation of some group of Americans, who wished to learn more about Vedanta Philosophy. Although the Vedanta Society of America is an extension of the Ramakrishna Mission of India, whose headquarters are at Belur, Calcutta, each center is a separate unit. Nearly all of them have their own boards of trustees, made up of American citizens. The swami in charge

gives lectures and holds classes for the study of Vedanta literature, including the Upanishads, the Bhagavad-Gita, the works
of Shankara and Patanjali's Yoga Aphorisms. In some centers,
there are resident students. At the present time, there are
thirteen centers in the United States, one in England, and
one in the Argentine.

The magazine from which this selection has been made was
started in January 1938, under the auspices of Swami Asho-
kananda of the San Francisco Center and Swami Prabhavananda of the Center in Los Angeles. During its first three
years, it was called *The Voice of India;* then the title was
changed to *Vedanta and the West.* It appears bi-monthly.
Swami Prabhavananda has been its editor throughout. He
has had a succession of assistant editors: Frederick Manchester, Percy H. Houston, Gerald Heard, Maud Alice Pig-
gott, and myself.

*Vedanta and the West* has always had an extremely small
circulation, a fact that we much regret, since there must be
many people in this country who would wish to subscribe to
it, if they knew of its existence. We hope to reach some of
them by publishing this book.

From another point of view, however, I cannot say I am
sorry that *Vedanta and the West* has always remained, as
it were, a parish magazine, a family affair. Our list of contents is quite innocent of window-dressing. Several of our
contributors have distinguished names, but their work has
not been hired. They have written for us simply because they
are interested in Vedanta and are our personal friends.

Very few of the essays included have been edited or
abridged. The reader will therefore find much repetition and
restatement. I do not apologize for this. Indeed, I think it is
desirable. The truths here discussed are, in a sense, decep-
tively simple. They may be overlooked at a first, a second, or
even a third reading. They need reiteration. They will bear
a great deal of thinking about, and acting upon.

Swami Prabhavananda—to whom I owe my own small
knowledge of the subject, and infinitely much else besides—
has helped me, from first to last, in preparing this book for
publication. I must thank all our contributors, both for their
original generosity and for permission to reprint what they

have written. Messrs. Harper and Brothers have kindly allowed us to include those essays which have since become portions of Aldous Huxley's "Grey Eminence" and "Time Must Have a Stop."

C. I.

October 1945.

## NOTE FOR THE COMPASS EDITION

I AM HAPPY TO SAY THAT *Vedanta and the West* is still being published and that its circulation increases continually. The assistant editors who have succeeded me are Amiya Corbin, John Yale, and Ursula Bond.

For this edition we have added, on page 453, notes identifying the contributors.

If you have any questions to ask in relation to this book, you are invited to write to the Corresponding Secretary, Vedanta Society of Southern California, 1946 Vedanta Place, Hollywood 28, California.

C. I.

January 1960.

# Is Mysticism Escapism?

## Gerald Heard

"Mysticism is simply escapism"—that little jingle has almost become a slogan of those who occupy most of the key posts in philosophy and religion. Even those who feel that there "may be something in it," shelter the mystics in their congregations or class rooms as though they were political suspects or at the very least feeble-minded people subject to fits and not to be teased. Now a slogan is a good "butt-end" of words with which, when the shot of reason misses fire, to bludgeon your opponent, but emotional attacks should have no part in religious or philosophical discussion. First and foremost philosophy stands for accurate definition of terms and religion, one used to think, for seeking above all else the Presence of God. We must therefore define these words and discover whether or no the procedure they describe leads to or away from the goal of our being.

The tremendous word mysticism cannot be defined until we have settled with the smaller but perhaps vaguer word escapism. Mysticism is a very old word, escapism one judges very new. But the verb to escape is clear enough—it means to leave a position which has become impossible. We can then ask: In the history of Christianity, was Benedict an escapist when he refused to become a consul in the dying empire, when he refused to believe there was any future for that bankrupt state and instead founded the order which revived the basic agriculture which the empire had ruined, salvaged the culture it could no longer protect, and did these things because and only because he had forged a new psychology or social psychotherapy whereby men of intentional living and good will might heal their own neurosis, create a true collectivism and put first the kingdom of God, then sound economics and finally the preservation of the intellectual wealth of western man? To escape is therefore a neutral term. It may be a wrong thing to do, or a right. "When they persecute you in one city flee into another" is an instruction which spread the Christian church. The man who leaves the ship to attempt to swim to shore with a rope, is escaping, but for the sake of the rest on the wrecked ship— and he is risking his life. Our motive therefore decides whether escape is good or bad and our motive, again, depends on what we think will happen and what we think the circumstances to be with which we are confronted. As a matter of fact the goal of most of those who charge others with "escapism" is an earthly Utopia. They don't believe in heaven and God is merely a means, if He is permitted any place, to make men better and happier. Now Utopianism can be called escapism, for it is a wish to live in the future, not in the present, and it certainly is as vague as "otherworldliness" because biologically and meteorologically we know it is impossible for any race of animals to achieve a permanent home, let alone a "heaven on earth," on this planet. As far as hard-fisted certainty is concerned there is then nothing to choose between the two futures which idealists put in front of themselves—neither can be proved to be manifestly evident. The pure idealist is able to retort to the "indefinitely postponed new worldist" that neither of them can prove his proposition. When the writer of the letter to the Hebrews remarked of the pioneers whose case he was making, they say openly that they seek another country, he was saying something which certainly today many people would call escapist but he knew what he was talking about. To escape then may or may not be right. That turns on whither we escape. That brings us to mysticism. The mystic says that this world is real in a way just as "token coinage" is not to be wasted but its reality depends on its being "quoted" on another currency and security. He does not call this life evil any more than he calls an egg evil but he says, with some common sense, that if an egg stays too long as an egg few things are more bad, more rotten, more evil. The mystic maintains that the only man who is a realist, is not the man who pursues imaginary ends, such as happiness by wealth or in some fanciful future—whether for himself or for others

—but the man who freeing himself of the delusions of regrets and anticipations, wins the power to see things as they are. Such realists, though their slit of vision was narrow, were the great impressionist painters who threw away livelihood, wealth, respect, who were called fools and knaves, in order that they might just see things as they actually were. Now most people do not believe that there is a reality "closer than breathing, nearer than hands and feet," a reality quite different from that of common sense. The religious should however have known that that was so. Because they lost their vision, its authenticity had to be vouched for by the artists—not by the clerics.

If then there is such a state of being, not in a future life (though there it may be also) but here and now, then the mystic is the realist. He maintains that there is such a state, that anyone may experience it who chooses to undergo the arduous training and athleticism of spirit to gain that insight, and that it was to attain that state that man was created, or to use our vernacular, the end of evolution is not the creation of bigger and more complicated societies and more elaborate economic structures but the attainment of a higher and intenser form of consciousness, a consciousness as much above that of the average man today as that is above the animals'.

Now all high religion has borne witness to this state, to its attainability and to it as being the goal set for man by God. It needs, however, a great creative effort to attain it. Creaturely activity, to use the Friends' phrase, may help one to attain this state, or it may hinder; again it depends on motive and knowelge. "If thou knowest what thou art doing blessed art thou, if not cursed." The rules whereby the process may be worked are clear—there is nothing soft or vague about them. "But don't they take men away from life?" If by life is meant helping others to follow and not thwart evolution—certainly not. If by life is meant building a more pleasant social order for those who do not wish to follow the stern path of evolution, even then the mystic way is probably the only way of ever getting a more efficient social order than we have today. It is sanction for which our social order waits. Who has the vision to tell us how to act, who can guarantee that "right action is prized at the heart of things?" Only the mystic; all others speak as the scribes. Our social order, as Lincoln Steffens pointed out, has gone as high as people of our characters can carry it—weak bricks can only make small arches for a larger arch will crush them and all will crash in ruin. If we want a more effective social order we must produce better men. How? By giving them that training whereby the innate egotism of the best of today is transcended, through what the mystic calls the vision of God, through what we may call an accurate, or painstaking, gradual enlargement of consciousness. The ants as they achieved their amazing socialist state found that it could not be done by leaving themselves as they once were. They go through three stages achieving their social structure. They hatch out as larvae, then they have to pass into pupation, and only after that second birth-and-death do they emerge as full adults adequate to sustain the state and not ruin it. The mystics have said the same thing. You must be born again. You begin by being a servant of God, then you must die even to all the things of that life that you may be born a friend of God and finally you may pass into an even higher state, if so be we suffer together with those who have so attained, that we may be glorified with them also. Such a scheme of things is daring, is curiously naturalistic, and is the only adequate answer to our present problem:—How find men adequate in character and powers to the enormous task which our sanctionless society (capsizing because its means have overbalanced its knowledge of ends, its physics, its psychology) now presents. The mystic may be too hopeful, too concerned with an attempt to salvage the unsalvable, but he, put beside the ordinary economically obsessed "secular" or "religious," is a realist and a daring man of action.

# The Minimum Working Hypothesis[1]

## ALDOUS HUXLEY

RESEARCH INTO SENSE-EXPERIENCE—motivated and guided by a working hypothesis; leading, through logical inference to the formulation of an explanatory theory; and resulting in appropriate technological action. That is natural science.

No working hypothesis means no motive for research, no reason for making one experiment rather than another, no way of bringing sense or order into the observed facts.

Contrariwise, too much working hypothesis means finding only what you already *know* to be there and ignoring the rest. Dogma turns a man into an intellectual Procrustes. He goes about forcing things to become the signs of his word-patterns, when he ought to be adapting his word-patterns to become the signs of things.

Among other things religion is also research. Research into, leading to theories about and action in the light of, non-sensuous, non-psychic, purely spiritual experience.

To motivate and guide this research what sort and how much of a working hypothesis do we need?

None, say the sentimental humanists; just a little bit of Wordsworth, say the nature-worshippers. Result: they have no motive impelling them to make the more arduous experiments; they are unable to explain such non-sensuous facts as come their way; they make very little progress in charity.

At the other end of the scale are the Catholics, the Jews, the Moslems, all with historical, one-hundred-per-cent revealed religions. These people have their working hypotheses about non-sensuous reality; which means that they have a mo-

[1] This article subsequently appeared as part of Sebastian's notebook in "Time Must Have a Stop."

tive for doing something about it. But because their working hypotheses are too elaborately dogmatic, most of them discover only what they were initially taught to believe. But what they believe is a hotch-potch of good, less good and even bad. Records of the infallible intuitions of great saints into the highest spiritual reality are mixed up with records of the less reliable and infinitely less valuable intuitions of psychics into the lower levels of non-sensuous reality; and to these are added mere fancies, discursive reasonings and sentimentalisms, projected into a kind of secondary objectivity and worshipped as divine facts. But at all times and in spite of these handicaps a persistent few have continued to research to the point where at last they find themselves looking through their dogmas, out into the Clear Light of the Void beyond.

For those of us who are not congenitally the members of an organized church, who have found that humanism and nature-worship are not enough, who are not content to remain in the darkness of ignorance, the squalor of vice or the other squalor of respectability, the minimum working hypothesis would seem to run to about this:

That there is a Godhead, Ground, Brahman, Clear Light of the Void, which is the unmanifested principle of all manifestations.

That the Ground is at once transcendent and immanent.

That it is possible for human beings to love, know and, from virtually, to become actually identical with the divine Ground.

That to achieve this unitive knowledge of the Godhead is the final end and purpose of human existence.

That there is a Law or Dharma which must be obeyed, a Tao or Way which must be followed, if men are to achieve their final end.

That the more there is of self, the less there is of the Godhead; and that the Tao is therefore a way of humility and love, the Dharma a living Law of mortification and self-transcending awareness. This, of course, accounts for the facts of history. People like their egos and do not wish to mortify them, get a bigger kick out of bullying and self-adulation than out of humility and compassion, are determined not to see why they shouldn't "do what they like" and "have a good time." They get their good time; but also and inevitably they get wars and syphilis, tyranny and alcoholism, revolution, and in default of an adequate religious hypothesis the choice between some lunatic idolatry, such as nationalism, and a sense of complete futility and despair. Unutterable miseries! But throughout recorded history the great majority of men and women have preferred the risk—no, the positive certainty —of such disasters to the tiresome whole-time job of seeking first the kingdom of God. In the long run, we get exactly what we ask for.

# Hypothesis and Belief
## CHRISTOPHER ISHERWOOD

IF A MEMBER of the so-called intellectual class joins any religious group or openly subscribes to its teaching, he will have to prepare himself for a good deal of criticism from his unconverted and more skeptical friends. Some of these may be sympathetic and genuinely interested; others will be covertly satirical, suspicious, or quite frankly hostile and dismayed. It will be suggested to the convert, with a greater or lesser degree of politeness, that he has "sold out," betrayed the cause of Reason, retreated in cowardice from "the realities of Life," and so forth. Henceforward, his conduct will be narrowly watched for symptoms of pretentiousness, priggishness, prudery and all other forms of puritanism. Certain topics will either be altogether avoided in his presence, or they will be presented in the form of a challenge, to see how he will take them.

The convert himself, self-conscious and badly rattled, is almost sure to behave unnaturally. Either he will preach at his old friends and bore them; thus confirming their worst suspicions. Or he will make desperate efforts to reassure them, by his manner and conversation, that he is still "one of the gang." He will be the first to blaspheme, the first to touch upon the delicate subject. And his friends, far from feeling relieved, will be sincerely shocked.

One question, especially, he must learn to expect. It will be asked by the most candid, by those who really want to know: "Yes, of course, I can quite understand why you did it, in a way . . . but tell me, do you actually *believe* all that?" This question is particularly distressing to the convert, because, if he is to be honest, he will have to answer: "No. I don't—yet."

The "all that" to which the questioner refers will vary in detail and mode of formulation, according to the religious

group the convert happens to have chosen. In essence, however, it can always be covered by what Aldous Huxley has
called "the minimum working hypothesis." This word "hypothesis" is extremely significant, but it will probably be
overlooked by the outside observer, who prefers to simplify
his picture of the world's religions by regarding their teachings as "creeds" and "dogmas." Nevertheless, a statement of
religious doctrine can be properly called a creed only by
those who know it to be true. It remains an hypothesis as
long as you are not quite sure. Spiritual truth is, by definition, directly revealed and experienced: it cannot be known
at second hand. What is revealed truth to a Christ is merely
hypothetical truth to the vast majority of his followers; but
this need not prevent the followers from trusting in Christ's
personal integrity and in the authenticity of his revelation,
*as far as Christ himself is concerned*. One can feel sure that
Einstein is neither a fraud nor a lunatic, and that he has actually discovered the law of relativity; and still fail, in a certain
sense, to "believe" in the conception of Space-Time, just because one has not yet personally understood it.

There is, even nowadays, a good deal of loose and unrealistic talk about "the conflict between religion and science."
I call this kind of talk unrealistic because it suggests that
"Science," and hence scientists, are one hundred per cent
materialistic; and that "Religion" is based upon the blind,
hundred per cent acceptance of dogmas which are incapable
of scientific proof. Modern Science is, of course, very far
from being materialistic. In the nineteenth century, it is
true, Science did pass through a phase of mechanistic materialism. But the scientist himself never has been, and never
could be, an absolute materialist. The scientist is a human being. The absolute materialist, if he existed, would have to
be some sort of non-human creature, completely lacking the
human faculty of intuition, a mere machine for measuring
and making calculations. If a human being could become a
truly convinced materialist, he would never have the heroism
to get up in the morning, shave, and eat his breakfast. His
world-picture would be too terrible for even the boldest heart
to contemplate; and, within twenty-four hours, he would
have committed suicide.

Similarly, a religion based upon blind faith could not possibly survive, as all the world-religions have survived, for hundreds and thousands of years. Religion lives, and is revived, from age to age, because of the direct revelation of the few, the saints, who win for themselves a personal knowledge of spiritual reality. Religion survives *in spite of* blind faith, priestly persecution, ecclesiastical politics; in spite of superstition and ignorance amongst the masses of its adherents. Most of us cannot understand this, because our imagination refuses to grasp the gigantic influence and importance of the saint as an historical phenomenon. Whereas the persecution and the ignorance stand out brutally from the pages of history in red and black, plain for all to see. Nine times out of ten, when we use the word "Religion," we are really referring to the crimes or follies committed in Religion's name.

There is no conflict between true Religion and true Science, but there is a great deal of bickering between religious dogmatists and scientific pedants. The dogmatist states his case, or rather, presents his dogmatic ultimatum. The scientifically trained pedant reminds him, none too patiently, that his assertions cannot be verified by the microscope, the slide-rule, or the laboratory experiment. Therefore, he continues, quite rightly, the dogma is merely another hypothesis. And, he will probably add that hypotheses which are incapable of scientific proof do not interest him, anyway. At this point, a deadlock is reached, and the two men part in mutual annoyance.

But now let us suppose that, instead of the tiresome, dogmatic convert (who is unconvincing because he has not personally experienced the truth of what he asserts) Christ himself should enter the scientist's laboratory, and make the very same statements which the convert makes. How would the scientist react? If the scientist were a pure, non-human materialist, he would, of course, remain completely unconvinced. But, since he is a creature of emotion and intuition as well as of reason, the chances are that he would be impressed, not rationally but emotionally, by the personality of Christ and the tremendous psychological impact of such a meeting. In spite of his scientific training, he would venture to trust his intuition. He would say to himself: "Although my scientific methods of analysis cannot deal with these statements, my intuition tells me that this man has some authority for his words."

This raises the question of what we may call "the credibility of the witness." The jury in a court of law does not, or should not, judge a case entirely by scientific (i.e. rational) method: it relies, also, on intuition. It decides to believe a witness or not to believe him—sometimes in defiance of considerable circumstantial evidence. There is, also, the factor of corroboration. If two or more witnesses support each other, and make an impression of being truthful, the case is apt to turn in their favour.

When we begin to examine the assertions of the great religious teachers, we shall have to behave like jurymen. Reason can help us, no doubt, and it must be brought to bear on the case; but Reason will not take us all the way. It can only deliver a provisional verdict. It can only say: "This is possible," or "Perhaps . . ." Next, we must ask ourselves: "What sort of men are telling us this? Are they charlatans? Do they seem sane? Do their lives bear out the truth of what they preach?" And, again: "Do they, substantially, agree with each other's testimony?" On this second point, however, there can be little argument. The basis of essential agreement between the great religious teachers of the world is very firm, and can easily be demonstrated by documentary evidence. Any student of comparative religion can reconstruct "the minimum working hypothesis." Nevertheless, it is quite possible to decide that Buddha, Christ, Shankara, St. Francis and Ramakrishna were all mad, or self-deluded, and therefore not to be taken seriously. If that is the verdict, then our inquiry ends.

But, if the world's teachers were not mad, then, as all must agree, their teaching has universal application, and implies an obligation to put it into practice, in our own lives. And so we are faced by the next question: "Am I dissatisfied with my life as it is at present? And, if so, am I sufficiently dissatisfied to want to do anything about it?"

Here the majority and the minority definitely part company. Buddha said that human life is miserable, but he did not say that everybody thinks it is. Not all the socially underprivileged are dissatisfied, as every reformer knows, to his despair. And this is even truer of spiritual poverty than of economic lack. Life contains a number of vivid sense-pleasures, and the gaps of despondency and boredom between them can be filled more or less adequately by hard work, sleep, the movies, drink and daydreaming. Old age brings lethargy, and morphia will help you at the end. Life is not so bad, if you have plenty of luck, a good physique and not too much imagination. The disciplines proposed by the spiritual teachers are drastic, and the lazy will shrink back from them. They are tedious, also, and this will discourage the impatient. Their immediate results are not showy, and this will deter the ambitious. Their practice is apt to make you appear ridiculous to your neighbors. Vanity, sloth and desire will all intervene to prevent a man from setting his foot upon the path of religious effort.

Disregarding all these obstacles, and they are tremendous, the beginner will have to say to himself: "Well, I am going to try. I believe that my teacher is sane and honest. I don't believe in his teachings with the whole of my mind, and I won't pretend that I do, but I have enough belief to make a start. My reason is not offended. My approach is strictly experimental. I will put myself into his hands, and trust him at least as far as I would trust my doctor. I will try to live the kind of life which he prescribes. If, at the end of three or four years, I can conscientiously say that I have done what was asked of me and had no results whatsoever, then I will give up the whole attempt as a bad jcb."

# *What Yoga Is*

## Swami Prabhavananda

PATANJALI, the father of Indian yoga philosophy, has defined yoga as "restraining the mind-stuff from taking various forms." What in the West is known as mind is called in Eastern psychology the *chitta,* or "mind-stuff." The chitta, according to this psychology, comprises the *manas,* or that which receives the impressions from the outer senses; the *buddhi,* or the discriminating intellect; and the *aham,* or the sense of ego. The chitta, or mind-stuff, despite the fact that it perceives and is conscious, is not the Self, but only the instrument of the Self. The Self is Intelligence itself, the Knower, the Seer, the Subject; the chitta reflects the divine illumination and so itself appears—but only appears—to see and to know. Knowledge or perception, according to Patanjali, is a *vritti,* a wave in the mind. All knowledge is objective: the Seer, the real Self, which is behind all knowledge, remaining unknown. What Western psychologists call introspection or knowledge of the subjective mind—even that Patanjali regards as objective, since the mind is not the Seer, but only an instrument of seeing, and is as much an object of perception as is the objective world. Man thinks that he knows himself, but that is an error which he falls into by identifying himself with his mind and with the waves that rise upon it. Something external impinges on his mind, and raises in it a wave of happiness or a wave of misery, with the result that he regards himself as either happy or unhappy. This delusion continues so long as he remains ignorant of the true nature of his Self—which is said to be *shuddha* ("pure"), *buddha* ("enlightened"), and *mukta* ("free"). Now the method of yoga is to control completely the waves of the mind, "restraining the mind-stuff from taking various forms," so that the real, free, and divine nature of the Self may at last be revealed.

In order to make clear what has just been explained, the commentators employ a simple image. If the surface of a lake, they say, is covered with ripples, or its water is muddy, the bottom cannot be seen. The lake is the chitta, and the bottom of the lake is the Self.

Whenever the waves of the mind are made tranquil, knowledge of the Self is revealed. This it was that Christ meant when he said: "Blessed are the pure in heart, for they shall see God."

The subdual of the waves that would possess the mind is not a superficial process, nor a momentary one, but a complete transformation. It is a change that can be achieved by yogic discipline. Doubtless St. Paul referred to this kind of restraint when he said, "Be ye transformed by the renewal of your own mind."

In order to achieve this renewal of the mind, yoga psychology considers not only the actual states (vrittis) of the mind-stuff (chitta), but also the latent states, called the *samskaras,* or "potentialities." Before we can hope to restrain the mind-waves successfully, we must endeavor to eradicate the potentialities, the root impressions which control the actual states of the vrittis. For when one mental state passes into another, it is not altogether lost, but leaves behind it an impression in the chitta—an impression, or samskara, which in turn tends to give rise to similar vrittis, or states. Thus the vrittis cause the samskaras, and the samskaras cause the vrittis. The samskaras are like deep roots in the soil of the chitta, from which grow the actual plants, the vrittis. To destroy the weeds, we must eradicate the roots, and to do this it is not enough to restrain the actual vrittis, but also, through yoga discipline, to overcome, weaken, and destroy the samskaras, the potentialities of the actual states.

Modern Western psychology, particularly Freudian, takes into consideration these potentialities. Freud postulates three "areas," or states of mind: the unconscious, the pre-conscious, and the conscious. The unconscious is the receptacle of such of our past experiences as have been definitely forgotten and cannot be recalled by the ordinary method of recollection.

The pre-conscious is that part of the mind in which are stored experiences which, though apparently forgotten, can be recalled by an effort of the will. Modern Western psychologists differ in their explanation of the unconscious mind, some holding that it is the receptacle of our individual past experiences, and of these alone, while others would include with them the common experiences of the race.

Yoga psychology agrees with the Western view that the unconscious is a depository of certain individual past experiences, but it differs radically as to the interpretation of those experiences. To Patanjali, our individual past is not limited to the present life, as all Western psychologists would assume, but extends indefinitely backward through a succession of incarnations. According to the law of karma, our birth is the result of our past lives, in each of which, and in the present, we possess the same chitta. In the "unconscious mind," if we may adopt the Freudian term, are stored the impressions and the tendencies which have been formed in our previous existences, and which, taken together, have made us what we are.

The samskaras, or potentialities, represent therefore the root impressions received from all our past experiences, including those of our former lives, and they have moulded our characters so that, even though largely forgotten, they still control or influence our every act and thought. They may also take on fresh life and potency without our conscious effort or will. Now yoga philosophy—and this is the very core of its doctrine—proposes a method of discipline whereby these root impressions may first be overcome, and then destroyed, and whereby a complete transformation of character may in the end be effected. Yoga psychology agrees with Freud that the conscious is controlled and guided by the unconscious, but it insists that there is a power inherent in the mind, through which, restraining itself, it can overcome the unconscious and all its tendencies, and achieve by so doing a complete renewal. Thus is its original purity restored—a purity that reflects the supreme purity and infinite knowledge of the Divine Self. Thus at last does the Self learn its true nature—its utter separateness from the non-self—and attain to freedom.

Any thought wave arising in the mind, or any perception apprehended by the mind, is a vritti. The objects of perception and of thought are innumerable: innumerable, therefore, are the vrittis. These Patanjali has roughly classified into two main divisions: *klishta,* those which lead towards bondage and suffering, and *aklishta,* those which lead towards freedom and illumination. This distinction is made by the great yogi because of an important psychological fact. Though the ideal is the attainment of a state in which "all modifications of the mind-stuff are controlled," such a state is not possible except through a twofold process. First, the thought waves that are impure and lead to bondage and suffering must be overcome by raising the vrittis that "lead towards liberation." Then these good vrittis themselves must be eliminated, so that all motion of the mind-stuff may cease and Pure Intelligence may stand revealed.

Now it is a characteristic of the chitta, or mind-stuff, that it tends both towards good and towards evil. Vyasa, an ancient commentator, compares it to a river that flows at the same time in opposite directions. Though, again, the chitta plays this dual rôle, its tendency towards good, the will to freedom inherent in every man, is the greater of the two forces. Having noted this superior strength of the will to freedom, Professor Das Gupta observes, in substance:

"This point is rather remarkable, for it gives the key to yoga ethics and shows that our desire for liberation is not actuated by any hedonistic attraction towards happiness, or even towards removal of pain, but by an innate tendency of the mind."

Could it be, one wonders, that the "will to liberation" described in yoga philosophy is the force which Freud wrongly interprets as the "death-instinct"? Freud finds within us two innate tendencies: the life-instinct and the death-instinct. But the death-instinct is not, he thinks, to be found in its pure form, but is inextricably mixed with its opposite, the life-instinct—a fact that explains the strange phenomena of sadism and masochism and the feeling of alternate love and hate towards the same object. We are not concerned, however, with the truth or falsity of Freud's explanation of the phenomena we have just mentioned, but rather with the fact that by his characterization of his two instincts as antithetical he almost arrived at the position taken by yoga psychology—and yet somehow failed to do so. Yoga mentions the two opposed instincts: the "will to live" and the "will to liberation." The "will to liberation" (Plato's "inner check" and Buddha's "higher will") exists, according to yoga, side by side with the "will to live" (the "will to desire"), though in some men it is weak and in others strong. It is the principal purpose of yoga psychology to show how the "higher will" may be strengthened and the "will to live" overcome.

As the "will to liberation" gains in strength, the "will to live," which Freud calls the "life-instinct," grows weaker. Evidence of this fact may be seen in the lives of all who check the lower craving. And, strange though it may seem, this craving can be completely overcome, though the "will to liberation" cannot. This latter, which Freud misnames the "death-instinct," is to be found mixed with the "life-instinct" in all souls.

The concrete means by which spiritual control is exercised Patanjali analyzes in considerable detail. Control, he says, is "by practice and non-attachment."

By "practice" is meant, he tells us, the exercise of the ethical and spiritual disciplines. These are *yama,* the cultivation of moral virtues, such as truthfulness, non-injury, continence; *niyama,* the acquiring of regular habits of study and worship; *asana,* the discipline of sitting quietly in order to achieve tranquillity; *pranayama,* the taking of breathing exercises in order to gain control of the mind; *pratyahara,* the gathering of the mind from the thraldom of the senses; *dharana,* concentration; *dyhana,* meditation; and *samadhi,* absorption.

These disciplines are to be practiced, and along with this practice, says the yogi, we must sow the seed of non-attachment in our hearts. In fact, practice and non-attachment must go hand in hand. Non-attachment, in Patanjali's words, is "that effect which comes to those who have given up their thirst after objects either seen or heard."

There are stages of non-attachment, the commentators point out, through which we pass as we practice the yoga disciplines and as we strive to attain to the supreme ideal of renunciation. There are four such stages. The first is *yata-man*, when there arises an inner struggle from not permitting the mind to seek gratification of the senses. The second is *vyatireka*, when through self-analysis we realize the measure of our own achievement in the field of self-control. We realize what desires we can control and what we as yet cannot. Then with vigor and enthusiasm we must continue to attack all desires that still remain in the way of illumination. The third is *ekendriya*, when greater self-control is achieved, and the heart, knowing their ephemeral and shadowy nature, no longer desires the objects of enjoyment; yet there may still remain in the heart a longing curiosity. When this longing also has been overcome, we attain the fourth and highest stage of renunciation. This is known as *basikar*.

This, the supreme goal of renunciation, is achieved only by him who has attained complete enlightenment. "That supreme non-attachment comes from knowledge of the Self," says Patanjali. And the Gita says: "Objects fall away from the abstinent man, leaving the longing behind. But when a man sees the Highest, his longing also ceases;"—and, again, summing up the whole truth of yoga: "With the heart unattached to external objects, he realizes the joy that is in the Self. With the heart devoted to meditation upon Brahman, he attains undecaying happiness."

# The Goal of Yoga

## Swami Prabhavananda

ALL RELIGIONS WITHOUT EXCEPTION hold that the Self is in-
nately pure and divine. "God made man in his own image."
All religions further hold that that innate, original purity
has somehow been lost. Christianity attributes the fall of
man from his pristine state of innocence to the fall of the
first man, Adam, so that now we are "born in sin and iniquity" through having inherited the sin of Adam, and can
only be saved through the grace of a merciful heavenly Father
as revealed in the sacrifice of His only Son, Jesus Christ our
Lord. Howsoever Christian theologians may interpret this
doctrine, the truth of this mythological story would seem to
be that man in his original nature is pure and is a perfect
image of God; but through some inexplicable cause, he seems
to have lost that perfection. This imperfection, however,
which the story of the Fall of Adam informs us we have inherited, cannot be real and permanent, cannot really have
altered our innate purity. For Christianity, again, offers us
the ideal goal of conquest over sin and the attainment of
liberation and a renewed perfection, "even as the Father in
heaven is perfect." This goal would be meaningless, for it
could never be attained had imperfection been our innate
nature. For it is not possible to change the innate nature of a
substance without destroying the substance itself. One cannot
change the nature of fire, which by that very nature must
radiate heat, except by destroying fire itself. But its inborn
nature, its heat, may be suppressed by a covering of ash. Remove the ash, and fan the fire, and you will again have both
fire and heat. The same thing is true of the Self—its innate
purity and divinity may be covered by ignorance but not lost.
Indian philosophy asserts: "You are for ever free and divine.
Your apparent imperfection is due to ignorance; realize what

you are, and be free." This same truth appears in Christian teachings, although theologians may differ in their interpretations; for does not the Bible say, "The light shineth in darkness; and the darkness comprehended it not"?

We are pure, free, and divine. Suffering, sin, limitations, and all imperfections are caused by *avidya*, the ignorance which veils the true nature of Self, causing us to identify ourselves with the non-Self. Patanjali, the father of Indian Yoga philosophy, says: "The pain-bearing obstructions are ignorance, egoism, attachment, aversion, and clinging to life. Ignorance is the productive field [the main cause] of the others that follow."

*Ignorance* has been defined as "taking the non-eternal, the impure, the painful, and the non-Self, for the eternal, the pure, the happy, and the Atman or Self." This ignorance is of course universal, and is the basis of our empirical lives, the cause of all conditioned experience. It is the "original sin" of Christian doctrine. Ignorance, says the great yogi, Patanjali, leads to egoism, attachment, aversion, and clinging to life—the immediate causes of suffering and the confusions of our empirical lives.

"*Egoism* is the identification of the seer with the instrument of seeing." The mind is the instrument of perception and experience, and the identification of the Self, the seer, with this instrument is called the ignorance of egoism. We say, "I am happy," or "I am suffering," but happiness or suffering are but waves of thought arising in the mind. Through the ignorance of egoism, the Self, becoming identified with the mind, identifies itself with the waves or thoughts in the mind, and either enjoys or suffers.

Through egoism there arises the desire for pleasurable experiences in the senses, and there grows *attachment* to them. Desire for sensory and emotional experiences and attachment to them cause suffering. Therefore attachment to those experiences and a desire for them must be avoided if we are to seek tranquillity of mind and heart. Opposed to attachment is *aversion*, which is also another cause of suffering, and to be avoided. Sri Krishna says in the *Gita*, "The self-controlled man, moving among objects with senses under restraint, and free from attraction and aversion, attains to tranquillity."

Neither a complete withdrawal of the senses from the world, nor a denial of the experiences of empirical life, is required for tranquillity of mind, but the right attitude of mind in freeing itself from both attraction and aversion.

The last of the "pain-bearing obstructions," according to Patanjali, is *clinging to life,* a term which may perhaps be correlated with Freud's "Life-instinct." Commentators have explained it as "fear of death," which exists instinctively in all living beings. This fear of death is another cause of unhappiness.

These five causes of suffering are the chief obstacles in the path of yoga; of them all, ignorance is the root cause. They exist universally in all beings, though in different states and degrees in different people. Patanjali says, "They are either dormant, attenuated, overpowered, or expanded." In most people these obstacles exist in an expanded state, in some in a repressed or overpowered condition. Through the practices of yoga and self-discipline, they may be attenuated and finally destroyed.

The goal of yoga is to eradicate these obstacles completely and thus to remove the causes of suffering. The root cause, as we have seen, is ignorance, which is the "productive field" for all other obstacles; and its removal is possible by means of its opposite, *vidya,* or knowledge. Patanjali says, "The means for destruction of ignorance is illumination." This knowledge or illumination that removes the ignorance is not intellectual knowledge, but rather an immediate, direct illumination in one's own soul. Patanjali declares that this illumination appears to us in a sevenfold manner. "His knowledge is of the sevenfold highest ground."

The first to appear will be the convincing realization that all knowledge is within ourselves; that what is to be known can be discovered not by seeking outside of ourselves but by turning our gaze within.

The second stage of illumination will be marked by the absence of suffering. Then it will be impossible for anything either within or without to disturb the equilibrium of the mind.

The third will be the attainment of full illumination, and in the fourth stage we become established in the knowledge of the Self, when the Self is no longer identified with the non-Self, the seer with the seen.

After attaining this stage, man realizes the fullness of life; there is no longer in him any lack or desire, or any sense of duty. This is known as *karya-vimukti,* or the attainment of liberation through one's own individual effort. After this follows *chitta-vimukti,* or the process of release of the Self from non-Self in three stages.

First we realize that the mind, the instrument of experience, and also the objective world (mother nature), both have ended their services to the Self by providing it with worldly experiences, and then by releasing it from all bondage and suffering, so that neither the mind nor nature has anything more to do with the Self.

Immediately, upon the attainment of this stage, all the stored-up impressions of the mind, all its struggles and vacillations, fall away from the Self as a stone rolls from the mountain-top into the valley below, never to return to its former position.

Lastly we find that we are established in the glory of our own Self. We know, in the words of Swami Vivekananda, "that we have been alone throughout the universe, neither body nor mind was ever related, much less joined, to us. They were working their own way, and we, through ignorance, joined ourselves to them. But we have been alone, omnipotent, omnipresent, ever blessed; our own Self was so pure and perfect that we required nothing else. We required nothing else to make us happy, for we are happiness itself. We shall find that this knowledge does not depend on anything else; throughout the universe there can be nothing that will not shine with our knowledge. This will be the last state, and the yogi will become peaceful and calm, never to feel any more pain, never to be again deluded, never to be touched by misery. He will know he is ever blessed, ever perfect, almighty."

# Vedanta as the Scientific Approach to Religion[1]

## GERALD HEARD

THE REVIVAL OF INTEREST in Religion is perhaps the most significant symptom of our time. For long we have been aware that materialism, whether true or false, is not going to win. There is a vast mass of people who, whether their intelligences are able to grasp the arguments of mechanistic science or no, are possessed of wills which are determined not to accept a doctrine which maintains that their lives are futile, that their existences mean nothing and that the spirit has no significance. We are not however concerned with this pathetic defiance nor with the childish defenses with which it would protect itself, except in so far as such efforts by their very absurdities prove how profound is the need which can provoke such reactions. We are concerned with far graver symptoms of a great social "deficiency" disease. It would not matter much—save for themselves—if a few millions of "oldsters," possessed no longer of livers which will stand drink or nerves which will endure gambling, take to fanciful cults to while away the boredom of retirement and make them forget a future which holds in it no further outstanding event save death. It is of immediate social concern when the young and highly vigorous start showing similar signs of the lack of spiritual vitamins. For they will not take to cults which only harm themselves nor practice illusions which end in the clinic or cult-house. For some time we have dismissed with a superior smile the neurotic vagaries of elderly introverts. With our utterly superficial psychology we have attributed such behavior to balked sex and the death-fear. Today the contagion has spread from the dozing dotards to the

[1] From a lecture, in 1939.

51

most athletic and energetic youthful extroverts. As Carl Jung
has pointed out, in the fanatical crusading enthusiasms of the
young storm-troopers of the Totalitarian States we have a
persecuting dogmatic faith, only to be compared with the
rise of Mohammedanism. Nationalism today has sprung up as
a force capable of destroying civilization because the lack of
religion—the lack of a discipline and goal in which the individual might transcend himself—left a vacuum in men's
minds—an emptiness and craving which, being without its
right satisfaction, seized upon a false one. Put men adrift at
sea in a boat without fresh water and however much you
warn them that to drink sea water is deadly, when the pangs
of thirst come upon them and they see the clear delusive
liquid near them, they drink it and die mad. Nor is this
thirst-madness merely a symptom of "neurotic Europe."
Nothing is giving educationalists in the United States greater
concern than just this—that there is an immense gap in the
national education. In technical education, in making men
and women experts and specialists, the United States has
nothing to fear. If improvements are required it is quite easy
to see how they may be provided. It is the other side of the
educational ledger which is causing a concern so grave that
here there is almost a conspiracy of silence; for no one knows
how that growing debit may be met. Lately a questionnaire
was circulated among prominent educationalists. It suggested—what is obvious—that American education was going
with an increasing "list," a list which if not remedied must
lead it to capsize. It gave a long series of suggestions as to
how this imbalance might be corrected. These ranged from
creative drama, through occupational therapeutic hobbies,
out to collectivised hiking. Indeed only two activities from
the Realm of Ends were omitted—Philosophy and Religion.
That is significant of the apprehension and the helplessness among progressive and influential educationalists. And
while they question and avoid the pressing issue—"Is life
possible without a philosophy, without a religion?"—the great
public and its government go on their way making the problem daily more difficult. For the man in the street and his
fellow whom he sends to Congress have not as yet awakened to
the fact that there is any imbalance at all. The men who make

public opinion and the laws are still in that pre-psychological condition of mind when it is assumed that, as life in the end must terminate in futility, you can make men content by increasing their means, until they will forget that there are no ends worth living for. As life has no meaning we shall increase amusements until everyone is so distracted that they won't be able to think even of their own deaths. This is of course pathetic nonsense and were it not such wishful thinking no rational being could maintain it for a moment. Here of course is religion's opportunity, yet we see Western religion is helpless to take it. Youth today when its hunger for meaning grows unbearable, will turn not to the churches but to those who preach crusading nationalism. Why is Western religion helpless? In the answer to that question there lies, it would seem, the case for Vedanta. Western religion has made three fundamental mistakes. Taking its cosmology from the rudimentary Hebrew world-view it tied itself to a crude Apocalypticism. By the sixth century Parousial expectations, long discouraged by the church, were given an *ad hoc* moral substitute by the invention of the doctrine of Purgatory. This doctrine, leading to ecclesiastical corruption, was repudiated by the Reformation. Henceforward Protestantism would have no world-view, unless it returned to Apocalypticism by becoming Fundamentalist. The Vedanta has a world-view infinitely vaster than the Hebrew and one which does not contradict the findings of science. The statement that the physical world is a construction of the human mind from a substratum, a basic unity which our animal senses break up into a manifold, is a statement which modern physics can support. The hypothesis that consciousness is *sui generis* and this particular temporal experience is an event in a series which extends beyond it in both directions, is an hypothesis which research into consciousness tends to establish. This brings us to the second great mistake of Western religion and it is even graver than the first. Western religion neglected psychology and psycho-physiology. Its conception of Deity, fluctuating between a humanised Jehovah (the loving Father of Jesus Christ) and a Trinity in which an anthropomorphised Logos mediates between man and the inflexible absolute Judge God, made Christianity's one praxis to be simple petitionary prayer. True, Eastern influences introduced a crude asceticism (such as the Thebaid) and an occasional second-hand knowledge of meditation, but psychical and psycho-physical knowledge was lacking and whenever there was any search for these things the church ruthlessly persecuted the seekers. In the Vedanta meditation and contemplation are basic and make a complete working psychology, while with this scientific knowledge there is, as a modern would expect and demand, a clear realisation of the body-mind relationship, of how man may and only may change the aperture of consciousness by a thorough understanding of that relationship. And all this rests, not on blind authority, but upon empirical work which any enquirer may repeat (indeed must repeat) and confirm for himself. As Dr. Babbitt has said, it is the West which has made experiment and religion seem an impossible combination. But once trust authority blindly and permit authority to rule that Deity is arbitrary power only revealing Itself in unchangeable dogmas, and the church must first condemn all experiment and then fall into the further, graver error of persecuting and striving to destroy all who differ from orthodoxy's rulings. This was the third and final blunder of Western religion. Tied to an inadequate world-picture, lacking a psychology, fearing experiment, it had to end in the last and worst mistake of brutal intolerance. The Vedanta, having a world-picture which counsels against impatience and rashness, and having a psychology which shows how men may test truth and, further, may change their characters and their consciousness, not only avoids intolerance but has a scientific case for tolerance. Tolerating other religions teaches a man to understand two great truths which the intolerant overlook to their cost. The first and more obvious is that men's characters are not changed by coercion—and yet to change character is the sole aim of religion. You may alter the forms but soon, though your labels may stick, even the forms have gone back to express the unaltered outlook of the so-called converted. The second and even more important truth that tolerance reveals is that there are not merely higher and lower types in the world, but that men of equal intelligence, integrity and devotion inherit different methods whereby they must make their initial approaches to the Inexpressible Ultimate. Some are, to borrow Dr. Sheldon's valuable nomenclatory classification, mainly cerebro-tonic, others viscero-tonic and a third large class principally somato-tonic. The first class will be predominantly intellectual and rational, having little use for symbols or conscious need for psycho-physical aids to concentration. The second will be much moved and helped by adequate and progressive symbolism. The third is very dependent on a co-ordination of mind and body in its religious practices and, obtaining this aid, may often outstep the intellectual who unwisely despises such techniques. The needs of these types are met by the three main yogas: Jnana Yoga for the intellectual, Bhakti for the predominantly devotional, and Raja Yoga for those who combine in their natures the need for a balanced approach, mental, emotional and physical, to the divine.

Such in brief are some of the outstanding advantages of the Vedanta for all interested in religion as a union of Truth and Goodness. The blend of Hebrew and Greek thought made the "armature" on which was built up that occidental way of life which has been called Christendom. It is today in ruins and even if it stood it would be too small an arch to span that diversity of mankind which today physical science brings into contact, though it cannot combine. That can only be done by a psychology, an applied knowledge of the human psyche, as comprehensive and as exact as is today the West's applied knowledge of physical science. It is this which India possesses and at last in the Vedanta Mission has shown an apostolic desire to give to mankind. Here then, and here alone, lies the hope, not of personal salvation (though that is an integral part of the training) but of a new and balanced philosophy and praxis of life which could provide sane and progressive living for a unified mankind.

# Dedication Ode[1]

## FREDERICK MANCHESTER

### I

In India long ago,
While yet the dreaming earth
Wore on her brow the glory of her birth,
   The Rishis saw
The high Himalaya lift amid the snow,
And lucid Ganga all her waters draw
In slow procession toward the expectant sea;
   In silent awe,
Awhile they gazed on flower and tree,
And flaming sun, and gentle moon, and star—
   Then, suddenly,
From their rapt vision, in a quiet hour,
Fell star and moon and sun, and tree and flower,
And purest Ganga's waters bright,
And great Himalaya's snowy height,
While to their being's depths, afar,
Forsaking outward things, they fled,
By some deep instinct inward led.

### II

"The courts of sense we left behind"—
Thus the saints their story told—
"And in the stillness, yet more bold,
Passed beyond the mortal mind;
Beyond the mortal mind we passed—
   Oh, listen well!—

[1] Composed for the dedication of the temple of the Los Angeles Vedanta Society, July 10, 1938.

Beyond the self, until at last
We came to THAT whereof no tongue can tell:
In a hidden place untrod,
Where death is dead, and grief unknown,
There, blissful on his royal throne,
We found the ATMAN—BRAHMAN—GOD!"

## III

Strange are the ways
Of this our life!
The word the Rishis spoke
In ancient days,
From sage to sage descending, woke
Reverberations through ten thousand years—
Heard now amidst the strife
Of noble kinsmen warring in their tears,
And now amidst the calm
By mighty monarch in his wisdom wrought;
Now heard in accents loud
Above the noisy crowd,
Now faintly where a few lone hermits sought
In leafy woodland cell their souls' eternal balm;
Heard latest from his honeyed lips whose name
From blessed Rama and from Krishna came:
And, lo, this joyous hour,
In this far-distant clime—
As 'twere a trumpet's tone,
From skyey tower
Across the continents and oceans blown—
Wondering, we hear that selfsame word sublime.

## IV

To-day a temple fair,
With immemorial chant and prayer,
Is dedicated to all sacred thought:
May from its shrine
A pure light shine
Above the darkness of a world distraught;

May from its brooding domes descend
   A gracious peace,
And to sore-burdened spirits lend
   A dear release;
Ah, may it ever work to make men truly free—
   May these things be!

# My Discoveries in Vedanta [1]

## Gerald Heard

I HAVE BEEN ASKED by the Swami again to address you on this anniversary. A year has passed, and in that year much of seeming importance has happened. What the world calls momentous events have taken place. Our reason for taking an interest in the work of this place is, however, due to the fact that we have become convinced that the world never understands what is taking place in it, it never traces consequences to their causes—let alone to their right causes—and that therefore it is always engrossed with accidents and never with the underlying Substance, with Reality. The work of this place is concerned with two things, two supremely important issues, the uncovering of Reality and the bringing of human life into line with that Reality. We are therefore making the only possible contribution to salvaging an almost derelict civilization when we work at those two issues. We are making the most vital of all returns when we attempt, at the completion of another year, to report on this the one possible progress, the only progress that can outbalance and reverse the world's decline toward chaos. What progress have we made? We are taught here that the only real progress we can begin by making is progress in ourselves. We have to heal ourselves before we can think of healing others—let alone whole nations. Otherwise we are simply operating with septic instruments. The patient might recover of himself if we left him alone, but, if we will try our surgery on him and our knives are infected, he must die of poisoning. That is why so-called Theocracies and Benevolent Tyrannies have been so much more hated and harmful than easy-going laissez-faire democracies and republics. When, then, we

[1] The Address was delivered on the second Anniversary of the Dedication of the Temple of the Vedanta Society of Los Angeles, 1940.

would review our progress we have to keep that fact in mind
—growth in spiritual vitality is the only true progress. But
that fact compels us to go further. Not only does it warn us
to attain first true spirituality in ourselves before we would
save the world: it warns each of us who are set on this path
and have seen this truth, not to judge our fellow seekers and
companions-in-training but to attend to our own development. If then I am to speak to you with any accuracy and
truthfulness about the process, if not the progress, of the
past year, I must lay before you the type of discovery and
the sort of application of discovery which one trainee has
made in the twelve months under review. After all, we are
much the same, and, though the self can only speak for
the self, nearly all of us go along the same path. Those of you
who are ahead will listen with patience to these novice notes.

I believe that the principal discovery I have made is so
simple and vast that at times I feel I have always known it
and at other times I feel that I shall never quite grasp it. I
can put it most familiarly in the words of our own Western
Avatar. Jesus the Christ seems to have been, like Gautama
the Buddha before him, a teacher most anxious to simplify
the Way for mankind. With that purpose in view he reduced
the Hebrew Ten Commandments—and indeed, as he said,
the whole Law and the Prophets, down to Two. We are, first,
to love God unlimitedly and, secondly, we are to love our
neighbor as ourself. But we in the West thought we could
go one better than our Teacher. We have tried to reduce the
Two Commandments to one. We have tried to teach that the
Second Commandment really included the First and that as
the First meant no more than the Second, the First was really
unnecessary, otiose. But Christ was an accurate thinker. The
Two Commandments cannot be reduced to one, and, further,
the Second Commandment cannot be put in front of the
First. Unless we begin by knowing and loving God we cannot love our neighbor. Once we have loved God we can—
and then only—love our neighbor as ourself. The First Commandment comes first because it alone can make the Second
possible. The First Commandment is and is meant to be unlimited. We love God without restriction. But is not that

what the Second Commandment says about loving our neighbor? No: and we would never have fallen into this mistake
had we ever thought of religion as a subject requiring as
much accuracy as chemistry. Our love to our neighbor is both
inspired and controlled, fed and restrained, energized and
directed by our love toward God. We should not have fallen
into the tragedies of persecution had we grasped the preci-
sion and accuracy of Christ's teaching on this essential instruction. For once we see that God is infinite being, infinite
wisdom, infinite love, then we see with that to Him and to
Him alone we owe an unlimited devotion and also we see
why, whereas there is no limit to what we may do for Him
in accord with his will and being, there is a limit to what
we may do for all others and to all others. I may love my
neighbor so that, and only so that, he may become what I
see from the First Commandment God wishes me—and all
his creatures—to become, one with God. I am therefore by
the First Commandment guarded from the two tragic mistakes which have ruined so much human love which assumed
that there was only one commandment and that was to love
my neighbor as I thought myself to be. The first mistake is
that mistaken love which wishes to give the fellow creature
it loves all those physical comforts which arrest the soul's
growth. That is the mistake of Humanism. If we aim at making human beings materially so well-off that they find their
life good enough in itself then all we do is to suffocate the
Soul. The second mistake is a blind reaction from the first:
it is to coerce the fellow creature to give up his comforts and
to go in the direction in which I say I have found God, or
some national or class idolatry which I put in the place of
God. Once we have begun to find God we realize two things.
First, that since He is the only real good, we dare not give to
others anything which might distract them from finding the
only real happiness and, secondly, that since He is the only
real Power and Being we dare not attempt to drive others to
find Him Who is the one guide and goal of all. If we have
found God we need not fear that we are not doing enough
to help others find Him. As we are taught here, "once the
flower has opened to the Sun the bees do not have to be
coerced, or preached at, to come to the nectar!"

The second thing taught here which has sunk month by month ever more deeply into my mind, may seem at first sight to have little connection with the first. I have found these two things, nevertheless, to be closely connected. The first is the Object of devotion—God in Himself, Absolute Reality beside which all the physical universe is only a significant dream. The second is the way of devotion, the method or technique of worship. Increasingly one has realized how partial and weak is much of our western devotion because we hardly ever worship with more than one-third of our nature. At the least we are tripartite creatures of body, mind, and spirit. In modern western religion the mind is almost the only aspect of consciousness which is used in devotion. Yet the body accompanies us everywhere. We can't leave it outside, parked like our cars. Rather are we like the Scotch countrymen who bring their collie-dogs into church: but whereas the dogs behave perfectly, few could claim such sedateness for their bodies. We have not taught them. To learn that the body too must worship or it must distract, this is a psycho-physical truth which grows in significance the more one practices. And as the body assists the mind to worship so does the soul. Further each has its own approach and utterance: the result is not unison but harmony, a chord, "not three notes but a star." How is this truth about the method of worship to be linked with that about worship's object? God is Reality; Reality is a Being so intense that, as we are, we cannot see Him. If we would experience Reality, know God, we must draw our entire being together, bring our scattered, dissipated and distended being into a single-pointed focus. "The single-hearted," those who want only one thing, so they have ceased to desire anything else, either appetites, or possessions, or recognitions, "see God." Unless we correlate our complete being, and desire Reality and nothing but Reality with the whole gamut and range of our being, from the highest range of the psyche to the most basic level of the physique, we shall not see God—we shall be devoted to something which is less than Reality and, in consequence, we shall never be wholly satisfied and we shall never be able convincingly to tell others about God, and about the way to find Him. As I have come to see the connection be-

tween these two truths taught here I have begun to grasp a
third which, to use again the simile from music, makes a
chord in the teaching. If God is Reality: if that Reality can
only be apprehended when he who would see has dedicated
his entire nature to seeing, then it must follow as the day the
night that God is not some Being infinitely distant, at best a
*post mortem* experience, but, if the seer will become single-
visioned, God, Reality, may be known here and now. His
very nature is Presence: it is only our obliquity of body—
mind—spirit that hides from us the instant, timeless splendour. These then are the three correlated truths that in the
past year have grown into a unity of understanding and begun to coordinate the three aspects and levels of one's being.
The first is that God alone is wholly Real—all other experiences are sustained on and by that base. The second is that
we fail to see Reality, though He is always Present, because
we are dissipated. Once we recollect and present our scattered being, bringing the facets into one focus, we cannot but
see the Presence. The third is that this transmuting Event is
not something which we have to wait for till we die, something which we may hope for after death, but which we may
have, cannot fail to have, the moment we can ask for it
wholly, with spirit, with mind, and with body. Then our self-
imposed ignorance vanishes and we see that God has always
been Present, closer than breathing, nearer than hands or
feet.

That these truths are taught here and that the way to practice them is indicated, is of the greatest value. Here is given
a system, when in the West we have only had fragments of
true gnosis: here is an empirical science, in comparison with
those happy insights and uncoordinated hints which are all
the guidance our own tradition can now yield.

# Divine Grace

## Swami Prabhavananda

How to attain salvation is the fundamental problem of every religion. The Christians believe that man is born in sin and iniquity, and that he must be saved from sin and attain eternal felicity in heaven. The Hindus and the Buddhists believe that man is born in ignorance and that he must save himself from ignorance, and thus from the bondage of life and death, and attain the kingdom of God which is within us. If we really analyze all the different doctrines of the religions of the world, we find that whereas they differ in language and expression they share the same ideal, the same goal. The Hindus, Buddhists and Christians all teach that the Kingdom of God is within, and that is what the mystics of all faiths emphasize—that heaven is within your very soul, and that by completely attaining to this divine realization you attain salvation, or liberation from ignorance and from the bondage of life and death.

Now again, the Vedantists point out that, because of the presence of God within us, there exists in everyone, whether sinner or saint, the urge to attain God. But a sinner is one who is unconscious of that urge, while a saint is one who understands that urge and consciously strives for its attainment. Now what is that urge? It is the hope to attain freedom from suffering, freedom from misery, freedom from ignorance, freedom from death. What is the sinner seeking by his sins? Happiness, freedom. In other words, he too is seeking heaven, only he is seeking it the wrong way. He can find freedom in himself. Christ and Buddha and all the great illumined souls, and all the scriptures point out to us this one truth: that there is salvation from the bondage in which we live; that we can be saved from our limitations and finitude and that we can attain that eternal life, that eternal felicity, if only we enter the kingdom of God which is within our very souls.

Now with this doctrine of salvation and the attainment of liberation and freedom, is closely allied the doctrine of grace. If you read the many scriptures of the world, you will find the idea of grace as the ultimate way by which we can attain that liberation, that illumination. True, Buddha did not speak of divine grace, but neither did he speak of God. What he taught, however, was not incompatible with the idea of divine grace. But Christ, Krishna, Ramakrishna all say that through divine grace alone one can attain that wisdom, that kingdom of God. Christ said: "Ye have not chosen Me, but I have chosen you." In the Upanishads we read: "By him whom the Self hath chosen is this truth of God attained." Without this choosing of God, without that divine grace, it is not possible to know Him, to attain Him. And all the greatest souls, in the highest stages of illumination, have unequivocally admitted, "Through divine grace alone could I have this illumination." Not one, whether he be Christian or Hindu, says, "By my own struggles have I attained."

It is very difficult, from our viewpoint of ignorance, when we hear that through divine grace alone can illumination be attained, to understand what is really meant by "divine grace." We get a little confused. The question arises: If I have to depend upon divine grace, if I have to wait until that grace descends upon me, what is the use of my efforts?

Then there arises the question: Is God partial, showering His grace upon some and withholding it from others? And then another question arises: What kind of a God is He? When we think of divine grace, we think of a personal Being, with human attributes, human feelings and emotions, an anthropomorphic God. Then again, those who believe in an Impersonal God think: How can there be any grace from the Impersonal? To them, the Impersonal is like an automaton, a mechanism, an abstraction; it has no response. But that also is a great misunderstanding. What *is* God? The Scriptures tell us that He is Consciousness itself. And whether we call Him personal or impersonal does not matter. The Infinite Consciousness, in which we all believe, cannot be a mechanism, an abstraction. Those who have realized God point out that God is personal, but not an anthropomorphic idea; He is also impersonal, but not an abstraction. He is Infinite Consciousness, beyond both personal and impersonal. Sri Ramakrishna used to say: "Never finitize the infinite." In other words, never think that what you conceive as God is the only conception, the only truth. I would say that the best expression, from our human standpoint, of that Infinite Reality is the Sanskrit word, Hari, which means, He who steals the hearts of mankind—the Eternal Beloved. That is God! That Eternal Beloved is within our very souls, and without the grace of the Beloved it is not possible to realize Him.

Now, in answer to the questions: what is the need of our struggling if we have to depend upon His grace? and is He partial, that He gives His grace to some and withholds His grace from others?—the Gita points out that He Who is within each one of us takes no note of the merit or demerit of anyone, but remains covered by our ignorance, and hence we become deluded. Now that explains the whole truth: that God is residing equally in the heart of the sinner and in the heart of the saint; but in the heart of the sinner He is covered by the ignorance of the sinner; in the saint that ignorance is removed.

Now, what is the cause of this covering? The cause is ego! Everyone of us thinks that he is independent of God, that we have free will. But as a matter of fact without God we are mere nothings. Man forgets that, although he is using God's life, God's consciousness, he creates, as it were, an independent ego. And then what happens? He is bound by Karma, earning merit or demerit within this Karma—but God remains unaffected.

In the words of Sri Ramakrishna, the breeze of God's grace is blowing continually. You have to set your sail to catch that breeze. If you simply say that, since it depends upon grace, you need do nothing, or that you can do nothing, or, even, that you can do something—that is because you think you have an independent will. And so long as that ego is there, so long as you feel you have a free will, how can you understand anything about divine grace?

So, what is the step we must take? The Gita again teaches:

"You must save yourself by your Self." You are your own friend and your own enemy. Forget about grace, while you have this ego, so great, so strong! Use your ego, your will, to overcome the ego, to surrender the will to the will of God. This is the struggle all must make.

My master used to repeat a beautiful verse from a Vaishnava saint: "There is the grace of the Guru, there is the grace of God, there is the grace of his devotees; but for the lack of one grace, man ruins himself." And what is that grace? It is the grace of your own mind. Unless you have the grace of your own mind, you cannot have that divine grace. Although there is the breeze of divine grace blowing, you cannot catch that breeze until you have the grace of your own mind. In fact, there are stages of development when this grace is tangibly felt.

In the first stage, one has to begin the spiritual life by striving, by using the will—one has to make an effort. You must have intense longing, intense desire to find God.

But simply to long to find Him will not do. You must proceed to the next stage. You must practice spiritual disciplines.

This brings you to the third stage: self-surrender. No more struggle, no more spiritual disciplines, for you completely surrender your ego to God! Then there is a continuous consciousness of God.

I will give you an illustration from the life of a disciple of Ramakrishna, G. C. Ghosh, a well-known dramatist. He is the ideal of self-surrender in this present age. He went to Sri Ramakrishna, who told him to practice certain spiritual disciplines. But he said he couldn't do it. Then Sri Ramakrishna asked him to meditate for ten minutes in the morning and ten minutes in the evening. He said he couldn't. Then Sri Ramakrishna said: "Very well, then just take the name of God once before you go to bed." "I can't promise to do that either, for I am a drunkard, and at times I have no consciousness of whether it is night or day." So Sri Ramakrishna said: "All right, give me your power of attorney and I will do everything for you. In other words, surrender yourself to me." G. C. Ghosh said: "That I will do gladly." But when he returned home, he began to think, "Oh, I shall have to do this. How can I do it? I have given myself to Ramakrishna, how can I have a will of my own?" You see, he was what we call a sinner, but he was sincere and frank, to the core. So, even when he was merely walking, he couldn't think that he was walking, but with every step he had to think of Ramakrishna. With every breath, he was forced to be conscious of the power of Ramakrishna. Once he remarked to some other disciples: "If you practice meditation at certain hours, that is very good; but with me it is different, I must practice meditation every moment of my life." That is self-surrender. And when that self-surrender comes, then it is that we realize what grace means.

Now then, what is the ideal that we must follow? I will repeat the same thing I have said again and again before. Try to fix your thought upon God. That is the only thing that man should do—nothing else. Keep your heart upon God. True, you will forget many times; but remember a few times each day, and gradually your mind will become fixed in God.

That is the struggle you must make—to keep your mind in God. I believe in practicing only such disciplines as will help us to keep our minds in God.

Sri Ramakrishna used this illustration: The policeman in the dark looks at others with his bull's-eye lantern but nobody can see him. With the help of the light, the others can also see each other. Now we have to ask this policeman to turn his lantern upon his own face. Then only can we see him. And this is the situation: we have that light in us which comes from God, which gives light to the senses, which makes us feel and be conscious, which enables us to experience this world. But the light's source we do not know. We use that light, but we forget that it is His light. We create an ego of our own, which experiences this world by the borrowed light of God; and we remain bound to the law of Karma, bound to birth and death, bound to those three miseries, suffering, death and ignorance. In order to free ourselves from these bondages we must learn to turn that light upon God Himself. The mind runs away, it runs here and there; but keep turning your mind toward God. Through practice alone can this be done. As you practice this self-surrender, practice thinking of God, meditate upon God, be conscious of Him. Then you will begin actually to realize His grace. It will be like a magnet drawing the needle unto itself.

Now, while you are thinking of the Presence of God, there are still distractions, there is still darkness, you still see nothing. You do not intensely feel that presence, there is a "dryness" in you. Then suddenly, when you are least expecting it, you feel that, in spite of yourself, your mind is being drawn to that magnet, you become unconscious of this world, you become conscious of the presence of the Reality, you feel the grace, you feel the magnet drawing you.

You, being trained in the western hemisphere, may say: "But, if we fix our minds upon God, what about our life in this world, our duties?" Your ideal is activity. That is only an excuse. You can think of God, you can love God, you can fix your heart absorbingly on God, and at the same time live in the world, attend to your duties in the world. What is the purpose of working and living? To find freedom from the bondages of misery and death. There is no other purpose. So let all your actions, let every moment of your life, even while you are attending to your so-called duties, be used as means to keep your mind in God, to attain illumination.

Philosophically, it is obvious that man's finite struggle cannot give him the attainment of God, since God is infinite. To this Shankara, the great saint-philosopher, points out very truly, that it is not through your finite struggles that you attain the Infinite, but through the grace of the Infinite. Our finite struggles are needed, however, to remove the finite obstacle of ignorance. The sun is shining, but the clouds have gathered and a gust of wind must come and remove the clouds so that the sun may shine upon us. God, the luminous sun, is shining within us, but there is a cloud of ignorance covering His light. Your finite struggle removes that finite ignorance. Liberation is not something you have to achieve, it is something you have, it is your very nature. Remove the cloud of ignorance, penetrate beyond that cloud and regard that which is beyond the cloud—that is the only way.

That truth is simply stated when we say: "Think of God." Pray to Him, worship Him, meditate on Him, and you will find that life becomes full of joy and sweetness. I don't see how people can live without thinking of God. What have they got in their lives?

You may say that I am a pessimist. Perhaps I am and see nothing but troubles and worries in this life. Life seems to go on smoothly for some time, but nobody escapes death. Where is the only true rest? If you try to rest in anything else, it moves away, for that is the nature of everything— flux, change. So how can any human being of intelligence live any other life but the life in God? All the nations of the world are committing suicide because they have no God, because they have forgotten God. But, I say, none will be lost. Hari, He Who steals the hearts of mankind, is within the hearts of all, and He will steal the heart of each one, at some time or other, in some life or other. Those who are awakened do not go to sleep again.

Strive, struggle, keep your thoughts in God, talk to God, sleep with God, eat with God; and I believe, if a few of us can do that, it will change the atmosphere of the whole world. You all feel, every child feels, that you have to do something for the world. Very good. The greatest thing that you can do for the world is to turn your face toward God. You will be a dynamo—you don't have to talk, you don't have to see people —but you will be a living dynamo. The life that you are living will be reflected upon men's souls, and they also will strive for the attainment of that goal.

# Towards Meditation

## Swami Yatiswarananda

### I

As in material affairs, so also in spiritual matters we should be perfectly clear and definite in our thoughts and actions.

The modern man says lightly: "Oh, God is everywhere." But when he really tries to think of this, he finds he cannot. All these hazy ideas are like those of the so-called worshiper of the formless God who, when he comes home from church, simply busies himself with his physical affairs as he cannot think of and have dealings with God, who to him is indefinite, abstract.

When we have strong body-consciousness, when we take our personality to be the only reality, we need a Holy Personality for our spiritual practice and growth.

On a lower plane the Absolute becomes abstract, although It is real on a higher plane. And remaining on the lower plane of form and personality as we do, we cannot counteract all bad and unwelcome pictures and thoughts that rise in the mind, by means of abstract ideas. We must be able to raise opposing good and holy pictures and thoughts to counteract them, and here the necessity of a Holy Personality comes in, in Whom we find our highest ideals realized. We need a definite holy form, so long as we consider our forms to be real. But at the same time we must find a connecting link between the form and the formless. Form is only a manifestation of the formless. The Holy Personality is a manifestation of the Principle that stands at the back of all.

The Holy Personality serves as the connecting link between the finite and the Infinite, and understood this way it satisfies the head and the heart. The intellect wants the Infinite, the feelings want the finite, and in the Holy Personality we find both, if we see it in the right light, i.e., as manifestation of the Principle, of which the personality is always conscious. Visualization plays a great and important part in spiritual life especially at the beginning, when we are still on a lower plane, the plane of forms and pictures, taking them to be real. The holy forms are always to be looked upon as luminous and living, forming parts of an Infinite Ocean of Light.

Think of the Holy Form as rising out of an Infinite Ocean of Light, and after that, if you want, you may think that it again gets merged into this Infinite Ocean of Light.

As the mind of the aspirant grows, it comes to have a very vivid imagination with reference to everything—good, bad and indifferent. And the best way to counteract the bad fantasies is to have good fantasies, which must be made even more vivid and strong than the others.

The Holy Personality calls up in us the sense of Purity, the sense of Divinity, and at the same time connects us with the Infinite, the Formless, the One Principle, in which all things have their being. In calling up this Holy Form, one may use the help of the sound-symbol: the Holy Name or Om. And this may be used first with reference to the form and then also to the formless.

Every time your mind threatens to lose its balance, repeat the sound and try to think of the Holy Form in the center of your consciousness. The sound is a symbol of Divinity, the form also is a symbol of Divinity. We use both the symbols to call up the Divine Consciousness. With the help of the Holy Personality, we try to realize the Principle, manifesting Itself as Name and Form, and we begin to feel that we too are a manifestation of that Principle, that everybody and everything is a manifestation of that Principle.

After getting a glimpse of the Immanent in the Holy Personality we get a glimpse of the Divine in ourselves and also in others. We have to learn to see the Divine in all forms, good and bad, without, of course, losing the distinction between good and bad. And then the bad forms cannot affect us at all. And we should try to see the Divine not only in the forms that dwell in the physical world, but also in those that rise in the mind.

For those that do not like to dwell on the form, the only way is to recognize the Divine in oneself and also in others. The body is a temple, in which the soul dwells: God is the Soul of the soul. One point is always to be borne in mind: we should stress the soul more than the body and God more than the soul. The body is the dwelling-house of the soul and God is the Soul of the soul. If you do not stress this, it becomes idolatry.

Even idol-worship with reference to a Holy Personality is far better than worship of our body.

The immanent aspect of the Divine is greatly to be stressed: without realizing the immanent aspect, it is not possible to realize the transcendent.

Visualization plays a very important part in the spiritual life of the beginner and in all this visualization a luminous and living form is to be called up. The Infinite Ocean of Light takes shape as the Holy Personality.

In Tantrika Sadhana the following method is used:

The aspirant, after taking his seat, tries to fix the mind at the center of his consciousness, thinks of it as luminous, thinks that this luminosity forms part of an Infinite Ocean of Luminosity, into which he merges his gross body as well as all physical forms, then his subtle body, as well as all subtle forms and finally his causal body, as well as all causal forms. He tries to think of that One Undivided Ocean of Luminosity, that is living, being the source of all life, that is conscious, being the source of all Consciousness. Then he tries to become merged in that. And if one could do that really, if one could really dwell on that, not as a mere imagination, then one gets Samadhi, a high spiritual consciousness. But most people have to be satisfied only with the thought of the Unity. Even that is helpful. Next you think that out of this Infinite Ocean of Luminosity rise your own form and also the form of the Holy Personality you have chosen as the object of your worship.

Think of your body as a luminous body, i.e., make the old perish and come to have a new body, fashioning it out of this luminosity. This is one of the steps in higher Tantrika Sadhana, with Unity at the background. One should forget one's own form, and should worship the Divine Personality.

One may dwell on this form along with the repetition of some holy sound-symbol. And when one is not in a meditative mood, one may go on with Japam, repeating the Holy Name or Symbol a thousand or two thousand times, without any break. It does not matter, even if it is a little mechanical. Practicing this way, one may later on find meditation easier.

Hold on to the sound and think of the meaning. If we are able to do this for some time, great steadiness will come. Then our muddled brain will become somewhat clearer, our thinking and feeling will become more definite. Japam removes many an obstacle and prepares the aspirant for meditation.

Whether you feel inclined or not, do it, go on with it. Why should you stop it, merely because your mind does not feel inclined to do it? Why own defeat? Why be deceived by your own mind? Go on repeating the Holy Name, or sound-symbol, and thinking of the ideal it represents, and never allow yourself to be defeated. Go on repeating it, so that your ear may hear the sound, and your mind may dwell on its meaning.

The Holy Sound gives a sort of support to the mind. When there is any great trouble, one should try to be a little calm and introspective, and should pray to the Divine from the very bottom of one's heart. Why allow yourself to be swept off your feet, when any trouble arises? The moment you let go the chain, you are lost.

When there is absolutely no help, the Divine is your only help, and by the Divine we mean that which is in us, the Soul of our soul, this Soul of all.

In our stage Japam is one of the most important practices. And it takes us nearer and nearer to the Soul of our soul.

Sri Ramakrishna says:

"Each Japam is like a link of a chain, and holding this chain, you reach the very end of the chain, that to which it is fixed."

So it is by proceeding step by step, as it were, holding on to the chain and never letting it go, and that, in course of time, we reach our goal. The sound calls up the thought, the thought brings us in touch with the Divine. And if Japam does not appeal, then you may have some prayer, constantly repeating this prayer, making the sound audible only to your ears. And also think of the Divine. Your prayer should not be aimless: it should be directed towards the Divine.

Even when we seem to be swept away, let us try to hold on to the chain. Very often we magnify the danger that threatens us. Afterwards we find that we have been enlarging it too much with our vivid imagination. The situation may seem bad, but usually it is not so awful as we suppose. Very often it does not take such an awful turn as we imagine. And even if matters are really awful, why give up the struggle and allow yourself to be defeated without any resistance? Always go on with your Japam, your prayer, in such cases, and try to meet the situation as well as you can. Even if you are defeated, your defeat will prove to be a stepping-stone to success.

When the storm is raging, we should hold on to the chain —Japam and prayer. If you do not, you cut yourself away from the higher forces and allow yourself to be defeated by the lower ones. And then you have to suffer.

When you try to be in tune with the higher forces, you may find the discrepancy between the higher and the lower forces. But then you don't feel any discrepancy between the higher forces and yourself. On the other hand, if you identify yourself with the lower forces, you find the discrepancy not only between the higher forces and the lower ones, but also between the higher forces and yourself. So you come to have a double discrepancy. The discrepancy between the higher forces and the lower ones cannot be avoided, but there need not be any discrepancy between the higher forces and yourself. We lose sight of the Divine and the higher path completely if we stop all struggle and are fully overpowered by the lower forces. The whole thing comes to this: you need a ladder, to take you up, but you kick it away just at the moment you need it most. And then you can never get up. And Japam, prayer and meditation form the ladder that should never be given up.

In our case Japam is the only thing we can really do, and it is out of courtesy that we sometimes give it the name of meditation. There can be no question of doing anything higher like real meditation, unless we prepare ourselves first through ethical culture, performance of duty, Japam, prayers, regular readings from the holy books, trying to dwell on their meaning as much as possible—these preliminary practices help us in withdrawing the mind from the manifold distractions, and then in making us dwell on holy thoughts, naturally with breaks in the beginning. Later on through persistent practice, we are able to continue the thought-current in an unbroken way.

As we become pure and purer in body and mind, in thought, word and deed, we are able to have greater and greater concentration, better and better meditation. And then, in course of time, we come in touch with the Divine, in both His Personal and Impersonal aspects. Then within our own selves, we feel the contact between the finite and the Infinite, between the soul and God, the Soul of our soul, the World-Soul. Meditation thus attains its goal, the highest state of superconsciousness, in which the soul comes into direct touch with the Divine Reality, its true Self, and attains its natural perfection and freedom, peace and blessedness.

## II

Both good and evil belong to the relative plane. There is a difference between good and bad, but both belong to the relative plane, the plane of phenomena.

The thin cloud reflects the light, the dark one also, but very little. And when the thick cloud becomes thin, then it reflects the light all the more. The real substance is not the cloud, neither the thin, nor the thick one, but the light. Both the thick and the thin clouds only limit the light, i.e., the cloud is the limitation that must be got rid of.

Even when we speak of God and the soul, this is limitation, but the highest form of limitation. Since we are still on the staircase and not on the terrace, we should think of the higher parts and the lower parts, stressing the steps very much, but always remembering that our goal is beyond all steps, beyond the whole staircase. So long as we worship, so long as there is the worshiper and the object of worship, even in the subtlest form, it is dualism. Monism is a state, an actual experience, but all these steps take us slowly to the final realization. It is a graduated course.

So, now, we need not worry about the One without a Second, about getting merged into the One, but we should see that we bring the One into the many. You need not be afraid of getting merged as this will take millions and millions of years. So there is no imminent danger of your losing yourself and getting merged into the One.

In the path of devotion, the aspirant always has something to support him, and all need an amount of personal support, a Holy Personality, to some extent.

If you feel that you are drowned in an Infinite Ocean of Consciousness you feel that your personality is something subtle, that has become gross. Think that both the vast mass of light, your object of worship, and the small particle of light are drowned in a vast, infinite ocean of light.

First we think more or less of the body only, and there is only an indefinite idea of the Principle of Life, standing at the back of ourselves, of everything, then we begin to stress the Principle of Life more than the body and try to see the Divine spark living in all bodies, and giving life to all.

It is possible for a devotee to love the Formless as much as God with form. This is only a question of temperament. In this, there are three steps:

1) with form and with attributes,
2) without form and with attributes,
3) without form and without attributes.

In the greatest Incarnations and Prophets you see a manifestation of the Purity, Knowledge, Love, etc., that are godlike. And at the nucleus of our small personality there is this same purity, knowledge, love, etc., but all covered with ignorance. Our personality is a combination of the True Self, and the false self. We forget the true Self and identify ourselves with the false self. The spark of light forgets its light-nature and identifies itself with the cloud-nature, and then all the troubles and miseries of life arise.

The body may be the center of our consciousness. The mind may be the center of our consciousness. The little soul may be the center of our consciousness. The Infinite may be the center of our consciousness. And our whole attitude, all our actions and thoughts depend upon what center of consciousness we have chosen, and where we have our center of gravity.

All our thoughts and ideas and imaginations must be clearcut, definite, not hazy and vague. Very often the church-goer goes to church and tries to pray there to something hazy, indefinite, vague, feeling himself to be nothing. But when he comes out again, he stresses his personality all the more in his every-day actions and thoughts and does not believe himself to be nothing. Our prayers, our worship, etc., must be directed towards something definite, be it in the form of a human personality or in some other non-human form.

So long as we take our personality to be real, we must also take other forms to be real and have a Holy Personality to center our thoughts and feelings upon. This may be a Christ, a Buddha, a Ramakrishna, etc.

We have got two forms of consciousness: we make the soul the center of our consciousness and feel the Infinite in that, or we make the Infinite the center of our consciousness and feel the soul as a manifestation of this Infinite. Making our soul the center of our consciousness, we feel this Infinite in the soul. Making the Infinite the center of our consciousness, we feel that the soul is its manifestation. We come to feel the Infinite Ocean of Light joining and combining every point of the circle.

At the beginning this may be a fantasy, but ultimately it becomes an experience.

As regards our spiritual practice we must be very definite, do away with all hazy thoughts and feelings. If you are able to catch the Formless, do it by all means. If not, take hold of the form and realize the formless in the form, next realize the formless in yourself, then the formless in all.

There are some devotees, who in a certain mood, would have the form and the attributes, and in another mood the formless with attributes. At every step we must be in touch with the Divine, whatever be our mood.

Sri Ramakrishna was very fond of a Sanscrit passage:

"When I think of myself as identified with the body, I am Thy servant and Thou art my Master, my will is controlled by Thy Will.

"When I think of myself as a Jiva (individualized soul) as distinct from the body, I am the part and Thou art the Whole.

"When I recognize the spiritual Principle in me as distinct from body and mind and Jiva, I realize that I am one with the Divine."

During all our practices we must take a definite standpoint, from whence to proceed. A dualist with experience is infinitely better than a monist without experience.

There are some aspirants who are not satisfied with having only one form of meditation. They think of the Infinite Ocean, in which there is the worshiper and the worshiped. The devotee thinks more of the Divine than of himself. Then he tries to think of the Principle in the object of worship and in himself. The next step will be that both these are merged, that the bubble and the wave are merged into the Infinite Ocean.

So long as there is even the slightest clinging to personality, one passes through birth and death. When this clinging stops, then the water-drop becomes one with the ocean.

Before we die, we must get at least some glimpses, and then move on. If in this life we don't succeed, begin again and again, move on life after life till you reach the goal.

If some day you are going to realize the Self, why not try to do it now? So the ideal of Vedanta is to realize Truth while we are alive. "Until you fall asleep, until you die, busy yourself with Vedantic thoughts."

# The Yoga of Meditation[1]
## SWAMI PRABHAVANANDA

MEDITATION IS THE very center and heart of spiritual life. It matters not whether you are a follower of the path of Karma, or of devotion or knowledge, whether you are a Christian or a Buddhist or a Hindu, sooner or later you have to practice meditation, you have to become absorbed in divine contemplation; there is no other way. You may begin in divergent ways according to your beliefs and temperament, but as you proceed, as you approach the center and heart of religion and religious practice, you come to that center which is called meditation.

The yoga of meditation was propounded by the great Yogi Patanjali. Patanjali was not the founder of this path of meditation. There were already existent different systems of spiritual practices which he studied and followed, and afterwards systematized, edited and compiled into aphoristic form which became known as the Yoga Aphorisms of Patanjali.

The outstanding peculiarity of this philosophy of Patanjali is that what he propounds has nothing to do with any theory or dogma or presupposition. Even whether you believe in God or not does not matter.

Patanjali was one of those philosophers who claimed that belief in God is not a necessary prerequisite for spiritual life. To him religion is experience; therefore, whether you have theories, or preconceived ideas, whether you believe in God or not, does not matter.

To the seeker after truth, who follows certain principles and makes the experiment, the truth will be revealed, because truth is truth, an existent factor, not anything imaginary, but a matter of fact and experience. Patanjali, how-

[1] Notes of a lecture.

ever, says that belief in God is one of the means to practice yoga.

What God is, what that Reality is, nobody has been able to express in words. To define God is to limit Him, to finitize Him.

So Patanjali tells us that our belief in God is one of the means, and not the only means, to reach the ultimate Reality, and also gives us various principles and methods of life and procedure to follow for the attainment of that reality. These principles can be accepted and practiced universally by the followers of any path or religion.

Yoga has been defined by Patanjali as the complete control of the waves of the mind. One who can control the waves of the mind attains Yoga, that state when the true nature of the Self becomes revealed.

This control of the waves of the mind is not so simple as it would at first appear. It is a complete transformation of the character, when the mind becomes absolutely pure and tranquil. St. Paul said: "Be ye transformed by the renewal of your own mind." That is it, and this control is the blessedness of purity which Jesus spoke of when He said: "Blessed are the pure in heart for they shall see God." He meant that complete transformation, that complete overhauling of the mind.

In every religion we find the same truth taught, that the Kingdom of God is within; the Reality is to be found within our own Self. As long as we forget this truth, as long as we seek the Reality outside of ourselves so long shall we be disappointed. We must learn to look within.

The question may well be asked, if the Kingdom of God is within, what obstructs our knowledge of that Kingdom? Why do we not experience that Heaven? The obstruction to this knowledge is the restlessness of the mind due to the waves or impressions that have accumulated there. There are innumerable impressions in the mind, because no thought, no action is ever lost. We send out a thought of love or a thought of hatred, and this thought creates a peculiar impression in the mind. A thought may be forgotten, but it is never lost. It leaves an impression in the mind. So we see that the mind is filled with countless impressions, not only of this life but of many past lives, and to control these impressions of the mind which we have accumulated by the very nature of our existence would seem a tremendous task.

These innumerable impressions have been classified by Patanjali into five divisions—the five causes of impurity that exist in the mind. The first is *avidya,* ignorance, which causes us to forget our true nature, and hides the vision of the real Self. From ignorance springs *ego.* With the sense of ego arise *attachment* or attraction, *repulsion* and the *will to live.* Buddha calls this *will to live, tanha,* or thirst for life and enjoyment. Christ referred to this thirst when He said: "He that loveth his life shall lose it."

These are the impurities, the impressions, the waves that exist in the mind and obstruct our vision of the Reality, our entrance into the Kingdom of God.

To show us how to overcome these distractions and achieve that blessed purity through which the truth of God may be revealed in our own souls, Patanjali evolved a system which he called the eight-limbed Yoga. These eight limbs are: *yama, niyama* (which include the ethical practices), *asana* (posture), *pranayama* (regulation of breath), *pratyahara* (the indrawing of the senses from sense objects), *dharana* (concentration), *dhyana* (meditation), and *samadhi* (absorption).

Before explaining these limbs of Yoga, it would be well to explain in brief the ideal of ethical life as taught by the Hindu seers. There have been scholars in the West who have brought charge against the Hindu philosophy that ethics play no important part in the religion of India; whereas, on the contrary, the Hindu philosophers and mystics clearly state that, in order to have the transcendental experience of the Reality, though it is necessary to go beyond both good and evil, beyond ethics, moral life is the very foundation of spiritual life. Nevertheless, we must rise above this foundation. This does not mean that we become unmoral. Just as a flower gives out fragrance without any consciousness of doing so, but because it is fragrant by its very nature, in the same way our natures must become such that we do what is good and moral without any consciousness of being good and moral; we become moral because holiness has become a part of our very nature. This is what is meant by transcending ethical life.

As a house that is built upon quicksand cannot stand, neither can a spiritual life stand unless it is built firmly on the rock foundation of ethical and moral life. All great spiritual teachers insist, however, that spiritual life is something far greater, far grander, far nobler than moral life.

Now let us consider *yama,* the first of these eight limbs of yoga. Yama includes *ahimsa* (not hurting any creature), *satya* (truthfulness), *asteya* (non-stealing), *brahmacharya* (chastity), and *aparigraha* (non-covetousness). In order that we can practice the virtue of *ahimsa,* we must not hurt any creature by word, thought or deed; we must learn to feel unity, oneness and sympathy with every living being.

Next comes *satya,* truthfulness in thought, word and deed. Speak the truth but do not tell a harsh truth. We must always consider why we are speaking the truth; is it to help or to hurt another? To tell a harsh truth which would hurt another is to go against the very first principle, *ahimsa,* and it is unethical. Truth must always be agreeable and beneficial.

*Non-stealing* comes next. This may seem quite strange to many, because the habit of stealing as we understand it belongs to a very few selfish individuals. Few of us would actually steal the possessions of another. Yet, according to Patanjali, we are all thieves at heart, every one of us. How? Every time we label anything as ours and call it our own, we are stealing. Nothing belongs to us. Everything belongs to Prakriti—nature. The idea of ownership comes through ignorance. Non-stealing therefore means the ideal of non-possession.

The next ideal that follows is *chastity, continence.* To attain the heights of spiritual realization there must be the practice of continence in thought, word and deed.

Then comes *non-covetousness.* We must covet nothing, possess nothing.

These constitute the ethical practices of life.

To know about the ethical practices, to grasp their importance intellectually is not enough. We must practice them. But the question is, how? We are all creatures of habit. If we are good it is because we have formed the habit of being good; if we are bad, we are bad in spite of ourselves, it has become our habit. Therefore, in order to rid ourselves of this present bundle of habits we have to create a new bundle of habits, which brings us to the next step:

*Niyama* consists of the practices of *purity, contentment, austerity,* and *self-surrender.*

The first of these regular habits which must be formed is *purity,* which means purification, both external and internal. External purification is a simple matter as we know. We bathe every day as a matter of course, but with little or no thought behind the action. Now our daily bathing must become a purification ceremony; the temple of God must be consciously purified that the God within may become manifest. That is the ideal of external purification.

As the body becomes unclean if it is not cleansed each day, so also does the mind. Therefore we must practice *inner purification* every day. Within everyone of us there is the sense of ego, of pride, jealousy, hatred, etc. The method of this inner purification by which we may be cleansed of these impurities is to feel the presence of the Divine within, and to feel that all the impurities and all ignorance have been consumed by that Presence. This must become a daily habit; we must feel that Presence, and meditate upon It.

Next comes *contentment.* Whenever conditions do not suit us we want to change them. We feel sure that if we but change our environment everything will be different, and we shall be happy. Outward conditions can never be changed. We cannot change the weather, so what do we do? We adapt ourselves to it. If it is cold outside we change the condition in the home. In the same way we must change our inner condition. The outward conditions exist because of the inner condition. Change that, reform yourself and the whole world becomes reformed. Before you try to reform another reform yourself.

*Study* is the next regular habit to be formed. By study is not meant merely the reading of books. The study of different books, of different scriptures and different philosophies is very good for a beginner, but when once we take to the spiritual life seriously and have a conclusive intellectual understanding, then study must be only of such as will help contemplation. Study also means *Japam,* or the repetition of the sacred word and meditation on its meaning. This practice of study brings great purity of heart.

Then comes the regular habit of *surrendering ourselves to the Reality.* Though you may not know what that Reality is, you must feel that there is a Reality, an infinite power, and you must surrender yourself to that. If you believe in God, surrender yourself to Him—every day. Make this self-surrender a regular habit.

The foregoing principles are the foundation of spiritual life.

The first step in the higher practices to be followed is called *Asana* or posture. Posture has been defined by Patanjali as that which is firm and pleasant. There are no gymnastics in this practice. The only principle is that the upper part of the body must be kept straight. As one proceeds, as one grows and there comes certain spiritual unfoldment, many experiences will be felt coming through the spiritual nerve in the spine. Therefore, the spine must be kept perfectly straight.

The next practice is known as *Pranayama* or regulation of breath. Breath controls thought. When you are restless, when you are angry, watch your breath. When you are calm, tranquil, watch your breath. As you watch your breathing, you will notice that there are different rhythms at different times, according to your thoughts. When you feel love you will see that the breath is different than when you feel anger or hatred. Therefore, Patanjali tells us that if we can change the regulation of our breath we can gain control over our thoughts, and to do this he gave certain methods for regulating the breath which would bring calmness and tranquility in our thoughts.

*Pratyahara* which is the next practice has been beautifully described by Sri Krishna in the Bhagavad-Gita: "When, like the tortoise withdrawing its limbs, he can withdraw his senses from their objects, then his wisdom becomes steady." The secret of this practice is that we must learn to be attached and at the same time detached. We must be able to apply our minds to whatever we do, and yet be able to withdraw the mind completely at will. When the tortoise withdraws its limbs nothing from outside can hurt it, so when we learn to withdraw our minds from sense objects they are freed from distracting thoughts. For this practice of *Pratyahara* Patanjali has given certain instructions and rules which, if followed, will lead to that "steady wisdom."

Now we come to the practice of *concentration*. Concentration does not mean fixing one's gaze upon any external object. It means we have to concentrate upon the Reality which is within. Within this body—which is the temple of God—there are spiritual centers of consciousness, not imaginary, but very real, and it is upon one or the other of these centers of consciousness that we have to concentrate.

For the practice of concentration it is very necessary to follow the instructions of a *Guru* or teacher who has known and realized these spiritual centers; and to follow these instructions one must have faith in the words of the teacher. Faith is an important factor in every department of life. Just as a student of physics, for instance, must have faith in the words of the professor until he has experimented and attained certain results for himself, so must the spiritual aspirant have faith in the words of his Guru, until he has experimented and attained certain results. The teacher will instruct him according to his growth and development, and if these instructions are followed faithfully and perseveringly, the aspirant will attain definite experiences for himself.

Patanjali did not insist upon one object of concentration for everybody, but suggested different forms to suit the beliefs and tendencies of the individual. One suggestion he gives is to concentrate upon the effulgent light which is within the heart. Another suggestion is to concentrate upon the heart of a perfected soul.

Patanjali also speaks of the knowledge which sometimes comes in dreams. These dreams are rare indeed, and in the heart of the spiritual aspirant who gets such a dream there is created a deep and lasting impression, and he points out that one blessed with such a dream could make that the object of his concentration.

Thus there are many ideals upon which to concentrate, depending upon the growth and the temperament of the individual. It is difficult for the student to decide for himself which ideal he should adopt. Concentration can never be learned from the study of books. There is not one method for all; what may help one may harm another. Therefore, the need of a spiritual teacher cannot be too strongly emphasized.

The next stage is reached through the practice of concentration. It is called *Dhyana,* meditation. Through the practice of meditation the mind flows towards the one object of concentration without a break.

The mind by its very nature is always in a state of flux. One thought follows another constantly. It is possible of course to limit the mind to one certain subject of thought. For instance, one may meditate upon the life of Christ or any great soul, or upon the ideas expressed in a beautiful poem, but that is not what is meant by meditation, though such practices are helpful aids to meditation. The mind is still in a flux, moving in a larger space, following a series of thoughts.

The practice of meditation is to hold the mind to one thought. In the beginning other thoughts will intrude, gaps will be created, but again it must be applied to the one thought, until gradually the gaps will be lessened and there will be no more intervals; the one thought will continue uninterruptedly. Just as each point of the electric current, though separate, flows in one continuous stream and produces a flickerless light, or just as oil being poured from one vessel to another does not break, so when the mind flows toward the object of concentration, toward the spiritual ideal, without break or interval, there comes that state known as *Dhyana* which has been translated as meditation or contemplation.

This state brings us to the next stage known as *Samadhi.* Ordinarily the word samadhi has been used to mean the transcendental consciousness, the revelation, but Patanjali uses it as a stage of absorption, the door that leads to the transcendental experience.

This samadhi means identity with the object of meditation. Thus we see how important it is that the object of our meditation be divine and uplifting.

From this absorption we reach the stage in spiritual progress which is technically called *Samyama,* which means the complete forgetfulness of everything external or internal; there remains nothing but the object of meditation. Time itself is annihilated.

At this point there come visions, spiritual experiences and sometimes occult powers. Many aspirants in the course of their progress stop here. When these visions and spiritual experiences come, when they experience that joy which the Christian mystics call ecstasy, they feel there is nothing greater, nothing superior to be experienced. So they stop, and make no further progress.

Visions, spiritual ecstasies, occult powers are great in themselves, but there is a realm far beyond visions and ecstasies. Occult powers may come, but if you are tempted to use them, the door to spiritual progress is closed and you have to learn the secrets by which these powers can be controlled, and become once more a simple and humble seeker.

By transcending these powers and visions, the door to spiritual life is opened, and we experience *samadhi,* the transcendental consciousness. We come face to face with the Reality; then we too can say with Christ, "I and my Father are one."

# The Return to Ritual

## GERALD HEARD

THE ATTITUDE of Western man is going through many changes, changes in regard to things which he took for granted were settled. Most Westerners have no doubt thought that their parents had cleared much rubbish out of their lives, rubbish which the grandparents had somehow tolerated. Whatever happened we should never again clutter ourselves with superstitions and tabus. The attitude was really not much in advance of the bitter couplet in Butler's "Hudibras":

> *He knew what's what; and that's as high*
> *As metaphysic wit can fly.*

Perhaps no subject shows more clearly the way in which casual and hasty rejection of the past is now giving place to reconsideration, than what is happening about ritual. In all progressive countries and especially among the democracies the thought of ritual, of expressing a condition, of creating a state of mind not by words but by behaviour, has seemed for long simply ridiculous. All that was a hang-over from effete feudalism. Of course you could dress up if you liked, stage a show on the campus, be a self-styled knight of this or that fancy order or even if you happened to be a Catholic carry on the old forms with a sense that it was just because they were genuine antiques that you liked them. The thought that a "behaviour pattern" could actually influence thought and will and character, *that* could not be entertained for a moment by a rationalist.

Yet it is psychology which has breached the bank of this self-assured belief. Psychology pointed out, first how little we are influenced by argument or oratory. The one method of influencing public opinion which the democratic rationalist had held to, was shown to be almost worthless. That led to the further inquiry: how are men influenced, how is it that change does come about? It became clear that we are influenced by habit formation, by what we do and especially by those particular behaviours which we regularly and precisely repeat. Further, such behaviours are all the more efficacious the less we attempt to interfere with them consciously. Everyone knows that reason will not prevent you falling off a bicycle however hard you argue with yourself and however clearly you understand the reason why you fall off, if you cross your hands putting the right hand on the left handle and the left hand on the right handle. There are certain deep motivations that can be set in motion only by physical practices and when they are in train can be kept going only by obeying rules and not letting the critical intelligence interfere as long as the action is being performed. This fact, of action depending on something deeper than argued thought, is illustrated by the doggerel distich:

> *The centipede was happy, until a frog in fun*
> *Said, which leg, please, comes after which?*
> *This raised her doubts to such a pitch,*
> *She fell confounded in the ditch,*
> *Not knowing how to run.*

It is with this strange paradox, that we do a thing the better by not knowing too much about it, that ritual deals and can deal as no other approach permits. For ritual is the recognition of "knack," that an art and craft, if it is in your hand is all the better for not being in your head, or at least in that part of it which is given over to the describing in words and the criticising by arguments the processes that go on in the rest of the body-mind.

Once, however, we allow that certain "behaviour patterns" are the best and perhaps the only way of getting the whole body-mind to take up a certain attitude and to maintain it, the question arises which of the many patterns we can choose is the best. They cannot all be equally valuable. Some, for instance, have in them much that is purely magical. That is not to discuss what is magic and whether it may not at times work. It is simply to point out that in any rite which includes magical practices, by so much the rite's value as a psychophysical training is impaired. Military drill is a very efficacious ritual, much more so than any number of orations on patriotism, but drill would be far less efficacious if some of the maneuvers were not intended to set up conditioned reflexes in those drilled but were supposed to cast a spell on the enemy. Other rituals have combined with them ancient practices which once had point but now have none. For instance were we thinking of reviving the religious rites of ancient Egypt we might well find some which were valuable for the purpose we have in view. But we should certainly not be able to take over the full ritual corpus; for example the Sed Festival, which had to do with the belief that the Pharaoh should and could be rejuvenated, we should have to omit. Therefore when we are considering a scientific revaluation of ritual and the selection of those rites and religious functions which are most effective on the body-mind we have to consider two main things. The first is Use and Wont. Certain symbols are familiar to us; others, which as far as we know are "objectively" as efficacious and inoffensive, awake in us misgiving and dislike simply because they are unfamiliar. We find in them associations which those who are used to them do not see. For example, take the two great rites from the Christian Church. To those who had never heard of Baptism a Baptist service would seem ludicrous. While to those who had never known of Totemism the sacrament of Communion through bread and wine thought of as flesh and blood would seem revolting. On the other hand the great Puritan revolution which swept the religious life of the Near East—the Nile and the Levant—in the 7th Century, B.C.—has made all those whose religious practices descend from that source unable to understand the sacramental and ritualistic worship of the generative function. To them such symbolism seems simply degraded and disgusting. We have, then, in the first place to choose those symbols which upset least the social heredity to which we belong. It is probably little use trying to teach ourselves to adopt a symbolism which is alien to us. By the time we have made ourselves by reason tolerant of forms which at first sight were puzzling, grotesque and even repulsive, all natural enthusiasm has gone. Deep devotion is not won by the way of indifferent toleration. Secondly, quite apart from our social heredity, each of us is personally affected to different degrees by different symbols. As the task before all those who would understand is to grasp, or rather to be grasped by, the idea of the Godhead Transcendent and equally Immanent, it follows that Deity is of His Nature inexpressible in our present state of consciousness. Whether, then, we think of Him as with form or as without form the very fact of our thinking of Him immensely lessens what He is. The Puritan, using no forms and feeling himself superior to the ritualist who uses forms, is not necessarily advanced. Indeed he may find that he has, in spite of his intentions but because of the limitations of his mind and the immensity of the Mystery he worships, fallen back behind the ritualist. Many a Puritan, as we see with the Jews for example, while refusing imagery nevertheless, in the mind, relapsed into a crude anthropomorphism which the more elaborate and ritualistic religions avoided. Yet though the Puritan must not impose his bareness and emptiness on the ritualist, he may claim a tolerance for himself and his *via negativa*. Probably also what he is asking for is not a complete banishment of form but for forms through another sense than through the eye. There are three great symbolic methods and ritual activities whereby man reminds himself of the Inexpressible. The first is through sight and touch, through relics, sacraments and functions. The second is through sound. Many Puritans are just as much symbolists as any Priest, but their symbol is conveyed through the ear. To such, music is the pattern through which Perfection delegates itself and poetry is also another aid. Music, however, is the purest help because in it no word interferes to limit the limitless, for all definition is limitation. The third great avenue of symbolism is not through the eye or through the ear but through the whole body—that is the kinesthetic expression of worship which is shown in the dance. We are probably too self-conscious to be able to revive that behaviour pattern and yet there seems little doubt that many of us are predominantly kinesthetic types. Dancing has seldom been more popular than it is today. A false rationalism makes us believe that we can only have a high and advanced experience if we use reason and logic with perhaps a little visual symbolism. The Sufis were not unsubtle thinkers nor unlofty livers yet they used the dance regularly in worship. It is also of interest to note in this respect that the Sufis being a branch of Islamism were denied visual symbolism. The line, however, along which ritual might follow up a promising research would be in the direction of music, of symbolism through the ear. Molinos the Quietist Mystic gave as a formula for approaching the Unnameable, "Silence of the mouth, silence of the mind, silence of the will." That silence, that allaying of the ego's tumult, that stilling of the waves of the mind is an art which needs every aid. Many, to whom visual symbolism is not a medium but a hindrance, not a lens but a thick stained-glass window, would find in carefully applied music an instrument whereby to draw aside the flashing meshes of maya.

# Religion and Temperament

## Aldous Huxley

"OUR HOLY FATHERS herebefore taught us that we should know the measure of our gift, and work upon that; not taking upon us by feigning more than we have in feeling. . . . Who hath grace, be it never so little, and leaveth wilfully the working thereof, and maketh himself to travail in another which he hath not yet, but only because he seeth or heareth that other men did so, soothly he may run awhile until he be weary, and then shall he turn home again; and unless he beware, he may hurt his feet by some fantasies ere he come home. But he that worketh in such grace as he hath, and desireth by prayer meekly and lastingly after more, and after feeleth his heart stirred to follow the grace which he desired, he may safely run if he keep meekness. . . . And, therefore, it is speedful that we know the gifts that are given us of God, that we may work in them, for by these we shall be saved; as some by bodily works and deeds of mercy, some by great bodily penance, some by sorrow and weeping for their sins all their lifetime, some by preaching and teaching, some by divers graces and gifts of devotion shall be saved and come to bliss."

These words from Walter Hilton's "The Scale of Perfection" were written by an English monk of the fourteenth century. But the message they convey is beyond any particular time or place. In one form or another it has been enunciated by all the masters of the spiritual life, Western and Oriental, present and past. Liberation, salvation, the Beatific Vision, unitive knowledge of God—the end is always and everywhere the same. But the means whereby it is sought to achieve that end are as various as the human beings who address themselves to the task.

Many attempts have been made to classify the varieties of

human temperament. Thus, in the West, we have the four-fold classification of Hippocrates in terms of the "humours" (phlegmatic, choleric, melancholic and sanguine), a classification which dominated the theory and practice of medicine for more than two thousand years, and whose terminology is indelibly imprinted upon every European language. Another popular system of classification, which has also left its trace in modern speech, was the seven-fold system of the astrologers. We still describe people in planetary terms—as jovial, mercurial, saturnine, martial. Both these systems had their merits, and there was even something to be said for the physiognomic classification in terms of supposed resemblances to various animals. All were based to some extent on observation.

In our own day a number of new essays in classification have been attempted—those of Stockard, of Kretschmer, of Viola, and, more satisfactory and better-documented than all the rest, of Dr. William Sheldon, whose two volumes on "The Varieties of Human Physique" and "The Varieties of Temperament" are among the most important of recent contributions to the science of Man.

Sheldon's researches have led him to the conclusion that the most satisfactory system of classification is in terms of three types of temperament, which he calls the viscerotonic, the somatotonic and the cerebrotonic. All human beings are of mixed type. But in some the various elements are evenly mixed, while in some one element tends to predominate at the expense of the other two. In some again the mixture is well balanced, whereas in others there is a disequilibrium which results in acute internal conflict and extreme difficulty in making adaptation to life. No form of hormone treatment or other therapy can change the fundamental pattern of temperament, which is a datum to be accepted and made the best of. In a word, the psycho-physical pattern is one of the expressions of karma. There are good karmas and bad karmas: but it is within the choice of the individual to make a bad use of the best karma and a good use of the worst. There is a measure of free will within a system of predestination.

A religion cannot survive unless it makes an appeal to all sorts and conditions of men. This being so, we must expect to find in all the existing world religions elements of belief, of precept, and of practice contributed by each of the principal categories of human beings. Dr. Sheldon's findings confirm these expectations, and provide new instruments for the analysis of religious phenomena. Let us now briefly consider the three polar types in their relations to the organized religions of the world.

The viscerotonic temperament is associated with what Dr. Sheldon has called endomorphic physique—the type of physique in which the gut is the predominant feature, and which has a tendency, when external conditions are good, to run to breadth, fat and weight. Characteristic of extreme viscerotonia are the following: slow reaction time, love of comfort and luxury, love of eating, pleasure in digestion, love of the ritual of eating in company (the shared meal is for him a natural sacrament), love of polite ceremony, a certain untempered quality of flabbiness; indiscriminate amiability; easy communication of feeling; tolerance and complacency; dislike of solitude; need of people when in trouble; orientation toward childhood and family relations.

The somatotonic temperament is associated with mesomorphic physique, in which the predominant feature is the musculature. Mesomorphs are physically strong, active and athletic. Among the characteristics of extreme somatotonia we find the following: assertiveness of posture and movement; love of physical adventure; need of exercise; love of risk; indifference to pain; energy and rapid decision; lust for power and domination; courage for combat; competitiveness; psychological callousness; claustrophobia; ruthlessness in gaining the desired end; extraversion towards activity rather than towards people (as with the viscerotonic); need of action when troubled; orientation towards the goals and activities of youth.

The cerebrotonic temperament is associated with the ectomorphic physique, in which the predominance of the nervous system results in a high degree of sensitiveness. Extreme cerebrotonia has the following characteristics: restraint of posture and movement; physiological over-response (one of the consequences of which is extreme sexuality); love of privacy; a certain overintentness and apprehensiveness; secretiveness of feeling and emotional restraint; dislike of company; shyness and inhibited social address; agoraphobia; resistance to habit formation and incapacity to build up routines; awareness of inner mental processes and tendency to introversion; need of solitude when troubled; orientation towards maturity and old age.

These are summary descriptions; but they are sufficient to indicate the nature of the contributions to religion made by each of the three polar types. In his unregenerate state, the viscerotonic loves polite ceremony and luxury, and makes a fetish of ritual eating in public. It is because of him that churches and temples are so splendidly adorned, that rituals are so solemn and elaborate, and that sacramentalism, or the worship of the divine through material symbols, plays so important a part in organized religion.

The ideal of universal brotherly love represents the rationalization, refinement and sublimation of the viscerotonic's native amiability towards all and sundry. Similarly, it is from his native sociophilia that the idea of the Church or fellowship of believers takes its origin. The various cults of divine childhood and divine motherhood have their source in his nostalgic harking back to his own infancy and earlier relations to the family. (It is highly significant in this context to note the difference between the ordinary, viscerotonic cult of the child Christ and the cerebrotonic version of it produced by the French Oratorians of the seventeenth century. In the ordinary cult, the infant Christ is conceived of, and represented as, a beautiful child about two years old. In the Oratorian cult, the child is much younger, and the worshipper is encouraged to think of infancy, not as a time of charm and beauty, but as a condition of abjection and helplessness only slightly less complete than that of death. Christ is to be thanked for having voluntarily taken upon himself the appalling humiliation of being a baby. Between this point of view, and the point of view implicit in one of Raphael's Madonnas and Infant Christs, there is fixed an almost unbridgeable temperamental gulf.)

To the somatotonic, religions owe whatever they have in them of hardness and energy. Proselytizing zeal, the courting of martyrdom and the readiness to persecute are somatotonic characteristics. So are the extremer forms of asceticism, and the whole stoic and puritanic temper. So is the dogmatic insistence on hell fire and the sterner aspects of God. So is the preoccupation with active good works, as opposed to the viscerotonic's preoccupation with sacraments and ritual and the cerebrotonic's with private devotion and meditation. Another significant peculiarity of the somatotonic is mentioned by Dr. Sheldon, who points out that it is among persons of this type that the phenomenon of sudden conversion is most frequently observed. The reason for this must be sought, it would seem, in their active extroversion, which causes them to be profoundly ignorant of the inner workings of their own minds. When religion opens up to their view the interior life of the soul, the discovery comes to them, very often, with the force of a revelation. They are violently converted, and proceed to throw themselves into the business of acting upon their new knowledge with all the energy characteristic of their type. Religious conversion is no longer common in educated circles; but its place has been taken, as Dr. Sheldon points out, by psychological conversion. For it is upon unbalanced somatotonics that psycho-analysis produces its most striking effects, and it is they who are its most fervent believers and most energetic missionaries.

Very different is the case with the cerebrotonic, who habitually lives in contact with his inner being, and for whom the revelations of religion and psychiatry are not startlingly novel. For this reason, and because of his emotional restraint, he is little subject to violent conversion. For him, change of heart and life tends to come gradually. Along with the viscerotonic, who lacks the energy to get himself violently converted, the cerebrotonic has a peculiarly wretched time of it when he happens to be born into a sect which regards violent conversion as a necessary condition of salvation. His temperament is such that he simply cannot experience the convulsion which comes so easily to his somatotonic neighbors. Because of this inability, he is forced either to simulate conversion by an act of conscious or unconscious fraud, or else to regard himself, and be regarded by others, as irretrievably lost.

The great cerebrotonic contribution to religion is mysticism, the worship of God in contemplative solitude without the aid of ritual or sacraments. Because he feels no need of it, the cerebrotonic is sometimes moved, with the Buddha, to denounce ritualistic worship as one of the fetters holding back the soul from liberation.

The unregenerate viscerotonic likes luxury and "nice things" around him. When he becomes religious, he gives up "nice things" for himself, but wants them in his church or temple. Not so the cerebrotonic. To him the life of voluntary poverty seems not only tolerable, but often supremely desirable; and he likes to worship in a shrine as austerely naked as his cell. When the cerebrotonic love of bareness and poverty becomes associated with somatotonic proselytizing zeal, we have iconoclasm.

Among cerebrotonic inventions are hermitages and contemplative orders. Most systems of spiritual exercises are devised by cerebrotonics as an aid to private devotion and a preparation for mystical experience. And finally the great systems of spiritual philosophy, such as those of Shankara, of Plotinus, of Eckhart, are the work of cerebrotonic minds.

So much, then, for the elements contributed to religion by the three polar types of temperament. Two questions now present themselves for our consideration. First, which of the types has been most influential in the framing of the world's great religions? And, second, which of the types is best fitted to discover the truth about ultimate Reality?

The religions of India are predominantly viscerotonic and cerebrotonic religions of ritual and mysticism, having little proselytizing zeal and intolerance, and setting a higher value on the contemplative life than on the active. The same seems to be true of the Taoism of China, at any rate in its uncorrupted forms.

Confucianism would seem to be predominantly viscerotonic—a religion of forms and ceremonials, in which the cult of the family is centrally important.

Mohammedanism is decidedly more somatotonic than any of the religions native to India and China. In its primitive form it is hard, militant and puritanical; it encourages the spirit of martyrdom, is eager to make proselytes and has no qualms about levying "holy wars" and conducting persecutions. Some centuries after the prophet's death it developed the Sufi school of mysticism—a school whose strict Islamic orthodoxy its theologians have always had some difficulty in defending.

In Christianity we have a religion of which, until recent years, the central core has always been cerebrotonic and viscerotonic, contemplative and ritualistic. But, to a much greater extent than is the case with Buddhism and Hinduism, these cerebrotonic and viscerotonic elements have always been associated with others of a strongly somatotonic nature. Christianity has been a militant, proselytizing and persecuting religion. At various periods of its history, stoicism and puritanism have flourished within the church, and at certain times active "good works" have been esteemed as highly as, or even more highly than, contemplation. This is especially the case at the present time. For, as Dr. Sheldon has pointed out, our age has witnessed a veritable somatotonic revolution. The expression of this revolution in the political field is too manifest to require comment. In the sphere of personal living the revolt against pure contemplation and the sacramental reverence for material things may best be studied in the advertising pages of our newspapers and magazines. Where religion is concerned, the revolt is not so much against the viscerotonic elements of Christianity as against the cerebrotonic or contemplative. The two key words of contemporary Western religion are respectively viscerotonic and somatotonic, namely "fellowship" and "social service." The things which these words stand for are good and precious; but their full value can be realized only when the contemplation of ultimate Reality gives meaning to the emotional warmth of fellowship and direction to the activity of service.

Risking a generalization, we may say that the main social function of the great religions has been to keep the congenitally energetic and often violent somatotonics from destroying themselves, their neighbors and society at large. Highly significant in this context is the Bhagavad Gita, which is addressed to a princely kshatriya, a hereditary and professional somatotonic. Its teaching of non-attached action was supplemented, in India, by the theory and practice of caste, with its all-important doctrine of the supremacy of spiritual authority over temporal power. Orthodox Christianity holds the same doctrine in regard to the supremacy of spiritual authority. During the last four hundred years, however, this doctrine has been assailed, not only in practice by ambitious rulers, but also in theory, by philosophers and sociologists. As far back as the sixteenth century, Henry VIII made himself, in Bishop Stubb's words, "the Pope, the whole Pope and something more than the Pope." Since that time his example has been followed in every part of Christendom, until now there is no organized temporal power which acknowledges even theoretically the supremacy of any kind of spiritual authority. The triumph of unrestrained somatotonia is now complete.

We now come to our second question: Which of the three polar types is best fitted to discover the truth about ultimate Reality? The question is one which can be referred only to the judgment of the experts—in this case, the great theocentric saints of the higher religions. The testimony of these men and women is unmistakable. It is in pure contemplation that human beings come nearest, in the present life, to the beatific vision of God. But the desire and the aptitude for contemplation are cerebrotonic characteristics. (But of course those who belong predominantly to the other polar types can always arrive at contemplation, if they fulfil the necessary conditions for receiving the grace of unitive knowledge. It may, however, be doubted whether persons of viscerotonic and somatotonic temperament would ever think of embarking upon the road which leads to contemplation, if the way had not first been explored by cerebrotonics whose soul is, in some sort, *naturaliter contemplativa*.)

To what extent is the viscerotonic justified in his claim that ritual, group worship and sacramentalism enable him to establish contact with ultimate Reality? This is a very difficult question to answer. That such procedures permit those who practice them to get in touch with something greater than themselves seems to admit of no doubt. But what the nature of that something may be—whether some mediated aspect of spiritual Reality, or possibly some kind of psychically objective crystallization of the devotional feeling experienced by the long succession of worshippers who have used the same ceremonial in the past—I will not venture even to try to decide.

One practical conclusion remains to be recorded. Analysis seems to show that religion is a system of relativities within an absolute frame of reference. The end which religion proposes is knowledge of the unalterable fact of God. Its means are relative to the heredity and social upbringing of those who seek that end. This being so, it seems extremely unwise to promote any one of these purely relative means to the rank of a dogmatic absolute. For example, an organized fellowship for the furtherance of spiritual ends and the preservation of traditional knowledge is, obviously and as a matter of empirical experience, a most valuable thing. But we have no right to proceed to a quasi-deification of Church and a dogma of infallibility. *Mutatis mutandis,* the same thing may be said of rituals, sacraments, sudden conversions. All these are means to the ultimate end—means which for some people are enormously valuable, for others, of different temperament, of little or no value. For this reason they should not be treated as though they were absolutes. That way lies idolatry.

The case of ethical precepts is different. Experience shows that such states of mind as pride, anger, covetousness and lust are totally incompatible with the knowledge of ultimate reality; and this incompatibility exists for persons of every variety of temperament and upbringing. Consequently these precepts may properly be inculcated in an absolute form. "If you want God, it is absolutely essential for you not to want to be Napoleon, or Jay Gould, or Casanova."

# Religion and Time

## Aldous Huxley

RELIGION IS as various as humanity. Its reactions to life are sometimes intelligent and creative, sometimes stupid, stultifying and destructive. Through its doctrines it presents sometimes an adequate picture of the nature and quality of ultimate Reality, sometimes a picture coloured by the lowest of human cravings, and therefore wholly untrue. Its consequences are sometimes very good, sometimes monstrously and diabolically evil.

In considering a group of organized religions, or the religious beliefs and practices of a group of individuals, how can we distinguish between the truer and the less true, the better and the less good? One of the answers given by all the great religious teachers is that "by their fruits ye shall know them." But, unfortunately, fruits often take a long time to observe; the full consequences of adherence to a given religion will not be manifested in all circumstances, and the would-be critic must often wait, before passing judgment, until external events provide the opportunity for making a crucial observation. Nor is this all. The fruits of certain less good practices and less true beliefs do not take the form of positive wrong-doings or obviously recognizable disasters. They are of a subtler, more negative kind—not sins, but failures to achieve the highest development of which the individual or group is capable; not catastrophes, but the non-attainment of the fruits of the spirit, love, joy and peace. But such failures and non-attainments can be measured only by observers of more than ordinary insight, or by those who are so placed that they can look back over a long span of the career of the individuals or groups under consideration.

It is clear, then, that, besides the criterion of fruits, we need another more readily applicable—a criterion by which to judge the roots and flowers from which the fruits spring. Thanks to the insight of specially gifted individuals and to the collective experience of generations of worshippers, such criterions for evaluating the doctrines and practices of religion have been discovered and only require to be intelligently applied.

The most elementary criterion is that which has reference to the unity or plurality of the object of worship. It has been found that the doctrines and practices of monotheism are, generally speaking, truer and better than those of polytheism, and lead to more satisfactory results, both for individuals and for societies. But the distinction between monotheism and polytheism is not enough. Two men may both be monotheists; but the nature of the God believed in by the first may be profoundly different from that of the God believed in by the second, and their religious practices may be as diverse as their theoretical conceptions. But the one God—and this is affirmed by all those who have fulfilled the conditions which alone make possible a clear insight into the nature and quality of Reality—is a God of love. In the light of these insights we may refine our criterion and assert that those beliefs will be truer, and those practices better, which have as their object a single God of love. But even a God of love can be conceived of, and therefore worshipped, in a variety of ways, and with diverse consequences for individuals and societies. To become fully adequate, our criterion requires to be further refined. Once again, the new qualification of the elementary criterion is provided by those theocentric mystics who alone have fulfilled the conditions upon which insight depends. The truer forms of religion are those in which God is conceived, not only as one and loving, but also as eternal (that is to say, outside time); and the better forms of religious practice are those which aim at creating in the mind a condition approximating to timelessness. (Reality cannot make itself known except to those who have fulfilled the necessary conditions of "mortification," and have rendered themselves commensurable with God by becoming, as far as they can, unified, loving and, in some measure, timeless.) Conversely, the less true forms of religious belief are those which emphasize God's everlastingness rather than his eternal presence in a non-temporal Now; and the less-good religious practices are those which stress the importance of petitionary prayer addressed to a temporal God for the sake of personal or social advantages in temporal affairs, and which, in general, substitute a preoccupation with future time for the mystic's concern with the timeless presence of eternal Reality.

In theory all the higher religions have insisted that the final end of man, the purpose of his existence upon earth, is the realization, partially in the present life, more completely in some other state, of timeless Reality. In practice, however, a majority of the adherents of these religions have always behaved as if man's primary concern were not with eternity, but with time. At any given moment several quite different religions go by the name of Christianity, say, or Buddhism, or Taoism—religions ranging all the way from the purest mysticism to the grossest fetishism.

In all the higher religions the doctrines about eternal Reality, and the practices designed to help worshippers to render themselves sufficiently timeless to apprehend an eternal God, bear a close family resemblance. Eckhart, as Professor Otto has shown in his "Mysticism East and West," formulates a philosophy which is substantially the same as that of Sankara; and the practical teaching of Indian and Christian mystics is identical in such matters as "holy indifference" to temporal affairs; mortification of memory for the past and anxiety about the future; renunciation of petitionary prayer in favour of simple abandonment to the will of God; purification not only of the will, but also of the imagination and intellect, so that the consciousness of the worshipper may partake in some measure of the intense undifferentiated timelessness of that which he desires to apprehend and be united with. For the theocentric mystics both of East and West, it is axiomatic that one must "seek first the kingdom of God" (the timeless kingdom of an eternal God) "and his righteousness" (the righteousness of eternity over and above the righteousness of life in time); and that, only if one does this, is there any prospect of "all the rest being added."

In the less true forms of the genuine religions and, still more, in the humanistic pseudo-religions of Nationalism,

Fascism, Communism and the like, the position is completely reversed. For here the fundamental commandment and its accompanying promise are, "Seek ye first all the rest, and the kingdom of God and his righteousness shall be added to you."

Among the religious, the seeking first of temporal values is always associated with the idea of a God who, being in time rather than eternity, is not spiritual but "psychical." Believers in a temporal God make use of passionately willed and intensely felt petitionary prayer for concrete benefits, such as health and prosperity before death and, afterwards, a place in some everlasting heaven. These petitionary prayers are accompanied by rituals and sacraments which, by stimulating imagination and intensifying emotions, help to create that psychic "field," within which petitionary prayer takes on the power to get itself answered. The fact that "spiritual healing" (more accurately, "psychic healing") often works, and that prayers for one's own or other people's health, wealth and happiness often get answered, is constantly put forward by the devotees of temporal religion as a proof that they are being directly helped by God. One might just as well argue that one is being directly helped by God because one's refrigerator works, or because somebody answers when one dials a number on the telephone. All one has a right to say of such things as "spiritual healing" and answers to prayer is that they are happenings permitted by God in exactly the same way as other natural psycho-physical phenomena are permitted. That the mind has extensive powers over and above those which are ordinarily used in everyday life has been known from time immemorial; and at all periods and in all countries these powers have been exploited, for good and for evil, by mediums, healers, prophets, medicine men, magicians, hatha yogins and the other queer fish who exist and have always existed on the fringes of every society. During the last two or three generations some efforts have been made to investigate these powers and the conditions under which they are manifested. The phenomena of hypnotism and suggestion have been carefully explored. Under the auspices of the Society of Psychical Research a thoroughly respectable and critical literature of the abnormal has come into existence. Research into Extra-Sensory Perception is carried on in a number of university laboratories; and now, in at least one of those laboratories, there is piling up significant evidence for the existence of "Pk," or the ability of persons to interfere with the movements of material objects by means of a purely mental act. If people working under the most uninspiring laboratory conditions can perceive clairvoyantly, exercise foreknowledge and affect the fall of dice by purely mental acts, then clearly we have no right whatever to invoke a direct intervention of God in the case of similar phenomena, just because they happen to take place in a church or to the accompaniment of religious rites.

In this context, it is highly significant that the great theocentric mystics have always drawn a sharp distinction between the "psychic" and the "spiritual." In their view, phenomena of the first class have their existence in an unfamiliar, but in no way intrinsically superior, extension of the space-time world. Spiritual phenomena, on the other hand, belong to the timeless and eternal order, within which the temporal order has its less real existence. The mystics' attitude to "miracles" is one of intellectual acceptance, and emotional and volitional detachment. Miracles happen, but they are of very little importance. Moreover, the temptation to perform "miracles" should always be resisted. For mystics, this temptation is particularly strong; for those who try to make themselves timelessly conscious of eternal Reality frequently develop unusual psychic powers in the process. When this happens, it is essential to refrain from using such powers; for the user thereby places an impediment between himself and the Reality with which he hopes to be united. This advice is given as clearly by the masters of Western spirituality as by the Buddhists and Vedantists. But, unfortunately for Christianity, the teaching of the gospels upon this subject is somewhat confused. Jesus denounces those who ask for "signs," but Himself performs many miracles of healing and the like. The explanation of this apparent inconsistency can probably be found in the passage, in which He asks His critics which is easier, to tell the sick man to rise and walk, or to tell him that his sins are forgiven him. The implication seems to be that physical "signs" are legitimate, if the person who performs them is so completely united with eternal Reality that he is able, by the very quality of his being, to modify the inner being of those, for whose sake the "signs" are performed. But this enormously important qualification has been generally neglected, and the adherents of the less true forms of the Christian religion attach enormous importance to such purely "psychic" phenomena as healing and the answer to petitionary prayer. By doing this they positively guarantee themselves against attaining that degree of union with timeless Reality which alone might render the performance of a "miracle" innocuous to the doer and permanently beneficial to the person on whom, or for whom, it is done.

Another form frequently taken by temporal religion is apocalypticism—belief in an extraordinary cosmic event to take place in the not-too-distant future, together with the practices deemed appropriate to this state of things. Here again intense preoccupation with future time positively guarantees the apocalypticist against the possibility of a timeless realization of eternal Reality.

In certain respects all the humanistic pseudo-religions, at present so popular, bear a close resemblance to the apocalyptic perversions of true religion. For in these also an intense preoccupation with hypothetical events in future time takes the place of the genuinely religious concern with Reality now, in the eternal present. But whereas believers in the approaching end of the world seldom find it necessary to coerce or slaughter those who do not agree with them, coercion and slaughter have formed an essential part of the programme put forward by the crusaders for the humanistic pseudo-religions. For the revolutionary, whether of the right or the left, the supremely important fact is the golden age of peace, prosperity and brotherly love which, his faith assures him, is bound to dawn as soon as his particular brand of revolution has been carried through. Nothing stands between the people's miserable present and its glorious future, except a minority, perhaps a majority, of perverse or merely ignorant individuals. All that is necessary is to liquidate a few thousands, or it may be a few millions, of these living obstacles to progress, and then to coerce and propagandize the rest into

acquiescence. When these unpleasant but necessary prelim-
inaries are over, the golden age will begin. Such is the theory
of that secular apocalypticism which is the religion of revolutionaries. But in practice, it is hardly necessary to say, the
means employed positively guarantee that the end actually
reached shall be profoundly different from that which the
prophetic theorists envisaged.

Happiness is not achieved by the conscious pursuit of happiness; it is generally the by-product of other activities. This
"hedonistic paradox" may be generalized to cover our whole
life in time. Temporal conditions will be accepted as satisfactory only by those whose first concern is not with time,
but with eternal Reality and with that state of virtually timeless consciousness, in which alone the awareness of Reality
is possible. Furthermore, in any given society, temporal conditions will be generally felt to be tolerable, and will in fact
be as free from the grosser evils as human conditions ever
can be, only when the current philosophy of life lays more
stress upon eternity than upon time, and only when a minority of individuals within the society are making a serious
attempt to live out this philosophy in practice. It is highly
significant, as Sorokin has pointed out, that a man born into
the eternity-conscious thirteenth century had a much better
prospect of dying in his bed than a man of our own time—
the obsessed and therefore nationalistic, revolutionary and violent twentieth century. *Si monumentum requiris, circum-
spice.* So runs the epitaph carved on Wren's tomb in St.
Paul's cathedral. Similarly, if you require a monument to
modern man's preoccupation with future time to the exclusion of present eternity, look round at the world's battle-
fields and back over the history covered by the life-time of a
man of seventy—the history of that late-Victorian "Generation of Materialism," so ably sketched in a recent volume by
Professor Carlton Hayes, and the history of the generation
which inevitably succeeded it, that of the wars and revolutions. Reality cannot be ignored except at a price; and the
longer the ignorance is persisted in, the higher and the more
terrible becomes the price that must be paid.

# The Problem of Evil

## Swami Prabhavananda

THE PROBLEM OF EVIL is a central one in every system of philosophy or religion, a problem that is usually explained away instead of itself being explained; and the difficulty of reconciling the conception of a God who is all good with the existence of evil remains. Monists of the West, in order to be consistent with their philosophy of absolutism, tend to deny the reality of evil; for, they declare, what we call evil is evil only because we do not view our lives *sub specie aeternitatis*. What appears to be evil is in reality good when viewed in this manner.

And yet we must ask, can evil really be changed into good merely by viewing it in a special manner? Can pain be labelled pleasure provided we view it absolutely? It is true that pain may be borne gracefully if we fix our gaze upon the ultimate goodness of God, but pain is a positive experience of suffering, at least during the duration of the experience. How then can a philosophy be at one with itself simply by denying evil or even more simply by affirming that it can be transformed into good when it is viewed "under the aspect of eternity"? The question remains unanswered in Western attempts to dodge this gravest of all ethical problems.

Vedanta meets the issue in a different way. In the first place, it asserts that, when viewed from the point of view of the Absolute, there is neither good nor evil, neither pleasure nor pain. Then evil no longer exists, not because the magical power of the Absolute changes evil into good, but because both good and evil have ceased to exist. So long, however, as we are experiencing pleasure and pain, so long do both good and evil exist as empirically real. The experience of evil is indeed as much a positive fact as the experience of good.

Vedanta thus recognizes both good and evil, and pleasure and pain, as positive facts of experience in our empirical lives, they being in effect the play of *Maya,* neither real nor unreal. They cannot be said to be real, for we no longer experience them when we touch absolute experience; and they cannot be said to be actually unreal, for they are experienced in our empirical lives.

Thus, if we accept finite experiences as but the play of Maya, the perfection of the Absolute is in no way tarnished. The experiences of pleasure and of pain within Maya are in fact due to the good and evil deeds of an individual's past; they are the direct result of karma operating in an individual's life. Shankara compares God to the giver of rain. As rain falls to the ground, various plants ripen and grow and differ from one another, not because the rain is partial but because the seeds are different. *Iswara* (God) in like manner is the dispenser of the Law, and individuals experience pleasure and pain according to the seeds of merit and demerit they have sown in themselves from a beginningless past.

So, again, the all-goodness of God is not contradicted by our own individual experiences of suffering and evil. Good and evil, that is to say, as they exist as Maya, are relative—in the sense that the one without the other is meaningless. Shankara, therefore, distinguishes Maya as being of two kinds—*avidya* (evil) and *vidya* (good). Avidya is that which causes us to move away from the real Self, or Brahman, drawing a veil before our sight of Truth; vidya is that which enables us to move towards Brahman by removing the veil of ignorance. As we receive illumination and come to know the Self, we transcend both vidya and avidya and cease to submit to the dominion of Maya.

# The Magical and the Spiritual

## ALDOUS HUXLEY

CREATION, EVIL, TIME—three mysteries, about which it is only possible, in the last analysis, to say that they are somehow interconnected, and that their relationship to the greater mystery of divine Reality is one of limitation. Creation and time are the results of some cosmic process of limiting the eternal spiritual substance, while evil is the name we give to a secondary process of limitation carried out by creatures within the order of creation—a limiting of individual creatureliness to its own self, to the exclusion of other creatures and to that which lies beyond all creatures.

Reality is present in all creatures; but all creatures are not equally aware of the fact. Those in which mind is rudimentary or only imperfectly developed can probably never become aware of Reality, except perhaps in its physiological aspect as normal and natural functioning, as the proper and perfect relationship between the parts of the organism, and between the organism as a whole and its environment. With man, however, the case is different. Thanks to their mental development, human beings can become aware of the presence of Reality within them, not only on the physiological level, but also by a direct spiritual apprehension. Though born into time and illusion, man has a capacity for Reality and Eternity. Whether he makes use of this capacity, or whether, on the contrary, he limits himself to the God-eclipsing activities of ordinary unregenerate life, depends upon his own choice.

In order to actualize their innate capacity for Reality and Eternity, human beings must undertake a course of detachment—detachment, first of all, from that limitation to self and to the creatureliness of creatures which constitute evil, and detachment, in the second place, from the cosmic limitations imposed upon creatures by the act of creation, namely separateness, individuality and time. The first kind of detachment is achieved by self-mortification, and practice of virtue, and the cultivation and exercise of love and compassion for one's fellow beings. The second kind of detachment is achieved through the practices of mystical contemplation. Or rather it would be more accurate to say that the practices of mystical contemplation are the means whereby we can prepare ourselves for receiving the grace of a direct intuition of Reality and Eternity. Experience has shown that this second detachment cannot be achieved except by those who are at least in process of achieving the first—that the mystical life, in other words, is closely associated with the ascetical.

Between Reality and Eternity on the one hand and, on the other, the limited and imperfectly real world of creatures and time there exists a kind of no-man's land—the world of what, for lack of a better name, has been called the world of psychic phenomena. This psychic domain is an extension of the world of creatures—a continuation of it, so to speak, into the ordinarily invisible infra-red or ultra-violet. Certain accidents of heredity permit of easy access to the psychic world; and there are a number of psycho-physical procedures which permit even those whose mediumistic or oracular gift is congenitally small to develop an ability to enter it and exploit its peculiar forces. Mystics, also, on their way towards Reality and Eternity, frequently find themselves in the region of psychic happenings. To these the masters of the spiritual life always give the same advice: pay no attention to these phenomena, however pleasant, interesting or extraordinary, but press forwards in the direction of that which lies beyond phenomena.

In the main, religion has always been concerned with the psychic world, and not directly with Reality and Eternity. The reason for this is simple. The search for Reality and Eternity imposes a discipline which the great majority of men and women are not prepared to undergo. At the same time it brings very few obvious rewards or concrete advantages to the searcher. Access to the psychic world can be attained without any painful "dying to self," and the exploitation of the forces existing in the infra-red and ultra-violet of our mental life frequently "gets results" of the most spectacular nature—healings, prophetic insights, fulfilment of wishes and a whole host of those miraculous "signs," for desiring which Jesus so roundly denounced the religious people of his time.

Psychic forces exist within an extension of the temporal universe of creatures, and their exploitation is permitted by God in exactly the same way as is the exploitation of such more familiar natural forces as electricity or heat, as cleverness or a strong will. Whether they are used to the glory of God and in accordance with God's will depends upon the choice of the individual at the moment of utilization. The only generalization that can justifiably be made is this: it is extremely dangerous to be able to exercise power or to get one's wishes fulfilled. By the successful exploitation of psychic forces one may do both these dangerous things. That is one of the reasons why religions have been a cause of evil as well as of good.

Contemplative prayer and mortification, not only of the passions but also of the intellect and, above all, the imagination—these are the means whereby men and women can fit themselves to receive the grace of a direct apprehension of Reality and Eternity. Very different is the procedure when our aim is the exploitation of the forces of the psychic world. Instead of mortifying the passions, the higher as well as the lower, we canalize them in the urgency of petitionary prayer; instead of doing all we can to die to our imagination, we deliberately intensify it by means of rituals, sacraments, images, music.

The exploitation of psychic forces need not of necessity be harmful or God-eclipsing. "White magic" and the liturgical and sacramental devices employed in order to make it work are compatible, as the history of many of the saints makes clear, with a high degree of holiness, a genuine apprehension of Reality and Eternity. The mass of ordinary worshippers, unsaintly indeed but reasonably respectable, may get certain insights into Reality through the psychic phenomena of non-spiritual religion and through the emotionally satisfying rituals and sacraments devised for the production of those phenomena. (In the same way, they may get certain insights into Reality through art and the beauty of nature.) Moreover, most of the highly developed religions possess a genuinely spiritual as well as a non-spiritual, psychic or magical side. Consequently it is always possible for its adherents to pass, if they so desire, from the orthodoxy of ritual and petitionary prayer to the other orthodoxy of contemplation, from the white magic of psychical phenomena to a detachment from all that is creaturely, including the psychic, and the single-minded search for Reality and Eternity. And even for those who do not take the spiritual path, it is probably true that adherence to a predominantly psychic religion of white magic is better, on the whole, than adherence to no religion at all, or to some idolatrous pseudo-religion, such as nationalism, communism or fascism. Meanwhile, it is vitally important that we should think clearly on this subject. At present there is a lamentable tendency to confound the psychic with the spiritual, to regard every supernormal phenomenon, every unusual mental state as coming from God. But there is no reason whatever to suppose that healings, prophecies and other "miracles" are necessarily of divine origin. Orthodox Christianity has adopted the absurd position that all supernormal phenomena produced by non-Christians are of diabolic origin, while most of those associated with non-heretical Christians are gifts of God. It would be more reasonable to regard all such "signs" as due to the conscious or unconscious exploitation of forces within the, to us, strange but still essentially creaturely psychic world. Examination of each particular case would be needed in order to determine whether the psychic phenomena in question were being manifested in accord with the will of God or for merely human purposes; for men can make use of psychic forces in good ways and in bad ways, just as they can do in the case of the more familiar forces of the material world. As things are, there is a tendency in the West to identify the merely unusual and supernormal with the divine. The nature of spirituality will never be generally understood until this mental confusion has been dispelled.

# How to Integrate Our Personality
## SWAMI YATISWARANANDA

THE SECRET OF STRENGTHENING the personality lies in its proper integration. I wish to tell you how this integration is brought about in spiritual life.

### THE MEANING OF PERSONALITY

First of all let us try to have, if possible, a clearer conception of what is meant by "personality." When the psychologist declares that "a man's personality is a collection of capacities, habits, and attitudes which distinguish him from other men," the question naturally arises—who is it that thinks, feels, wills and acts? What is the constant factor that persists and enables a man to consider himself to be the same person in the midst of changes—changes in the body, mind, ego, and environment? Philosophy and religion cannot stop with the psychological view. They want to go deeper.

In man—in ourselves—we find that the ego, the mind, the senses and body all combine to form a "complex." Now, what is the most important factor in man? It is his consciousness. First, "I am" and then I think, I feel, I will, I perceive, I act. We experience our consciousness directly and that of others indirectly. Whatever it is, all our individual consciousnesses seem to be made of the same stuff, although this stuff naturally gets associated or identified with other things which vary from person to person.

### THE INDIVIDUAL AND THE UNIVERSAL

Did you ever consider that the laws of thought ordain that it is not possible for us to have an idea of individual consciousness without having, at least, an indefinite idea of infinite consciousness? What to us is a logical necessity, we found well established in the great disciples of Sri Ramakrishna. In them the individual consciousness was a part, an expression of the universal consciousness. It is this that made them cosmo-centric instead of ego-centric. And they made us feel that the cosmic consciousness—including all forms of individual consciousness—was a unity in diversity.

To hold that consciousness is the essence of personality does not imply any denial of the mind, the senses and the body, which are the instruments of knowledge and action.

Our mind is one amongst many similar minds; our body is one amongst many bodies; so here, too, comes the question of the individual and universal—of the microcosm and macrocosm on the planes of mind and matter. Hindu teachers speak of three kinds of Akasha, space or plane. Mahakasha—the elemental or physical plane; chittakasha—the mental plane; chidakasha—the plane of knowledge or the spiritual plane. The individual body is a part of the cosmic body—or the ocean of matter. The individual mind is a part of the cosmic ocean of mind, the individual ego or consciousness is a part of the cosmic consciousness. The macrocosm is like the ocean; and the microcosm is like the wave. Now, of the two, the ocean and the wave, which is more real? The ocean is certainly more real than the wave. The wave, too, has its reality —but it is a dependent reality—a reality dependent on that of the ocean. This is also true of our "personality"—our individual consciousness, our individual mind, and our individual body which form part of a universal consciousness, a universal mind and a universal body.

Here we come to the ancient conception of the Cosmic Being—out of which all beings and things have come into existence and in which they all live and move. The Vedas say, "The Cosmic Being has innumerable heads, innumerable eyes and innumerable feet. It is He that has encompassed the whole universe and it is He again who transcends it. . . . That Being is this whole cosmos, all that is, all that was, and all that will be. He manifests Himself in the form of all. He also is the Lord and Giver of Immortality. The manifested universe forms but a small portion of His Being, in the main He remains unmanifest and immortal."

Am I losing myself too much in mysticism or metaphysics? I do not think so. In order to understand the individual we must know something of the universal. Do you know the ancient story of Socrates and the Brahmin sage? A Brahmin sage from India went to Greece and met Socrates who told him, "The greatest study of mankind is man." But the Brahmin asked, "How can you know man until you have known God—the All-Pervading Being?" We can get a correct idea of the individual being only in the background of the universal. We can understand personality only in the background of the cosmic Personality.

### WHAT IS INTEGRATION?

Now let us consider what we mean by integration. An integer is a complete unity—a whole, not a fractional or mixed number. To integrate is to form into a whole; to unite or become united so as to form a complete or perfect whole.

There are various kinds of integration. According to modern physical science a mass is composed of molecules; molecules of atoms, atoms of electrons and protons. Modern physicists tell us that atoms are composed of protons or positive units of electricity and of an equal number of electrons or negative units. The protons are concentrated in the nucleus which also contains a portion of the electrons. The remaining electrons are extra-nuclear or planetary and surround the nucleus.

Do you realize that this means that each atom is like a solar system—all the components uniting to form a whole? These in their turn form part of a greater whole. Similarly every cell in our body is like a tiny solar system and an organization by itself. All such units form parts of a greater unit we call a member; all the members in their turn form part of a greater unit we call the body. In an integrated body, while all the members have their individual movements, they all must coordinate with the general movement. When this is not the case, disharmony or illness is the result, so it is necessary for us to see that our body is properly integrated or harmonized. All our members should be healthy and strong and must work in harmony.

Let me now come to our mind. Our mind is a synthetic whole consisting of the faculties of cognition, feeling and willing. How often our reason and feeling, willing and action are at war with one another and create terrible confusion within ourselves. There may be conflict of duties, conflict of moral standards, conflict of spiritual ideals. We may become a whirlpool of emotions. So here, too, lies the need of integration which stands for purity and strength and harmony.

Let me now consider our ego. We all know that the ego is perverse; how it is constantly changing its center of gravity. It is now identified with outside things, next moment with the body, then with the senses or the mind. It is mad and is running the risk of tumbling down every moment. How at times it becomes much too one-pointed, centered on itself! We forget that our individual consciousness is part of an infinite consciousness, we forget that the welfare of our fellow beings is inseparable from ours, we become egocentric, selfish and mean—a danger to ourselves, to our family and society. So here too we need another kind of integration.

So integration has its physical aspect, its mental aspect, and also its spiritual aspect. In a properly integrated personality the ego or individual consciousness is in tune with the universal consciousness; and the integrated individual consciousness directs and guides the mind and the body in a harmonious, intelligent, and spontaneous way. This is what we understand by proper integration.

### STEPS TOWARD INTEGRATION

I am too ambitious, some of you may think. It is good to have a high ideal instead of a low one. But having the high ideal in view we must follow the path step by step with infinite patience and perseverance. In order to start on our journey we must find out where we stand. This is what we do when we wish to climb the mountains. This is also what we should do when we want to achieve a high ideal in our own lives. We must be realistic—find out the real condition of our body, mind, and ego. One of the greatest lessons I learned sitting at the feet of my Master and other disciples of

Sri Ramakrishna was the ideal of an harmonious growth—growth physical, intellectual, moral, and spiritual.

The body—our physical instrument—must be kept fit and efficient. It is necessary for us to have a new attitude towards the body. It is neither an instrument of sense gratification, nor a mass of filth to be hated and neglected. The body is primarily a temple of the Divine Spirit and must be kept clean and strong. A Sanskrit passage says—"The body is like a raft with the help of which we cross the ocean of phenomenal existence, with the help of which we attain spiritual illumination and immortality." The body must be nourished with pure food which brings energy, strength, health, and cheerfulness. Along with proper food we must take fresh air and exercise, avoiding drugs, stimulants, and intoxicants.

### THE "MIDDLE" PATH

In our present state of consciousness our body and mind are very much interconnected and affect each other and so we should take care of both. Remember the story of Buddha. He became tired of the pleasures of the palace, left his home and practised a terrible asceticism. One day as he was about to stand he fell down unconscious. On reviving, he heard a charming song:—

*"The string o'er stretched breaks, and the music flies,*
*The string o'er slack is dumb and music dies,*
*Tune us the Sitar neither low nor high."*

Self-indulgence and self-mortification—both are to be avoided. Buddha discovered the middle path of right comprehension, right living, and right meditation. Centuries before Buddha, Sri Krishna had preached the same message. "To him who is temperate in eating and recreation, in his work, in sleep and wakefulness, Yoga—spiritual practice—becomes the destroyer of misery." In still earlier times, the ancient sages sang: "May all the members of my body, the organ of speech, breath, eye, ear and all senses be strong and peaceful." The food that we eat with our mouths must be pure; so also the food that we take through the other senses must be pure. There must also be moral culture.

### MORAL DISCIPLINE

Moral disciplines have come to be too much connected with repression and suppression, to use modern psychological terms. The ancient Hindu sages believed in giving a higher direction to the senses,—"May we hear with our ears what is pure. May we see with our eyes what is holy. May we praise and worship the Divine Spirit and enjoy with strong and steady limbs and body the life allotted to us."

One really feels harmonized and integrated when one is master of one's own senses, master of one's own mind, when one follows the spiritual life without conflicts and in a spontaneous way. The process of mental purification is called "purgation" in mystic language and "sublimation" in psychological terms. It is a process of giving a higher turn to the desires or "primary instincts."

### MODERN AND ANCIENT PSYCHOLOGICAL METHODS

Modern psychology has discovered a technique which was known to the ancient spiritual teachers of India in a more thoroughgoing way. In modern analytic technique the main task is to bring into consciousness or awareness the underlying and deep-seated causes of the patient's mental troubles. Some unscrupulous psychologists may advocate a free play of the morbid tendencies in the patient but as Dr. Fosdick quotes in his admirable book "On Being a Real Person" an eminent psychiatrist holds, "From the point of view of cure the advice to go and 'express your instinct' is foolish. In actual experience I have never known a true neurosis cured by sexual libertinism."

In the psychological method as discovered by Freud—this is true of all psychologists—the patient is asked either (1) to regard the disturbing desire in a new light, accept it wholly or in part without fear or disgust, or (2) to face the trouble deliberately and reject it without feeling too much sense of guilt, or (3) to direct it along a higher channel to a higher goal.

Adler always advocates the pursuit of what he calls a healthier style of life, useful to the community. The

Hindu spiritual teacher also wants us to give a higher turn to all our "passions." Says Sri Ramakrishna, "Direct the passions to God. The impulse of lust should be turned into a desire to have communion with the Divine Spirit. Seek the company of the holy, be angry at those who stand in the way of God, be angry with your anger, feel greedy for Him. If you have the feeling of I and mine, then associate it with God. If you must have pride, then feel proud thinking that you are a servant of God, a child of God." How truly does the modern psychologist, Adler, remark: "By changing our opinion of ourselves we can also change ourselves." Swami Vivekananda said, "Teach yourself, teach everyone his real nature. Power will come, goodness will come, purity will come, everything that is excellent will come." The Hindu teacher goes to the very logical conclusion of this ideal—to a point beyond the scope of the ordinary psychologist.

### FROM DISINTEGRATION TO INTEGRATION

By becoming a slave of passions, a human being—in whom the higher moral consciousness has awakened—whose "spirit is willing but whose flesh is weak"—creates a great discord and disharmony within himself. His personality becomes disintegrated. On the other hand, by giving a spiritual turn to the passions, by sublimating and purifying them, the aspirant comes to possess a greater and greater harmony and integration within himself.

Now we must aim at a still higher integration and try to coordinate our thinking, feeling and willing. Our consciousness is usually associated with one of these faculties which dominates the rest. We may be over-intellectual or too emotional or it may be we have too strong a will and want to be active without caring for reason or higher emotions. This creates a cleavage within ourselves. We must coordinate the faculties, but how? We must learn to disassociate ourselves from all the faculties and come to our individual consciousness, make it the subject of our meditation and keep it steady. When from this detached state we come back to the faculties, we are able to coordinate them and make them work in a spirit of harmony for the common good. This is a great achievement.

But from the standpoint of our highest ideal, this ego-centric meditation—however useful it may be in giving our ego a mastery over the mind, senses and body—is not enough. We have not yet striven for the highest integration, this we must do next. Dr. Jung writes, in his "Modern Man in Search of a Soul": "The ego is ill for the very reason that it is cut off from the whole and has lost its connection with mankind as well as with the Spirit." In his "The Integration of Personality" he makes a still more significant remark: "To be in Tao means fulfilment, wholeness . . . complete realization of the meaning of existence innate in things. Personality is Tao." Tao is the invisible, ungraspable, infinite Source of life—the abode of truth, the origin of all things. Tao corresponds to the cosmic spirit, the Universal Being of the Hindu sages.

## INTEGRATION OF PERSONALITY IN THE IMPERSONAL SPIRIT

How are we to bring the ego in touch with the universal? With the help of prayer or hymns, spiritual texts or holy, mystic words, by repeating them and dwelling on their meaning, by meditating on the Divine Reality, we can create such a "music" in our soul—such a harmonious state, that we rise above our little personality, our little ego, above our individual consciousness. Then we feel the touch of the Super-ego, the cosmic consciousness that lies in us all. It is in this state that the cosmic is realized to be more real than the individual consciousness. Here the deepest integration takes place. When the soul comes back to normal consciousness, to the plane of the ego, mind and body—it feels a remarkable integration. Individual consciousness remains rooted in the universal and the spiritualized ego is in tune with the mind and the body which act as most obedient servants. Here personality remains integrated in the One Impersonal and Universal Being.

Such a rare and blessed "personality" sees the Supreme Spirit within himself and in all beings. His mind is not shaken by misery, nor upset by happiness. He becomes free from attachment, fear and anger. His body has become a veritable Divine temple. He radiates purity and love and becomes a source of abiding inspiration and blessing to all. We have heard from our spiritual teachers that real spiritual life begins after the obtainment of the superconscious state. But let us not dwell too much on the ideal. Having found the ideal, let us follow the path and move from lesser integration to higher integration. We are assured that as we proceed higher and higher in the scale of perfection and integration, we shall enjoy greater and greater poise and harmony, peace and blessedness. Therefore let us awake, arise and move on till the goal is reached.

# *Distractions—I*[1]

## ALDOUS HUXLEY

THE PETITION, "Thy Kingdom come," has a necessary and unavoidable corollary, which is, "Our kingdom go." The condition of complete illumination is complete purgation. Only the purified soul can realize identity with Brahman; or, to change the religious vocabulary, union with God can never be achieved by the Old Adam, who must lose the life of self-will in order to gain the life of the divine will. These principles have been accepted as fundamental and axiomatic by all mystics, of whatever country, faith and period.

When these principles are applied in practice, it is found that the personal kingdom which has to go, if the divine kingdom is to come, consists mainly of two great provinces, Passions and Distractions. Of the passions it is unnecessary to say much here, for the good reason that so much has been said elsewhere. Furthermore, it is, or should be, self-evident that "Thy kingdom" cannot possibly come for anyone who inhabits a home-made universe created for him by his own fear, greed, malice and anxiety. To help men to overcome these passions is the aim of all ethical teaching; and that overcoming is an essential preliminary and accompaniment to the life of mystical spirituality. Those who imagine that they can achieve illumination without purgation are extremely mistaken. There is a letter addressed by St. Jeanne Chantal to one of the nuns of her order, a letter which should be placed in the hands of every beginner in the art of yoga or mental prayer. "I' faith," writes the saint, "I can well believe it when you say that you do not know what to answer those novices who ask you what is the difference between union and contemplation. Lord God, how is it that

[1] Portions of these two articles later formed part of a chapter in the author's "Grey Eminence."

my sister the Superior permits them such a thing, or that you permit it in her absence? Dear Jesus, where is humility? You must stop this at once, and give them books and lectures that treat of the practice of the virtues, and tell them that they must first set themselves to doing, and then they can talk about these exalted matters."

But enough of this first and all-too-familiar province of our personal kingdom. It is not of the passions, but of those less frequently publicized impediments to the unitive life, distractions, that I mean to write in this place.

Contemplatives have compared distractions to dust, to swarms of flies, to the movements of a monkey stung by a scorpion. Always their metaphors call up the image of a purposeless agitation. And this, precisely, is the interesting and important thing about distractions. The passions are essentially purposeful, and the thoughts, emotions and fancies connected with the passions always have more reference to the real or imaginary ends proposed, or to the means whereby such ends may be achieved. With distractions the case is quite different. It is of their essence to be irrelevant and pointless. To find out just how pointless and irrelevant they can be, one has only to sit down and try to recollect oneself. Preoccupations connected with the passions will most probably come to the surface of consciousness; but along with them will rise a bobbing scum of miscellaneous memories, notions and imaginings—childhood recollections of one's grandmother's Yorkshire terrier, the French name for henbane, a White-Knightish scheme for catching incendiary bombs in mid air—in a word, every kind of nonsense and silliness. The psycho-analytic contention that all the divagations of the sub-conscious have a deep passional meaning cannot be made to fit the facts. One has only to observe oneself and others to discover that we are no more exclusively the servants of our passions and biological urges than we are exclusively rational; we are also creatures possessed of a complicated psycho-physiological machine that is incessantly grinding away and that, in the course of its grinding, throws up into consciousness selections from that indefinite number of mental permutations and combinations which its random functioning makes possible. Most of these permutations and combinations have nothing to do with our passions or our rational occupations; they are just imbecilities—mere casual waste products of psycho-physiological activity. True, such imbecilities may be made use of by the passions for their own ends, as when the Old Adam in us throws up a barrage of intrinsically pointless abstractions in an attempt to nullify the creative efforts of the higher will. But even when not so used by the passions, even in themselves, distractions constitute a formidable obstacle to any kind of spiritual advance. The imbecile within us is as radically God's enemy as the passionately purposeful maniac, with his insane cravings and aversions. Moreover, the imbecile remains at large and busy long after the lunatic has been tamed or even destroyed. In other words, a man may have succeeded in overcoming his passions and replacing them by a fixed, one-pointed desire for enlightenment—he may have succeeded in this, and yet still be hindered in his advance by the uprush into consciousness of pointless and irrelevant distractions. This is the reason why all advanced spirituals have attached so much importance to such imbecilities and have ranked them as grave imperfections, even as sins. It is, I think, to distractions—or at least to one main class of distractions—that Christ refers in that strangely enigmatic and alarming saying, "that every idle word that men shall speak, they shall give account thereof in the day of judgment. For by thy words shalt thou be justified and by thy words shalt thou be condemned." Verbalized idiocies, spoken irrelevances, all utterances, indeed, that do not subserve the end of enlightenment must be classed as impediments, barriers between the soul and ultimate reality. They may seem harmless enough; but this harmlessness is only in relation to mundane things; in relation to spiritual and eternal ends, they are extremely harmful. In this context, I would like to quote a paragraph from the biography of that seventeenth-century French saint, Charles de Condren. A pious lady, named Mlle. de la Roche, was in great distress, because she found it impossible to make a satisfactory confession. "Her trouble was that her sins seemed to her greater than she could say. Her faults were not considerable; nevertheless she felt unable, so she said, ever to express them. If the confessor told her that he was content with her accusation of herself, she would answer that she was not satisfied and that, since she was not telling the truth, he could not give her absolution. If he pressed her to tell the whole truth, she found herself utterly incapable of doing so." Nobody knew what to say to this unfortunate woman, who came in time to be regarded as not quite right in the head. Finally she addressed herself to Condren, who relieved her of her misery by an explanation of her case which is of the highest interest. "It is true," he said, "that you have not adequately expressed your sins; but the fact is that, in this life, it is impossible to represent them in all their hideousness. We shall never know them as they really are, until we see them in the pure light of God. In your case, God has given you an impression of the deformity of sin, by which he makes you feel it to be incomparably graver than it appears to your understanding or can be expressed by your words. Hence your anguish and distress. You must therefore conceive of your sins as faith presents them to you, in other words, as they are in themselves; but you must content yourself with describing them in such words as your mouth can form." All that Condren says about poor Mlle. de la Roche's no doubt very trifling sins applies with equal force to our distractions. Judged by ordinary human standards, they may seem of no account. And yet, as they are in themselves, as they are in relation to the light of God (which they are able completely to eclipse, as the sun is darkened by a dust storm or a cloud of grasshoppers) these seemingly trifling imperfections are seen to have as great a power for evil in the soul as anger, or an ugly greed, or some obsessive apprehension.

It is because they mistrust the imbecile who, in the body of every human being, cohabits with the criminal lunatic, the easy-going animal, the good citizen and the potential, unawakened, deeply latent saint, it is because they recognize his truly diabolic power, that the contemplatives have always imposed upon themselves and their disciples such rigid self-denial in the matter of all distracting and irrelevant stimuli. The Old Adam's restless curiosity must be checked and his foolishness, his dissipation of spirit turned to wisdom and one-pointedness. That is why the would-be mystic is always told to refrain from busying himself with matters which do not refer to his ultimate goal, or in relation to which he cannot effectively do immediate and concrete good. This self-denying ordinance covers most of the things with which, outside business hours, the ordinary person is mainly preoccupied—news, the day's instalment of the various radio epics, this year's car models and gadgets, the latest fashions. But it is upon fashions, cars and gadgets, upon news and the advertising for which news exists, that our present industrial and economic system depends for its proper functioning. For, as ex-President Hoover pointed out not long ago, this system cannot work unless the demand for non-necessaries is not merely kept up, but continually expanded; and of course it cannot be kept up and expanded except by incessant appeals to greed, competitiveness and love of aimless stimulation. Men have always been a prey to distractions, which are the original sin of the mind; but never before today has an attempt been made to organize and exploit distractions, to make of them, because of their economic importance, the core and vital center of human life, to idealize them as the highest manifestations of mental activity. Ours is an age of systematized irrelevances, and the imbecile within us has become one of the Titans, upon whose shoulders rests the weight of the social and economic system. Recollectedness, or the overcoming of distractions, has never been more necessary than now; it has also, we may guess, never been so difficult.

# Distractions—II
## ALDOUS HUXLEY

IN AN EARLIER ARTICLE I gave some account of the psychological nature of distractions and of their significance as obstacles in the path of those who seek to attain enlightenment. In the paragraphs which follow, I shall describe some of the methods which have been found useful in overcoming these obstacles, in circumventing the tricks of the imbecile whom we carry about with us as a secondary personality.

Distractions afflict us not only when we are attempting formal meditation or contemplation, but also and even more dangerously in the course of our active, everyday life. Many of those who undertake spiritual exercises, whether yogic or Christian, tend all too frequently to confine their efforts at concentrating the mind strictly to business hours—that is to say, to the hours they actually spend in meditation. They forget that it is possible for a man or woman to achieve, during meditation, a high degree of mental concentration and even a kind of subjectively satisfying pseudo-ecstasy, while remaining at bottom an unregenerate ego. It is not an uncommon thing to meet with people who spend hours of each day doing spiritual exercises and who, in the intervals, display as much spite, prejudice, jealousy, greed and silliness as the most "unspiritual" of their neighbors. The reason for this is that such people make no effort to adapt to the exigencies of ordinary life those practices which they make use of during their times of formal meditation. This is, of course, not at all surprising. It is much easier to catch a glimpse of reality under the perfect conditions of formal meditation than to "practice the presence of God" in the midst of the boredoms, annoyances and constant temptations of family and professional life. What the English mystic, Benet Fitch, calls "active annihilation" or the sinking of the self in God at every moment of the day, is much harder to achieve than "passive annihilation" in mental prayer. The difference between the two forms of self-annihilation is analogous to the difference between scientific work under laboratory conditions and scientific work in the field. As every scientist knows, a great gulf separates the achievement of results in the laboratory and the application of one's discoveries to the untidy and disconcerting world outside its walls. Laboratory work and work in the field are equally necessary in science. Analogously, in the practice of the unitive life, the laboratory work of formal meditation must be supplemented by what may be called "applied mysticism" during the hours of everyday activity. For this reason I propose to divide this article into two sections, the first dealing with distractions in times of recollection, the second with the obscuring and obstructive imbecilities of daily life.

All teachers of the art of mental prayer concur in advising their pupils never to struggle against the distractions which arise in the mind during recollection. The reason for this is simple. "The more a man operates, the more he is and exists. And the more he is and exists, the less God is and exists within him." Every enhancement of the separate personal self produces a corresponding diminution of the consciousness of divine reality. But the voluntary struggle against distractions automatically enhances the separate personal self and therefore reduces the individual's chance of coming to an awareness of reality. In the process of trying forcibly to abolish our God-eclipsing imbecilities, we merely deepen the darkness of our native ignorance. This being so, we must give up our attempt to fight distractions and find ways of circumventing and evading them. One method consists in simply "looking over the shoulder" of the imbecile who stands between us and the object of our meditation or our imageless contemplation. The distractions appear in the foreground of consciousness; we take notice of their presence, then lightly, without effort or tension of will, we shift the focus of attention to the reality in the background. In many cases the distractions will lose their obsessive "thereness" and gradually fade away.

Alternatively, when distractions come, the attempt to practice imageless contemplation or the "simple regard" may be temporarily given up, and attenion directed to the distractions themselves, which are then used as objects of discursive meditation, preparatory to another return to the "simple regard" later on. Two methods of making profitable use of distractions are commonly recommended. The first consists in objectively examining the distractions, and observing which of them have their origins in the passions and which of them arise in the imbecile side of the mind. The process of following thoughts and images back to their source, of uncovering, here the purposive and passional, there the merely imbecile manifestations of egotism, is an admirable exercise in mental concentration, as well as a means for increasing that self-knowledge which is one of the indispensable pre-requisites to a knowledge of God. "A man," wrote Meister Eckhart, "has many skins in himself, covering the depths of his heart. Man knows so many other things; he does not know himself. Why, thirty or forty skins or hides, just like an ox's or a bear's, so thick and hard, cover the soul. Go into your own ground and learn to know yourself there." The dispassionate and scientific examination of distractions is one of the best ways of knowing the "thirty or forty skins" which constitute our personality, and discovering, beneath them, the Self, the immanent Godhead, the Kingdom of Heaven within us. Discursive meditation on the skins passes naturally into a simple regard directed to the ground of the soul.

The second method of making use of distractions for the purpose of defeating distractions is merely a variant on the first. The difference between the two methods is a difference in the quality of the emotional tone accompanying the examination of the disturbing thoughts and images. In the first method, the examination is dispassionate; in the second, it is accompanied by a sense of contrition and self-humiliation. In the words of the author of "The Cloud of Unknowing," "when thou feelest that thou mayest in no wise put them (distractions, imbecile and passional) down, cower then down under them as a caitiff and a coward overcome in battle, and think that it is but folly to strive any longer with them, and therefore thou yieldest thyself to God in the hands of thine enemies. And feel then thyself as though thou wert overcome forever. . . . And surely, I think, if this device be truly conceived, it is naught else but a true knowing and a feeling of thyself as thou art, a wretch and a filthy thing, far worse than naught: the which knowing and feeling is meekness. And this meekness meriteth to have God himself mightily descending, to venge thee on thine enemies, so as to take thee up and cherishingly dry thy ghostly eyes, as the father doth his child that is on the point to perish under the mouths of wild swine or mad biting bears."

We now come to the problem of dealing with distractions in common life—in the field rather than in the laboratory. Active annihilation or, to use the phrase made familiar by Brother Lawrence, the constant practice of the presence of God at all moments of the day, is a work of supreme difficulty. Most of those who attempt it make the mistake of treating field work as though it were laboratory work. Finding themselves in the midst of things, they turn away from things, either physically, by retreat, or psychologically, by an act of introversion. But the shrinking from things and necessary external activities is an obstacle in the way of self-annihilation; for to shrink from things is to assert by implication that things still mean a great deal to one. Introversion from things for the sake of God may, by giving them undue importance, exalt things to the place that should be occupied by God. What is needed, therefore, is not physical flight or introversion from things, but the capacity to undertake necessary activity in a spirit of non-attachment, of self-annihilation in reality. This is, of course, the doctrine of the Gita. (It should be noted, however, that the Gita—if it is meant to be taken literally, which one hopes it isn't—suggests that it is possible to commit murder in a state of self-annihilation in God. In various forms, this doctrine of non-attachment has been used by aberrant sectaries of every religion to justify every kind of wickedness and folly, from sexual orgies to torture. But, as a matter of plain psychological fact, such activities are entirely unannihilable in God. Going to war, like the heroes of the Gita, indulging in unlimited sexual promiscuity, like some of the Illuminati of the West, are activities which cannot result in anything but an enhancement of the separate personal self and an eclipsing of divine reality. Non-attachment cannot be practiced except in relation to intrinsically good or ethically neutral actions; the idea that it can be practiced in relation to bad actions is a delusion, springing from the wish of the ego to go on behaving badly, while justifying such behavior by means of a high and apparently spiritual philosophy.)

To achieve the active annihilation, by which alone the distractions of common life may be overcome, the aspirant must begin by avoiding, not merely all bad actions, but also, if possible, all unnecessary and silly ones. Listening to the average radio program, seeing the average motion picture, reading the comic strips—these are merely silly and imbecile activities; but though not wicked, they are almost as unannihilable as the activities of lynching and fornication. For this reason it is obviously advisable to avoid them.

Meanwhile, what is to be done in the psychological field? First, it is necessary to cultivate a constant awareness of the reality that is everything and the personal self that is less than nothing. Only on this condition can the desired non-attachment be achieved. No less important than the avoidance of unnecessary and unannihilable activities and the cultivation of awareness is emptying of the memory and the suppression of foreboding. Anyone who pays attention to his mental processes soon discovers that a large proportion of his time is spent in chewing the cud of the past and foretasting the future. We return to the past, sometimes because random memories rise mechanically into consciousness; sometimes because we like flattering our egotism by the recalling of past triumphs and pleasures, the censoring and embellishing of past pains and defeats; sometimes, too, because we are sick of ourselves and, thinking to "repent of our sins" return with a gloomy satisfaction to old offences. As for the future, our preoccupation with it is sometimes apprehensive, sometimes compensatory and wishful. In either case, the present is sacrificed to dreams of no longer existent or hypothetical situations. But it is a matter of empirical observation that the road to spiritual eternity is through the immediate animal eternity of the specious present. None can achieve eternal life who has not first learned to live, not in the past or in the future, but now—in the moment at the moment.

Concerning the God-eclipsing folly of taking anxious thought for the future the Gospels have much to say. Sufficient unto the day is the evil thereof—and, we might add, sufficient unto the place. We make a habit of feeling disquietude about distant evils, in regard to which we can do no good, and we think that such disquietude is a sign of our sensibility and compassion. It would probably be more nearly true to say, with St. John of the Cross, that "disquietude is always vanity, because it serves no good. Yea, even if the whole world were thrown into confusion, and all things in it, disquietude on that account would still be vanity." What is true of things remote in space and in the future is also true of things remote in the past. We must teach ourselves not to waste our time and our opportunities to know reality by dwelling on our memories. Let the dead bury their dead. "The emptying of the memory," says St. John of the Cross, "though the advantages of it are not so great as those of the state of union, yet merely because it delivers souls from much sorrow, grief and sadness, besides imperfections and sins, is in itself a great good."

Such, then, in briefest summary, are some of the methods by which distractions can be overcome, not merely in the laboratory of formal meditation, but also (which is much harder) in the world of common life. As always, it is enormously easier to write and read about such methods than to put them into practice.

# Dryness and Dark Night

## Gerald Heard

Once anyone realizes that real growth of the spirit can be made he becomes interested in method. He sees that he need no longer leave his life to accident, nor drift and look to amusement to give living whatever meaning it may have: he sees that he must set about intentional living, he must undertake training, he must coordinate all his activities and his whole way of life along the path which has appeared and toward the goal at which that path aims. This insight, or foresight, raises a number of questions. How is he to set about his new task? How much of his past life, which was based upon deliberate distraction and amusement, can remain? When anyone changes over from a way of living in which it was taken for granted that however you lived, the fundamental fact was that Life meant nothing and went nowhere, to a way of living in which the meaning of Life is apprehended and the place of the individual in that scheme has been discovered, then there must be very considerable modification of the things that are done as well as of the thoughts that are thought. Right Livelihood, the fifth step in the Eightfold Path to Liberation and Enlightenment, is something more than abstention from certain debarred occupations and professions such as armament manufacturing or white slave trafficking. It is even something more than abstaining from gambling in Stocks and Bonds or from being absorbed in the advertising business. It is getting rid of everything which may distract one's attention from the one end and purpose of living. Many things which are obviously of no particular harm to any one else have to be put out of the way not because they are harmful in themselves but because they take up too much time and attention when all the time one has and all the attention which one can command is required for the one main purpose which now makes meaning of every moment. Most people think that as long as what they do harms no one else and is not unhealthy for them there is no reason why they should not enjoy themselves whatever way they please. This familiar standard of morality cannot, however, satisfy those who have found the meaning of their life. For them every moment is precious and every ounce of attention is husbanded to bring them as soon as may be to their goal.

But once that is clear to them, and once they have resolved that only so they can live, they have to ask, How best may I get to my End? Most of us find that the discovery that life has a meaning, a meaning as urgent as it is vast, breaks on us with a shock of surprise and also delight. "So after all that we see about us, the pointless lives of most individuals, the blind clash of classes, the hideous anarchy of the nations, Life has a meaning, it goes somewhere, we can go with it." That is the huge wave of relief. The accepted nightmare which drives men to addictions, to possessiveness, to pride and violence and despair, is false. Then comes also the wave of counter-concern. If that is true, then there is not a moment to be wasted. Already one has wasted so much. "Work while ye have the light; the night cometh when no man may work." It is urgent not to waste a moment more of the all-too-few hours of daylight. So there is a double pressure urging us to use every second. There is the attraction of the goal and there is the rapidly passing opportunity of working on the means to the goal. This sense of stress and attraction undoubtedly sometimes makes beginners suffer from anxiety and a kind of febrile haste. This may be one of the causes of disappointment and that giving-out of interest which is generally called "dryness." There is much need here, it is obvious, for good teaching and wise guiding. Even if we start young, which is uncommon in the West, we are by nature an impatient lot and all human beings, whether of the East or the West seem to have this factor in common that their lives are run on what we may call an "alternating" rather than on a "continuous" current. With the best will in the world and with the wisest training it does not seem possible for them to avoid a certain, and perhaps a necessary fluctuation. Now this it is which is so difficult for the ardent and anxious beginner to endure and it is here therefore that it is very interesting to try and compare the findings both of the masters of the West and also of the East as to how far this ebb and flow is necessary and how far the fluctuations—like those of unemployment—may be "flattened out" as the economists say, so as to save the booms and slumps. The obvious question here is whether the slumps— as in employment—might not be saved, by "back-pedalling" when the booms are on. Psychologists have taught for a long while those of their patients who have a tendency to too big a fluctuation, and so are honored with the fine frenzied title of Manic-Depressive Types, to check the moment of elation and so save themselves from the moment of depression. But, beyond this very natural and practical advice, may we not learn more? Quite obviously there are a number of rules for the spiritual life which apply to all of us whether we are stolid or excitable. There is a lower limit of observance and practice which if we go under it we shall be simply slothful and not making any real effect on the will and the character. After all, we are like people in a ship which has a leak and which is making for the shore. We must work at a certain pace at the pumps or the water will gain on us, rising in the hold and we shall founder before we can be safely beached. But there is also a higher limit, a limit above which strain comes on. To use the same simile again: there comes a time when the crew may wear itself out in pumping and so have to abandon their labor before the shore is reached. The leak cannot be wholly stopped, what we have to do (at least we beginners) is to keep the water level down, to keep on pumping out more or at least as much as is coming in. Now our question is where do those limits lie? To take another simile, this time from Alpine climbing. The young when they go out with an experienced guide are always surprised at the slow and almost loitering pace at which he starts. They cannot endure this dilatoriness. They swing off ahead but when the sun is up and the higher slopes are reached, he passes them for they have to sit down exhausted in order to get back their strength. His set pace is a thought-out balance between fatigue and the distance to be covered and the time for covering that distance. It is significant that all Alpine distances are given not in kilometers but in hours and minutes—it is a well-thought-out race, however slow it looks, a race between the time before the sun will set and the energy at the climber's disposal. Some violent fluctuations would therefore seem to be due to lack of foresight on our part. After all, risks are nearly always taken and accidents nearly always happen because we will not look ahead. Instead we suddenly see an oncoming difficulty and try to get out of it without sufficient time in which to make the necessary change.

But there are deeper rules of fluctuation and of ebb and flow which do not seem due to our present mistakes and carelessness. Nor under our present control. In learning a language, a golf-swing, the piano, in every skill where knowledge has to combine with knack and blend into skill, there seems a wave-motion, an ebb and flow. There is a period of rapid surface-mind learning and then a disappointing ebb when even that which was thought to have been mastered disappears. It seems possible that during this disappointing time some deeper process is going on, what may perhaps be called a period of storage and profound modification and, again it may be, no new knowledge or knack could safely be taken in unless first of all the first load had been safely stowed and room and relation found for it in the ways and means, the methods and functions of the body-mind. We are probably far more full up than we know and a new knowledge and power must always mean a modification of old ones. But still again beyond this recognition of gaps, and waits and periods when we seem to "lose way" as sailors say and "hang fire," there are deeper dips. What of those states which the western saints and contemplatives call the Dark Nights of the Soul? Here a number of difficulties confront the researcher. First there is the difficulty of the words themselves. Do all the writers mean the same thing when they use this same title? It seems difficult to think that they do. For example a textual authority on Western Mysticism such as Dr. W. R. Inge gives in his collection of Excerpts from various spiritual authorities ("Freedom, Love and Truth," pp. 160-161) as examples of the Dark Night passages from Ruysbroek and the Theologia Germanica—two sources near one another in date and place. But the Ruysbroek passage where he talks of an Autumn of maturing fruits after the lush springing of summer seems to refer to Dryness and a fruitful dryness at that, a rich reflection after a high experience, and not to deep despairs and utter emptiness. Ruysbroek mentions physical losses and hardships as being part of his "Autumn." The desolation of the Night seems in other cases so profound that they would be quite unaware if they were given all the health in the world or lost their closest relations. The Theologia Germanica says the Soul is sent to Hell, and medievalists did not use that term lightly. The loss of the Presence—*that* alone counts and to regain *that* is the one hope. In these latter cases, then, there does not seem a storage, an autumn harvesting going on. Rather, it would seem we might say, the very barn itself is being harvested, cut down and taken to pieces. Here we seem past the acquiring of virtues and the abandonment of vices and specific weaknesses. It is the very Self itself which is being challenged and attacked. Eckhart, who does not seem to say much about the Dark Night as a specific term—perhaps because he welcomed it—yet teaches a path which certainly with most good people would lead to acute distress. He says that there are three things which keep us from God and, it would seem, three stages whereby we may and do return to Him. The first is by loosing ourselves from our specific sins, the second is by loosening ourselves from all sense of self and the third by loosening ourselves from Time. Many a Westerner when he reads even those introductory lines of Emerson's

> *The strong gods pine for my abode,*
> *And pine in vain the sacred Seven;*
> *But thou, meek lover of the good!*
> *Find me, and turn thy back on heaven.*

feels a certain chill. And certainly Christianity has never been comfortable with what its teachers called Oriental Nihilism, though, it is all the more important to note, all the master saints of Christendom as they climb beyond a certain height seem to view the same prospect which so daunts those on the lower levels.

Perhaps such high matters should not concern beginners. Perhaps all we on our level have to fear is quite common laziness, the wish for comfort and excitement, the impatience with the slow assimilation, the lack of advance because we will not let fall much that makes, by its weight and back-pull, our advance necessarily slower than it need be, would we abandon more. Still the problem remains as one of interest to all students of humanity. How much of our difficulties, even the difficulties of the advanced, is due to ignorance, which greater knowledge could remove, and how much is due to the necessities of the case? An entomologist was particularly anxious to hatch out successfully a valuable moth which had been found in its cocoon stage. The moment came when it began to emerge. It was watched with delighted care. But just when the dangerous emergency seemed safely over, one of the beautiful wings, which made so largely the value of the specimen, remained caught in the husk of the cocoon. In vain the moth seemed to struggle to get free and at last it seemed quite clear to the anxious watcher that the insect's strength was failing and that it must die in the vain struggle. As it lay helpless and exhausted on its side, trapped and inert, the watcher snipped with sterilized scissors the stiffened edge of the cocoon. The wing was released. The insect crawled out free. But it could not fly; the specimen was ruined. The wing remained curled and shrivelled. That final struggle to the limits of life and strength seems to have been necessary. The circulation was not driven into the delicate veins of the wing and so it could not expand. The agonizing effort was not merely to get free but to grow whole, not merely to get out into the new world of winged flight but to have, full of power and energy, the fully unfolded wings, without which the new and larger life was vain and a mockery. So it may be with our struggles. We may be made, not merely to win the larger life, but, through the agony of effort, to attain the powers and capacities and the quality of consciousness to function fully and rightly in that life.

# Realize the Truth

## Swami Yatiswarananda

### DEFINITE IDEA OF THE PATH AND GOAL

WE SHOULD HAVE THE IDEAL fixed that neither worldly nor heavenly pleasures are our goal and that our ultimate goal is Self-Realization. It is neither this world nor heaven, nor any other world we seek. Heavenly enjoyment is no better than earthly enjoyment, and so long as there is hankering after heavenly enjoyment, we can never attain the goal. We must yearn for God more than for His creation either in heaven or on earth.

Before we actually begin our spiritual life in real earnest, we must decide if we are really fully prepared to pay the price. We must fix once for all our ideal, our conduct of life, and then stick to it whatever happens. If we wish to transcend all the unrealities, there must always be a certain amount of the dare-devil in us, a certain amount of fearlessness and true heroism. Unless we are prepared to sacrifice all our worldly desires and our sense of I-ness, we can never hope to realize the higher ideal. "Give us discrimination, give us renunciation, give devotion and knowledge"—let us pray to the Divine.

### DISCRIMINATION

We should practice a certain amount of control and discrimination regarding the food we take. And so long as we are in the body, the body must be properly taken care of and nourished to keep it a fit instrument for the realization of the Divine and for the Divine's work. There is much more body-consciousness in the person who is ill or weak than in the perfectly healthy and normal person, and we have to see that our body-consciousness is reduced to a minimum if we want to make good progress in spiritual life.

Unless our mind is to be to some extent pure and non-attached and prepared for renunciation, we can never even think of God-Realization. Try to purify your heart, to purify your mind as much as possible. Then the blazing fire of spiritual realization will burn away all desires.

### MEDITATION ON THE HOLY PERSONALITIES

Few people can begin their spiritual practice with the meditation on the Formless and Attributeless Aspect of the Divine. Even the conception of God without form but with attributes is beyond the grasp of the many. So long as it is impossible for us to form even an idea of the Divine in both His transcendent and immanent aspects, we should first of all try to think of the Divine Glory as manifest through the Holy Personalities—the great incarnations and Prophets of mankind. It is very easy for us to speak of worshiping God in truth and in spirit. But since, as a matter of fact, we cannot do so, it becomes a meaningless phrase and nothing more.

We think in terms of our small, limited, impure, individual consciousness, but the Great Ones think in terms of the Infinite Consciousness. We are like small, tiny, self-forgetful bubbles, while they are like mountain-high waves that always are conscious of their ocean-origin. The ocean never comes to be limited by the wave-form.

The Incarnation is a glorious manifestation, but never the whole of God who is the reality at the back of ordinary beings also.

Tiny bubbles that we are, we find it difficult to understand even a full-wave-consciousness. By worshiping and meditating on the Great Ones, we are raised to a realization of their higher consciousness. This breaks the bonds of our limited existence and brings in a new light, a deeper awareness that lies hidden in the depths of our being. The waves bring us in contact with the ocean. By lifting ourselves consciously to the plane of their knowledge, we get rid of all our false notions, of our being identified with the body, of being men and women. Dropping the limiting adjuncts, we get a new and purer sense of existence—a universal consciousness that gives the true meaning to our individual existence and life.

### THE INDIVIDUAL AND THE UNIVERSAL

In trying to separate itself from the ocean the bubble runs the risk of bursting its bubble-form, as it can never exist without the contact of the ocean. But the trouble is that we are not conscious of this great fact. We consider ourselves to be separate entities, separate from the ocean, separate from one another. When this initial mistake is made through ignorance, all other mistakes follow as a matter of course and make our life one of endless misery.

Although we may take our limited existence to be absolutely real at first, we find, on deeper consideration and experience, that it is not so. The false conception of reality is wholly due to ignorance. It is through this that we come to cherish many a petty and ignoble idea and suffer because of that. However, by getting rid of the false conception, we rise above all illusory, limiting adjuncts and regain our true nature, the true dignity and glory of the Divine in us,—who is not only our Self but is the Self of all.

### HINTS FOR MEDITATION

In the beginning of our spiritual life we have to create our own images, but these should always be images of which the pattern is right, *i.e.*, imaginations of something that is real, not of something wholly imaginary. Some stress the sense of the Presence more than the form, although they, too, may call up the form. The same Being permeates both the form called up and the devotee, as It is the devotee's own eternal Being—his true Self.

Just think that your heart or head is permeated with the Divine Effulgence, and that His Light is part of the Infinite Light that pervades everything. Melt away your whole personality, your I-ness, into That. Melt away your body, your senses, your emotions, into That. Just imagine this very vividly. And then this infinite ocean of Light takes shape as part of this Light and becomes solidified in the form of your Ishtam (chosen Deity), but never lose sight of the Infinite background of which your Ishtam and you, yourself, as well as all others are parts and which permeates all these. The ocean, the One Eternal Principle, lying at the back of both yourself and the whole universe, must never be lost sight of, because it is That which is to be fully realized by you one day.

But one who does not lead a pure life and is not disciplined, ought never to follow this instruction, because meditation becomes dangerous in the case of a person who is not properly prepared and has not gone through the proper preliminary training.

### SELF-SURRENDER

Only one who has really passed through strenuous self-effort can give himself up and surrender himself wholly and unconditionally at the feet of the Divine. All forms of striving make the mind pure and fit for the Divine touch. And self-surrender can be accomplished only after having gone through one's spiritual practice with great perseverance and doggedness. Self-surrender can come only when our wings are dead-tired like those of the bird sitting on the ship's mast who flies off in search of land and, finding none, returns to the mast again.

Too much activity is very dangerous, because it usually becomes like the aimless activity of the monkey. This kind of activity is just restlessness, and we see it in people who are terribly afraid to be left to themselves. But on the other side we find a form of so-called self-surrender, that is nothing more than inertness, indolence, lethargy. And this is just as bad as aimless activity. The true aspirant should always try to combine both: activity of the right kind, and self-surrender.

### STUDY AND PRACTICE!

Religion is something different from, and something more than, book-knowledge. Through mere scholarship, through mere intellectual study you can never learn the Truth. When we think too much and too highly of intellectual life, we can never realize the essential truths of religion.

"Let one study as well as he can, master the subjects, but after becoming a great scholar, let him renounce desires and try to live upon the strength which comes from knowledge."

One must be free from all guile, from all falsehood, all lack of uprightness, from all the perversities of the mind, and then become a man of meditation, if one wants to make real spiritual progress.

Having known the essentials of spiritual life, having formed a clear idea of the Divine, you should try to practice the disciplines. Do not read too many empty words. That creates only disturbance and trouble. Now, this does not mean that you should not go in for studies, but you should make it a point to study with a view to realize the Truth, and along with your studies there must be some real spiritual practice day by day. You must always train your intellect and have your fixed studies, thinking deeply on the studies, so that you would feel uncomfortable the day that you have not studied anything deeply, pondering over it and over the truths it contains. This daily study is to be made an important item of your spiritual practice.

### LUST AND GREED

Sri Ramakrishna's message is: "Be spiritual and realize the Truth yourself." By living the spiritual life, we can make the Divine living in our own life. The Master shows us how we may overcome sex and greed, our greatest obstacles on the path of all spiritual progress. He wishes us to have a new outlook towards ourselves and others; men as well as women must have the Divine outlook and not think of themselves in terms of sex and body. To see the Divine in oneself and in all others, men and women, is the only solution for the world-problem of sex and the relation between the sexes. This is a most vital point to note for the spiritual aspirant. You can never rise above the sex-idea by just hating woman or man, as many mystics of the Middle Ages tried to do. Something more is needed: The Divine is in me, in all, in everything. "I am not a man, I am not a woman, I am the Self."

### BUDDHA'S PRACTICAL INSTRUCTIONS

It was the mission of Buddha's life to ask people not to think too much of philosophies and metaphysics, of rites and ceremonies, but to make religion—the Spiritual Law—a living force in their lives by leading a life of purity, meditation, spiritual discipline and control. What did Buddha say of

God? He was silent on the point. It is not essential to speak of God so much, but far more essential to follow God's path, to live the spiritual life. What is the use of saying: "O Lord, how beautiful Thou art! How beautiful are Thy skies, Thy stars, Thy whole creation!" The Creator is always greater than His creation and does not feel proud of it. Seen from our human standpoint we find it great, but to God it is insignificant. So it is more important to follow God's path than to praise God eternally, without ever doing anything. This lip-service is of no use to the aspirant.

Once Buddha was asked, "Sir, is there a God?"—"Did I say there is a God?"—"Then there is no God, Sir?"—was the question. "Did I say there is no God?"—came the reply. Buddha wanted to stop all empty and hair-splitting discussions and speculations and make people do something. So he said, "When a house is on fire, do you first go and trace the origin of the fire or do you try to extinguish it?" But we in our foolishness very often try to trace the origin first, but before we have succeeded in the attempt, the whole house is burnt down and nothing remains of it but a heap of ashes.

We always want everything to be done for us by somebody else. There can be no vicarious salvation without self-effort on the part of the aspirant. Most so-called religious people are mere parasites in the world of religion and spiritual life. It would be better for them to take up something else.

### AVOID TEMPTATIONS

During the period of our spiritual training we must try as much as possible to avoid all temptation, both in its gross and subtle forms. We should salute anything that may become an object of temptation to us, from a safe distance. Let us not go near it. We must not rely too much on our own strength for a long time to come. We have such a dirty mind full of filthy impressions that once it is really stirred up it may create no end of troubles. Lust and hatred, greed, vulgarity, all these are lying hidden in us and waiting to make us their prey. And so we must be on our guard.

Always the trouble arises through our being too little aware of the danger in the form of a tiny and apparently insignificant ripple in the mind. The outer stimulus, even if it be a very subtle and scarcely perceptible one, gradually affects the mind. Sometimes even the memory of some old impure impression is enough to upset us, because the germ or the seed is always inside, never outside. Unless the seed be inside, it can never sprout.

Attachment in any form may be enough to muddle the brain and bring about the spiritual ruin of the aspirant, but when attachment and anger combine, the whole mind becomes chaotic, and all progress is stopped. All struggle for the Higher Life comes to an end when passion has its way over a person. That is why we should carefully avoid any harmful stimulus, even if it be a very subtle one, and keep our mind engaged with the higher thoughts. We should not give an opportunity to the lower propensities and impulses, and avoid as much as possible the company of persons of the other sex as well as that of those of our own sex who do not lead a strictly moral life, at least during the period of our spiritual training.

"Fill the mind with Vedantic thoughts until you fall asleep or until this body of yours drops off."

We should not give an opportunity to the passions to sway us. It is the nature of the mind to think, and if we do not give good and pure thoughts to the mind by avoiding all old impure associations, it is bound to think of bad and impure ones. So be up and doing: Always be on your guard and follow the path intelligently and assiduously.

## PRAYERS

O Lord, with the passing of every day the duration of life is seen to shorten, and youth to decay. The days that are gone never come back; time verily is the devourer of the world. Fortune is fickle and short-lived as ripples on the surface of water; while life is momentary like a flash of lightning. Therefore, O Thou refuge of all, do Thou even now protect me who seek refuge in Thee.

May the wicked become virtuous. May the virtuous attain tranquillity. May the tranquil be free from bonds. May the freed make others free.

# The Mystic Word "OM"

## Swami Prabhavananda

FROM VEDIC TIMES until the present day the word "OM" has been taken as a symbol and as an aid to meditation by spiritual aspirants. It is accepted both as one with Brahman and as the medium, the Logos, connecting man and God. It *is* God, and by its aid man may realize God. The entire history of the syllable is in the revelations of the Vedas and the Upanishads, and this history in the hands of the later philosophers developed into what became known as Sphota-vada, or philosophy of the Word. Later also than the Vedas and the Upanishads we discover the doctrine of the Logos among Greek metaphysicians, and this in turn influenced the writer of the Fourth Gospel.

The Sphota-vada, however, is not precisely the philosophy of the Logos of the Greek philosophers. The Greeks first conceived of the Logos as a bridge over the gulf that separates man and God, the known and the unknown. The earliest Greek conception of the Logos was a crude one. It was identified with one or another of the physical elements, according as the source of the universe was thought to have been one or another of these. Heraclitus, who lived in the sixth century B.C., was the first to break away from a purely physical conception of creation, substituting for the material first cause of his predecessors a principle which he called intelligence. This principle of intelligence was the Logos. The advance Heraclitus made, however, was rendered somewhat equivocal by his identification of the Logos with the physical element fire.

With Plato the theory of the Logos underwent a complete transformation. He regarded the Logos, or Word, as the supersensual image, the "idea" or "thought" in God, word and thought being inseparable. And the visible universe, he thought, is the imperfect shadow of the idea, the Logos.

The Stoics denied the validity of Plato's supersensual archetypes, accepting rather the essential theory of Heraclitus and freeing it from the illogicality to which attention has been drawn. Like Heraclitus, the Stoics perceived the principle of reason immanent and active in the universe. This eternal reason, "made concrete in the endless variety of the physical world," became the Logos of the Stoics, and this Logos in reality resided in the soul of man, who might rise above all limitations by realizing its presence within him.

Somewhat later came Philo of Alexandria, a Jewish philosopher and contemporary of Jesus of Nazareth, who attempted to harmonize Stoic reason with the transcendentalism of Plato. Philo declared that the Logos was not only immanent in the universe but was transcendent as well, one with God.

According to the Stoics, the Eternal Reason was the ultimate principle, and the necessity of its transcendental existence they did not admit. Stoicism may in fact be regarded as an attempt to escape from an admission of the existence of a transcendental God. Philo, on the contrary, insisted on the existence of a supreme self-existent Deity, and on the Stoic Logos, or Reason, as related subordinately to Him, this relation being, however, of the nature of identity. Philo called this Logos the "Son of God," and "the only begotten Son of God," as being God's first manifestation. Later the Logos assumed concrete form as the universe.

The author of the Fourth Gospel accepted this conception of the Alexandrian Philo but gave it new expression to serve the theological needs of Christianity.[1] The Logos, that is, which is identical with God, and through which the universe was created, was "made flesh" in Jesus Christ. Thus Jesus, one with the Logos, became the "only begotten son of God," and in Jesus, therefore, there was identity of being with God the Father. "In the beginning was the Word, and the Word was with God, and the Word was God." This verse is almost identical with a verse in the Vedas: *"Prajapatir vai idam agre asit*—In the beginning was Prajapati (Brahman); *Tasya vag*

[1] Cf. J. Reville, *La Doctrine du Logos dans la quatrième Evangile et dans les Oeuvres de Philon.*

*dvitiya asit*—With whom was the Word; *Vag vai Paramam Brahma*—And the Word was verily the Supreme Brahman."

The Philonic and Johannean conceptions of the **Logos** may conceivably owe no debt to Indian thought, for the truth is no monopoly of any race or nation, and with spiritual growth the same truth is often realized by different peoples independently of one another. Yet it is also possible that both Greek philosophers and Christian theologians were in some degree under obligations to India for their initial ideas, since it is a well-known fact that Hindu philosophy exercised a strong influence upon the minds of early Western thinkers.

Not only, however, are there general points of similarity between the Eastern conception of the Logos and that which took root in the West, but there are also differences between the Greek and Christian Logos and the Hindu Sphota-vada that are quite as great. To the Hindu mind, the expressed sensible universe is the form behind which stands the eternal inexpressible, the Sphota, the manifester as Logos, or Word. This Eternal Sphota, the essential material of all ideas or names, is the power through which God creates the universe.[1] Iswara, Brahman conditioned by Maya, first manifests Himself as the Sphota, the inexpressible Word, out of which He evolves as the concrete, sensible world. The Christian Logos is not, however, regarded as the material cause of the Universe, for God according to Christianity is only an efficient cause.

The Christian Logos, as we read in the Fourth Gospel, "was made flesh, and dwelt among us (and we behold his glory, the glory as of the only begotten of the Father), full of grace and truth." There is here a second interesting difference between the Christian and the Hindu Logos. The Christian Logos was incarnate once, in the person of Jesus, whereas the Sphota of the Hindus was and is and will be incarnate in all persons—and not in persons only but in all

---

[1] Patanjali, the author of Yoga philosophy, did not admit this last statement, for the universe was to him a product of Prakriti. Vedanta accepts the Samkhya-Patanjali view, and then reduces the dualism of Samkhya-Patanjali to non-dualism by regarding Prakriti as Maya, or the power of God—the power to create, preserve, and dissolve the universe.

beings, throughout the universe, each of whom may directly realize God through His power, the power of Sphota. "This Sphota," says Swami Vivekananda, "has one word as its only possible symbol, and this is OM. And as by no possible means of analysis can we separate the word from the idea, this OM and the eternal Sphota are inseparable; and therefore it is out of this holiest of all holy words, the mother of all names and forms, the eternal OM, that the whole universe may be supposed to have been created. But it may be said that, although thought and word are inseparable, yet as there may be various word-symbols for the same thought, it is not necessary that this particular word OM should be the word representative of the thought out of which the universe has become manifested. To this objection we reply, that this OM is the only possible symbol which covers the whole ground, and there is none other like it. The Sphota is the material of all words, yet it is not any definite word in its fully formed state. That is to say, if all the particularities which distinguish one word from another be removed, then what remains will be the Sphota; therefore this Sphota is called the Nada-Brahman, the Sound-Brahman. Now, as every word-symbol intended to express the inexpressible Sphota will so particularize it that it will no longer be the Sphota, that symbol which particularizes it the least and at the same time most approximately expresses its nature, will be the truest symbol thereof; and this is the OM, and the OM only; because these three letters A, U, M, pronounced in combination as OM, may well be the generalized symbol of all possible sounds. The letter A is the least differentiated of all sounds. Again, all articulate sounds are produced in the space within the mouth beginning with the root of the tongue and ending in the lips—the throat sound is A, and M is the last lip sound; and the U exactly represents the rolling forward of the impulse which begins at the root of the tongue, continuing till it ends in the lips. If properly pronounced, this OM will represent the whole phenomenon of sound production, and no other word can do this; and this, therefore, is the fittest symbol of the Sphota, which is the real meaning of the OM. And as the symbol can never be separated from the thing signified, the OM and the Sphota are one. And as the Sphota, being the finer side of the manifested universe, is nearer to God, and is indeed the first manifestation of Divine Wisdom, this OM is truly symbolic of God."

More than this, the Yogis claim that through meditation one may hear this word OM vibrating through the universe. In Patanjali's words, the worship of God and meditation upon Him can be effected by repeating OM and meditating upon its meaning.

# The Power of the Word

## SWAMI ADBHUTANANDA[1]

SOME KIND OF EXCUSE will always be found by those who do not perform japam, yet if one will make a practice of repeating the holy Name, the Name itself will take hold of the mind.

Of a surety the mind is restless, drunk with worldly attachment, and it is this attachment that drags it down. This is why Sri Krishna taught Arjuna non-attachment to objects and actions, and why he taught him the practice of devotion.

Through the regular practice of repeating the holy Name the mind will gradually become tranquil. Practice discrimination, and whenever the mind runs after sense-objects discriminate between the Real and the unreal. Know every sense-object to be transitory; today it is, tomorrow it is not. You will find that though you add together all the transitory, finite objects that this world can give you, you cannot find the Reality, you cannot find the Infinity. There is one infinite existence: That is Brahman—That is the Reality. All else is unreal.

Impress these thoughts again and again upon the mind, and as the mind receives the impressions, true discrimination will arise.

Once Rama gave a string of pearls to his devotee Hanuman. Hanuman examined each pearl carefully, opened one of them with his teeth, and then threw them away. When

[1] Translated from the teachings of Swami Adbhutananda as recorded by a disciple. Swami Adbhutananda, or Latu Maharaj, as he was known to the circle of devotees of Sri Ramakrishna, came to the Master when quite young. He was the servant boy of a devotee of Sri Ramakrishna. He became one of the monastic disciples of the Master. Latu Maharaj never knew how to read or write. From Sri Ramakrishna he learned the art of reading the book of knowledge which is within every human soul. Whatever he himself taught later came directly from that same source-book of wisdom—the knowledge of God.

Lakshmana, who had been watching him, saw this, he angrily exclaimed: "The value of a pearl necklace cannot be recognized by a fool!" Rama then asked Lakshmana to enquire of Hanuman the reason for his action, and upon being questioned Hanuman replied: "I opened the pearl to see if the holy Name was there. The necklace is worthless if Rama is not in it."

Always discriminate between the Real and the unreal. To keep the power of discrimination awake in the mind is the greatest exercise of tapas (austerity). He who has learned to discriminate can successfully overcome lust and craving. First of all, the mind must be swept clean of all the undesirable thoughts which arise, they must not be allowed to enter through the doors of the senses, and as they creep in, the power of discrimination must be brought into play; the lower mind must be conquered by the discriminating mind. Then alone will the heart be purified, and then alone will God be revealed.

Until the heart and mind are consecrated to God through meditation, one cannot completely overcome lust and craving.

The mind alone is the field wherein is planted the seed of lust. This seed is nurtured by the sense organs within and the sense objects without. Thus it increases and multiplies. The weeds that grow from it have to be uprooted, the seed has to be destroyed, and the holy Name of God sown in its place. Constant repetition of the holy Name will nurture the seed and cause it to bring forth much fruit. Sri Ramakrishna used to say: "Where there is craving there is no Rama, where there is Rama there is no craving."

There is another saying of Sri Ramakrishna: "Put on the armor of the holy Name and overcome the enemy of lust." The seeds of lust and craving may be burnt by japam; for such is the power of the holy Name of God. The Word is God. The Word is the Reality. Through the practice of japam its magnetic atraction is felt, and as the mind becomes more deeply drawn into the spiritual current which flows toward the Real, lust, which is unreal, loses its hold and is swept away.

It is also true that the power of the Word works even while one sleeps. He who practices japam continues to repeat the

Name in all states of consciousness—waking, dreaming, and dreamless sleep. Just as the body continues to breathe, so does the mind continue to repeat the Name even in sleep. Thus the aspirant is able to overcome the evil impressions of the subconscious mind also.

The mind is a storehouse of lust and craving. From this storehouse some evil elements rise to the surface, while others may remain hidden, dormant, unrecognized. Now the more one practices spiritual disciplines, the nearer one moves toward the light of God, the purer one becomes in body and mind, the more clearly will the evil impressions of one's many, many past lives be revealed. The "heat" produced by the practice of japam will draw them out, and that same "heat" will destroy them. The power of the Word is supreme.

No more will the mind be troubled by the restless waves of lust and craving; by the power of the Word the mind becomes pure, transformed, renewed. Upon the pure mind the power of God descends. Unto the pure heart Reality is revealed.

# Meditation

## Swami Adbhutananda

MANY AND VARIED are the forms of meditation. One form is that in which Brahman is likened to a boundless ocean, and the jiva to a fish, swimming happily about, feeling the soothing, living presence everywhere. In another form the body is regarded as a vessel, and the mind as water—pure as crystal—upon which is reflected the sun of Satchidananda—Existence, Knowledge and Bliss. Yet again Brahman may be meditated upon as the limitless ocean, and the jiva as a vessel submerged in it, the water of Brahman within and without—everywhere. Again one may think of oneself as a bird soaring blissfully through the sky of Satchidananda. These and many other forms are known to the followers of the path of knowledge.

God is with form and without form. God in His absolute, formless aspect is meditated upon by the followers of the path of knowledge; but the devotee holds on to the name and form of God, and meditates upon Him with form. Various are the names and forms of God, which are but different aspects of the one Reality.

The guru and the Avataras are also forms of God, and the devotee takes one form and meditates upon that as his Chosen Ideal. While absorbed in meditation the devotee may have visions of the different forms of God. These must be regarded as but different aspects of the one Chosen Ideal. Forms are many, but the Reality is one. To emphasize this truth Sri Ramakrishna would give the simile of the chameleon—which changes its color, yet remains the same. Thus by devotion to the Chosen Ideal the devotee soon realizes that God assumes many forms, and yet is also formless.

The devotee meditates on the Holy Name and form of God, and the follower of the path of knowledge meditates on the relation and identity of jiva with Brahman. But whichever path is followed, the one and the same state of spiritual consciousness is attained by each. When, by meditating on name and form one attains a depth in meditation, both name and form vanish; when, by meditating on the relation of the jiva and Brahman one attains a depth in meditation, relation also vanishes. There remains in both a spiritual current which words cannot describe.

Sri Ramakrishna once said that in the depths of meditation there arises the consciousness of the impartite, the indivisible Reality. Body is forgotten, mind ceases to function—there remains pure Consciousness.

There is a difference between ecstasy and samadhi. In ecstasy the aspirant *experiences* bliss, he sees the play of the Divine; in samadhi the aspirant *becomes* blissful. The experiencer, the experience, and the experienced become one.

To see the light in vision during meditation is not enough, though it is true that such a vision or any other vision serves to strengthen the faith, and encourage the aspirant to go deeper and deeper. Only when the physical consciousness is gone, when the heart becomes pure, can one really know that there is a deeper and vaster realm beyond the realm of spiritual visions.

The knowledge of the existence of this realm cannot be grasped by the human mind, nor can words define it. The grace of the Guru alone can open the gates to that blissful realm. One day while massaging the head of Sri Ramakrishna the door to that realm suddenly opened before me. What I saw, the eyes could not hold, what I tasted the tongue could not express. It was a definite experience beyond all expression.

If you would know and enter into that kingdom, let the tongue tirelessly chant the name of God, let the heart and mind become absorbed in His meditation. Sooner or later, through His grace, you will surely know and enter into that blissful realm.

Be absorbed in meditation. Be absorbed so that the world becomes annihilated, and only you exist, you and your Beloved shining in your heart. As one becomes established in the meditative life there comes a control over the mind.

Then alone can one know his own mind, how and in what devious ways it works. He becomes immediately aware of any tricks the mind would try to play. The old habits of hatred, jealousy, and all the passions will no longer have the power to raise any wave in the mind. They will gradually recede, and eventually disappear.

Many changes come in one who lives the contemplative life. The character becomes transformed, the body also changes, the voice becomes sweet; he breathes differently. A truly meditative man can be recognized by his movements, his face, his eyes. He has wonderful poise, his mind is tranquil. With eyes opened or with eyes closed, engaged in whatever occupation, he meditates constantly and continuously. The current of thought flows unceasingly toward his Beloved. Just as a person suffering from acute toothache is constantly reminded of it, so is the aspirant constantly aware of the living Presence.

Do not sleep the sleep of ignorance. Keep yourself constantly awake by the practice of spiritual disciplines. Without spiritual practice life is meaningless, the truth of God remains unknown. People quarrel over theories and dogmas of religion, but those who devote their lives to the attainment of the bliss of God, and know the Reality, have no quarrel with other faiths, nor do they antagonize them, for they speak the same tongue.

# Brahman and Maya

## SWAMI ADBHUTANANDA

THE TRUE BEING in man is ever free, ever pure, and remains ever untouched by good or evil. Good and evil have no absolute reality. They exist only so long as man identifies himself with the ego, the false self. When the ego is completely annihilated, man is freed from the false knowledge of duality or relativity—of good and evil.

Good and evil exist only so long as man thinks himself to be the doer of actions. If through the grace of the Infinite Being he is freed from this consciousness of ego, then the idea of good or bad no longer exists for him.

Merit and demerit are the effects of karma. Because of the sense of attachment to the false ego, man is subject to this law. As a man sows, so does he reap. The law of karma operates within the realm of Maya. Man, identifying himself with the ego, becomes bound by Maya.

In creation and destruction, in happiness and misery, in success and failure, in every domain of duality is Maya's play. Such is her nature, and man, because of ignorance, is caught in the play. But he who is freed from the bondage of Maya is guided by the Infinite Being, and in His guidance finds everlasting joy, everlasting peace, everlasting blessedness. There no waves of duality can arise. There is only the one Infinite Ocean of peace and joy.

Maya of itself has no independent existence. As Sri Ramakrishna has said: "The wave is of the ocean, not the ocean itself." Similarly Maya is of the Infinite Being, but is not the Infinite Being Itself. Therefore, the bondage and control of Maya cannot be said to be the same as the control and guidance of God. Yet true it is that the ultimate purpose of the play of Maya is to lead man Godward—to the Infinite Reality. All will ultimately reach God.

Unattached and with perfect balance Maya plays her dual role. On the one hand it is she who lulls man into forgetfulness of his true nature, and again it is she who awakens him to the consciousness of God. Within her domain are all the dual throng. And why? That man may overcome evil with good and finally transcend both. So we see that while Maya appears to bind, yet by this same bondage man is led toward freedom, albeit along a winding and tortuous pathway, for only after many births and much suffering does he finally recognize the inscrutable play of Maya and surrender himself to her liberating power.

One truth is certain. Whether he wills to find God in this present life, or after many more lives of suffering and bondage, sooner or later man must seek to find God with wholehearted devotion. And as he seeks Him, he finds Him.

God is the Infinite Existence. In Him there is neither east nor west, neither within nor without, neither above nor below. He permeates all space—he is woven warp and woof into all things. He is immanent, all-pervading—unaffected by forms or boundaries. He is all and He transcends all. Sri Ramakrishna used to say: "Everything but the Truth of Brahman has been defiled through the lips of man." No words can express the glory of God. Sri Ramakrishna would often wish to reveal the truth of Brahman to his disciples but his lips were sealed as it were by the Divine Mother Herself.

Brahman is Truth, and whosoever observes truthfulness and wills to know Truth shall surely attain it. The power to will is the greatest gift bestowed upon man, and nothing can stand against one whose will is awakened. Will and impulse or desire, however, must not be confused. Impulse or desire is a degeneration of the will. What is it that man truly wills? It is the attainment of *Ananda,* that everlasting peace, and this is attained only by finding the *Satchidananda*—the Infinite Being, the Infinite Wisdom, and the Infinite Love.

The true purpose of human birth is to fulfill this one, this only will, to realize God—which is truly the motive power behind all other desires. Unhappy is the man who forgets this purpose, and loses himself in the meshes of petty desires and impulses. Desiring first one thing, then another and yet again something else is but impulse, and can be likened unto a man, who, desiring to sink a well, digs first in one place and then in another, never completing one well, and never reaching the water. Not by such impulses and desires can the thirst for God be quenched. Therefore, I say unto you, *will* to attain the Truth, the Kingdom of Self.

This Kingdom is never lost. It may lie hidden, covered with dirt, but it is forever within. Brahman is ever pure, ever free, self-luminous, and that Brahman is one's very Self. Just as a gold vessel may be covered with dirt, yet lose nothing of its true nature, so the true Self lies hidden within, and remains forever unaffected by the dirt of ignorance covering it.

Man is ever conscious of the existence of this Self. Every time he says "my body," "my mind," "my intelligence," etc., he unconsciously admits the existence of an "I," of a "Self." Because of this ignorance which clouds man's true Self, he is unable to manifest his real nature. Hence the necessity of spiritual disciplines, and the firm will to unfold this latent divinity.

# Seven Meditations

## ALDOUS HUXLEY

### BEING

GOD IS. That is the primordial fact. It is in order that we may discover this fact for ourselves, by direct experience, that we exist. The final end and purpose of every human being is the unitive knowledge of God's being.

What is the nature of God's being? The invocation to the Lord's Prayer gives us the answer. "Our Father which *art* in heaven." God is, and is ours—immanent in each sentient being, the life of all lives, the spirit animating every soul. But this is not all. God is also the transcendent Creator and Law-Giver, the Father who loves and, because He loves, also educates His children. And finally, God is "in heaven." That is to say, He possesses a mode of existence which is incommensurable and incompatible with the mode of existence possessed by human beings in their natural, unspiritualized condition. Because He is ours and immanent, God is very close to us. But because He is also in heaven, most of us are very far from God. The saint is one who is as close to God as God is close to him.

It is through prayer that men come to the unitive knowledge of God. But the life of prayer is also a life of mortification, of dying to self. It cannot be otherwise; for the more there is of self, the less there is of God. Our pride, our anxiety, our lusts for power and pleasure are God-eclipsing things. So too is that greedy attachment to certain creatures which passes too often for unselfishness and should be called, not altruism, but alter-egoism. And hardly less God-eclipsing is the seemingly self-sacrificing service which we give to any cause or ideal that falls short of the divine. Such service is always idolatry, and makes it impossible for us to worship

God as we should, much less to know Him. God's kingdom cannot come unless we begin by making our human kingdoms go. Not only the mad and obviously evil kingdoms, but also the respectable ones—the kingdoms of the scribes and pharisees, the good citizens and pillars of society, no less than the kingdoms of the publicans and sinners. God's being cannot be known by us, if we choose to pay our attention and our allegiance to something else, however creditable that something else may seem in the eyes of the world.

## BEAUTY

Beauty arises when the parts of a whole are related to one another and to the totality in a manner which we apprehend as orderly and significant. But the first principle of order is God, and God is the final, deepest meaning of all that exists. God, then, is manifest in the relationship which makes things beautiful. He resides in that lovely interval which harmonizes events on all the planes, where we discover beauty. We apprehend Him in the alternate voids and fullnesses of a cathedral; in the spaces that separate the salient features of a picture; in the living geometry of a flower, a sea shell, an animal; in the pauses and intervals between the notes of music, in their differences of tone and sonority; and finally, on the plane of conduct, in the love and gentleness, the confidence and humility, which give beauty to the relationships between human beings.

Such then, is God's beauty, as we apprehend it in the sphere of created things. But it is also possible for us to apprehend it, in some measure at least, as it is in itself. The beatific vision of divine beauty is the knowledge, so to say, of Pure Interval, of harmonious relationship apart from the things related. A material figure of beauty-in-itself is the cloudless evening sky, which we find inexpressibly lovely, although it possesses no orderliness of arrangement, since there are no distinguishable parts to be harmonized. We find it beautiful because it is an emblem of the infinite Clear Light of the Void. To the knowledge of this Pure Interval we shall come only when we have learnt to mortify attachment to creatures, above all to ourselves.

Moral ugliness arises when self-assertion spoils the harmonious relationship which should exist between sentient beings. Analogously, aesthetic and intellectual ugliness arise when one part in a whole is excessive or deficient. Order is marred, meaning distorted and, for the right, the divine relation between things or thoughts, there is substituted a wrong relation—a relationship that manifests symbolically, not the immanent and transcendent source of all beauty, but that chaotic disorderliness which characterizes creatures when they try to live independently of God.

### LOVE

God is love, and there are blessed moments when even to unregenerate human beings it is granted to know Him as love. But it is only in the saints that this knowledge becomes secure and continuous. By those in the earlier stages of the spiritual life God is apprehended predominantly as law. It is through obedience to God the Law-Giver that we come at last to know God the loving Father.

The law which we must obey, if we would know God as love, is itself a law of love. "Thou shalt love God with all thy soul, and with all thy heart, with all thy mind and with all thy strength. And thou shalt love thy neighbor as thyself." We cannot love God as we should, unless we love our neighbors as we should. We cannot love our neighbors as we should, unless we love God as we should. And, finally, we cannot realize God as the active, all-pervading principle of love, until we ourselves have learnt to love Him and our fellow creatures.

Idolatry consists in loving a creature more than we love God. There are many kinds of idolatry, but all have one thing in common: namely, self-love. The presence of self-love is obvious in the grosser forms of sensual indulgence, or the pursuit of wealth and power and praise. Less manifestly, but none the less fatally, it is present in our inordinate affections for individuals, persons, places, things and institutions. And even in men's most heroic sacrifices to high causes and noble ideals, self-love has its tragic place. For when we sacrifice ourselves to any cause or ideal that is lower than the highest, less than God Himself, we are merely sacrificing one part of our unregenerate being to another part which we and other people regard as more creditable. Self-love still persists, still prevents us from obeying perfectly the first of the two great commandments. God can be loved perfectly only by those who have killed out the subtlest, the most nobly sublimated forms of self-love. When this happens, when we love God as we should and therefore know God as love, the tormenting problem of evil ceases to be a problem, the world of time is seen to be an aspect of eternity, and in some inexpressible way, but no less really and certainly, the struggling, chaotic multiplicity of life is reconciled in the unity of the all-embracing divine charity.

## PEACE

Along with love and joy, peace is one of the fruits of the spirit. But it is also one of the roots. In other words, peace is a necessary condition of spirituality, no less than an inevitable result of it. In the words of St. Paul, it is peace which keeps the heart and mind in the knowledge and love of God.

Between peace the root and peace the fruit of the spirit there is, however, a profound difference in quality. Peace the root is something we all know and understand, something which, if we choose to make the necessary effort, we can achieve. If we do not achieve it, we shall never make any serious advance in our knowledge and love of God, we shall never catch more than a fleeting glimpse of that other peace which is the fruit of spirituality. Peace the fruit is the peace which passes all understanding; and it passes understanding, because it is the peace of God. Only those who have in some measure become God-like can hope to know this peace in its enduring fullness. Inevitably so. For, in the world of spiritual realities, knowledge is always a function of being; the nature of what we experience is determined by what we ourselves are.

In the early stages of the spiritual life we are concerned almost exclusively with peace the root, and with the moral virtues from which it springs, the vices and weaknesses which check its growth. Interior peace has many enemies. On the moral plane we find, on the one hand, anger, impatience and every kind of violence; and, on the other (for peace is essentially active and creative), every kind of inertia and slothfulness. On the plane of feeling, the great enemies of peace are grief, anxiety, fear, all the formidable host of the negative emotions. And on the plane of the intellect we encounter foolish distractions and the wantonness of idle curiosity. The overcoming of these enemies is a most laborious and often painful process, requiring incessant mortification of natural tendencies and all-too-human habits. That is why there is, in this world of ours, so little interior peace among individuals and so little exterior peace between societies. In the words of the *Imitation:* "All men desire peace but few indeed desire those things which make for peace."

### HOLINESS

Whole, hale, holy—the three words derive from the same root. By etymology no less than in fact holiness is spiritual health, and health is wholeness, completeness, perfection. God's holiness is the same as His unity; and a man is holy to the extent to which he has become single-minded, one-pointed, perfect as our Father in heaven is perfect.

Because each of us possesses only one body, we tend to believe that we are one being. But in reality our name is Legion. In our unregenerate condition we are divided beings, half-hearted and double-minded, creatures of many moods and multiple personalities. And not only are we divided against our unregenerate selves; we are also incomplete. As well as our multitudinous soul, we possess a spirit that is one with the universal spirit. Potentially (for in his normal condition he does not know who he is) man is much more than the personality he takes himself to be. He cannot achieve his wholeness unless and until he realizes his true nature, discovers and liberates the spirit within his soul and so unites himself with God.

Unholiness arises when we give consent to any rebellion or self-assertion by any part of our being against that totality which it is possible for us to become through union with God. For example, there is the unholiness of indulged sensuality, of unchecked avarice, envy and anger, of the wantonness of pride and worldly ambition. Even the negative sensuality of ill health may constitute unholiness, if the mind be permitted to dwell upon the sufferings of its body more than is absolutely necessary or unavoidable. And on the plane of the intellect there is the imbecile unholiness of distractions, and the busy, purposeful unholiness of curiosity about matters concerning which we are powerless to act in any constructive or remedial way.

From our natural state of incompleteness to spiritual health and perfection there is no magically easy short cut. The way to holiness is laborious and long. It lies through vigilance and prayer, through an unresting guard of the heart, the mind, the will and the tongue, and through the one-pointed loving atention to God, which that guard alone makes possible.

### GRACE

Graces are the free gifts of help bestowed by God upon each one of us, in order that we may be assisted to achieve our final end and purpose; namely, unitive knowledge of divine reality. Such helps are very seldom so extraordinary that we are immediately aware of their true nature as God-sends. In the overwhelming majority of cases they are so inconspicuously woven into the texture of common life, that we do not know that they are graces, unless and until we respond to them as we ought, and so receive the material, moral or spiritual benefits, which they were meant to bring us. If we do not respond to these ordinary graces as we ought, we shall receive no benefit and remain unaware of their nature or even of their very existence. Grace is always sufficient, provided we are ready to co-operate with it. If we fail to do our share, but rather choose to rely on self-will and self-direction, we shall not only get no help from the graces bestowed upon us; we shall actually make it impossible for further graces to be given. When used with an obstinate consistency, self-will creates a private universe walled off impenetrably from the light of spiritual reality; and within these private universes the self-willed go their way, unhelped and unillumined, from accident to random accident, or from calculated evil to calculated evil. It is of such that St. Francis de Sales is speaking when he says, "God did not deprive thee of the operation of his love, but thou didst deprive His love of thy co-operation. God would never have rejected thee, if thou hadst not rejected Him."

To be clearly and constantly aware of the divine guidance is given only to those who are already far advanced in the life of the spirit. In its earlier stages we have to work, not by the direct perception of God's successive graces, but by faith in their existence. We have to accept as a working hypothesis that the events of our lives are not merely fortuitous, but deliberate tests of intelligence and character, specially devised occasions (if properly used) for spiritual advance. Acting upon this working hypothesis, we shall treat no occurrence as intrinsically unimportant. We shall never make a response that is inconsiderate, or a mere automatic expression of our self-will, but always give ourselves time, before acting or speaking, to consider what course of behaviour would seem to be most in accord with the will of God, most charitable, most conducive to the achievement of our final end. When such becomes our habitual response to events, we shall discover, from the nature of their effects, that some at least of those occurrences were divine graces in the disguise sometimes of trivialities, sometimes of inconveniences or even of pains and trials. But if we fail to act upon the working hypothesis that grace exists, grace will in effect be non-existent so far as we are concerned. We shall prove by a life of accident at the best, or, at the worst, of downright evil, that God does not help human beings, unless they first permit themselves to be helped.

### JOY

Peace, love, joy—these, according to St. Paul, are the three fruits of the spirit. They correspond very closely to the three essential attributes of God, as summarized in the Indian formula, *sat, chit, ananda,* being, knowledge, bliss. Peace is the manifestation of unified being. Love is the mode of divine knowledge. And bliss, the concomitant of perfection, is the same as joy.

Like peace, joy is not only a fruit of the spirit, but also a root. If we would know God, we must do everything to cultivate that lower equivalent of joy, which it is within our power to feel and to express.

"Sloth" is the ordinary translation of that *acedia,* which ranks among the seven deadly sins of our Western tradition. It is an inadequate translation; for *acedia* is more than sloth; it is also depression and self-pity, it is also that dull world-weariness which causes us, in Dante's words, to be "sad in the sweet air that rejoiceth in the sun." To grieve, to repine, to feel sorry for oneself, to despair—these are the manifestations of self-willing and of rebellion against the will of God. And that special and characteristic discouragement we experience on account of the slowness of our spiritual advance—what is it but a symptom of wounded vanity, a tribute paid to our high opinion of our own merits?

To be cheerful when circumstances are depressing, or when we are tempted to indulge in self-pity, is a real mortification—a mortification all the more valuable for being so inconspicuous, so hard to recognize for what it is. Physical austerities, even the mildest of them, can hardly be practised without attracting other people's attention; and because they thus attract attention, those who practise them are often tempted to feel vain of their self-denial. But such mortifications as refraining from idle talk, from wanton curiosity about things which do not concern us, and above all from depression and self-pity, can be practised without anybody knowing of them. Being consistently cheerful may cost us a far greater effort than, for example, being consistently temperate; and whereas other people will often admire us for refraining from physical indulgences, they will probably attribute our cheerfulness to good digestion or a native insensibility. From the roots of such secret and unadmired self-denials there springs the tree whose fruits are the peace that passes all understanding, the love of God and of all creatures for God's sake, and the joy of perfection, the bliss of an eternal and timeless consummation.

# Spiritual Maxims

## SWAMI SHIVANANDA[1]

THE ONLY WAY to lasting peace is complete surrender to the will of God. Restlessness destroys all peace of mind. When the mind becomes restless one should pray earnestly to God, for He alone is the abode of peace.

Constant recollection of God will bring an overflowing blessedness.

The only real purpose of human life is the search for Reality. To know the Reality we must meditate. Therefore, the spiritual aspirant should make the practice of meditation a regular habit. The early morning is the best time for spiritual practices. The sacred hours before sunrise are better than any other time of the day or night for the practice of inwardness.

The tribulations of the world indirectly drive the mind toward God. The more you are troubled and tortured in the world the more you will think of God, and know it for certain that loving remembrance of God severs all our attachments to the world.

As long as a man remains satisfied with earthly enjoyments and attainments, he has not started on the spiritual path; and when the pangs of separation from God pierce the mind, the time for God-vision is at hand.

A true devotee asks nothing of God but pure love for Him. Even as a child depends entirely upon its mother, so the devout soul depends entirely upon God.

God is with form, and also without form; again, He is beyond both. He transcends all our conceptions of Him. He can be meditated upon in any one of His multifarious aspects.

[1] One of the direct disciples of Sri Ramakrishna, Swami Shivananda succeeded Swami Brahmananda as head of the Ramakrishna Order.

When the mind is overcome by a feeling of monotony, one should resort to scriptural study, repetition of the Name of God, prayer, and holy company. But of all the means for purification and realization, meditation is the highest. Constant remembrance of God makes us "whole."

Kindle the fire of renunciation in your heart, dive deep in the ocean of His love, then alone will spiritual experiences come.

When you have succeeded in enshrining God within your heart you will see Him everywhere.

Everything depends upon the Grace of God—even the desire for spiritual practice. Eventually His vision too comes as a result of His blessing.

Dreams of holy men and holy places are very auspicious. One should shun all evil association by all means.

If you sincerely adhere to your spiritual exercises with faith, purity and devotion, you will surely be illumined.

Spiritual life must be lived in absolute secrecy; publicity hinders our attempts. To give expression to divine emotions is to lessen them, and it is unwholesome. The more they are concealed, the more they are intensified.

Be ever prayerful, then evil thoughts, even if they come to the mind, cannot linger long. A prayerful man is ever peaceful.

The power of a divine Incarnation is infinite. Unflinching reliance on the Chosen Ideal is the religion of the devotee. For him the veil of ignorance is quickly removed.

Liberation in life, as contrasted with liberation after death, is like standing on the threshold of a room, with one foot placed inside and the other outside. In this state everything of the inner and the outer world is visible, while in the latter state one enters the inner world and sees nothing of the outer world; the outward consciousness is totally eliminated from the mind.

To think of a divine form within the heart is one kind of meditation. Imagine that the form is very gracious and is looking at you with deep affection and kindness. Such thoughts will fill the soul with love, hope and peace, and you will be blessed.

It is the nature of the mind to become restless and unsteady at times. But we must not allow ourselves to be unsettled or upset by this. When the mind is restrained, such occasional reactions will strengthen rather than weaken it.

Patient and regular practice is the whole secret of spiritual realization. Do not be in a hurry in spiritual life. Do your utmost, and leave the rest to God.

Past tendencies will be uprooted and obliterated by the constant remembrance of God, and the heart will be filled with peace. The mind is stilled by His grace alone.

The building of a pure life and character is the sole concern of the spiritual aspirant. It is the primary object of his life; everything else is secondary.

The more you call upon God the nearer will you be to Him. Overflowing devotion is the only condition of His Grace.

A pure and spotless life is a source of real welfare to the world. When such a life is actually lived, there is no need for oral teaching. Example is more potent than precepts.

The Lord gives us difficulties only to test and strengthen our faith. Look to Him for help and guidance. Love all equally. Do not wound the feelings of others.

It is difficult to turn the course of our mind towards God after it has been steeped in worldliness for so long, but if you are resolute never to abstain from thinking of Him, it will change. The Lord is most merciful. He rejects no prayer. Be regular and sincere in your daily meditation, and never allow despair to overwhelm your mind.

# Control of the Subconscious Mind
## Swami Prabhavananda

**WHAT IS THE SUBCONSCIOUS MIND?** We all know something
about the nature of the conscious mind. We think, we feel,
we act, and we are conscious of our thoughts, feelings, and
actions. And whatever we think and feel and do, in short, all
our experiences, are stored in the subconscious mind. You
can remember certain things you did. Why can you remember? Because what you did remained imbedded in the mind.
Every thought, every feeling, every action leaves its impression on the mind. Nothing is lost. The sum-total of those
impressions is what we may call the *character* of an individual. You are the result of what you have thought, felt and
done. In turn, your accumulated tendencies determine and
control your conscious thoughts, feelings, and actions. Your
reactions to this objective universe are governed by your individual character, which is the deposit of your past reactions. That is why individuals vary in their reactions to
experience. To take a crude illustration: nowadays the papers
carry headlines reporting many thousands of people killed.
To some minds, these headlines bring a reaction of joy; to
other minds, a reaction of pain and suffering. The reaction
varies according to the character of the individual, which has
been formed by past thoughts, feelings, and actions, which
remain imbedded in the mind.

But what about free-will? Can we not choose the way we
will react to given conditions and circumstances? Yes, we can
choose; but the will is not absolutely *free* will. The will, by
which I make choices, behaves in accordance with my character, that sum-total of all my past deeds, thoughts, and feelings. And not alone of this present life. The subconscious
mind carries the record of many, many past lives.

So then, we are what we have made ourselves, not in this

one life, but in many, many past lives. We have this sub-conscious mind, carrying our whole record, past and present, defining the character and the tendencies we are born with, which in turn determine the way we react to present conditions. The subconscious, that part of the mind below the level of the conscious or surface mind, is a very influential factor in our present life.

We all realize the power of the influence exerted by the subconscious mind. Through experience, a certain growth takes place in the ideas held by the conscious mind. You grow a sense of good and evil. Certain new ideals and principles come into your conscious mind. You realize that you must live according to these new ideals and principles. In other words, you begin to know a better way of life. But you find yourself helpless to live in that better way. This is an experience everyone of us has had. We know, but we cannot do. A thief, for example, wants to reform himself; he does not wish to steal any more. Then he goes to a place where he sees that it would be very easy to steal without being caught. He knows better, but he steals. So with any other bad habit. We have become slaves to our own subconscious minds, to our own characters.

Is there no way out of this? Yes, there is. I have already pointed out that the so-called free-will is also controlled by your character, so that the term "free-will" is really a mis-nomer. There is, however, a certain freedom, which is not of the will or of the mind or of the intellect, but it is a *freedom of the spirit* within us which says, "I cannot will, yet I *must* will." Although our mind says, and our character says, "I cannot do it," the spirit says, "You must do it." That is the freedom left in every one of us, and through that freedom of the Spirit each one of us may find salvation.

We recognize that there is something greater, something higher we have to achieve. Because of our habits and tendencies built up by past actions, we find it almost impossible—but not completely impossible. If it were completely impossible, then life would not be worth living for any of us. But, because of that freedom of the Spirit, though we may fail many times, still we struggle, and this struggle is life. And, whether we know it or not, the real struggle is to overcome the subconscious mind, to be free again.

Now, how are we to achieve that? The psychology of religion goes to the root of this. In my opinion, the only way to overcome the subconscious mind is to follow the psychology of religion. Just to analyze yourself and to recognize this slavery does not help you. You have to root out completely your impressions and your character—and that is the psychology of religion. What does Saint Paul say? "Be ye transformed by the renewal of your own mind." This complete transformation, this complete renewal of the mind is what is taught in the psychology of religion. The very first aphorism in *Patanjali's Yoga* is: *Yoga-schitta—vritti nirodha.* This defines Yoga as complete control of the modifications of the mind. The word "modifications" means the thoughts and contents of the mind. A complete overhauling of the mind. Emptying the mind of all its contents—that is Yoga!

Now, before we can learn the methods and means of doing this, the question arises: "What do we achieve by this complete emptying and renewal of the mind?" Patanjali says that by this renewal of the mind you realize your true being, you live in your kingdom. In the words of the Christian Bible, you realize the Kingdom of God within.

Simply to try to overcome your past and be good in the future does not work. It cannot work, because, however you may try, your tendencies are left. The only way is to change your whole mind completely—wipe out the whole past, the whole content of consciousness. That is the only way. And what is the effect when you do that? What happens then? In the words of Vedanta philosophy, you realize the Kingdom of Self. In the words of the Christian Bible, you realize the Kingdom of Heaven which is within you. Now, what is this true nature that we realize? What is this Kingdom of God? It is said to be perfection. Christ says: "Be ye perfect, even as the Father in heaven is perfect." This perfection is to be achieved. And it is not a relative perfection. The theologians interpret this perfection which Christ speaks of as a relative perfection toward which we grow eternally, but never fully achieve. Christ did not mean that. He said definitely, "Be ye perfect." Not relatively perfect. Relative perfection is imperfection. Perfection, to be perfection, must be an absolute perfection, nothing less. And this perfection is to be achieved, attained, as we empty ourselves of all the contents of consciousness.

The mind is like a lake of dirty water, lashed into waves. The reflection of the sun in that lake is not clear. But make the water of the lake clear and calm, and there is a perfect reflection of the sun. The sun, the light of God, shines within each of us, shines on the lake of the mind, but because of the imperfections of that mind, the light is imperfectly reflected.

Now what are those imperfections? They are the *Samskaras,* or the impressions that we have created, which, in turn, create thoughts in us that lash the mind into waves, so that the sun within us, the light of God, cannot be properly reflected, and we are not even conscious of that sun within. But the moment you free yourself you purify yourself of all those tendencies you have carried over from the past. The moment you attain to that tranquillity of mind that Christ calls purity of heart, God can be seen. "Blessed are the pure in heart, for they shall see God." And not until we have seen God, not until we have realized pure consciousness, can we say that the subconscious mind has been overcome.

Now, what is really meant by those phrases, "making the mind tranquil" and "freeing the mind of all its content of thought and consciousness"? The Brahman or God is said to be eternally existent. He *is.* Then He is Chit: consciousness itself; and He is Ananda: happiness, or love, itself. That Brahman, that God, is in some way reflected in our minds. You are always carrying God with you and within you, every moment of your life. This Sat, this *am,* or Existence, is reflected in every one of us by the knowledge: *I am, I exist.* We are all conscious of that existence; none of us can imagine non-existence. We must exist even to try to think of ourselves as not existing. We exist then, and we have knowledge of that existence; but this knowledge embraces only the contents of our minds, not of Reality, that which is. There is only a partial reflection. Only when we can free ourselves from this content of consciousness can we become aware of pure consciousness, that is, God, the Infinite Consciousness.

Again, we all feel. What is it we wish to feel? We wish to feel love, we wish to feel happiness. These are the two strong desires that exist in us, the desire for love and happiness. And that also is a reflection; but, when we free ourselves from the waves that arise in the mind and go to the bottom of it, to that pure consciousness, then we realize the *fulfilment* of the desire for love and happiness, which is infinite love and infinite happiness!

It seems so easy to say, "Free yourself from the contents of consciousness and be pure in heart, and you will reach God." But, owing to our different states of consciousness, we find that it is quite impossible to reach freedom, to reach God. In our waking state of consciousness, with our physical senses, with our human minds which can only become conscious of objects and things, we cannot reach that pure consciousness, however we may try. Then we go to sleep, we dream. There again, in the sleep of dreams, we cannot realize that pure consciousness. Then we go into deep sleep, we become unconscious; but, although we seem to be freed of the content of consciousness, it is only because there is a veil of darkness covering our consciousness. We do not realize pure consciousness. So long as we live and move within these three states of consciousness, it is not possible to reach the realization of pure consciousness. We cannot see God, cannot realize God, within the province of these three states of consciousness that are known to us.

In order to free ourselves from the contents of consciousness we must reach a state beyond these three states of consciousness. This state is called in the Upanishads *Turiya*, the Fourth. And it is possible to reach that Fourth State while living on earth. In the Fourth State of pure consciousness you lose the contents of consciousness, you are freed from your own character and from all your past, and you become one with infinite and pure consciousness. That is what is meant in the psychology of religion when we are taught to become pure in heart that we may see God, to empty ourselves of all our past impressions and live in the Kingdom of the Atman.

But how is that to be achieved? As the goal is made very plain, so also the means to attain it are made very clear and simple. It is done by uniting our minds with pure consciousness by the practice of *Dhyana* or constant meditation, a flow of meditation, when in the mind there is nothing but God. That is the method, and it develops with practice. It takes practice to grow into that stage where there is a constant flow of thought towards pure consciousness.

Through ignorance many teachers have taught that the mind must be made blank in meditation. They think that, since the mind must be made empty of all objects of consciousness, if they can become unconscious and thus make the mind a blank, they will attain Samadhi, that state of transcendental consciousness. They do not stop to consider that, when we go into deep sleep, we are unconscious and there is no content of consciousness in the mind, and yet we do not attain Samadhi. What is the nature of Samadhi, and what is the difference between it and deep sleep or becoming unconscious? A fool goes to sleep and he comes out still a fool; but, if even a fool should go into Samadhi, he would come out a wise man, an illumined soul. That is the difference.

Likewise, in your meditation, if you try to make the mind a blank, try not to think of anything at all, what happens? A fool you went in, or tried to go in; the same fool you come out—even a worse fool, for you become lazy, what we call *Tamasic*. This laziness is not meditation. Meditation requires a great, strenuous effort to concentrate the mind definitely upon pure consciousness, upon God. It does not matter just what the conception, the ideal of the Godhead, may be. But there must be a positive something to concentrate upon. We have to raise one strong wave of thought to the exclusion of the rest. That is the right practice. Never try to make your mind blank—then you will remain a blank. But think of God, concentrate upon some conception of God, and you will become God!

This is what the Hindu means by meditation, a constant flow of thought toward that one ideal. In other words, you walk with God, you sleep with God, you eat with God, you live with God. Struggle to maintain that constant flow of the mind toward God. When the mind is constantly united with God, when it is established in the constant remembrance of

God, you have achieved that stage of meditation called *Dhruba Smriti*. To reach that stage you must acquire a certain purity of the mind by the control of the outgoing senses. You have to practice bringing the senses back from sense objects, so that your attention may be fastened upon God.

Suppose you had the problem of cleaning a dirty ink bottle that is made fast to the table. You can't take it up and empty the ink out. So what do you do? You pour clean water in and the ink and dirt spill out. And you keep on pouring in the clean water until all the ink and dirt have been washed out and the bottle contains nothing but clear water. So in the same way, it is not possible to empty the mind by throwing out the contents of consciousness and making the mind blank; but what you *can* do is to keep on pouring the clear water of the thought of God into your mind until the dirt spills out. That is the experience of everyone in the beginning. At first you find yourself worse in character than you ever thought you were. Such horrible thoughts and distractions arise when you try to meditate, that you say, "Surely I was not as wicked as that before. Why should such wicked thoughts come into my mind just now when I try to meditate?" That is a universal experience. In the beginning, it seems as if greater passions arise, because, as you pour in the clear water, the dirty ink flows out. Your whole subconscious mind is disturbed. Just as in a lake with a layer of mud at the bottom, if you stir up that mud, the whole lake becomes muddy for some time. We all pass through that stage of muddy water, muddy character. It quite often happens that, when a person starts to lead a spiritual life, his character apparently grows worse instead of better. All the worst things come to the surface. That is inevitable. Let them come up and then get rid of them. With patience and perseverance we have to go on pouring in that clear water of God. Distractions—evil thoughts, wicked desires—will arise in your mind. Struggle! Struggle to bring back the thought of God into the mind again and again. *Dhruba smriti:* practice constant recollection.

When Arjuna learned of this ideal, he said to his teacher, Sri Krishna, "Yes, what you say seems all right, but I consider this control of the mind more difficult than the control of the elements." Then Sri Krishna replies, "Yes, I know it is difficult, but it is not impossible; through practice and struggle it becomes easy." You do not achieve it in a moment, nor in a day; but keep your ideal high, shoot high, aim high. You will fail many times—it doesn't matter—get up again, struggle. That is life! If there is no struggle in life, if life goes on smoothly, either you are an illumined soul, which you are not, or you are an unawakened soul. But you are at neither end of the path. You are midway on the path. And there life is struggle, struggle is life! My Master used to say, "Do or die!" Keep that in mind. Struggle—and you are sure to overcome.

# Thoughts by a Stream

## Allan Hunter

FRESHNESS, ALIVENESS, SELF-GIVINGNESS, ONGOING GLADNESS—
these are some of the qualities you hope never to forget, as
you sit beside Dana stream. If only at this instant you could
see the meaning of this small river, the channel of your own
life might ever after be less choked, more open, less inhibited, more glad. For we are glad when fixations have been
removed, and life itself has its way through us without the
usual timidities. Then why not begin to order all your interests, activities, pleasures and reveries in unreluctant accord with it?

You see right now, at least you see a little, that the secret
of this mountain stream's vitality is the secret we are all
meant to live up to and enjoy. Your life, too, is a water-
course. What feeds it comes from a high glacier out of sight
behind that topmost mountain peak. You did not produce
the thoughts, the drives, the energies, even the motivations
that impel you. They all had their source higher upstream.

Perhaps this beauty is "an expression of the spiritual essence of the world," urging you even at this instant to be
aware and to feel at home. That lupine waving on the opposite green bank—can any trout's spotted skin be lovelier? The
pines, incessantly drawing power from the air and sun and
soil—power turned to starch and sugar that feed the world—
are never thanked. Only God has the glory. Their creative
patience shames you. But you need not take much time out
to be ashamed. These little eddies that seem to go in exactly
the opposite direction to the main movement of the stream—
you could go off your head just worrying about such conflicts,
such denials of the current of life. It's better simply to raise
one's eyes to where the bubbles indicate great vitality, as
wave after wave runs up against a boulder, then around, then

down toward the center of the stream. Even the color on the bottom, the russet, the green, the grey, the iridescent: it is all a reflection of a glory that only the single-minded can grasp.

As for the white ever-changing radiance formed anew each instant of time—what is that but the light of the eternal broken into infinitesimal but infinitely many fragments of beauty? The rock at your feet keeps its special long-drawn-out tempo. The ant crawling across your shoe keeps his own short rhythm. This body, through which you are now trying to respond, marches to quite a different beat. The conscious-ness that you ignorantly say is cooped up within the bonebox called your skull moves to a still different cadence. The main thing is the music to which each in its own way keeps in harmony.

If you could enter into that music, if you could become a part of it, just give yourself to it utterly, then your little hour down on the jostling street would be as cool and satisfy-ing as this living mountain water is to that doe over there, whose nose, dipped into a pool, thrills with a fresh sense of life.

In that perspective, within this frame of reference, you sit here on a rock under the sun, sadly realizing that never again will you see precisely that bubble wandering downstream, past that lupine that beckons to it. Never will there be just this unique combination of movement, consciousness and time. But why be so troubled by this inescapable fact? "Time's arrow never turns back": thank God for that. Kagawa, we are told, rarely talks or thinks about the past. He lives in the future and the moment now. While in prison, Gandhi wrote: "Sing with thy every breath the praise of God." This trout-stream, Dana Creek, will always be telling you: "Live as I do—for you can. Live in this instant now."

# Prayer

## John van Druten

THE FIRST TIME that I can remember going to church was when I was about fifteen. My parents never having been in any way religious, nor having attempted, except for an isolated instance, to teach me anything of religion, it was left for a slightly older woman friend to suggest that I should at least go and see what church was like, and for that purpose to take me to a Sunday morning Church of England service. I was, I remember, uncomfortable and embarrassed over my ignorance of church etiquette, and I remember her telling me: "When you first sit down, you have to kneel and say a little silent prayer." Now the only prayers that I knew were the Lord's Prayer, learned at school, and one that my mother, on the isolated instance that I have mentioned, had taught me. When I was about six and had been guilty of some wrongdoing, probably telling a lie, she had come to my bedside, talked to me gravely on my misbehavior, and then had said: "And now you must say a little prayer, which I am going to teach you." The prayer was as follows: "Please God, make me a good boy. Teach me always to tell the truth and to do what is right. God bless Mother, Father, Brother and everyone. For Jesus Christ's sake. Amen." Having learned it, it soon became a nightly habit, which persisted until after I was grown. That was the prayer that I silently voiced that morning in Church, and whenever I have been to church since, I have wondered whether all the other people, in those first moments on their knees, were not, in all probability, saying something just as childish and habitual.

The phrase "say a little prayer," used both by my mother and by the friend who took me to church, is an odd one, because I doubt whether anyone who truly believed in or understood the function or mechanism of prayer could ever use it, even to a child. To a poet, no poem can be a "little poem"; nor, if he wanted his child to value poetry, could he speak of one to him as such; it is like "a piece of poetry"— a phrase no poet would ever dream of employing. You cannot belittle, even verbally, what is holiest to you. There is poetry, and there is prayer; a little poem is a jingle, and a little prayer is—what? Perhaps only a jingle, also.

Yet there can be merit in jingles, so long as you do not take them for poetry, obscuring your vision of the highest, and the same is true, perhaps, of "little prayers." It was true, I think, of mine, giving it some merit when, in later years, needing something, some leaven, perhaps, in the adolescent dough of cynical materialism, I would find myself repeating it as the only prayer I knew. I tried, even, to mean it, to feel and think it instead of repeating it mechanically; really asking God to make me a good boy, and *wanting* to be a good boy, even though I did not ask myself what God was, or what was meant by His blessing people, and was irked by the jolting of the old, familiar rhythm, caused by the necessity of omitting Father from the last sentence, after he had died. The main virtue, as it seems to me, of my "little prayer," is that it asked for nothing, except goodness, and in that at least approximated to the dictum about true prayer of Meister Eckhart when he said: "When I pray for something, I do not pray; when I pray for nothing, I really pray. To pray for anything except God might be called idolatry or injustice." The habit of praying for *things* was never taught me, although I suppose I must have done it now and then as a seemingly logical deduction from the teaching that God was all-powerful, but I was most probably speedily discouraged by lack of result. In any case, I have little memory of it, although it is still, I imagine, what prayer (a different thing, by the way, from "saying one's prayers") means to most people.

In the Journal of the Goncourts, the following is quoted as a prayer of an old man of their acquaintance: "O Lord, let the water I pass be less cloudy, let the little flies not sting me, let me live long enough to pile up another hundred thousand francs, let the Emperor not be overthrown so that my government securities may rise, and let the rise in Anzin

Coal shares be maintained." His housekeeper had orders to read this aloud to him every night, he repeating it with hands palm to palm. "Grotesque," comments the diarist. "Sinister! Wouldn't anybody say? And at bottom, what is it but prayer, naked and unashamed?"

Yes, it is prayer, as it is normally conceived—petitionary prayer—naked and unashamed. It is even in essence the same kind of prayer that, in moments of agony or extremity, can rise to such urgency that it gets itself answered. We have lately been reading in the magazines, stories of men rescued from rafts in the Pacific, who are "not ashamed to admit" that they prayed for deliverance and, receiving it, have been converted to or confirmed in a belief in God, Whom, they swear, they will never more forget, just as they could never forget a pal who came to their help in a desperate moment. God, from now on, is their Pal, or their Co-Pilot.

It is easy to smile at such declarations, and easy, too, to be saddened by them. There can be value in such experiences as there is value in any experience that teaches man to look above and beyond his previous conception of himself; and there is danger, too, as Aldous Huxley and Gerald Heard have pointed out, in mistaking the source of such intervention, and in confusing either a passionate and intense exercise of human will, or an unconscious employment of latent psychical rather than spiritual powers, with divine intervention. Indeed, all petitionary prayer must involve the same danger, which is perhaps why it has been so heavily discouraged by the mystics. As Aldous Huxley wrote in a previous article in these pages: [1] "The practical teaching of Indian and Christian mystics alike is identical in such matters as . . . renunciation of petitionary prayer in favor of simple abandonment to the will of God." There seems to me, however, a danger of misapprehension lurking in this last phrase, suggesting as it does the passive attitude of "Christian Resignation," when what is needed surely is an active and unceasing longing and struggle to learn what the will of God is, and indeed what God, Himself, is.

Petitionary prayer, dictated by human needs, even if not consciously directed by human will, though it may produce

[1] *Religion and Time*, p. 103.

results, does so *at best* through a simple and unreasoning belief in an uncomprehended power, the same kind of belief
which has occasioned many "faith cures." These faith cures
have frequently been assumed to be similar to, if not identical with, the healings of Christian Science, those healings
which, just as the miracles of Christ have obscured the tenets
of Christianity, have done so much harm to the teachings of
Christian Science, reducing it for so many observers from a
religion to a system of spells and mumbo-jumbo in which
headaches, cancer and poverty are made to disappear by the
repetition of such phrases as "God Is Love."

It is interesting in this connection to read what Mrs. Eddy,
the founder of Christian Science, herself said of such faith
cures, admitting that they were sometimes more speedy than
healings in Christian Science. "Faith," she wrote, "is belief,
and not understanding, and it is easier to believe than to
understand Spiritual Truth. . . . Belief is a virtual blindness
when it admits Truth without understanding it. Blind belief
cannot say with the apostle 'I know whom I have believed.' "
And in another place, "The common custom of praying for
the recovery of the sick finds help in blind belief, whereas
help should come from the enlightened understanding." It
is for this reason that Scientists will seldom agree to help
anyone who does not voluntarily and of himself come for
assistance, and will not give that assistance without some
instruction in the principles of the religion. Healing without
understanding, without knowledge of who and what heals,
and how, is as dangerous as the answered prayers of desperation and extremity, and in exactly the same way. The practice of petitionary prayer at all, in fact, is as foreign to Christian Science as it is to any of the "higher religions" of which
Aldous Huxley speaks in the article referred to. "God," says
Mrs. Eddy, "is not influenced by man." And again: "In order
to pray aright, we must . . . close the lips and silence the
material senses."

Among other definitions, God, in Christian Science, is explained as "Principle," and in the chapter on "Prayer," on
the third page of the text-book, the author asks: "Who would
stand before a blackboard, and pray the principle of math-
ematics to solve the problem? . . . Shall we ask the divine

Principle of all goodness to do His own work?" Prayer, then, it would seem, is learning rather than asking; a means of learning and affirming the divine nature, through the understanding of which our human problems will themselves be solved, arising as they do only from a misunderstanding of our existence as a part of God.

# *From a Notebook*[1]

## ALDOUS HUXLEY

### THE KNIFE EDGE

"DELICATE," "DELICACY"—the words are of constant occurrence in the writings of Christian mystics. So too among the Zen masters. What an insistence on un-violence, on non-emphasis, on the all but invisible knife-edge that must be so lightly trodden if one is to reach the goal! "Try not to seek after the true" (that would be to make the fatal claim that you knew in advance what it was); "only cease to cherish opinions." More subtly, "Do not pursue the outer entanglements, and do not dwell in the inner void; be serene in the oneness of things." Again, "The Sravaka fails to perceive that Mind in itself knows no stages, no causation, no imagination. Disciplining himself in the cause, he has attained the result and abides in the *samadhi* of Emptiness itself for ever so many ages. But however enlightened in this way, the Sravaka is not at all on the right track. From the point of view of the Bodhisattva, this is like suffering the torture of hell. The Sravaka has buried himself in emptiness and does not know how to get out of his quiet contemplation; for he has no insight into the Buddha-nature itself." In other words, for the fully enlightened person, *nirvana* and *samsara* are one. God is perceived as being in creatures and creatures in God. But if, as an average sensual man or woman, you start with this belief and go about "leading a well-rounded life," like a good liberal churchman, you will remain unenlightened and undelivered. To come to the realization that God is in creatures and creatures in God, you must begin by behaving as though they were different, as though *nirvana* were something other

[1] These passages were originally included in the manuscript of "Time Must Have a Stop," but they do not appear in the published version of the novel.

189

than *samsara*. But remember that this *als ob* dualism must be acted upon with an artist's tact—as though you were playing Mozart or painting a water colour. Otherwise, like the earnest but ever-simplifying Sravaka, you'll get stuck in an emptiness that isn't ultimate, an emptiness subtly different from the genuine unmanifested principle of all being. No wonder if, out of the many who are called, so few in any given life are ever chosen.

### POWER

"Power," said Lord Acton, "always corrupts. Absolute power corrupts absolutely. All great men are bad." And he might have added, "All great nations, all great classes, all great religious or professional organizations are bad"—bad in exact proportion as they are powerful.

The first and ever-present problem of social life is power. For power makes devils of those who possess it; power is insatiable; power is aggressive and, by its very nature, intolerant of rival power—therefore intrinsically bellicose, cruel, oppressive.

Politically, power can be kept in check by a system of checks and balances—the parliamentary system, the American constitution.

Economically, it can be limited by the wide distribution of ownership in the means of production, permitting individuals and groups to live in independence of centralized political or industrial authority.

Or else there can be a purely social sanction, in the form of a generally accepted convention that power is undesirable, that ambition is in bad taste, and the social climber a vulgar and dangerous departure from the norm.

But political checks and balances can work only in a stable society, and in times of peace. Widely distributed ownership of the means of production is incompatible with the kind of industrial and financial system we now possess. The social conventions deploring ambition and the will to power are, in actual fact, not found except among certain small "backward" communities. For our part, we admire the manifestations of power—that is, when we are not the victims of power. After the war, of course, the concentration of power will become even greater and its manifestations even more ruthless than in the immediate past. Absolute chaos and destruction cannot be dealt with except by absolute power. And all history is there to show that absolute power corrupts absolutely.

In the last analysis there is no way out, except the way indicated at the close of the Lord's Prayer. "For *thine* is the kingdom and the power and glory." The results of regarding these things as *ours* constitute the evil from which, in the preceding clause, we have begged to be delivered. The principle can be enunciated in eleven words; but to translate it into action requires from everybody unsleeping thoughtfulness and heroic self-abnegation. In other words, any general solution to the problem of power is indefinitely remote.

### LITTLE THINGS

"Little things done in a spirit of fervent love are infinitely more precious than much greater things done with less love."

"Some people measure the worth of good actions only by their natural qualities or their difficulty. The dignity or difficulty of a good action certainly affects what is called its accidental worth, but all essential worth comes only from the love of God."

And note two further points. First, paradoxically enough, difficult works are often easier to accomplish than trifling ones. Most people behave well in the occasional crises of life, badly or indifferently in the inter periods of humdrum routine. But if, at ordinary times, we chose to behave only a quarter as well as we do in times of crisis, most of the crises (being strictly home-made, a product of innumerable small, customary omissions of good and commissions of evil) would never arise.

Second, works of essential worth tend to produce good consequences. Desirable social and personal conditions are the by-products of actions performed, not for the sake of creating such conditions, but for the love of God.

## MEANING

To complain, after listening to fifteen seconds of Rosenkrantz and Guildenstern, that *Hamlet* makes no sense, makes no sense. And yet we do just this in regard to the universe and human life—do just this and call it realism.

Mozart was sometimes aware in one instant of a symphony that it would take an hour to play. How? By ceasing to be the phenomenal Long Body known to the world as "Mozart" and becoming a timeless awareness. This awareness was of a particular musical duration perceived and comprehended as a point. The very similar mystical intuition is, among other things, a knowledge of cosmic duration perceived and comprehended in the same timeless way. And when not I, but the eternal Not-I in me, achieves this punctiform awareness of duration as a whole, man's life and the universe at large are understood as making sense, even though my poor old Long Body sees nothing more of the play than those fifteen seconds of Rosenkrantz and Guildenstern.

# Thoughts

## George Fitts

EVERY GREAT TEACHER, every scripture has impressed upon us again and again the necessity of belief. What is the problem of belief? What must we believe? Whom shall we believe—and why?

We are repeatedly told that "whoso believeth shall never thirst—shall have everlasting life." We read these words in the scriptures, we hear them from spiritual teachers, we repeat them over and over, we try to meditate upon their meaning, yet still there remains for many of us that cloud of doubt, that cloud of incomprehension, that cloud of unbelief.

Is it that we intellectually grasp the significance of the words, but that the feeling of their reality and of their attainability and of their present immediate practicability seem so lifeless to our world-trained senses and our out-going desires and our physical fixated minds and our educated ignorances?

We live and are apparently controlled by the misconception, the inherited belief of many centuries, that the Spiritual world is a world of illusion. The mass mind has accepted the physical, outer, apparent world as the reality, and the spiritual inner real world as the illusion. Hence comes our unbelief. We instinctively refuse the Truth. Our feelings are attached to the illusions of ignorance.

These shackles must be broken. This veil must be removed. This can be done by creating the right feeling toward God, the right feeling toward the inner world, the right feeling toward the promises of the scriptures and the spiritual teachers. In short, the right feeling toward the Self. The Upaniṣhads tell us: "With the thought 'why do I fear' disappears all fear, for fear comes of duality." In the same way it would seem that by questioning "why do I disbelieve," by realizing the intensity of our ignorance, this unbelief is gradually lessened, and finally it disappears.

Through discrimination, we no longer ignore the fundamental Truth, the Supreme Principle of existence, of life, bliss and knowledge, of Self, which lies hidden within the world-heart of each and every one of us, and which is attainable and to be known even in this very life. This attainment may be experienced by all who have a living faith in God, in the spiritual teacher, in the scriptures, and a living faith in the permanently unblemishable purity of one's own soul, concealed though that purity is, temporarily, by the mask of materialism.

It is then only, through the grace of the Lord, the grace of the Guru, and the grace of the individual mind—or Self, that the variety of aspects, the multiples of the One are realized to be but different aspects of the same Substance, the One unchanging principle of Light, of Consciousness, of Bliss.

The Self in one is the Self in all; the Lord in one is the Lord in all; the Substance in one is the Substance in all. We have to seek to find the shadowless light, the flickerless light, the silent light of eternity. And by this light we shall consciously realize that the light, the lighted and the lighter—the seen, the seer and the sight—the hearer, the heard, and the word are One, have always been One, and always will be One. The omnipresent light of Consciousness is the omnipresent presence of God, the source of all.

May we nourish, cultivate, and intensify our belief in the Word, and by so doing may we conquer our racial, inherited and acquired beliefs. May we realize God here and now. May we seek Him whole-heartedly. May He teach us to believe in His holy name, the true Self. May we consciously dwell in Him, even as He dwells in us. May our famished souls be nourished by that Bread of life, which is our very Self.

# Warnings and Hints to the Spiritual Aspirant
## SWAMI YATISWARANANDA

### CONCENTRATION AND MEDITATION

WITHOUT PREVIOUSLY HAVING ATTAINED to a certain amount of sublimation and purification of our feelings and desires, concentration becomes very dangerous. In the case of persons who have not prepared themselves properly for the higher life, it may lead to very bad effects. In a way, we all make the mind concentrated, but then we do not know how to manipulate it. This concentrated mind will run after sensual enjoyment and all kinds of worldly distractions and objects with a greater intensity for having become concentrated. So if we do not know how to handle it in the right way, it becomes a great danger. It is far better not to have concentration if one does not attain sublimation and purification at the same time. Therefore the necessity of purity, of non-injury, truthfulness, continence, etc., in thought, word and deed, has to be stressed very much. Without sublimation of all our desires and feelings we cannot progress in the spiritual path. It is after we have followed a strict code of ethics and morals that we should attempt concentration. The concentrated mind, if it is not purified, becomes a veritable demon and creates untold troubles for the spiritual aspirant.

The concentration of a worldly man on his gross material gain, profit and enjoyment; the concentration of the scientist on his experiments, for instance, on the structure of the atom or the constitution of the plant; the concentration of the Yogi upon his analysis of the ego and the non-ego—all these are but different forms of concentration, judged from the objective standpoint. But considered from the subjective point of view their contents differ very widely, and they lead to altogether different experiences and results.

The Yogic seeker after Truth, having no faith in God as ordinarily understood, may begin with concentration and meditation on gross elements associated with time and space. He may next take up the subtle elements as the objects of his concentration and meditation, at first within time and space, and later beyond their limits. Proceeding further, he may first make the mind, or "inner organ" and afterwards the ego, the objects of this concentration and meditation. Knowing the true nature of these objects he ceases to identify himself with these limiting adjuncts, and having come nearer to his real Self he enjoys a wonderful state of bliss and illumination.

The Vedantic aspirant who believes in the existence of the Divine, may at the beginning meditate on the physical form of some great, holy personality, image or picture or symbolic representation of the Divine, first associated with time and space, and then without these limitations. Advancing further, he may meditate on the "heart" of the holy personality or on the Divine Mind, and gradually imbibe the noble attributes associated with it. Later, he may pass on to Pure Consciousness, individual or cosmic, and thereby succeed in purifying and expanding his impure, limited consciousness, and come in touch with the Infinite Being within his Self, and even proceed to the highest Divine Realization in which the meditator, like a salt-doll coming in contact with the ocean, gets merged into the Absolute Divine Principle. Thus beginning with different forms of concentration and meditation associated with individualised consciousness, he may reach the highest Superconsciousness—the Absolute Reality, the One Undivided Principle—in which all subject-object relationship, nay, all relativity, is completely transcended.

By themselves concentration and meditation may not have any spiritual value. As already said, they may even be dangerous if the person who practices them has not already attained a certain amount of mental purification and does not continue the process of sublimation at the same time. Concentration and meditation become spiritually effective to the extent to which the mind is purified of its dross, of all the dirt and filth and bad impressions and tendencies it has been allowed to accumulate through successive evil thoughts and actions. With the attainment of great dispassion and purity alone can the aspirant take up successfully the higher forms of concentration and meditation, ultimately leading to the highest Divine experience and freedom.

### THE GODWARD TURN

Every average person has the capacity to practice concentration and meditation, although these are usually directed towards persons or objects of gain and enjoyment presented to us by the world. In order to follow the spiritual life, no new faculties need be created all of a sudden. The old capacities and tendencies are to be given a Godward turn without diminishing their intensity, and then the worldly man is transformed into a spiritual man. So the true devotee prays, "Lord, may I think of Thee with that strong love which the ignorant cherish for the things of the world, and may that love never cease to abide in my heart."

The ego asserts itself again and again. So, says Sri Ramakrishna, make it the servant of the Lord. Desires and passions refuse to be controlled. Give a Godward turn to them, maintaining their intensity; so advises the spiritual teacher. Instead of yearning for the company of men and women, yearn for union with the Divine. See Him in all, but take care that you do not cheat yourself. He alone can satisfy the hunger of the soul. He alone can fill its void and give it permanent peace and joy.

Instead of being angry with those standing in the way of your sense-enjoyments, gross or subtle, be angry with all the obstacles lying in the path to the Divine. Learn to be angry with your lower desires, with your turbulent passions, with your very anger, and avoid them all as your great and relentless enemies. Instead of wishing to possess another "human doll" or fleeting worldly wealth, covet the Divine and His inexhaustible wealth which can never be lost and is alone able to give abiding peace. So, says the Bhagavatam: "Lust, anger, fear, affection, fellowship and friendship, when directed towards the Divine Being, lead to union with the Divine."

At the touch of the philosopher's stone all the base metals of desires and passions, of greed and anger, lose their evil nature and are transmuted into pure devotion bringing Bliss and Immortality to the soul. "Even if the very wicked worships Me—the Divine—with devotion to none else, he should be regarded as good, for he has rightly resolved. Soon does he become righteous and obtain eternal peace. Boldly canst thou proclaim that My devotee never comes to grief," says the Bhagavad-Gita.

Time and again, Sri Ramakrishna says, "Give a Godward turn to all your tendencies." Especially in the path of devotion, all desires and passions should be consciously given a higher direction without allowing them to decrease in intensity.

#### THE PROCESS OF SELF-PURIFICATION

Let us take, *e.g.*, the question of anger. Why are we angry? Only because some one or other is standing in the way of what we think to be the object of our enjoyment. This is the only reason for all our anger. Always we find that anger is closely connected with the overstressed ego or a strong sense of personality, and without this strong sense of the ego and an inordinate desire for enjoyment, physical and mental, anger could never even rise in our hearts. So this ego, this desire of enjoyment, is the only cause of our becoming angry. If we do not desire any enjoyment, if we do not expect anything from anybody, but just give and act without ever expecting any return, giving up all expectations, there can never be any rise of anger. So we should get angry with our desires for sense-enjoyment and not with the objects as such. This is the only practical way of uprooting anger and eventually eliminating it. And without eliminating anger and other associated evils to a great extent, we can never make progress in spiritual life. Lust and anger are the two greatest enemies in the spiritual path. So they should be carefully avoided by all aspirants.

Thus, whenever there is anger there is some attachment or other, some inordinate desire or affection, for, truly speaking, without attachment to some person or thing there can never rise any form of anger. It is only our thwarted will to enjoyment that brings anger. But this should be understood more in a subtle sense than in a gross one. It need not necessarily be any craving for the grosser forms of enjoyment that lies as the root-cause of anger.

It may happen that a person is fully convinced of the evil effects of desires, but still is not able to rid himself completely of them. What is such a person to do? How can he rise above them? He can direct them all, directly or indirectly, to the Divine, give every desire, every sensual impulse, every passion a Godward turn, consciously and knowingly, with an effort of the will. If he cannot rid himself of the inordinate desire for music, let him listen to devotional, holy music, and all the time he is so doing, let him think of the Divine. If his artistic sense and his desire to enjoy are very strong, he should take up some holy form of art and make that a stepping stone for rising to the plane of the Divine. If he is very fond of the sweet fragrance and beauty of flowers and wishes to enjoy them, let him pluck the flowers, offer them to the Divine and decorate the holy altar artistically with them. If he desires to love somebody, feels greatly attracted towards somebody, let him love the Divine in that person and be thereby directly drawn towards the Divine. If done consciously and knowingly, all this acts as a great controlling factor, as a great regulating agency, helping us in sublimating our desires and in giving them a higher and higher turn and attaining a greater and greater purity. But even here the ultimate goal to be attained by the aspirant is perfect control and Divine Realization. Everything else serves only as a stepping-stone to that. Following the graduated steps we must be able to rise to the Highest sooner or later.

Unless all the filth and foulness which has gathered in the mind is removed from it, from all nooks and corners, our problem is not really solved. If some light just enters a room through a chink in the door and the rest of the room remains shrouded in darkness and continues to be dirty, nothing is achieved. There is no real spiritual illumination if just a tiny bit of light enters our mind and all the dirt and filth lying there is pushed away for the time being into some far-off corner. In such a case the man remains just what he was before he had this kind of "glimpse." Mere theories and philosophies do not help us in any way, however wonderful they may be. What is essential is the practical application, the sublimation, the removal of all the dirt lying hidden in the dark corners of the mind, not merely attempting to make the mind an absolute blank as some people would have it, which only leads to self-induced sleep in the beginner, but not to any form of real illumination. People talking of the complete stopping of all the mental modifications at the very beginning of their spiritual life do not know what they mean.

Very often there is in us a certain amount of external control, but as distinct from this there should be real internal control. If we are outwardly controlled, but are not able to stop the activity in the sense-organ or in the mind, there is still a struggle ahead for us. If the senses have been controlled, but are still eager to come in touch with the sense-objects, real control has not been achieved, but only its outward form. Even then a step has been taken in the right direction.

One form of control is to draw oneself away completely from the objects of the senses. Another form is to allow the senses to come in touch with things that are pure and not likely to harm the aspirant by rousing fresh desires in him. This is the better and easier method for most people.

"O my mind, worship the Mother and repeat day and night the great Mantram (the mystic word) that you have received from your Guru. When you lie down, think that you are meditating on Her. When you eat, think that you are offering food to Her. With great joy Ramprasad proclaims, 'Mother dwells in all bodies. When you walk in the city think that you are going round the Mother Divine.'"

The idea of this beautiful song is this:—To connect consciously every thought and every single act of our life either directly or indirectly with the Divine, to practice the Presence of God at all times.

### RECOGNITION OF THE ALL-PERVADING DIVINE PRINCIPLE

The Divine is everywhere and in everything, but we should learn to discriminate and act accordingly. We should learn to become more wide-awake and conscious. We should be more reflective and act less on the impulse of the senses and of our instincts, be they good or bad. We are so careless and easy-going in all this, that we follow the opposite course and bring no end of trouble on ourselves.

We should fully recognise this idea of Unity but in the right way. At present we recognise this so half-heartedly. And properly speaking, without acquiring true dispassion and detachment we cannot recognise it whole-heartedly and live up to it. If we were convinced that the One Undivided Principle exists in all, we could not have any strong hatred or any animal love for anybody, separate from the rest, but would only turn our eyes towards the Principle at the back of him. This does not mean that we are to be like fools. No, we still should know that the tiger is a tiger, in spite of its being a manifestation of this One Undivided Principle. So we should not go and shake hands with it. We should know the Principle to be present both in man and woman, but this knowledge should not prevent us from discriminating and being careful so long as we are on this phenomenal plane. We should see the One Principle at the back of the worldly person leading an impure and immoral life, but we should not go and have association with him. This is very, very essential. And if we do not live up to this rule, our feet will slip one day, and we shall seriously come to grief. The aspirant can never be careful enough in this. To the extent that we recognise the One Undivided Principle in all, our hatred, our so-called human love, our attachment, would be diminished and lose all strength and influence. Wherever we find in an aspirant the desire to mix indiscriminately with worldly-minded people and with members of the opposite sex, there is something seriously wrong. His desire for worldly things and enjoyment have not yet lost their tenacity and no purification has been attained. So spiritual progress and realization are altogether out of the question.

Ordinarily our attachment clouds our whole understanding. We must be able to stress the spirit more than the form, more than the personalities and sense-objects, but so long as our craving for sense-enjoyment, our clinging to this little personality of ours, continues to cloud our understanding, we can never really think of this One Undivided Principle, and thus we go on committing the same old mistakes over and over again. So dispassion should be cultivated as much as possible by all aspirants. Without it nothing positive can be achieved.

### THE WAY TO DIVINE REALIZATION—THE HIGHEST GOAL OF LIFE

Christ says, "He who loves father and mother more than Me, is not worthy of Me." And that is perfectly true. Not only that, but also he who allows another to love him more than the Divine is not worthy of God. He who allows another to be more attracted by him than by the Divine is not worthy of God and cannot attain Him. When we make another person love us in such a way by not being sufficiently reserved, we are not worthy of God. So, in this, too, we should be very careful and wide-awake. We feel flattered, no doubt, we like being attractive to others, we like being loved by others as objects of enjoyment. But we are too impulsive and too unreflective to know that from the spiritual standpoint we create troubles both for ourselves and for others and prevent our progress. We should be dignified and well guarded. We should take such an attitude that others do not dare to approach us in a wrong way. In short, we should try to possess greater and greater discrimination.

Dispassion has both its negative and its positive aspect. We should try to disconnect ourselves from others as much as possible and then connect ourselves with the Divine. So that later on all connection with others can be made only through the Divine, but never again in a direct way. Human love connected with the Divine can be gradually transmuted, but if it is not so connected, it degenerates and always ends in disaster and misery, whatever we may think to the contrary. All our relationships, if they be direct relationships, are only carried on through the medium of the body and its physical contacts. There is nothing lasting in them that could ever bring peace and real blessedness to any of us.

It is really very strange that people suffer so much and still are not brought to their senses, but cling to all these false identifications. Very often we forget the goal and take the means to be the goal. The whole world is bound by the desire for wealth and by the desire for sex. But we should learn to develop a new attitude towards both. We make money the highest goal of our life, and then we come to grief. We make love of a man or a woman the ultimate aim of our life, and end our life in misery. We should become introspective and know what is the real goal of life and then try to realize it.

Ordinarily there is in us such an awful identification with our body and our senses and passions that we just brush God aside. Whenever there is skepticism with reference to the Divine, there is some inordinate clinging to the self and to the senses and their objects, because of which God is pushed out. So long as the individual is full of sense-enjoyment, desire for possession, of egoism and vanity, God has no place in his life. The Divine is pushed away by our creature-consciousness. If the mind becomes perfectly free from desires and passions, one realizes the Divine then and there. So if we do not realize God, if we do not even get a glimpse of the Truth, we need not ask why it is so. We should know that in the conscious and in the subconscious mind there are still strong desires, and we should first rid ourselves of these obstructions. So long as we allow them to remain, the question does not even arise.

We should break the sway of our impulses over us. The very moment these impulses rise in us, we should try to expand ourselves, for then these impulses at once disappear just as the waves disappear in the ocean. The man who knows how to expand his consciousness, who knows how to attain a higher form of consciousness, is not affected by such impulses that rise in the mind. One of the most effective means to rise above one's impulses is to come in touch with the Divine Consciousness, with the Infinite Presence which is always in us. And without knowing how to rise above our instincts, without knowing how to control and curb our passions and cultivate true renunciation and dispassion, without having tried to attain the purity of mind and body, there can be no spiritual life for anyone. So we should become more reflective and more discriminating. We are not consistent enough in our thinking and in our actions. There should never be any haziness in the Vedantic aspirant. Vagueness and indefiniteness have no place in true spiritual life. Everything should be clear. We must have definite and right thoughts, definite and right emotions and feelings, definite and right actions, then alone can we proceed to the Divine goal and realize it.

# Renunciation and Austerity

## SWAMI PRABHAVANANDA

QUESTION: Should not a spiritual teacher manifestly demonstrate that he has, for the love of God, given up everything—should he not live with only the barest necessities?

*Answer:* You would then identify the life of renunciation with a life of poverty and discomfort, and you would say that if a spiritual teacher lives in comfort and in a plentiful household he is evidently not living the consecrated life. Your view has no doubt a surface plausibility, but it is too simple. A man of true renunciation concerns himself neither with poverty nor with riches. One person may live in dire poverty, and another may live in luxury, and yet both be steeped in spiritual ignorance and confirmed in worldliness. What *is* renunciation? Renunciation is *the giving up of everything*. The rich must give up his riches, and the poor must give up his poverty. If the poor man hugs his few trivial possessions and clings greedily to his meagre earnings, he is as much attached, and is as much a worldly man, as the rich man with his limousines and his princely income. Only the poor man is the worse off—because of his envy! To be a man of renunciation one must completely give up everything, without thought of keeping for himself even the barest necessities of life. He must possess nothing but God. How can one really achieve such a state? Only by fully realizing that the ideal is to renounce, utterly, *me* and *mine*. Attachment—whether to a rag and a hut or to silk robes and palaces—does not come from a quality in objects, but from a possessive taint in the soul. Everything belongs either to nature or to God. The moment you label anything as *yours,* you begin to suffer from attachment. The ideal monk, therefore, subdues all *craving* for possessions, renounces the ego-sense, and becomes content to live either in the midst of poverty or in the midst of plenty.

"He who is everywhere unattached," says the Gita, "not pleased at receiving good, not vexed at evil—his wisdom is fixed."

The vow of a monk is not a vow of poverty—as the expression would be generally understood in the West: it is a vow to cease craving for things.

"That man who lives devoid of longing"—if we may return to the Gita—"abandoning all craving, without the sense of 'I' and 'mine'—he attains to peace."

Remember: the ideal of renunciation is nothing that can be vulgarly demonstrated. It is the inner life, hidden from the eyes of all; for renunciation is in the mind and not in the object. A spiritual man is never eager to convince people of his spirituality. It is only the fakirs and the hypocrites who try to show their renunciation and their austerity by practicing mortifications of the flesh, and this they do either to gratify some selfish desire or to gain recognition for themselves.

Thus, again, the Gita:

"The austerity which is practiced with the object of gaining notoriety, honor, and worship, and with ostentation, is said to be *rajasika*, unstable and transitory.

"That austerity which is practiced for some foolish purpose, for self-torture or for the purpose of harming another, is declared to be *tamasika*."

A man who seeks the spiritual ideal always seeks to please God and never seeks to please man.

*Question:* What is austerity then? Should we not practice austerity?

*Answer:* In Sanskrit it is called *Tapas,* which literally means that which generates *heat* or energy. In other words, it is the practice of conserving energy and directing it towards a single goal—illumination in one's own soul. It is not by observing an externally austere life, in the Western sense of living in discomfort and poverty, or by torturing the flesh, that one can achieve this goal. Mere outward austerity is a degenerate form of ritualism, and is condemned by illu-

mined souls. As to external observances, both Krishna and
Buddha teach moderation.

Again I quote the Gita:

"Success in Yoga is not for him who eats too much or too
little—nor, O Arjuna, for him who sleeps too much or too
little.

"To him who is temperate in eating and recreation, in his
activity, and in sleep and wakefulness, Yoga becomes the
destroyer of misery."

If by observing certain forms of living, or by undergoing
some physical discomfort, one could gain self-control, religious life would be very easy. Degeneration in organized
monasticism began only after the introduction of that kind
of ritualism. Instances are not wanting of monks who to all
appearance lived an austere life, yet who, having learned no
self-control, even in the loneliness of their cells were guilty
of abominations. The ideal, the spirit, is forgotten: the form
is all.

Thus speaks the Gita:

"Worship of the higher powers, service to the teacher and
to the wise, cleanliness, external and internal, straightfor-
wardness, continence, and care not to injure any being—
these things are known as the austerity of the body.

"Speech which causes no vexation, and is true, and also
agreeable and beneficial, and regular study of the Scriptures
—these are said to constitute the austerity of speech.

"Serenity of mind, kindliness, silence, self-control, honesty
of motive—this is called the austerity of the mind."

In short: passionless peace can be had only by control of
the passions and by devotion, in meditation, to God.

One point in this connection needs to be emphasized: we
should never forget that the ideal of life is neither austerity
nor renunciation, nor even meditation, but to know God, to
be illumined within one's own soul. The means must never
be confused with the end.

*Question:* Should not the life of a spiritual man be confined to communion with God and instruction of seekers, so
that the most casual worldling can have no doubt of his sincerity? Should not his only comfort be unmistakably in one
thing—exclusive communion with God?

*Answer:* Yes, truly, the life of such a man must be a continuous communion with God. He must live, move, and have his being in Him. Without devotion, in meditation, to God, no illumination is possible. With closed eyes must he meditate, and with open eyes also he must commune with God. In work, in leisure, even while asleep, he must learn to live in God.

But, again, his communion with God must be such that not even his friend would know that he is communing with God—to say nothing of a casual worldling.

"And when thou prayest, thou shalt not be as the hypocrites are: for they love to pray standing in the synagogues and in the corners of the streets, that they may be seen of men. Verily I say unto you, they have their reward.

"But thou, when thou prayest, enter into thy closet, and when thou hast shut thy door, pray to thy father which is in secret."

No, a spiritual soul never makes any demonstration either of his renunciation or of his communion with God. He even sometimes raises external barriers to shield himself from the eyes of the curious. He does not desire to attract the attention of the frivolous. In the long, long line of illumined souls and teachers, nowhere do we find any that were recognized as such by worldlings. Buddha was denounced as an atheist; Christ was crucified as an impostor; Ramakrishna was shunned as a madman.

# *On a Sentence from Shakespeare*[1]
## ALDOUS HUXLEY

IF YOU SAY ABSOLUTELY EVERYTHING, it all tends to cancel out into nothing. Which is why no explicit philosophy can be dug out of Shakespeare. But as a metaphysic-by-implication, as a system of beauty-truth, constituted by the poetical relationships of scenes and lines, and inhering, so to speak, in the blank spaces between even such words as "told by an idiot, signifying nothing," the plays are the equivalent of a great theological *Summa*. And of course, if you choose to ignore the negatives which cancel them out, what extraordinary isolated utterances of a perfectly explicit wisdom! I keep thinking, for example, of those two and a half lines in which Hotspur casually summarizes a whole epistemology, a whole ethic, a whole theology.

> *But thought's the slave of life, and life's time's fool,*
> *And time that takes survey of all the world*
> *Must have a stop.*

Three clauses, of which the twentieth century has paid attention only to the first. Thought's enslavement to life is one of our favorite themes. Bergson and the Pragmatists, Adler and Freud, the Dialectical Materialists and the Behaviorists—all tootle their variations upon it. Mind, we are told, is nothing but a food-gathering mechanism; controlled by unconscious forces, either aggressive or sexual; the product of social and economic pressures; a bundle of conditioned reflexes.

All this is quite true so far as it goes; quite false if it goes no further. For obviously, if mind is only some kind of a nothing-but, none of its affirmations can make any claim to a general validity. But all nothing-but philosophies actually

[1] This passage subsequently appeared in "Time Must Have a Stop."

make such claims. Therefore they cannot be true; for if they were true, that would be the proof that they are false. Thought's the slave of life—yes, undoubtedly. But if it weren't also something else, we couldn't make even this partially valid generalization.

The significance of Hotspur's second clause is mainly practical. Life's time's fool. By merely elapsing, time makes nonsense of all that life consciously schemes for in the temporal order. No considerable action has ever had all, or nothing but, the results expected of it. Except under strictly controlled conditions, or in circumstances where we can abstract from reality, ignore individuals and concern ourselves only with vast numbers and the law of averages, any kind of accurate foresight is impossible. In all actual human situations more variables are involved than the human mind can take account of; and with the passage of time the variables tend to increase in number and change their character. All this is a matter of everyday experience. And yet the only faith of a majority of twentieth-century Americans and Europeans is faith in the Future—the bigger and better Future which they *know* that Progress is going to produce for them, like white rabbits out of a hat. For the sake of what their faith tells them about a Future, which their reason assures them to be almost completely unknowable, men are prepared to sacrifice their only tangible possession, the Present. During the last thirty years about fifty millions of Europeans have been liquidated in wars and revolutions. Why? The nationalists and revolutionaries all give the same answer. "In order that the great-great-grandchildren of those who are now being liquidated may have an absolutely wonderful time in A.D. 2043." And (choosing, according to taste or political opinion, from among the Wellsian, Marxian or Fascist blueprints) we solemnly proceed to visualize and describe the sort of wonderful time these lucky beggars are going to have. Just as our Victorian great-great-grandfathers solemnly visualized and described the sort of wonderful time *we* were going to have in the middle years of the twentieth century.

True religion concerns itself with the givenness of the timeless. And idolatrous religion is one which substitutes time for eternity—either past time, in the form of a rigid tradition, or else future time, in the form of Progress towards Utopia. And both are Molochs, both demand human sacrifice. Spanish Catholicism was a typical idolatry of past time. Nationalism, Communism, Fascism, all the twentieth-century pseudo-religions, are typical idolatries of future time.

What have been the consequences of Western man's recent shift of attention from past to future time? An intellectual progress from the Garden of Eden to Utopia and the Classless Society; a moral and political advance from compulsory orthodoxy and the divine right of kings to military and industrial conscription for everybody, the infallibility of the local political boss and the deification of the State. Before or behind, time can never be worshiped with impunity.

But Hotspur's summary has a final clause: time must have a stop. And not only *must*, as a prophecy or an ethical imperative, but also *does* have a stop, in the present indicative tense and as a matter of brute empirical experience, here and now, for all who so desire. It is only by taking the fact of eternity into account that we can deliver thought from its slavery to life. And it is only by deliberately paying our attention and our primary allegiance to eternity that we can prevent time from turning our lives into a pointless or diabolic foolery. Brahman, the Ground, the Clear Light of the Void, the Kingdom of God are all one timeless reality. Seek it first, and all the rest—from an adequate philosophy to a release from the compulsion to stultify and destroy ourselves —will be added. Or, to put the matter in Shakespearean language, if we cease to be "most ignorant" of what we are "most assured, our glassy essence"—the indwelling spirit, the principle of our being, the *Atman*—then we shall be other than that dreadful caricature of humanity who

> *like an angry ape,*
> *Plays such fantastic tricks before high heaven*
> *As make the angels weep.*

# I Am Where I Have Always Been

## JOHN VAN DRUTEN

ONE AFTERNOON, about four years ago, I was asleep on my bed in an hotel in Beverly Hills. My sleep was a deep one, so deep that when I awoke from it, I could not momentarily remember where I was. I had travelled a good deal in the preceding years, living in a number of places, and as I lay with my eyes still closed, I found myself struggling to lay hold of the continuity of life and to remember whether I was in California, New York, London or Mexico. After a moment, the knowledge came to me: "I am in California. This body lying beside me (for so it seemed at that moment) on the bed; this thing called 'me,' that I accept as 'me'; *that* is in California; but I am where I have always been." Then I opened my eyes; the body became me; and I was in California.

But the phrase remained with me, haunting me, asking to be thought of, to have its fullest meaning dug out of it, offering itself as a means of illumination in dark places. What exactly does it mean? If I knew, and knew to the utmost, I should, I suppose, have reached that full enlightenment that dispels illusion, the illusion of materiality and of the phenomenal world. There is little need to say that I do not know, but it may be worth trying to record what has glimmeringly emerged from my reflections upon it.

The phrase suggests at first the same knowledge that comes to us sometimes in a dream—the knowledge that one is dreaming, and that the experiences then being undergone are not real. This knowledge, while it can mitigate a dream, however, seldom serves to dispel it; and the same would seem to be exactly true of the knowledge that the experiences of the material world are illusory. One can know that one is "where one has always been," but the phenomenal world continues to assert itself; the illusion is not broken by the knowledge that it is an illusion. But the world is changed, no matter how little, as anyone who has had a glimpse of any such experience will know. From then on, it is never quite the same; its stuff is never quite so tough and unyielding; its colour is tinged always, no matter how faintly, with the hue of those faint intimations of immortality. That much, at least, is achieved.

"Where I have always been." The immediate question is: "Where?" and the answer, equally immediate, is "With God," meaning thereby, whatever one's training, learning or personal inclination tells one that God may be. "He that dwelleth in the secret place of the Most High shall abide under the shadow of the Almighty," says the psalmist. And also, "Lord, thou hast been our dwelling place in all generations." Which last is the exact equivalent of the phrase with which I awoke that afternoon.

For some years, both before and since that experience, I have been a student of that most widely misconceived religion, Christian Science. I say "misconceived," because the general impression is that it is a method of healing and of getting material benefits; a religion devoted exclusively to making itself a substitute for surgery, aspirin or personal endeavor. Read its testimonies (one is tempted sometimes to call them advertisements), and the impression is confirmed. "I had a headache." "My life was despaired of." "My small son was declared incurable by the doctors." These sound exactly like the testimonials for patent medicines. I, myself, went to Christian Science first, for just such a purpose—to ask for a healing and a miracle. The fact that I did not receive them was my salvation; had I done so, in all probability I should never have gone further, never opened my mind to try and learn what the religion meant or what it was that had healed me. It would have remained a surgery-substitute to me from then on.

It was, I think, Bernard Shaw who said that the miracles were the greatest stumbling-block to Christianity, since what Christ appeared to be saying was something like: "You should love your neighbour as yourself, and to prove what I say, I will now cure this gentleman of cataract." The same is true of Christian Science, or of any unexplained use of a non-material power; the miracles and the teaching seem unconnected. Only as one turns to the teaching, not for results, but for its own sake, does the connecting link appear.

In Science much is heard about "demonstration," a very ill-used word. "I demonstrated supply." "I demonstrated freedom from indigestion." Even, "I demonstrated a car." That is the kind of thing, and it is just as ridiculous and wrong as it sounds to the lay ear. Anyone with an understanding—I will not say merely of what Science stands for, but of what religion stands for—knows that demonstration can never be of material things. As a recent writer has pointed out, the only thing that can be demonstrated is God, and Man's oneness with God. That oneness—that coincidence of Man with God—is the whole basis of Christian Science teaching, as of all religious teaching, obscured though it has become. "The desire to *get* must be replaced by an understanding and acknowledgment of that which one already spiritually is." That is a composite quotation from an article by one of the most modern of Christian Science teachers.

What does that mean? Only, surely, that Man is "where he has always been"—a part of God—and that the understanding, acknowledgment and expression of that fact is what is demanded of Man; is his duty and his purpose. This I had learned imperfectly enough before that afternoon's experience, although after many years in which I had closed my eyes to it. The experience strengthened the knowledge, though there are still long stretches of unwatchfulness when it recedes, eluding one, when the sense of duality (at best) persists, and one seems to be compounded of materiality and spirit, if not fashioned of materiality alone. Only by flashes, or from constant meditation, can the reality be laid hold of— the true sense of being where one has always been, and *what* one has always been—namely, spirit.

It is this last statement, coupled with the fact that I have written in such pages as these of the religion of Christian Science, which makes me wish to add a final paragraph to try to bring that religion a little further into line with the

Hindu teachings. I would like to quote two passages; one from the textbook "Science and Health"—a passage which is the basic statement in the whole book—and the other a passage that I recently came upon in Sankaracharya's "Atma Bodha." "There is no . . . truth in matter," says Mrs. Eddy. "All is Infinite Mind and Its Infinite Manifestation, for God is All-in-All. Matter is the unreal and the temporal; Spirit is the real and the eternal, Spirit is God, and Man is His image and likeness. Therefore Man is not material; he is spiritual." And, from the other: "All that belongs to the body must be considered as the product of ignorance; it is visible; it is perishable as bubbles of air on the surface of water; but that which has not these signs must be recognized as pure spirit, which says of itself 'I am Brahman.' . . . The Yogin . . . knows that all this movable world is spirit, and that beyond spirit there is nothing; as all varieties of vases are clay, so all things he sees are spirit."

It is surely a first announcement of this theme, as the concert programme notes might call it, an announcement needing always to be held fast, reflected on and understood, that comes to one in such instants of awareness as the knowledge that, no matter where one's material body may be, the true self remains "where it has always been."

# Samadhi or Transcendental Consciousness

## SWAMI PRABHAVANANDA

THE INDIAN PHILOSOPHY of religion is based upon the transcendental, supersensuous experience of sages and seers, and Indian sages and philosophers have further insisted that the final goal of life must be the attainment of transcendental consciousness. The different systems of Indian thought, and the various teachings of Indian philosophers, deal with the practical ways and means by which this transcendental realisation is made possible. From the seers of the Vedas and the Upanishads down to Sri Ramakrishna in our modern age, the history of Indian philosophy of religion is thus a record of the discovery and re-discovery of the eternal verities of life as they find their consummation in transcendental consciousness.

It should, however, be pointed out in this connection, that India has never claimed that such experience is limited only to the seers of India, for we find, for example, that Yaksha, the well-known Vedic commentator, stated the fact that attainment of the highest plane of superconsciousness is not always confined to the votaries of Vedic religion alone, but the same kind of experience is also found among those professing non-Vedic religions.

Sri Ramakrishna again emphatically proved the truth that transcendental experience may be had not only by following the Vedic religion but also by following the gospel of Christ or Mahomet.

What this transcendental consciousness is, we hope to make clearer than ever by a study of the life and teachings of Sri Ramakrishna who for twelve years actually practiced the spiritual disciplines as laid down by various religions and through each of them attained the same illumination in transcendental consciousness.

Before we try to explain the nature of transcendental consciousness, let us try to explain what God is, because it is the truth of God that the seers realise when they enter into transcendental consciousness.

Various are the conceptions which men have held of God. Yet not only Indian seers, but great teachers like Christ or Mahomet or Zoroaster claim that God is not a mere conception of the human mind, but that He *is*, and that He can be realised. Why is it then that these teachers and various systems of thought speak of Him differently? The Rig Veda gives the answer: "Truth is one, sages name it variously." Sri Ramakrishna used to say, "God, Allah, Brahman, Self, Mother and so forth are the various names given to the same reality, as the one and the same substance 'water' can be called by various names, such as water, pani, jala, etc." And so great religious teachers differ in form though not in actuality, chiefly because they try to express in human terms their experience of the highest consciousness.

Sri Ramakrishna throws great light on the subject, as he harmonizes the various conceptions of God in the following words:

"What God is, none can define in words. Everything else has been defiled, as it were, like the leavings of food. The Vedas, the Tantras, the Puranas, the systems of philosophy— all are defiled; they have been studied by men, and they have been uttered by human tongue. In a sense, therefore, they are no longer pure. But there is one truth, one substance, that has never been defiled, and that is the truth of God. None has ever succeeded in describing that in words.

"When one attains samadhi (transcendental consciousness), then only comes to him the knowledge of Brahman. Then only does he attain the vision of God. In that ecstatic realisation all thoughts cease. Perfectly silent he becomes. No power of speech is left by which to express Brahman. He comes back from his ecstatic consciousness, and thereafter, it may be, talks; but he talks only that he may teach humanity. The bee buzzes until it lights in the heart of the flower. It becomes quiet as soon as it begins to sip the honey. Then again, after it has its fill, when it is at last drunk with honey, it makes a sweet, murmuring sound.

"Brahman, whom the Vedas proclaim the Impersonal, is also the Divine Mother, the source of all power, the repository of all blessed qualities. The true knower of Brahman knows that He who is impersonal, without attribute, beyond the gunas, is again the personal God, the God of love, the repository of all blessed qualities.

"He who lives continuously in the consciousness of God, and in this alone, knows Him in His true being. He knows His infinite expression, His various aspects. He knows Him as Impersonal no less than as Personal.

"Brahman, absolute existence, knowledge, and bliss, may be compared to an infinite ocean, without beginning or end. As through intense cold some portions of the water of the ocean freeze into ice, and the formless water appears as having form, so through the intense love of the devotee the Formless, Absolute, Infinite Existence manifests Himself before him as having form and personality. But the form melts away again with the rise of the sun of knowledge. Then, also, is the universe no more. Then is there but one infinite Existence."

In short, Sri Ramakrishna declared, "There can be no finality to the infinite." And he taught men how to realise God in one's own soul. To quote his words again: "Only when his heart becomes purified through the practice of spiritual disciplines does a man attain to wisdom. He then becomes convinced of the existence of God through realising Him in his own soul. There is, however, something greater than this attainment. To become convinced that fire lies hidden in the wood is one thing but greater is it to light the fire, cook food, and satisfy one's hunger.

"He indeed has attained the supreme illumination who not only realises the presence of God, but who knows Him as both Personal and Impersonal, who loves Him intensely, talks to Him, partakes of His bliss. Such an illumined soul realises the bliss of God while he is absorbed in meditation, attaining oneness with the indivisible, impersonal Being; and he realises the same bliss as he comes to normal consciousness and sees this universe as a manifestation of that Being and a divine play."

So not only do the seers of the Vedas but also modern prophets claim that God as the ultimate reality can be experienced in one's own soul. This experience, let me repeat, is not the experience of the senses, nor of the emotions, nor of the mind. This experience of God is the experience in samadhi or transcendental consciousness, which can be attained only by diligent, earnest, and strenuous practice of spiritual disciplines.

What is samadhi? Is it like the visions which an aspirant may occasionally experience? As one practices spiritual disciplines, sometimes wonderful visions of an ethereal light, or of spiritual forms of gods and goddesses or of Christ or Krishna or any saint or seer of the past, or of one's own Guru may appear. One may hear or see many truths which are not normally experienced. These are mystic visions and should not be confused with the attainment of samadhi. These are real experiences no doubt; that is, they are not to be discarded as dreams or hallucinations. But the great seers who have attained the highest spiritual illumination point out to us that too much importance must not be placed on these visions. They are indications of spiritual progress, or as Swami Vivekananda said, they are "mile-stones on the way to progress"; but they are not the experiences one attains in samadhi. We must also note that such visions may not come to every spiritual aspirant, yet an aspirant may be progressing toward spiritual illumination. Once a disciple of Sri Ramakrishna appealed to the master with the request that he might have mystic visions such as many other disciples were having. To him Sri Ramakrishna replied: "Why are you anxious to get visions? Do you think that visions make up the whole substance of spiritual illumination? Try to cultivate devotion to God and learn perfect control of self. These are much greater than visions."

These mystic visions have value in spiritual life inasmuch as with their appearance, greater self-control and purity of heart are achieved; therefrom arises greater faith in spiritual attainment and the aspirant finds encouragement to proceed with his spiritual practices.

Samadhi, however, is a much higher stage, beyond the mystic visions, and that this is so is known by its effects upon the life of the aspirant. When one attains samadhi, his whole life becomes completely transformed. As Sri Ramakrishna says, a man then touches God, who is like the philosopher's stone, and is turned into gold. All doubts and ignorance then forever vanish away. In the words of the Mundaka Upanishad: "All the knots of the heart are unloosened, all doubts cease to exist—when one attains illumination." Swami Vivekananda has humorously declared that even if a fool by any chance were to enter into samadhi, he would come back a wise man. Can one then relate what he experiences in samadhi?

Let me quote in this connection what Father Poulain in interpreting Christian mystic experiences writes: "Noble scenes, profound ideas are offered to their spirits. But they are unable to explain what they have seen. This results not from any lethargy of their intelligence, but because they have been elevated to the vision of truths that the human spirit cannot attain to, and for which they have no terms. Will you ask a mathematician to express the profundities of the infinitesimal calculus with the vocabulary of a child?" [1] Professor James B. Pratt thinks "it is usually lack of memory rather than lack of terms that makes it impossible for the mystic to communicate to others the truths revealed to him in his ravishment." [2]

Though I am quite sure some of the great Christian mystics had attained the height of realisation we call samadhi, yet the above description of Father Poulain of the experience of "noble scenes, profound ideas" is not the description of the experience of samadhi. In this connection let me also quote two other descriptions of ecstasy as cited by Professor Pratt. One relates the experience of Herman Joseph: "Suddenly God enlarged the field of his insight; He showed him the firmament and the stars and made him understand their quality and quantity, or to speak more clearly, their beauty and immensity." Another quotation is from St. Francis

[1] Quoted by Professor James B. Pratt in his valuable book, "Religious Consciousness."
[2] "Religious Consciousness." p. 409.

Xavier: "This state of intuition lasted about twenty-four hours; then, as if the veil had fallen again, I found myself as ignorant as before." These are certainly not the experiences in samadhi; I would simply interpret them as mystic visions. In samadhi the experience is not of many ideas or many truths, but rather the *one* truth of God. In the lower form of samadhi, the idea of ego, separate from God, is there, but only in relation to and in connection with God. The universe of many is then obliterated. And after one returns from samadhi, he does not find himself as ignorant as before, but he finds that "he lives, moves, and has his being in God." To quote Sri Ramakrishna: "When one has attained the supreme illumination, he lives always in God. With eyes closed, transcending the senses, absorbed in samadhi, he sees Him; and he sees Him with eyes open. For he sees Him as becoming all. Sri Chaitanya lived in three states of consciousness: the inner consciousness, wherein he would remain absorbed in samadhi, attaining his oneness with the Supreme Being; the middle consciousness, between the inner and the outer, wherein he would see the universe as the playground of Krishna, and Krishna playing in many forms and ways; and the outer consciousness, wherein he would sing the praises of God."

I would say that Father Poulain's explanation of the reason why these mystic visions cannot be communicated—that ordinary language lacks sufficient terms for a true account—and Professor Pratt's conclusion that want of memory of the visions was the cause are probably both correct, as some visions may have fled from the memory as soon as the subject returned to normal consciousness, and again he may have been quite unable to tell what he had seen. Many mystic visions are, however, remembered, and many visions may be communicated to others. With regard to the experience of samadhi, however, may I emphatically assert that I have heard it directly from certain great souls who to my knowledge have attained samadhi, that there is no lack of memory of one's experience in that state after one has returned to normal consciousness. Some part at least of that experience is moreover carried back into the normal state.

Can the experience of samadhi be communicated to

others? Yes, and no. The reason why it cannot be expressed by word of mouth is not far to seek. To express is to define and limit. In samadhi is experienced the indefinable and unlimited Existence, knowledge, and bliss. Let me quote in this connection what the great neo-Platonist Plotinus says: [3] "How, then, are we to speak of the One? How can we speak of it at all, when we do not grasp it as itself? . . . The answer is that though the One escapes our knowledge, it does not entirely escape *us*. We have possession of it in such a way that we speak of it, but not in such a way that we can express it. . . . We are like men inspired and possessed who know only that they have in themselves something greater than themselves— something they know not what—and who therefore have some perception of that which has moved them, and are driven to speak of it because they are not (wholly) one with that which moves them. So it is with our relation to the Absolute One. When we use pure intelligence we recognise that it is the mind within the mind, the source of being and of all things that are of the same order with itself; but we see at the same time that the One is not identified with any of them but is greater than all we call being, greater and better than reason and intelligence and sense, though it is that which gives them whatsoever reality they have."

Perhaps in similar words will a Hindu mystic, who has the savikalpa samadhi (lower samadhi), describe his experience.

Though, however, the experience in samadhi cannot be related by tongue, it can be communicated in silence to others more directly and perhaps more tangibly. In Krishna, Buddha, Christ, and Ramakrishna this power to transmit the spiritual experience, even to give samadhi to others, was most manifest, and this power has been proved and testified to, as we shall see later, most effectively by Ramakrishna in our modern era. In lesser souls, also, this power to communicate in silence has often been witnessed. This is the reason why scriptures advise living in the society of the holy.

Samadhi is chiefly of two kinds: savikalpa, lower samadhi, and nirvikalpa, the higher kind. In the lower form of samadhi, there exists the sense of "I" as distinct though not

[3] As quoted by Professor Pratt in "Religious Consciousness."

separate from God, wherein is realised the personal aspect of God. God the Creator, God the Father, God the Mother, God the Friend, God the Beloved—any or all of these aspects of God may then be realised in their completeness.

Nirvikalpa is the higher form of samadhi, wherein no sense of the separate ego is left, and there is realised the one-ness of the self with God, the Impersonal. In that experience, there is neither *I* nor *you*, neither *one* nor *many*. Patanjali defines it as the cessation of all waves of the mind, that is, the complete stoppage of all thoughts and impressions of the mind, conscious and subconscious. Patanjali advises that the means to the attainment of this samadhi is the practice of concentration through which may come cessation of all the waves of the mind. The Christian mystic Meister Eckhart mentions the same method of attainment in "Mystische Schriften." "Memory, understanding, will all tend toward diversity and multiplicity of thought, therefore you must leave them all aside, as well as perception, ideation, and everything in which you find yourself or seek yourself. Only then can you experience this new birth—otherwise never." [4]

Sri Ramakrishna points out that in the attainment of nirvikalpa samadhi all sense of ego is completely wiped out and though this sense of ego is repossessed by the individual as he returns from samadhi, his ego is no longer the same "unripe" ego as before; it has "turned into gold by the touch of the philosopher's stone." It remains as the "servant of the Lord, as the child of God."

Nirvikalpa samadhi, however, is not to be confused with unconscious trance. Sri Ramakrishna tells a story to illustrate the difference between nirvikalpa and unconscious trance. "A story," he says, "is told of a magician who was once showing tricks before a king, and was repeating, 'King, give me money, give me food and dress.' Suddenly his tongue turned upward and was joined to the throat inside. As a re-sult he attained the state of Kumbhak (suspension of breath). He was silent, and there was apparently no sign of life. So he was buried. After a time when somebody dug into the burial place, the magician was found seated in yoga posture. There-upon he was brought up out of the grave, and people flocked

<hr>
[4] Quoted by Professor Pratt in "Religious Consciousness."

to the place where he was, thinking that he was a holy man. Then he regained his consciousness and once more began to repeat, 'King, give me money, give me food, give me dress.' "

The crucial test of nirvikalpa or of savikalpa samadhi is that when a man returns from samadhi, he is not the same ignorant man as before his experience, for his whole life has become transformed with the attainment of illumination, and he now lives always in God and experiences the joy and freedom of a man in whom the divine side of his nature is expressed. After unconscious trance, on the contrary, or after deep sleep wherein the ego seems to have vanished, when a man returns to normal consciousness, his ego returns and he is the same ignorant individual. In contrast to unconscious trance and sleep, nirvikalpa samadhi is full of light. It is consciousness *itself*, without the contents of consciousness, such as of me or thee or of outer objects.

That this contentless consciousness is not the same as the unconsciousness which occurs in sleep is brought out very clearly in the Upanishads.

The Mandukya Upanishad, for instance, speaks of the three states of consciousness—waking, dreaming, and dreamless sleep—and in contrast to these is the Turiya—the fourth, the transcendental consciousness. The Chandogya Upanishad, by the famous story of how Indra and Virochana went to learn of the knowledge of Brahman from the teacher Prajapati, reveals how the unconsciousness of deep sleep serves no purpose in the knowledge of the Self, but that if we would attain our goal we must rise above and beyond the three states into the Turiya, the fourth.

# Chant the Name of the Lord[1]
## SRI CHAITANYA

CHANT THE NAME of the Lord and His Glory unceasingly
That the mirror of the heart may be wiped clean
And quenched that mighty forest fire,
Worldly lust, raging furiously within.
Oh Name, stream down in moonlight on the lotus-heart,
Opening its cup to knowledge of Thyself.
Oh self, drown deep in the waves of His bliss,
Chanting His Name continually,
Tasting His nectar at every step,
Bathing in His Name, that bath for weary souls.

Various are Thy Names, Oh Lord,
In each and every Name Thy power resides.
No times are set, no rites are needful, for chanting of Thy
    Name,
So vast is Thy mercy.
How huge, then, is my wretchedness
Who find, in this empty life and heart,
No devotion to Thy Name!

Oh, my mind,
Be humbler than a blade of grass,
Be patient and forbearing like the tree,
Take no honor to thyself,
Give honor to all,
Chant unceasingly the Name of the Lord.

---

[1] Translated from the original Sanskrit by Swami Prabhavananda and
Christopher Isherwood. Sri Chaitanya (1485–1533) is one of India's greatest
saints. He is famed for his ecstatic devotion to Krishna.

Oh Lord and Soul of the Universe,
Mine is no prayer for wealth or retinue,
The playthings of lust or the toys of fame;
As many times as I may be reborn
Grant me, Oh Lord, a steadfast love for Thee.

A drowning man in this world's fearful ocean
Is Thy servant, Oh Sweet One.
In Thy mercy
Consider him as dust beneath Thy feet.

Ah, how I long for the day
When, in chanting Thy Name, the tears will spill down
From my eyes, and my throat will refuse to utter
Its prayers, choking and stammering with ecstasy,
When all the hairs of my body will stand erect with joy!

Ah, how I long for the day
When an instant's separation from Thee, Oh Govinda,
Will be as a thousand years,
When my heart burns away with its desire
And the world, without Thee, is a heartless void.

Prostrate at Thy feet let me be, in unwavering devotion,
Neither imploring the embrace of Thine arms
Nor bewailing the withdrawal of Thy Presence
Though it tears my soul asunder.
Oh Thou, who stealest the hearts of Thy devotees,
Do with me what Thou wilt—
For Thou art my heart's Beloved, Thou and Thou alone.

# *An Unpublished Lecture*
## Swami Vivekananda

(This hitherto unpublished lecture was delivered by Swami Vivekananda to the Shakespeare Club of Pasadena, California, on January 27, 1900. It was recorded in a notebook which has recently been given to the Editors by Mrs. Ida Herman, a personal friend of the Swami. Although this transcription was unedited, it has been thought best to make as few cuts and alterations as possible—in order to preserve the charm and force of Vivekananda's characteristic idiom.)

Now, LADIES AND GENTLEMEN, the subject for this morning was to have been the Vedanta Philosophy. That subject itself is interesting, but rather dry and very vast.

Meanwhile, I have been asked by your president and some of the ladies and gentlemen here to tell them something about my work and what I have been doing. It may be interesting to some here, but not so much so to me. In fact, I don't quite know how to tell it to you, for this will have been the first time in my life that I have spoken on that subject.

Now, to understand what I have been trying to do, in my small way, I will take you, in imagination, to India. We have not time to go into all the details and all the ramifications of the subject; nor is it possible for you to understand all the complexities in a foreign race, in this short time. Suffice it to say, I will at least try to give you a little picture of what India is like.

It is like a gigantic building all tumbled down, in ruins. At first sight, then, there is little hope. It is a nation gone and ruined. But you wait and study, then you see something beyond that. The truth is that so long as the principle, the ideal, of which the outer man is the expression, is not hurt or destroyed, the man lives, and there is hope for that man. If your coat is stolen twenty times, that is no reason why you should be destroyed. You can get a new coat. The coat is unessential. The fact that a rich man is robbed does not hurt the vitality of the man, does not mean death. The man will survive.

Standing on this principle, we look in and we see—what? India is no longer a political power; it is an enslaved race. Indians have no say, no voice in their own government; they are three hundred millions of slaves—nothing more! The average income of a man in India is two shillings a month. The common state of the vast mass of the people is starvation, so that, with the least decrease in income, millions die. A little famine means death. So there, too, when I look on that side of India, I see ruin—hopeless ruin.

But we find that the Indian race never stood for wealth. Although they acquired immense wealth, perhaps more than any other nation ever acquired, yet the nation did not stand for wealth. It was a powerful race for ages, yet we find that that nation never stood for power, never went out of the country to conquer. Quite content within their own boundaries, they never fought anybody. The Indian nation never stood for imperial glory. Wealth and power, then, were not the ideals of the race.

What then? Whether they were wrong or right—that is not the question we discuss—that nation, among all the children of men, has believed, and believed intensely, that this life is not real. The real is God; and they must cling unto that God, through thick and thin. In the midst of their degradation, religion came first. The Hindu man drinks religiously, sleeps religiously, walks religiously, marries religiously, robs religiously.

Did you ever see such a country? If you want to get up a gang of robbers, the leader will have to preach some sort of religion, then formulate some bogus metaphysics, and say that this method is the clearest and quickest way to get to God. Then he finds a following. Otherwise, not. That shows that the vitality of the race, the mission of the race is religion; and because that has not been touched, therefore that race lives.

See Rome. Rome's mission was imperial power, expansion. And as soon as that was touched, Rome fell to pieces, passed out. The mission of Greece was intellect; as soon as that was touched, why, Greece passed out. So in modern times, Spain, and all these modern countries. Each nation has a mission for the world. So long as that mission is not hurt, that nation lives, despite every difficulty. But as soon as its mission is destroyed, the nation collapses.

Now, that vitality of India has not been touched yet. They have not given up that, and it is still strong—in spite of all their superstitions. Hideous superstitions are there, most revolting, some of them—never mind. The national life-current is still there—the mission of the race.

The Indian nation never will be a powerful, conquering people—never. They will never be a great political power; that is not their business, that is not the note India has to play in the great harmony of nations. But what has she to play? God, and God alone. She clings unto that like grim death. Still there is hope there.

So then, after your analysis, you come to the conclusion that all these things, all this poverty and misery, are of no consequence—the man is living still, and therefore there is hope.

Well! You see religious activities going on all through the country. I don't recall a year that has not given birth to several new sects in India. The stronger the current, the more the whirlpools and eddies. Sects are not signs of decay, they are a sign of life. Let sects multiply, till the time comes when every one of us is a sect, each individual. We need not quarrel about that.

Now, take your country. (I don't mean any criticism.) Here the social laws, the political formation, everything, is made to facilitate man's journey in this life. He may live very happily so long as he is on this earth. Look at your streets—how clean! Your beautiful cities! And in how many ways a man can make money! How many channels to get enjoyment in this life! But, if a man here should say, "Now look here, I shall sit down under this tree and meditate; I don't want to work," why, he would have to go to jail. See? There would be no chance for him at all. None. A man can live in this society only if he falls in line. He has to join in this rush for the enjoyment of good in this life, or he dies.

Now let us go back to India. There, if a man says, "I shall

go and sit on the top of that mountain and look at the tip of my nose all the rest of my days," everybody says, "Go, and God speed to you!" He need not speak a word. Somebody brings him a little food; somebody else brings him a little cloth, and he is all right. But if a man says, "Behold, I am going to enjoy a little of this life," every door is closed to him.

I say that the ideas of both countries are unjust. I see no reason why a man here should not sit down and look at the tip of his nose if he likes. Why should everybody here do just what the majority here does? I see no reason.

Nor why, in India, a man should not have the goods of this life and make money. But you see how those vast millions are forced to accept the opposite point of view by tyranny. This is the tyranny of the sages. This is the tyranny of the great, tyranny of the spiritual, tyranny of the intellectual, tyranny of the wise. And the tyranny of the wise, mind you, is much more powerful than the tyranny of the ignorant. The wise, the intellectual, when they take to forcing their opinions upon others, know a hundred thousand ways to make bonds and barriers which it is not in the power of the ignorant to break.

Now, I say that this thing has got to stop. There is no use in sacrificing millions and millions of people to produce one spiritual giant. If it is possible to make a society where the spiritual giant will be produced and all the rest of the people will be happy, as well, that is good; but if the millions have to be ground down, that is unjust. Better that the one great man should suffer for the salvation of the world.

In every nation you will have to work through their methods. To every man you will have to speak in his own language. Now, in England or in America, if you want to preach religion to them, you will have to work through political methods—make organizations, societies, with voting, balloting, a president, and so on, because that is the language, the method of the Western race. On the other hand, if you want to speak of politics in India, you must speak through the language of religion. You will have to tell them something like this: "The man who cleans his house every morning will acquire such and such an amount of merit, he will go to heaven, or he comes to God." Unless you put it that way, they won't listen to you. It is a question of language. The thing done is the same. But with every race, you will have to speak their language, in order to reach their hearts. And that is quite just. We need not fret about that.

In the Order to which I belong we are called Sannyasins. The word means, "a man who has renounced." This is a very, very, very ancient Order. Even Buddha, who was 560 years before Christ, belonged to that Order. He was one of the reformers of his Order. That was all. So ancient! You find it mentioned away back in the Vedas, the oldest book in the world. In old India there was the regulation that every man and woman, towards the end of their lives, must get out of social life altogether and think of nothing except God and their own salvation. This was to get ready for the great event—death. So old people used to become Sannyasins in those early days. Later on, young people began to give up the world. And young people are active. They could not sit down under a tree and think all the time of their own death, so they went about preaching and starting sects, and so on. Thus, Buddha, being young, started that great reform. Had he been an old man, he would have looked at the tip of his nose and died quietly.

The Order is not a church and the people who join the Order are not priests. There is an absolute difference between the priests and the Sannyasins. In India, priesthood, like every other business in social life, is a hereditary profession. A priest's son will become a priest, just as a carpenter's son will be a carpenter, or a blacksmith's son a blacksmith. The priest must always be married. The Hindu does not think a man is complete unless he has a wife. An unmarried man has no right to perform religious ceremonies.

The Sannyasins don't possess property, and they do not marry. Beyond that there is no organization. The only bond that is there is the bond between the teacher and the taught —and that is peculiar to India. The teacher is not a man who comes just to teach me and I pay him so much and there it ends. In India it is really like an adoption. The teacher is more than my own father, and I am truly his child, his son in every respect. I owe him obedience and reverence, first, before my own father, even; because, they say, the father gave me this body, but *he* showed me the way to salvation, he is greater than father. And we carry this love, this respect for our teacher all our lives. And that is the only organization that exists. I adopt my disciples. Sometimes the teacher will be a young man and the disciple a very old man. But never mind, he is the son and he calls me "Father" and I have to address him as my son, my daughter, and so on.

Now, I happened to get an old man to teach me, and he was very peculiar. He did not go much for intellectual scholarship, scarcely studied books; but when he was a boy he was seized with the tremendous idea of getting truth direct. First he tried by studying his own religion. Then he got the idea that he must get the truth of other religions; and with that idea he joined all the sects, one after the other. For the time being, he did exactly what they told him to do—lived with the devotees of these different sects in turn, until interpenetrated with the particular ideal of that sect. After a few years he would go to another sect. When he had gone through with all that, he came to the conclusion that they were all good. He had no criticism to offer to any one; they are all so many paths leading to the same goal. And then he said: "That is a glorious thing, that there should be so many paths, because if there were only one path, perhaps it would suit only an individual man. The more the number of paths, the more the chance for every one of us to know the truth. If I cannot be taught in one language, I will try another, and so on." Thus his benediction was for every religion.

Now, all the ideas that I preach are only an attempt to echo his ideas. Nothing is mine originally, except the wicked ones, everything I say which is false and wicked. But every word that I have ever uttered which is true and good, is simply an attempt to echo his voice. Read his life by Prof. Max Muller.

Well, there at his feet I conceived these ideas. There, with some other young men. I was just a boy. I went there when I was about sixteen. Some of the other boys were still younger, some a little older—about a dozen or more. And together we conceived that this ideal had to be spread. And not only spread, but made practical. That is to say, we must show the spirituality of the Hindus, the mercifulness of the Buddhists, the activity of the Christians, the brotherhood of the Mohammedans, by our practical lives. "We shall start a universal religion now and here," we said. "We will not wait."

Our teacher was an old man who would never touch a coin with his hands. He took just the little food offered, just so many yards of cotton cloth, no more. He could never be induced to take any other gift. With all these marvelous ideas, he was strict, because that made him free. The monk in India is the friend of the prince today, dines with him; and tomorrow he is with the beggar, sleeps under a tree. He must come into contact with everyone, must always move about. As the saying is, "The rolling stone gathers no moss." The last fourteen years of my life, I have never been for three months at a time in any one place—continually rolling. So do we all.

Now, this handful of boys got hold of these ideas, and all the practical results that sprang out of these ideas. Universal religion, great sympathy for the poor, and all that. are very good in theory, but one must practice.

Then came the sad day when our old teacher died. We nursed him the best we could. We had no friends. Who would listen to a few boys, with their crank notions? Nobody. At least, in India, boys are nobodies. Just think of it—a dozen boys, telling people vast, big ideas, saying they are determined to work these ideas out in life. Why, everybody laughed. From laughter, it became serious; it became persecution. Why, the parents of the boys came to feel like spanking every one of us. And the more we were derided, the more determined we became.

Then came a terrible time—for me personally and for all the other boys as well. But to me came such misfortune! On the one side was my mother, my brothers. My father died at that time, and we were left poor. Oh, very poor, almost starving all the time. I was the only hope of the family, the only one who could do anything to help them. I had to stand between my two worlds. On the one hand, I would have to see my mother and brothers starve unto death; on the other, I had believed that this man's ideas were for the good of

India and the world, and had to be preached and worked out. And so the fight went on in my mind for days and months. Sometimes I would pray for five or six days and nights together, without stopping. Oh, the agony of those days! I was living in hell! The natural affections of my boy's heart drawing me to my family—I could not bear to see those who were the nearest and dearest to me suffering. On the other hand, nobody to sympathize with me. Who would sympathize with the imaginations of a boy? Imaginations that caused so much suffering to others! Who would sympathize with me? None—except one.

That one's sympathy brought blessing and hope. She was a woman. Our teacher, this great monk, was married when he was a boy, a mere child. When he became a young man, and all this religious zeal was upon him, he came to see his wife. Although they had been married as children, they had not seen very much of each other until they were grown up. Then he came to his wife and said: "Behold, I am your husband; you have a right to this body. But I cannot live the sex life, although I have married you. I leave it to your judgment." And she wept and said: "God speed you! The Lord bless you! Am I the woman to degrade you? If I can, I will help you. Go on in your work."

That was the woman. The husband went on and became a monk, in his own way; and from a distance the wife went on helping as much as she could. And later, when the man had become a great spiritual giant, she came—really, she was the first disciple—and she spent the rest of her life taking care of the body of this man. He never knew whether he was living or dying, or anything. Sometimes, when talking, he would get so excited that if he sat on live charcoals he did not know it. Live charcoals! Forgetting all about his body, all the time.

Well, that lady, his wife, was the only one who sympathized with the idea of those boys. But she was powerless. She was poorer than we were. Never mind! We plunged into the breach. I believed, as I was living, that these ideas were going to rationalize India and bring better days to many lands and foreign races. With that belief, came the realization that it is better that a few persons suffer than that such ideas should die out of the world. What if a mother or two brothers die? It is a sacrifice. Let it be done. No great thing can be done without sacrifice. The heart must be plucked out and the bleeding heart placed upon the altar. Then great things are done. Is there any other way? None have found it. I appeal to each one of you, to those who have accomplished any great thing. Oh, how much it has cost! What agony! What torture! What terrible suffering is behind every deed of success, in every life. You know that, all of you.

And thus we went on, that band of boys. The only thing we got from those around us was a kick and a curse—that was all. Of course, we had to beg from door to door for our food—got hips and haws—the refuse of everything. A piece of bread here and there. We got hold of a broken-down old house, with hissing cobras living underneath; and, because that was the cheapest, we went into that house and lived there.

Thus we went on for some years, in the meanwhile making excursions all over India, trying to bring about the idea gradually. Ten years were spent without a ray of light! Ten more years! A thousand times despondency came; but there was one thing always to keep us hopeful—the tremendous faithfulness to each other, the tremendous love between us. I have got a hundred men and women around me: if I become the devil himself tomorrow, they will say: "Here we are still! We'll never give you up!" That is a great blessing. In happiness, in misery, in famine, in pain, in the grave, in heaven or in hell, he who never gives me up is my friend. Is such friendship a joke? A man may have salvation through such friendship. That brings salvation, if we can love like that. If we have that faithfulness, why, there is the essence of all concentration. You need not worship any gods in the world if you have that faith, that strength, that love. And that was there with us all throughout that hard time. That was there. That made us go from the Himalayas to Cape Comorin, from the Indus to Brahmapootra.

This band of boys began to travel about. Gradually we began to draw attention: ninety per cent was antagonism, very little of it was helpful. For we had one fault: we were boys—in poverty and with all the roughness of boys. He who has to make his own way in life is a bit rough, he has not much time to be smooth and suave and polite—"my lady and my gentleman," and all that. You have seen that in life, always. He is a rough diamond, he has not much polish, he is a jewel in an indifferent casket.

And there we were. "No compromise!" was the watchword. "This is the ideal and this has got to be carried out. If we meet the king, though we die, we must give him a bit of our minds; if the peasant, the same." Naturally, we met with antagonism.

But, mind you, this is life's experience: if you really want the good of others, the whole universe may stand against you and cannot hurt you. It must crumble before your power. You have all the power of the Lord Himself in you, if you are sincere and really unselfish. And those boys were that. They came as children, pure and fresh from the hands of nature. Said our Master: "I want to offer at the altar of the Lord only those flowers that have not even been smelled, fruits that have not been touched with the fingers." The words of the great man sustained us all. For he saw through the future life of those boys that he collected from the streets of Calcutta, so to say. People used to laugh at him when he said: "You will see—this boy, that boy, what he becomes." His faith was unalterable. "Mother showed it to me. I may be weak, but when She says this is so—She can never make mistakes—it must be so."

So things went on and on for ten years without any light, but with my health breaking all the time. It tells on the body in the long run: sometimes one meal at nine in the evening, another time a meal at eight in the morning, another after two days, another after three days—and always the poorest and roughest thing. Who is going to give to the beggar the good things he has? And then, they have not much in India. And most of the time walking, climbing snow peaks, sometimes ten miles of hard mountain climbing, just to get a meal. They eat unleavened bread in India, and sometimes they have it stored away for twenty or thirty days, until it is harder than bricks; and then they will give a square of that. I would have to go from house to house to collect sufficient for one meal. And then the bread was so hard, it made my mouth bleed to eat it. Literally, you can break your teeth on that bread. Then I would put it in a pot and pour over it water from the river. For months and months I existed that way—of course it was telling on the health.

Then I thought, I have tried India; it is time for me to try another country. At that time your Parliament of Religions was to be held, and someone was to be sent from India. I was just a vagabond, but I said, "If you send me, I am going. I have not much to lose, and I don't care if I lose that." It was very difficult to find the money, but after a long struggle they got together just enough to pay for my passage —and I came. Came one or two months early, so that I found myself drifting about in the streets here, without knowing anybody.

But finally the Parliament of Religions opened and I met kind friends, who helped me right along. I worked a little, collected funds, started two papers, and so on. After that I went over to England and worked there. At the same time I carried on the work for India in America, too.

My plan for India, as it has been developed and centralized, is this: I have told you of our lives as monks there, how we go from door to door, so that religion is brought to everybody without charge, except, perhaps, a broken piece of bread. That is why you see the lowest of the low in India holding the most exalted religious ideas. It is all through the work of these monks. But ask a man, "Who are the English?" —he does not know. He says perhaps, "They are the children of those giants they speak of in those books, are they not?" "Who governs you?" "We don't know." "What is the government?" They don't know. But they know philosophy. It is a practical want of intellectual education about life on this earth they suffer from. These millions and millions of people are ready for life beyond this world—is not that enough for them? Certainly not. They must have a better piece of bread and a better piece of rag on their bodies. The great question is, how to get that better bread and better rag for these sunken millions.

First, I must tell you, there is great hope for them, because, you see, they are the gentlest people on earth. Not that they are timid. When they want to fight, they fight like demons. The best soldiers the English have are recruited from the peasantry of India. Death is a thing of no importance to them. Their attitude is, "Twenty times I have died before, and I shall die many times after this. What of that?" They never turn back. They are not given to much emotion, but they make very good fighters.

Their instinct, however, is to plow. If you rob them, murder them, tax them, do anything to them, they will be quiet and gentle, so long as you leave them free to practice their religion. They never interfere with the religion of others. "Leave us liberty to worship our gods, and take everything else!" That is their attitude. When the English touch them there, trouble starts. That was the real cause of the '57 mutiny—they would not bear religious repression. The great Mohammedan governments were simply blown up because they touched the Indians' religion.

But aside from that, they are very peaceful, very quiet, very gentle, and, above all, not given to vice. The absence of any strong drink, oh, it makes them infinitely superior to the mobs of any other country. You cannot compare the decency of life among the poor in India with life in the slums here. A slum means poverty, but poverty does not mean sin, indecency, and vice in India. In other countries, the opportunities are such that only the indecent and the lazy need be poor. There is no reason for poverty unless one is a fool or a blackguard—the sort who want city life and all its luxuries. They won't go into the country. They say, "We are here with all the fun, and you must give us bread." But that is not the case in India, where the poor fellows work hard from morning to sunset, and somebody else takes the bread out of their hands, and their children go hungry. Notwithstanding the millions of tons of wheat raised in India, scarcely a grain passes the mouth of a peasant. He lives upon the poorest corn, which you would not feed to your canary birds.

Now there is no reason why they should suffer such distress—these people; oh, so pure and good! We hear so much talk about the sunken millions, and the degraded women of India—but none come to our help. What do they say? They say: "You can only be helped, you can only be good by ceasing to be what you are. It is useless to help Hindus." These people do not know the history of races. There will be no more India if they change their religion and their institutions, because that is the vitality of that race. It will disappear, so, really, you will have nobody to help.

Then there is the other great point to learn: that you can never help, really. What can we do for each other? You are growing in your own life, I am growing in my own. It is possible that I can give you a push in your life, knowing that, in the long run, all roads lead to Rome. It is a steady growth. No national civilization is perfect, yet. Give that civilization a push, and it will arrive at its own goal: don't strive to change it. Take away a nation's institutions, customs and manners, and what will be left? They hold the nation together.

But here comes the very learned foreign man, and he says: "Look here: you give up all those institutions and customs of thousands of years, and take my tom-fool tin pot and be happy." This is all nonsense.

We will have to help each other, but we have to go one step farther: the first thing is to become unselfish in help. "If you do just what I tell you to do, I will help you. Otherwise not." Is that help?

And so, if the Hindus want to help you spiritually, there will be no question of limitations: perfect unselfishness. I give, and there it ends. It is gone from me. My mind, my powers, my everything that I have to give, is given: given with the idea to give, and no more. I have seen many times people who have robbed half the world, and they gave $20,000 "to convert the heathen." What for? For the benefit of the heathen, or for their own souls? Just think of that.

And the Nemesis of crime is working. We men try to hoodwink our own eyes. But inside the heart, He has remained, the real Self. He never forgets. We can never delude Him His eyes will never be hoodwinked. Whenever there is any impulse of real charity, it tells, though it be at the end of a thousand years. Obstructed, it yet wakens, once more to burst like a thunderbolt. And every impulse where the motive is selfish, self-seeking—though it may be launched forth with all the newspapers blazoning, all the mobs standing and cheering—it fails to reach the mark.

I am not taking pride in this. But, mark you, I have told

the story of that group of boys. Today there is not a village, not a man, not a woman in India that does not know their work and bless them. There is not a famine in the land where these boys do not plunge in and try to work and rescue as many as they can. And that strikes to the heart. The people come to know it. So help whenever you can, but mind what your motive is. If it is selfish, it will neither benefit those you help, nor yourself. If it is unselfish, it will bring blessings upon them to whom it is given, and infinite blessings upon you, sure as you are living. The Lord can never be hoodwinked. The law of Karma can never be hoodwinked.

# Sri Ramakrishna, Modern Spirit, and Religion

## SWAMI PRABHAVANANDA

### I

AMONGST THE STUDENTS of religion who are acquainted with the life of Sri Ramakrishna, perhaps only a few regard his life in all its phases as historically true. To these few, what appears to the rest as belonging to the class of legend and mythology becomes living spiritual truth. To them even the lives of Krishna, Buddha, or Christ which seem lost in the mist of myth and legend become true and living in the light of the life of Ramakrishna. But apart from these few, however, to most people who have drunk deep of the modern spirit, who refuse to accept anything as true which is beyond the realm of their personal discoveries and thus are circumscribed by their own limitations, much that is told of Sri Ramakrishna's life appears as legendary, and his supernormal experiences as fantastic, or, at best, the hallucinations of a disordered brain.

A strange fact emerges here, however, which is, that certain people, while rejecting the supernormal experiences of Ramakrishna, and regarding samadhi as an hallucination, are the very ones who revere and honor him as a rare soul, nay, a man-god. As an example of such admiration one may cite the name of Pandit Shivanath Shastri, a most learned man, and contemporary of Ramakrishna, who was also one of the co-founders of the Sadharan Brahmo Samaj. The Pandit became a regular visitor to Ramakrishna, learning at his feet, and esteeming him as one of the greatest men alive. Yet the state of samadhi still remained to him an abnormality.

In this connection one may also mention Professor Max Muller, and Romain Rolland, biographers of Ramakrishna, and two of the greatest thinkers of our age. They were attracted to and admired the superior spiritual genius of the man Ramakrishna, yet viewed many of the incidents of his life as legendary, and some of his spiritual experiences as delusions, or mental aberrations.

Let us, therefore, analyze why there is this contradiction in the estimation of Ramakrishna; why he is accepted as a spiritual genius by those very people who at the same time reject some of the most important experiences of his life—experiences which made him what he was. Is it true that Sri Ramakrishna had to pass through a "period of hallucination . . . whence his spirit was to rise in the fullness of joyous and harmonious power to mighty realizations for the benefit of humanity" as Romain Rolland says; or may it be that the modern man sees these contradictions in Ramakrishna's life, only because he himself is the product of an age which has failed in the understanding of, and application to life, of the true spirit of religion?

To find an adequate answer, let us examine more closely this modern age and its reactions to the standards of religion; then we shall better be able to consider whether it, rightly or wrongly evaluates the life of this great saint.

The modern spirit can be defined as utilitarian and rationalistic or scientific. The history of the last four hundred years in Europe, since the age of the renaissance, marks the attempt at progress politically, economically, socially and intellectually from the standpoint of utilitarianism. The world today, however, is rudely shaken by the confusion that it is facing in every phase of life and human activity. The basic structure upon which we built the civilization of the West seems to be hopelessly collapsing. And we ask ourselves, "Have we progressed?" or, are we not moving in a circle within an "endless whirl of vain appearances."

Though many of us are aware of the failure of the utilitarian standard, and though we may admit, as we face the stark reality of events in the history of the world, that there has been no real progress, yet again, we cling in substance tenaciously to the same philosophy of utilitarianism and of progress. For the basic philosophy of the Western world is still the philosophy of flux. Life is ever changing, life is ever progressing—this is the cry of today. That there is an unchangeable reality, that there is "one in the many," that there is a supreme goal attained in life—these fundamental truths are completely ignored by the man in the street as well as by the progressive philosophers and thinkers of today. The result is that the modern man rests content with this world; to him this world is all. He knows only life on earth and goodness and happiness are limited to creature comforts. In short earthly life is the object and sole purpose of all his struggles and actions. Even his religion is made subservient to fulfil his purpose on earth.

This last statement, of course, does not apply to Christianity in its original form. The central idea in the teachings of Christ, like all true religions, is the evanescence of earthly life, and the transcendent reality of God, the one unchangeable Being above all the changes of life. So my remarks in this essay do not apply to those devout Christians who having realized the vanities of earthly life live in constant communion with God.

But this "other-worldly" attitude of Christ and Christianity has been largely discarded by the West in her interpretation of the teachings of Jesus as something impractical and useless. To make Christianity practical to the modern man, it has been identified with humanitarianism and social service. The religion of the majority of the intellectuals of today is doing good to and loving one another! True, they profess faith in God, but to them such a faith is only a means to inspire mankind to live harmoniously and happily on earth. This attitude has so permeated all strata of society, that it has become an accepted goal, so much so, that by now my readers will be asking themselves, what is wrong with this ideal? Should not religion inspire man to love and serve humanity?

Bear patiently with me for a moment. I am not saying that the ideal of service and love is wrong; merely the fact that religion has been identified exclusively with this conception;

and with such completeness that some theologians go so far as to say that God needs our help to straighten this world and its affairs.

Thus there is no gainsaying that the religion of today may be termed humanist ethics. The other day I read how a well-known modern thinker (I am sorry to admit, he is an Indian —but a disciple of the modern West) remarked that communism as he has seen it in Russia is the true practical religion, for it does not merely believe in doing good, but it actually helps and does good to mankind. It is not that I have anything against communism, or as a matter of fact against any form of government. It is not within my sphere to judge any system. But to identify any existing form of government with religion is going too far. And the reason for this misunderstanding is that religion has been identified with humanist ethics.

Does not modern Christianity teach adoration of God, a personal relationship with God? Certainly it does. But to what extent? Is it only "tinged by emotion," to borrow a phrase of Matthew Arnold? If the modern man prays at all, his prayer consists of petitions to enrich himself on earth, and he hands God over a few thanks for allowing him to live on earth. In short he professes faith in God but does not care to devote himself to Him, nor does he care to understand the words of Jesus when he said: "Thou shalt love the Lord thy God with all thy heart, and with all thy soul, and with all thy mind." In fact, if a modern man dares to love God with the intensity that Christ speaks of he will be considered a spiritual freak.

I have defined Western religion as humanist ethics. This ethical life of the majority of the intellectuals of today is, however, guided by customs and social behavior, external to himself. Stress is laid not upon self-control, or inner check, with a view to regenerating one's own self, but upon external decorum. Truly has it been remarked by Antoine De Rivarol: "People mean nowadays by a philosopher not the man who learns the great art of mastering his passions or adding to his insight, but the man who has cast off prejudices without acquiring virtues."

Now the question is, do not religions teach service to mankind, love for one another? Is it not a fact that the lives of Buddha, Christ, Ramakrishna and other spiritual souls have been the inspiration in every age to deeds of love and benefit to humanity? Very true. They were the inspirers; for who could have been drawn to such great ones if their deep love for mankind were not seen? Their very lives were sacrifices on the altar of God as humanity. Pandit Shivanath, though he denounced the samadhi of Ramakrishna, yet was attracted to him for his great love, his great sympathy and toleration. Romain Rolland saw how the spirit of Ramakrishna rose "in the fullness of joyous and harmonious power to mighty realizations for the benefit of humanity." Ramakrishna's heart indeed bitterly wept at the suffering and ignorance of mankind. The disciple Vivekananda, the torch bearer of his master's message, said that he did not even care for his own liberation if only he could give liberation to one individual soul. Christ died on the cross for suffering humanity. Buddha denied himself the throne of a mighty kingdom that he could bring eternal life to mankind. Indeed the lives of spiritual men and women bring immense blessings to all.

But the question still remains, what kind of benefit and blessings do these great ones bring? Are they philanthropists, and are their lives devoted to social, political and economic regeneration? In short, are they interested in our world and its affairs? The modern man will undoubtedly see in a Christ, a Buddha, or a Ramakrishna a lover of humanity, and a philanthropist, and thus appreciate these spiritual giants. But such appreciation is misinterpretation. This may appear to many a very strange and rather bold statement. Nevertheless the fact remains that all spiritual souls know that this world is a vanishing dream. They know that they are "not of this world." Thus they are interested neither in the world nor straightening its affairs. But what they are concerned about is you and me and every individual. Not to do us any earthly good, not to give us the taste of life that ends in death, not to give us happiness that lasts for a moment; but their concern is to lead us to that life which is eternal, to that joy which knows no sorrow, to that knowledge which brings liberation. They give their life-blood for humanity that man may wake up from his dream of ignorance of an earthly life and be born in the life in spirit. Therefore, such spiritual souls are by no means humanists in the sense of those who believe that "this world is all and we must rest content with it."

In the words of Swami Vivekananda the world is like a "dog's curly tail." You straighten it and it curls again; which does not mean that we are to be indifferent to the world's sufferings any more than these great ones were indifferent.

As they were not humanists in the accepted sense, what may we ask is their attitude to this problem? Vivekananda taught man to serve man *as God*. To quote the words of Christ: "For inasmuch as ye have done it unto the least of these my brethren, ye have done it unto me." This teaching of Christ is often quoted to inspire people to philanthropy and humanitarian works. Emphasis is laid upon doing and not upon the attitude with which we do. And that makes a world of difference. "Ye have done it unto *me*"—thus Christ taught us to worship God in suffering humanity. The object, the ideal is to worship God, to serve Him. The building of hospitals and schools, and feeding the poor, are but means to that end. The modern man takes up the means as an end; the ideal is completely forgotten. Sri Ramakrishna once said to a rich disciple of his, who was bent upon philanthropy: "If you see God, would you ask Him to build hospitals and schools?" About Vidyasagar, who was well-known for his humanitarian work and was literally regarded as "the ocean of kindness," Sri Ramakrishna remarked: "That man does not know that he has the jewel within himself. When he knows it, his work in the outside world will drop away from him."

In this connection it would be interesting to pass a few remarks on the philanthropic and social service that the Ramakrishna Mission is doing in India and which the intelligentsia and visitors to India speak of highly. They recognize and praise our work as a great philanthropic deed. The monks of the Ramakrishna Order are regarded by many, who do not know our inner attitude, as great humanitarians. But the fact is, none of the monks of the Ramakrishna Order regards himself as a humanitarian. His one ideal in life is to know God, and he knows that worship and meditation are the means to that end. When he is engaged in the service of man he knows he is worshipping God. Which brings to my memory a very interesting incident which throws light on the subject. A young disciple of Swami Vivekananda, being inspired by the ideals of renunciation and service, devoted himself to the nursing of the sick and helping of the poor. From a very humble beginning his work grew into a huge organization. The disciple was the head of the institution for many years, which is one of the largest homes of service in India under the Ramakrishna Mission. Swami Brahmananda, an immediate disciple of Ramakrishna, and who was the leader of the Ramakrishna Mission at that time, kept watch over the spiritual progress of all the disciples and monks of the Order. When Swami found out that to this disciple, who was the head of the home of service, work became more important, he relieved him of his duties and sent him away to practice austerities and live exclusively the life of meditation. I record this incident here to point out that the ideal of the Ramakrishna Mission has been from its inception to help man to attain God, to help him to be devoted to God and be absorbed in His love and knowledge. Service to mankind is the worship of God, and as such is a means to that end. Therefore, serving man, let us not forget that this is but a form of worship.

Now let me ask those who preach brotherly love and forget to love God with all their heart, soul and mind, why is it that in spite of this teaching of love for mankind and service to humanity, when it actually comes to living, it does not work? How is it that though one may sincerely wish to love the world, the reaction is the complete opposite, despite one's will to the contrary? And man finds, by his contact with people, that the ideal of universal love is not practical. Yet as he looks at the lives of Christ or Buddha or Ramakrishna he finds that they had this love in their hearts and to them it was practical. To take an illustration from the life of Sri Ramakrishna: There were times in his life when he would feel that treading the grass, the very grass itself would be hurt; for he saw everywhere the one life, his own Self. One time a boatman was severely beaten by a cruel person and Ramakrishna cried out: "Oh! how painful!" and the disciples saw marks of the beating on Ramakrishna's person. Can we feel such unity? Can we feel for humanity that way? We admire this love, we want to imitate such lives; but in practice we fail. And why?

Today the philosopher and the man in the street talk about unity and expansion; and they try to reach this unity by expanding themselves, as it were, into space. But they fail. To attain unity with all beings and to love humanity, two things are needed which the modern man and thinker lack. The first is the check of inner passion, or self-control; and the second is the art of diving deep within one's own soul; in other words, the following of the first commandment of Christ, which is to love God with all one's soul, heart and mind. Shun ego or selfishness and learn to dive deep within yourself, for the Kingdom of God is within your own soul; then you find that it is the same God dwelling in the hearts of all. Universal love is thus attained, for "in that realization," to quote the words of the Upanishads, "you know that the one Self has become all." (Yashmin Sarvani bhutani Atmaibabhut vijanatah.) "Love thy neighbor as thyself," because thy neighbor is thine own Self. Know this Self.

Herein lies the cause of man's confusion. Emerson hit the nail on the head when he said:

> *"There are two laws discrete*
> *Not reconciled—*
> *Law for man, and law for thing;*
> *The last builds town and fleet,*
> *But it runs wild,*
> *And doth the man unking."*

The superficial humanists of today who regard this world as important, and earthly pursuits as paramount, by seeing man merely as a physical and mental being, know only of the "law for things" and are ignorant of the "law for man." For they ignore the truth that there lies in man something more real, something greater than is apparent in his everyday consciousness; they forget that there is the Self in man, the Spiritual presence, which is the source of life, thought and consciousness. And thus in the phraseology of Emerson they "un-king the man."

Because of the ignorance of the Spiritual presence in man,

the moderns have no supreme purpose, no ideal or goal, in life. And as such life to them has become meaningless, and meaningless it will remain so long as they take the physical self as the real man and earthly pursuits as the be all and end all of life. The hunger for the eternal, the immortal longings have thus been stifled by them. True it is that preachers of religions ask man to look forward to eternity in the midst of his earthly pursuits, but this looking forward is an expectation to achieve the kingdom of God after he has lived his allotted time on earth. Though they may quote every day the teachings of Christ that the "Kingdom of God is within" and "is come nigh unto you," many do not believe that it can be attained while living on earth. The result is that the "Kingdom of heaven" has begun to be looked upon as a grandma's story.

To understand the true spirit of any religion and to appreciate the greatness of teachers like Christ, Buddha, or Ramakrishna, there is one thing most important which we must know and recognize and which unfortunately the modern thinker, as I have just mentioned, does not know and believe; and it is just this: that there is a supreme purpose, a supreme goal, which can be achieved in life, "having attained which no other acquisition seems of any value" (Gita). The immortal longing of mankind is expressed in the prayer of the Upanishads: "Lead us from the unreal to the real; lead us from the darkness to light; lead us from death to immortality." The immortal longing of humanity is to attain the "eternal amongst the non-eternals of life, the abiding, infinite joy in the midst of the fleeting pleasures of life" (Upanishads). And we must know that this longing can really be satisfied on earth. The greatness of a spiritual soul lies in the fact that he has achieved this reality. The central theme of all true religions, and of all philosophy of life, in one Sanskrit word, is *jivanmukti*, which can be interpreted as liberation in life, tasting the bliss of Brahman, or attaining the Kingdom of God. Liberation from the bondages of life, the Kingdom of God, is not a far-off ideal which may or may not be realized after death, but it is perfection to be attained on this earth, while living in the body, moving and acting apparently like all ordinary human beings. "On this earth, the mortal becomes immortal," says the Katha Upanishad. In the words of Christ: "But whosoever drinketh of the water that I shall give him . . . shall be in him a well of water springing up into everlasting life." Buddha says: "Verily I say unto thee, the Tathagata lives in the pure land of eternal bliss even now while he is still in the body." Samkara, in his commentary on the Brihadaranyaka Upanishad writes: "One attains Brahman; and he attains It here on earth and not after death of the body." (Ihaiva Brahmaiva san Brahma apyeti na sharira patat uttarakalam.)

Is it then any wonder that man should worship Christ, Buddha, or Ramakrishna as embodiments of Godhead who not only had attained this liberation in life and entered the Kingdom of God but could give that liberation to others by their touch? In our modern times we have witnessed the lives of the disciples of Ramakrishna who as they came to the Master testified how their bonds of ignorance were severed and how they were illumined by his grace, by a mere touch.

All true religions and all spiritual teachers worth the name are emphatic in pointing out that the one and only purpose of human life and existence is to attain *moksha* or liberation, which is the same as perfection and which is attained by entering the Kingdom of God within. "Be ye perfect," says Christ. "You are complete in Godhead," comments St. Paul.

All spiritual wisdom in the world tells man that he can consciously unite himself with the divine while living in this body and thus may attain perfection. For in each man is God concealed. Purity, freedom, illumination, peace, perfection are all identical with the immortal Self which only remains to be uncovered. "As people ignorant of a golden treasure that has been hidden underground may walk over it again and again and yet never find it, so all beings, though every moment living in Brahman, never find him, for he is hidden by a covering of ignorance. . . . Brahman is the Self within, untouched by any deed, ageless, and deathless, free from grief, free from hunger and thirst. The etheric center within the heart, where dwells Brahman, is like a boundary which separates That from the mundane world. Day and night do not cross that boundary, nor old age, nor death;

neither grief, nor pleasure, nor good deeds, nor evil deeds reach That. All evil shuns That, because That is free and can never be touched by any impurity." [1]

St. Augustine wrote: "I, Lord, went wandering like a strayed sheep, seeking thee with anxious reasoning without, whilst thou wast within me. . . . I went round the streets and squares of the city of this world seeking thee, and I found thee not, because in vain I sought without for him who was within myself."

To seek for the perfection in Godhead, to seek for the truth that gives us freedom, is to seek for our true Self. Religion is not anything extraneous to ourselves that we have to acquire, neither is it something which we may or may not believe, but it is something living in the soul of each man. And as no man can jump out of himself, so no man can free himself from this living religion. Only it remains hidden in most men and it awaits their finding. Mother Nature, however, is patient and she gradually leads each man by the hand to awaken in him ultimately that which is his birthright. Man may incarnate again and again until he has learned his lesson and is awakened to the worth, the golden treasure, the Kingdom of God which lies within the depths of his own soul.

The man who loves and worships God as separate from himself really gives devotion to Him who is the Self within. The followers of the path of Love worship God as Father, Mother, Friend, or Beloved. All Hindu worshippers know, however, that God whom they love and worship dwells within the Shrine of their own hearts. They call him *dehabhritam atma*—the Self hidden within the body. St. Augustine was aware of it as also are other true Christian devotees. What is this Self which is identical with Brahman? A distinction should be made between the apparent, phenomenal self, and the real Self, which is divine. The Katha Upanishad which I quote here clearly explains the philosophy of Self:

"Both the individual self and the universal Self, the Atman, have entered the cave of the heart, the supreme abode of the Most High. Of these the former enjoys the pleasures within the realm of the body. The knower of Brahman, to-

[1] Chandogya Upanishad.

gether with the householders who observe the fire sacrifices, sees a difference between them as between the darkness and the light.

"Of the two selves—the illusory or individual self, of which all are aware, and the real Self, which few know—it is as unchangeable being that the real Self is first recognized. He who has recognized it as unchangeable being—to him will be revealed its innermost nature.

"That which is awake in us even while we are asleep, shaping (in dream) many objects of desire, That indeed is pure, That is Brahman, and That verily is called Immortal. All the worlds have their beings in That and none can transcend That. That is the Immortal Self.

"As fire, though one, filling the world, takes the shape of each object it burns, so the indwelling Self in all, though one, takes the form of each object it fills, yet transcends all.

"As air, though one, filling the world, takes the shape of each object it enters, so the indwelling Self in all, though one, takes the form of each object it fills, yet transcends all.

"As the sun, the revealer of all objects to the seer, is not touched by the sinful eye nor by the impurities of objects it gazes upon, so the one Self, dwelling in all, is not touched by the miseries of the world. For He transcends all.

"He is One, the Lord, the innermost Self of all; of one form he makes many forms. The wise man who sees Him revealed in his own soul, to him belongs eternal happiness; to none else, to none else.

"The eternal among non-eternals, the intelligence of the intelligent, He, though one, fulfills the desires of many. The wise man who sees Him revealed in his own soul, to him belongs eternal peace; to none else, to none else."

The immortal longing of man is thus realized in his own being, which is the one Self of the universe—the God we seek. "Town and fleet" are not eternal. They live and die. Man must live and struggle for that which is eternal in him.

We offer our deep homage to Christ, Buddha, or Ramakrishna not because of their *accomplishments* in the external world—of which they had practically none—but because of their *attainment*. They were the children of Light; they became one with the Light.

# St. Francis and Sri Ramakrishna

## GUIDO FERRANDO

WHILE READING the "Gospel of Sri Ramakrishna." a truly remarkable book which brings so vividly before our eyes the figure of the great Indian saint, I was continually reminded of the purest, the gentlest, the most beloved and lovable of all the Christian saints, Francis of Assisi. There is a striking similarity between these two divine men who belong to different ages, different races and different faiths; a similarity which is most illuminating as it proves the fundamental unity of true Religion.

They both seem to have had the same mission in this world. They were not founders of a *new* religion, but rather revivers and restorers of the Eternal Faith in an all-pervading God who can and must be realized in our earthly life. They were "living embodiments of godliness," as Mahatma Gandhi says of Ramakrishna, or, to use a beautiful expression of one of St. Francis' biographers, they were "perfect images of God in the mirror of humanity." St. Francis, at the beginning of the thirteenth century, was the Saviour of the Christian church, then on the verge of collapse, threatened outwardly by the struggle with the Emperor and inwardly by corruption, dissension and heresy; and he saved the Christian religion simply by living the Gospel of Christ in a spirit of obedience, of purity and love. Ramakrishna, during the latter part of the nineteenth century, played the "noble role of the Saviour of the Eternal Religion of India, and fulfilled the spiritual aspirations of three hundred millions of Hindus for the last two thousand years." They both had followers: St. Francis founded a religious order which spread rapidly all over the world, exercised an incalculable influence on Western civilization and is still flourishing after more than seven centuries. Sri Ramakrishna had a number of devoted disciples who, after the death of the Master, renounced the world and formed a monastic order which is spreading over land and sea, bringing the message of India to Europe and America, and helping towards the spiritual unity of mankind.

When we consider these two great Teachers in their human aspect, we find that they both had the purity and the simplicity of a child. It was the child in them that gave them their irresistible charm, their instinctive ability of winning the hearts of those around them. They never lost the sublime naïveté of childhood; they were happy natures always desirous to share their joys with others. They were also intellectually simple; they were not scholars and did not attach any importance to learning; on the contrary they sometimes looked upon it as an obstacle to God. Ramakrishna was an almost illiterate man and was always telling his disciples not to waste time in reasoning and worldly knowledge. Francis, in an age of great theologians, was not a man of great culture; true knowledge for him consisted in being, not in possessing intellectual learning. I do not mean to say that these two supreme religious Masters were ignorant men; they had a marvelous spiritual intelligence, and possessed the divine wisdom that comes from the love of God. And they never attacked learning. Francis was most respectful to the Doctors of the Church, and when compelled to relinquish the active leadership of the Order, he chose as his successor a man thoroughly versed in theology and canon law. He did not scorn culture; he merely felt that it was impossible for one to be devoted both to the pursuit of learning and to the cultivation of the mystical side of one's nature. Moreover, among his followers were some of the famous scholars of his age, and he became the inspirer of the greatest of poets, Dante, and of one of the supreme artists of all times, Giotto, both of whom painted for us, one in exquisite lines and the other in marvelous frescoes, the life of their spiritual master. Ramakrishna, though he was not a cultivated man and took no interest in science and philosophy, had among his dearest friends some learned pundits and teachers; and his most beloved disciple, Narendra—universally known under his monastic name of Swami Vivekananda—whom he chose to carry on his teaching and to bring his message to the Western world, was one of the most brilliant and scholarly minds of our time.

St. Francis believed that the greatest obstacles to God were lust and greed, which Ramakrishna so vividly personified in "woman and gold"; and he founded his Order on chastity, poverty and obedience. It is in the interpretation of these spiritual rules that the medieval Italian and the modern Hindu masters reveal their likeness. Chastity for St. Francis is not simply a negative virtue, the refraining from lust; and it is much more than a mode of living; chastity is the broadening of the scope of life so as to take in the whole world. It is carnal passion that fetters love. No one who looks back on his own life, can fail to realize what vast stores of enthusiasm, faith and gaiety are dissipated through the betrayal of our senses. Francis, in the vow of chastity, saw the means of preserving for, or of restoring to oneself the purity, the intensity and the independence of the child who is always free to pursue any object of his affections. Also for Ramakrishna chastity was much more than abstinence from carnal love. "To me," he used to say over and over again, "every woman is a mother." And the image of a mother, the idea of motherhood lifted his mind to the vision of the Divine Mother, Kali, to whom he was completely devoted.

Poverty for the Italian saint was not simply renunciation of earthly riches and power. No one saw more clearly than St. Francis how most of us are slaves to money, whether we possess it or not, and how the accumulation of riches corrupts the soul more than anything else; for him riches and fetters are synonymous. But it is most important to understand that for Francis poverty was a spiritual attitude, not a material state. Fidelity to poverty signified for him the negation of all desire for worldly honour or bodily comfort, since thus alone was the soul's freedom to be secured. The external sacrifice was a mere symbol of the inward renunciation. It was not only a casting away of worldly encumbrance for a life of liberty, it was a shedding of spiritual obstructions for the soul's union with God. Ramakrishna undoubtedly had the same understanding of the great spiritual meaning of poverty.

The vow of obedience, which has as its symbol a yoke, serves not to fetter, but to free the soul. It is only through spiritual obedience that one can attain complete freedom from the illusion of our ego. Just as moral freedom is the result of our obedience to reason, so spiritual freedom, the surrender of our individual self, comes to us only through renunciation of our personal will and obedience to the will of God. Francis saw very clearly how necessary it is for all who seek union with God to be humble, to trust Divine Providence, to obey their spiritual guide. Ramakrishna, in his talks with his disciples, continually reminds them that they cannot attain divine wisdom without the help and the guidance of a Guru, and that they must obey their Master completely, with the same trust that a child has for his mother. It is, however, in another trait of their nature that these two great Masters revealed their wonderful likeness; both were unconsciously supreme religious artists. An English biographer of the Italian saint rightly emphasizes this quality of St. Francis. "Probably the particular human quality" he says, "in which Francis lives with the modern world, is as a supreme religious artist, with an exquisite sensibility as to spiritual value and a unique power of dramatic self-expression. All through his life he is either the hero of episodes that seize the imagination and impress themselves indelibly upon the memory, or he is uttering parables or inventing images, which no one, having read or heard them, can easily forget. It is manifest he had all the shining virtues: courage and humility, love and purity, joy and compassion, courtesy and holiness; so had other saints. It is in the expression of these qualities that he excels them all. No human soul so bright as his ever shone out so clearly through the fleshly veil; there seems to be an actual radiance about him. By reason of this heavenly quality he ranks with the great poets as the creator of the common imagination of mankind; and the simple stories of his life take their place in the world's literature with those of Dante and the Bible." Ramakrishna shared with Francis this divine quality; he was a poet at heart and he explained to his disciples the deepest truths of religion, not in an abstruse, philosophic language, but by using, with telling effect, simple and homely parables and images full of charm and beauty.

They both loved music and song, because, living in direct communion with God, only in song they could express, at least in part, the ecstatic love and the unutterable joy that filled their hearts. Ecstatic love and joy is probably the nearest description we can give of the plane of consciousness on which they lived. Ramakrishna saw God in everything, in the loftiest and noblest as well as in the humblest and meanest form; he believed in the Absolute, indivisible and formless, but he loved His manifested world the *lila*, with its infinite variety of created forms. He especially loved and worshipped Kali, the Divine Mother, a living reality for him, full of compassion and tenderness for all; and it was through this all-permeating and embracing love for every single manifestation of God, that he attained union with the Absolute. He used to sing many times a day hymns of praise to God and chant His name and glory, and he used to ask his devotees and his visitors to join in the songs, and, almost invariably, while singing or listening to a beautiful song, he entered samadhi, communion with God.

Among the many songs recorded in "The Gospel of Sri Ramakrishna," there is one, especially dear to the Master who loved to sing it while dancing in a circle with his disciples, which recalls to our minds the Italian saint, as it is full of the Franciscan spirit:

*In Wisdom's firmament the moon of Love is rising full*
*And Love's flood-tide, in surging waves, is flowing everywhere.*
*O Lord, how full of bliss Thou art! Victory unto Thee!*

*On every side shine devotees, like stars around the moon;*
*Their Friend, the Lord All-merciful, joyously plays with*
*   them.*
*Behold! the gates of paradise today are open wide.*

*The soft spring wind of the New Day raises fresh waves of*
*   joy;*
*Gently it carries to the earth the fragrance of God's love,*
*Till all the yogis, drunk with bliss, are lost in ecstasy.*

*Upon the sea of the world unfolds the lotus of the New Day,*
*And there the Mother sits enshrined in blissful majesty.*
*See how the bees are mad with joy, sipping the nectar there!*

*Behold the Mother's radiant face, which so enchants the heart*
*And captivates the universe! About Her Lotus Feet*
*Bands of ecstatic holy men are dancing in delight.*

*What matchless loveliness is Hers! What infinite content*
*Pervades the heart when She appears! O brothers, says*
  *Premdas,*
*I humbly beg you, one and all, to sing the Mother's praise!*

Francis would have loved this beautiful song; it has something in common with his great hymn: "Laudes Creaturarum," the Praises of Creatures. Francis was a born poet. As a young man, before his conversion, he loved the troubadours' songs, which he probably learnt from the lips of his mother, who was French by birth; later on, after he had renounced the world, he went on singing; no longer the praise of woman, but of God. Among his followers there was a brother who, before he entered the Order, had been a troubadour; and it was he who set to music the songs that Francis composed, so that the brethren might chant them morning and night in praise of God. Of all his songs, the most famous and the only one that has been preserved to us in its complete form, is the "Hymn of Created Things," a poem beyond the realms of art, in which one senses immediately the simplicity and spirituality of the author. It was composed shortly after Francis had attained the highest state of samadhi, the complete realization of God, of which he bore a visible sign in the stigmata. "I will make a new song," he said to his brethren; "a praise of all creatures which daily minister to us and without which we could not live, and among which man much offendeth his Creator by reason of his gross ingratitude, though in the midst of so much grace and benefit." Thomas of Celano, his first biographer, says that he invited the Creatures and the Elements to praise God, their Creator, in certain verses that he composed after the manner of the Benedicite. The title of the poem explains the aim: it is the praises of the Creatures, and not merely the praise of man for them; and the Creatures consist of the heavenly bodies and the four elements. To these praises, which form the main body of the hymn, Francis added later on two brief stanzas, one in praise of those who suffer in peace all human infirmities, and the other, composed just before his passing away, in praise of bodily death. This beautiful hymn, which expresses in a naïve and moving way the true religious spirit, and which, I recall with deep emotion, was chosen at the World Congress of Religion held in London in the summer of 1931 as the one song that representatives of all creeds would gladly sing together in praise of God, has been often misunderstood by modern interpreters. The majority of the students of St. Francis believe that for him the heavenly bodies and the elements were brothers and sisters of man: our brother sun, our sister moon, and so on; which is not correct. Only one verse of the poem contains the possessive pronoun "our," and that is in the praise of mother Earth, "our mother," as he calls her, and not "our sister," because she could not be both. For Francis "our brothers and sisters" were the animals, especially the birds, the larks above all, to which he used to preach and which he dearly loved because they soar up into the sky and express in their song the joy of life and their gratitude to the Creator. The heavenly bodies and the elements, in Francis' poetic imagination, formed a divine Order which was, in a certain sense, a counterpart of the religious order he had founded on earth. It is the brethren and sisters of this higher and far more glorious Order that he invites to praise his Lord as men could not do worthily.

Here is the hymn, which I have translated literally, hoping to preserve some of the wonderful simplicity of the original.

### LAUDES CREATURARUM

*Most High, Omnipotent, good Lord! To Thee*
*The praises, the glory, the honour be!*
*All blessings, Most High, befit only Thee,*
*And no man is worthy to mention Thee.*

*Be praised, my Lord, by all Thy creatures,*
*Especially by Monsignor brother Sun*
*Who brings us day and through whom Thou illuminest us.*
*Fair is he and radiant with great splendour;*
*Of Thee, Most High, he bears significance.*

*Be praised, my Lord, by sister Moon and by the Stars;*
*In heaven Thou hast made them clear, precious and fair.*

*Be praised, my Lord, by brother Wind,*
*By air and cloud and serene sky and all weather*
*By whom Thou givest sustenance to Thy creatures.*

*Be praised, my Lord, by sister Water*
*Who is very useful and humble, precious and chaste.*

*Be praised, my Lord, by brother Fire*
*By whom Thou lightenest us in the night;*
*And fair is he and merry, strong and full of might.*

*Be praised, my Lord, by our mother, sister Earth*
*Who sustaineth and governeth us and giveth birth*
*To divers fruits, coloured flowers and herb.*

*Be praised, my Lord, by those who pardon for Thy love*
*And bear infirmity and tribulation;*
*Blessed are they who shall endure in peace*
*For by Thee, Most High, they will be crowned.*

*Be praised, my Lord, by sister Death-of-the-body*
*From whom no living man can escape.*
*Woe to them who die in mortal sin;*
*Blessed they who are found in Thy most holy will,*
*For to them the second death will work no ill.*

*Praise and bless my Lord and thankful be*
*And serve my Lord with great humility.*

# *The Marriage of Sarada Devi*

## Amiya Corbin

"THEY'RE GONE! Mother, all my pretty ornaments are gone! Oh, Mother, *please* where are they? I had them last night when I went to bed, I know I did, because I wore them right in bed! And now they are all gone! When you put them on me yesterday you said how pretty I looked; that nice man said I looked pretty too. Now they are gone, and I am not pretty any more!" Sobbing bitterly, the little Indian girl tugged frantically at her mother's sari, almost pulling it off in her grief.

Tearfully the poor mother tried to explain what had happened to the ornaments that had so delighted her daughter.

"You see, my darling, yesterday was your wedding day, and when a girl becomes a bride she must always look her very prettiest, because it is the most important day of her life. We are very poor, my dearest, and had no money to buy ornaments for you. Those you wore were borrowed and had to be returned to their owner. Your husband took them away from you while you were sleeping. But never mind, my darling, don't cry, he will buy others for you when you are a big girl and go to live with him."

"Who is my husband, Mother? Was that nice man my husband? Why am I married to him? Where is he now?" But it was only after many years that Sarada found the answers to her childish questions. How could she, a child of five, understand that she had been married to a "mad priest," in the hope that marriage would cure his madness?

Many years passed before the young bride saw her husband again, and then only for three months. But the memory of that association with him left an indelible stamp on her mind, and she spent many happy hours alone, remembering his gentleness and great thoughtfulness. She felt quite sure

261

that he would call her to his side when the proper time came, and until then she would wait. The years of waiting were not idly spent. Her earliest memories were those of helping her mother, who, with tireless patience taught her how to cook, almost is if she knew that her daughter's life would be spent in cooking and in the service of others.

Gradually the gossip of the village people, and the rumors about her husband's insanity began to reach her ears. At first she tried to ignore it, until the people began to whisper about her as she passed. "They say he is *mad!*" she thought to herself. "They say that he has forgotten me, and that I am no better off than a widow! They say that all he does is shout the names of God and go about naked like a lunatic! Well, if that is really true, my place is beside him! He needs me. I shall go to him!"

So it was that this shy, modest village girl defied all the conventions, and set out on foot to join her husband. Her vigil was ended. But he had not forgotten her. Rather it seemed that he was expecting her, and the moment she saw him she knew that her fears for his sanity were groundless. She found in him the same kindliness and saintliness that she had always remembered, and from the moment of their first meeting at Dakshineswar, Sarada Devi dedicated her life to the service of her husband, Sri Ramakrishna.

During the first part of her stay with Sri Ramakrishna, Sarada shared with him the supreme test he was bound to make as her husband and as a spiritual aspirant. His Guru, Totapuri, had told him that a wife presented no obstacle to one really established in Brahman. But *was* he established in Brahman? He must find out for himself. He knew that one so established could see no distinction in the sexes, therefore the question did not arise; but, since the question had arisen he lost no time in putting himself to the test. Gazing at the sleeping form of his beautiful wife, Sri Ramakrishna boldly asked himself which it was he wanted, that or God, knowing he was free to take either. While yet discriminating, he became suddenly absorbed in Samadhi, which lasted throughout the night. And, later, when asked by her husband if she wished that their marriage be consummated, Sarada's answer was characteristic of her own saintliness: "Why should I wish

that?" she asked, "I have come only to help you in your
spiritual life."

Knowing nothing of Samadhi at that time, poor Sarada
spent many sleepless nights watching over Sri Ramakrishna.
Night after night he would spend absorbed in that state, and
even though he had taught her special mantrams to repeat
which would restore him to normal consciousness, she could
never quite get over her anxiety for his safety. Learning of
her fears and constant vigil, Sri Ramakrishna insisted that
she sleep at the *Nahabat,* an apartment somewhat removed
from the main building. This she did, living and sleeping
and cooking in the one room it provided for the greater part
of thirteen years.

The upper room of the apartment was occupied by her
mother-in-law, whom Sarada served with unswerving devotion as long as she lived. She was never known to have complained of her congested surroundings, which, from her own
description, would have tried the patience of a lesser saint to
the point of rebellion. Not only did she live, cook, and sleep
in the same room, but as it was the only place of storage she
had, every corner was stacked with sacks of rice and lentils
and other provisions, while the cooking pots and pans swung
from the ceiling which, to use her own words, "was so low
that I used to bump my head every time I entered the room,
until my head got used to it and would bend of itself the
moment I entered the door. Many stout Calcutta ladies came
to visit me, but they never came into the room!"

Because of her extreme shyness, Sarada strictly observed
*Purdah,* and to insure her privacy, a bamboo screen reaching
above her head was erected all around the veranda. This
made it absolutely impossible for any sunlight ever to enter
the dark, narrow room. Yet she never complained. After a
while she developed pains in her legs, which she admitted
were caused by her standing for hours peeping through the
holes she had picked in the screen through which to watch
the fun that went on in Sri Ramakrishna's room among the
devotees. Sri Ramakrishna knew that she did this, and always
made a point of leaving the door of his room open whenever
there was any fun, or dancing, or music going on there.

One day while Sarada was massaging Sri Ramakrishna's

feet, she suddenly looked up at him and asked: "How do you look upon me?" A natural and utterly feminine question, to which he gave the astounding answer: "The Mother who is worshipped in the temple, and the mother who gave birth to this body is now massaging my feet. I look upon you as the very manifestation of Motherhood." And indeed, in the years that followed the passing away of Sri Ramakrishna, it was to her, their "Holy Mother," that many of his young monks turned for counsel and advice. It was also upon her decision and with her blessing that Swami Vivekananda sailed for America to represent Hinduism at the World's Parliament of Religions at Chicago in 1893.

Sarada Devi had been staying at Dakshineswar with her husband about a year when one day he asked her to come to his room that evening at nine o'clock. She silently assented, asking no questions. Was not his will hers also? Had she not dedicated herself, heart, soul, and body to his service? Yet she could not help wondering what it was he wanted. It was such an odd hour to choose if he intended to scold her or instruct her in any matter, spiritual or domestic. She had tried always to be obedient to his teachings, and circumspect and right in all her conduct. Had her mother-in-law complained about anything, she wondered? If so, what? She seemed always to be satisfied with the food, and was never kept waiting, even for an instant, whenever she called, no matter how busy Sarada happened to be at the time. No, it couldn't be that. And why had he chosen this particular night? The whole place was alive with people and preparations for the *Kali Puja,* the worship of God in the form of Woman, which was to be celebrated that night. Would he not be taking some part in that?

All through the hours of waiting the one question "Why?" must have filled the mind of the young wife, and, as evening fell and the hour of her tryst drew nearer, surely her hands must have trembled as she brushed her long black hair and draped her red-bordered sari about her. And as she put on her earrings and a few of the bracelets her husband had given her, she probably recalled the criticism that had been made about her for wearing so many ornaments when her husband was a man of such strict renunciation! She soon learned that it was impossible to please everybody, but even so, she never again wore so many at a time.

The hour had come at last. Silently stealing through the crowds that had gathered in the temple grounds, Sarada reached her husband's room. Opening the door, she was amazed to see him already seated and beginning the worship which had been prepared beforehand. He appeared not to notice her arrival, and, not wishing to disturb him, she stood watching him as he performed the preliminary purification of the vessels and other things necessary for the ceremony. She noticed that the seat prepared for the Deity was vacant, and while she was vaguely wondering why, Sri Ramakrishna turned and motined to her to be seated there. Unquestioningly she obeyed. Like one in a dream she watched him, and soon her mind began to soar, until, as from a great way off she heard the invocation: "O Divine Mother, Eternal Virgin, Mistress of all powers and abode of all beauty, do Thou unlock for me the gate of perfection. Sanctifying the body and mind of this woman, do Thou manifest Thyself through her and do what is auspicious."

By the time the ritualistic part of the worship was over each of them had reached a state of deep absorption in which they realized their complete identity with Brahman, and so with each other. Thus was their marriage brought to its spiritual consummation.

Many hours passed before Sri Ramakrishna regained sufficient physical consciousness to enable him to complete the worship. When all was finished he prostrated himself to the embodied Deity before him, laying at her feet the fruits of all his years of austerities, his rosary, himself, and everything he owned, thereby sharing with her all his spiritual attainments, and making her a co-partner in his mission.

And Sarada Devi, what of her? Who can say? For silently, as an obedient and devoted wife, she had come. Silently she had accepted the worship of herself as the manifestation of the Divine Mother whose presence had been invoked in her by Sri Ramakrishna. Silently through this worship she had attained the highest spiritual union with her husband. And now she had stolen away, as silently as she had come.

# The Gospel of Sri Ramakrishna

## CHRISTOPHER WOOD

"THE GOSPEL OF SRI RAMAKRISHNA? It's awfully long—what's it all about? It certainly weighs enough! And what a strange looking man!"

"It's a fascinating piece of biography," I answered, "quite extraordinarily honest. And as for its being long, the truth about anyone is never dull. Try it; I don't think you'll be disappointed." And, I added to myself, maybe you'll get something more than pleasure out of it.

Which made me wonder what I, also an outsider, had got out of it! But, of course, there really are no outsiders. For the more I think about Ramakrishna and his disciples the more I am aware of a growing conviction that sooner or later, by some route or other, this is the way we all must go. "How lucky," one is tempted to say, "the disciples were to have such an inspiration before them; how easy it would have been—even for me!" forgetting that by the inevitable workings of Karma they had almost certainly previously earned their privilege.

But at least we have this book in which Ramakrishna and his disciples come vividly, unmistakably to life. M., the sympathetic author, has faithfully recorded all that he heard, and all that he saw during the last years of the Master. It is impossible to read the book with an open mind and not be convinced that Ramakrishna was a mystical genius; that he loved God because he could not do otherwise; and that because he so loved he reached union with God. Whether or not he was a divine incarnation does not seem to me to matter. . . . After all it is a question of degree. God is in all of us to a greater or lesser extent. But Ramakrishna was like a flaming torch pointing the way to God. He was in addition an extremely lovable man. He had such grace, such ease.

There was never any feeling of strain, as of someone torturing himself in order to be good. One feels instinctively that his way of life, his belief, his teaching are right; somehow they are inevitable, they need no argument. Yet Ramakrishna had a gift for words, as his parables and his conversation show; nor was he at a loss when assailed by intellectual philosophers. Somehow it all seems so simple. And in a way it is—if you want God enough you will find Him. Which do you want the most—"woman and gold," or God? Another side of Ramakrishna which seems to me important is that he had a sense of fun, and that he was joyous. It is a tragic mistake that the popular idea of a good person is so often that of someone rather dull and sombre, someone who rarely laughs. Whereas in actual fact it seems that the joy, the sheer pleasure even, of approaching to God surpasses anything we know. There are some minor actions of Ramakrishna faithfully reported by M. which may seem hard to understand. But one is such a prig, one is so sure of what behaviour is permissible or not! What does it matter! Ramakrishna repeatedly said of himself that he was a child. And since, as one of the parables points out, God takes on the characteristics of any being in which He is carnate, occasional childishness is a very small price to pay for an immeasurable help to mankind—the life of Ramakrishna.

And when at last, ceasing to reason, one stills one's mind, there is something more. For there steals over one a strange nostalgia, and almost-memory of something once known, long since forgotten. And one wonders, all too well aware of the answer, what has one in place of that which is lost? Vanity, illusion; just nothing.

# Vivekananda and Sarah Bernhardt

## CHRISTOPHER ISHERWOOD

IN PARIS, during the late summer of 1900, Swami Vivekananda had a conversation with the most famous woman
of the Western world. It was probably, but not certainly, their
first meeting. The two-volume Life of Vivekananda, by his
Eastern and Western disciples, refers somewhat vaguely to an
earlier occasion, in the United States, on which Bernhardt
"sought an interview with him" (that hardly sounds like the
imperious Sarah, who had made royalty take its hat off in
her presence!) "and expressed her admiration and intense
interest in the sublime teaching of the philosophy he so
eloquently and truly represented." The date given for this
encounter, 1895, would seem, in any case, to be wrong. Bernhardt was not in the States that year, though she visited them
for a six-month tour in 1896. Moreover, Swamiji himself,
writing in 1900 about the people he has met in Paris, particularly mentions that he and Madame Calvé, the singer,
were previously acquainted, but speaks of Bernhardt as
though they had just been introduced.

His correspondent was Swami Trigunatita, back home in
India, and the tone of these travel-letters, which were intended for publication, is instructive, gossipy, explosive, fa-
cetious, affectionate and prophetic by turns: they are among
the most characteristic things Vivekananda ever wrote. "Madame Bernhardt," he tells his brother-monk, "is an aged
lady; but when she steps on the stage after dressing, her
imitation of the age and sex of the role she plays is perfect!
A girl, or a boy—whatever part you want her to play, she is
an exact representation of that. And that wonderful voice!
People here say her voice has the ring of silver strings!"

In a couple of months the "aged lady" was going to be fifty-six years old. Even the unkind camera shows us that, "on the stage after dressing," she did not look a day over thirty. Her photograph in the role of *L'Aiglon*, the Duke of Reichstadt, which she played for the first time in March of that year, presents an astonishingly slender and erect little personage in a riding-coat and high boots with spurs, neither boy nor girl, woman nor man, sexless, ageless, and altogether impossible by daylight, outside the walls of a theater. Some later references in another of the letters to the story of Napoleon's tragic son suggest that Vivekananda must almost certainly have seen Sarah in this, her greatest dramatic triumph after *La Dame aux Camélias*.

Bernhardt was then on the final peak of her mountainous career. Her acting was probably better than it had ever been before: better, certainly, than in the nineties, when her hit-or-miss noisiness, ranting and hamming had provoked the brilliant scolding of the young theater-critic Bernard Shaw, and his unfavorable comparisons between her and the more modern restraint of Eleanora Duse. She had disciplined herself, artistically and emotionally. The crazy days of her publicity—of the balloon-trip, the coffin, and the shooting of the St. Louis Bay bridge—were far behind her. The shameful tragedy of her marriage with Damala had been ended, long ago, by his death from morphine poisoning. Her extravagance was still immense, but so were her earnings. And the accident in Rio de Janeiro which was to result in her gradual crippling was still five years ahead.

Swamiji seems to have been taken round to visit her in her dressing-room at the theater after a performance. One wonders who introduced them, what word was used to describe the Swami's occupation to the actress, and whether she had already heard of him. "Madame Bernhardt," writes Vivekananda, "has a special regard for India; she tells me again and again that our country is *'très ancien, très civilisé'*—"very ancient and very civilised." There must have been a gleam in Swamiji's eye as he politely received this flattering information.

They talked, as was natural, of the only play Sarah had ever produced with an Indian setting. It was *Izéil*, by Morand and Silvestre, an expensive flop. Bernhardt had always obstinately liked this piece, perhaps because it displayed her undoubted talent for theatrical décor. "She told me that for about a month she had visited every museum and made herself acquainted with the men and women, and their dress, the streets and bathing ghats and everything relating to India."

"Madame Bernhardt," the letter concludes, "has a very strong desire to visit India. '*C'est mon rêve*—It is the dream of my life,' she says. Again, the Prince of Wales has promised to take her over to a tiger and elephant hunting excursion. But then she said, she must spend some two lacs of rupees if she went to India! She is of course in no want of money. '*La divine Sarah*'—the divine Sarah—is her name—how can she want money?—She who never travels but by a special train! That pomp and luxury many a prince of Europe cannot afford to indulge in! One can only secure a seat in her performance by paying double the fees, and that a month in advance! Well, she is not going to suffer want of money! But Sarah Bernhardt is given to spending lavishly. Her travel to India is therefore put off for the present."

Underneath these few mock-serious, bantering sentences, one senses the warmth of an immediate sympathy and liking. You can picture Swamiji sitting opposite the vivid, Semitic little Frenchwoman, large and jolly, his amused glance taking in the whole luxurious setting, the jewels, the mirrors, the silks, the cosmetics, the marvelous robes. Here, as in all women everywhere, he saluted his own daughter, sister, mother: here, as always, he bowed to the eternal Godhead, beneath yet another of those queer disguises which bewilder our wanderings toward Self-realisation. Here, also, he surely recognized, to an unusual degree, the virtue he prized so highly: courage. Courage was, perhaps, the one quality which these fantastically dissimilar personalities had in common: the courage which had supported Vivekananda in the blackest hours of spiritual torment, of his Master's loss, of all the early struggles and trials of the Order, and which had never deserted him in the jungle or the mountains or the drawing-rooms of American millionaires: the courage which had nerved Sarah in her battles to raise her child, in her work during the siege of Paris, in her defence of Dreyfus, in her return to the stage at the age of seventy-two after the amputation of her right leg. Swamiji must have been aware of this, and loved her for it.

And how did Bernhardt think of him? Perhaps, curiously enough, as a kind of colleague. Had not he, also, appeared triumphantly before the public? Many actors and actresses, including Sarah herself as Joan of Arc, have represented saints—at any rate, to the satisfaction of the audience beyond the footlights. Swamiji, on the other hand, with his superb presence and sonorous voice, might well have been mistaken for a great actor.

In a photograph of this period, we see how the eyes of the young sannyasin, burning almost intolerably with mingled devotion and doubt, have softened and deepened in the face of the mature man. The big lips and the lines spreading from the wide nostrils have a curve of watchful humor, in which there is neither irony, nor bitterness, nor resignation—only a great calm, like the sea, with certainty dawning over it, an absolute, arising sun. "Are you never serious, Swamiji?" somebody asked him, rather reproachfully, and was answered: "Oh, yes. When I have the belly-ache." Even this was an overstatement; for the smiling, joking Vivekananda of 1900 was already a very sick man.

He and Bernhardt never saw each other again. In October, the Swami's party left Paris for Austria, the Balkans and Egypt, whence he sailed to India, arriving home at the Belur monastery early in December. Thus ended his last journey to the West. The longer journey, also, was nearly over. One day in July 1902, wishing perhaps to spare his friends the agony of a goodbye, he passed, by stealth as it were, into *samadhi*, and did not come back.

Sarah survived him for twenty-one years, survived the first world-war, lived on into the era of Chaplin and Pickford and the Keystone Cops, appeared in two or three movies herself, and died in action, getting ready to rehearse a new play.

In the half-dozen Bernhardt biographies I have been able to consult, the name of Vivekananda is not even mentioned. In fact, this brief anecdote of their meeting, with its exchange of conventional small-talk and politeness, would seem to have no point whatsoever. That is just what makes it so fascinating and so significant. When poets or politicians foregather, we expect epigrams and aphorisms; for talk is their medium of expression. But talk is not, primarily, the medium of the man of illumination. His way of approach is more direct, more subtle and more penetrating. He makes contact with you below the threshold of everyday awareness. No matter whether he speaks of the Prince of Wales, or of God, or only smiles and says nothing; your whole life will be, to some degree, changed from that moment on.

That is why—despite the biographers' silence, and the lack of high-class philosophical conversation—one dare not say that Swamiji's visit made no great or lasting impression upon Sarah. The spotlight of history, which reveals a tiny area of surface-action so brightly, cannot help us here. All we can venture to say is this: "One day, the two human mysteries known to this world as Bernhardt and Vivekananda met, exchanged certain signals which we do not understand, and parted, we do not know why. All we *do* know is that their meeting, like every other event in this universe, did not take place by accident."

# Man and Reality

## Aldous Huxley

FOR THOSE WHO live within its limits, the lights of the city are the only luminaries of the high sky. The street lamps eclipse the stars, and the glare of the whisky advertisements reduces even the moonlight to an almost invisible irrelevance.

The phenomenon is symbolical, a parable in action. Mentally and physically, man is the inhabitant, during the greatest part of his life, of a purely human and, so to say, home-made universe, scooped by himself out of the immense, non-human cosmos which surrounds it, and without which neither it nor he could exist. Within this private catacomb we build up for ourselves a little world of our own, constructed of a strange assortment of materials—interests and "ideals," words and technologies, cravings and day-dreams, artifacts and institutions, imaginary gods and demons. Here, among the magnified projections of our own personalities, we perform our curious antics and perpetrate our crimes and lunacies, we think the thoughts and feel the emotions appropriate to our man-made environments, we cherish the crazy ambitions that alone make sense in a madhouse. But all the time, in spite of the radio noises and the neon tubes, night and the stars are there—just beyond the last bus stop, just above the canopy of illuminated smoke. This is a fact which the inhabitants of the human catacomb find it all too easy to forget; but whether they forget or remember, a fact it always remains. Night and the stars are always there; the other, non-human world, of which the stars and night are but the symbols, persists and is the real world.

*Man, proud man, drest in a little brief authority—*
*Most ignorant of what he's most assured,*

> *His glassy essence—like an angry ape,*
> *Plays such fantastic tricks before high heaven*
> *As make the angels weep.*

So wrote Shakespeare in the only one of his plays which reveals any deep concern with the ultimate spiritual realities. It is the "glassy essence" of man that constitutes the reality of which he is most assured, the reality which sustains him and in virtue of which he lives. And this glassy essence is of the same kind as the Clear Light, which is the essence of the universe. Within us, this "spark," this "uncreated depth of the Soul," this *atman,* remains unsullied and unflawed, however fantastic the tricks we may play—just as, in the outer world, night and the stars remain themselves in spite of all the Broadways and Piccadillies, all the searchlights and the incendiary bombs.

The great non-human world, which exists simultaneously within us and without, is governed by its own divine laws— laws which we are free to obey or disobey. Obedience leads to liberation; disobedience to a deeper enslavement to misery and evil, to a prolongation of our existence in the likeness of angry apes. Human history is a record of the conflict between two forces—on the one hand, the silly and criminal presumption that makes man ignorant of his glassy essence; on the other, the recognition that, unless he lives in conformity with the greater cosmos, he himself is utterly evil, and his world, a nightmare. In this interminable conflict, now one side gains the upper hand, and now the other. At the present time we are witnessing the temporary triumph of the specifically human side of man's nature. For some time now we have chosen to believe, and to act on the belief, that our private world of neon tubes and incendiaries was the only real world, that the glassy essence in us did not exist. Angry apes, we have imagined ourselves, because of our simian cleverness, to be angels—to be indeed, more than angels, to be gods, creators, framers of our destiny. What are the consequences of this triumph of the purely human side of man? The headlines in the morning papers furnish an unequivocal reply: the destruction of human values either by death or degradation or perversion to the ends of politics, revolution and war. When we think presumptuously that we are, or shall become in some future Utopian state, "men like gods," then in fact we are in mortal danger of becoming devils, capable only (however exalted our "ideals" may be, however beautifully worked out our plans and blue-prints) of ruining our world and destroying ourselves. The triumph of humanism is the defeat of humanity.

Fortunately, as Whitehead has pointed out, the moral order of the universe consists precisely in the fact that evil is self-stultifying. When evil is given free rein, either by individuals or by societies, it always ends by committing suicide. The nature of this suicide may be either physical or psychological. The evil individuals or societies may be literally killed off, or reduced to impotence through mere exhaustion; or else they may reach a condition, if the orgy of evil is too much prolonged, of such weariness and disgust that they find themselves forced, by a kind of sanguinary *reductio ad absurdum*, to surrender to the obvious truth that men are not gods, that they cannot control the destiny even of their own home-made world and that the only way to the peace, happiness and freedom they so ardently desire is through the knowledge of and obedience to the laws of the greater, non-human cosmos.

"The further you go towards the East," Sri Ramakrishna was fond of saying, "the further you go away from the West." This is one of those apparently childish remarks, which we meet with so often among the writings and recorded sayings of religious teachers. But it is an apparent childishness that masks a real profundity. Within this absurd little tautology there lies, in a state of living, seminal latency, a whole metaphysic, a complete programme of action. It is, of course, the same philosophy and the same way of life as were referred to by Jesus in those sayings about the impossibility of serving two masters, and the necessity of seeking first the kingdom of God and waiting for all the rest to be added. Egoism and alter-egoism (or the idolatrous service of individuals, groups and causes with which we identify ourselves so that their success flatters our own ego) cut us off from the knowledge and experience of reality. Nor is this all; they cut us off also from the satisfaction of our needs and the enjoyment of our legitimate pleasures. It is a matter of empirical experience and observation that we cannot for long enjoy what we desire as human beings, unless we obey the laws of that greater, non-human cosmos of which, however much we may, in our proud folly, forget the fact, we are integral parts. Egoism and alter-egoism advise us to remain firmly ensconced in the West, looking after our own human affairs. But if we do this, our affairs will end by going to pot; and if our alter-egoistic "ideals" have been very lofty, we shall, as likely as not, find ourselves liquidating our neighbors on a gigantic scale—and, incidentally, being liquidated by them. Whereas if we ignore the counsels of egoism and alter-egoism, and resolutely march towards the divine East, we shall create for ourselves the possibility of receiving the grace of enlightenment and, at the same time, we shall find that existence in our physical, Western home is a great deal more satisfactory than it was when we devoted our attention primarily to the improvement of our human lot. In a word, things in the West will go better because, as we go towards the East, we are further from them—less attached to them, less passionately concerned about them, therefore less liable to start liquidating people on account of them. But, alas, as the author of the "Imitation" remarks: "All men desire peace, but few there are who desire the things that make for peace."

A measure of detachment from egoism and alter-egoism is essential even if we would make contact with the secondary aspects of cosmic reality. Thus, in order to be fruitful, science must be pure. That is to say, the man of science must put aside all thoughts of personal advantage, of "practical" results, and concentrate exclusively on the task of discovering the facts and co-ordinating them in an intelligible theory. In the long run, alter-egoism is as fatal to science as egoism. Typical of alter-egoistic science is that secretive, nationalistic research which accompanies and precedes modern war. Such science is dedicated to its own stultification and destruction, as well as to the destruction of every other kind of human good.

These are not the only detachments which the man of science must practice. He must liberate himself not only from the cruder egoistic and alter-egoistic passions, but also from his purely intellectual prejudices—from the trammels of traditional thought-patterns, and even of common sense. Things are not what they seem; or, to be more accurate, they are not only what they seem, but very much else besides. To act upon this truth, as the man of science must constantly do, is to practice a kind of intellectual mortification.

Analogous mortifications and detachments have to be practiced by the artist, when he is making his attempt to discover and express that divine relationship between the parts of the cosmos, which we call beauty. Similarly, on the plane of ethical conduct, the manifestations of goodness cannot be made by oneself or elicited from others unless there is an inhibition of personal and alter-egoistic cravings and aversions.

When we pass from the realm of the manifested and embodied aspects of reality to that of reality itself, we shall find that there must be an intensification of detachment, a widening and deepening of mortification. The symbol of death and rebirth recurs incessantly in the sayings and writings of the masters of the spiritual life. If God's kingdom is to come, man's must go; the old Adam has to perish in order that the new man may be born. In other words, ascetical self-mortification, at once physical, emotional, ethical, and intellectual, is one of the indispensable conditions of enlightenment, of the realization of divine immanence and transcendence. True, no amount of ascetic practices or of spiritual exercises can automatically guarantee enlightenment, which is always in the nature of a grace. The most we are justified in saying is that the egoism and alter-egoism, which ascetic practices are designed to root out, automatically perpetuate the state of non-enlightenment. We cannot see the moon and the stars so long as we choose to remain within the aura of street lamps and whisky advertisements. We cannot even hope to discover what is happening in the East, if we turn our feet and faces towards the West.

# Words and Reality

## ALDOUS HUXLEY

*Wishing to entice the blind,*
*The Buddha has playfully let words escape his golden mouth;*
*Heaven and earth are ever since filled with entangling briars.*
*Oh, my good worthy friends gathered here,*
*If you desire to listen to the thunderous voice of the Dharma,*
*Exhaust your words, empty your thoughts,*
*For then you may come to recognize this one essence.*

SO RUNS ONE OF THOSE paradoxical utterances, of which the masters of Zen Buddhism were so fond. In its startling and rather perverse way, it sums up the whole thorny problem of the relationship between direct religious experience and the words in which that experience is described, explained and related to other experiences in a generalized philosophy. Obviously the Buddha and the other founders of religions never had any desire to play practical jokes on bewildered humanity; nevertheless, the fact remains that their words have served to "entice the blind" as well as to enlighten, to "fill heaven and earth with entangling briars" as well as to point out the path of liberation. The history of even the most advanced religions is horribly checkered. Their teachings have inspired some men to sanctity; for others, they have served as the justification for every kind of destructive and diabolic activity. The compassionate saint and the ruthless crusader, the heresy-hunter and the contemplative are all characteristic products of religion, and all derive inspiration for their actions from the words recorded in some sacred scripture. In other, equally characteristic cases, the contrast is less extreme. The same words inspire one man to become a mystic and another, a theologian—inspire one, that is to say, to give up words in an attempt to get to know God directly,

278

inspire another to devote himself to an intensive analysis of words in the hope of getting to know *about* God, indirectly, through discursive reasoning. All men of great religious insight are agreed in regarding the theologian's preoccupation with words as being almost as dangerous to the individual's chance of liberation as are the preoccupations of the crusader and the inquisitor with violent action. Its evil effects on others will not, of course, be so immediate as in the latter cases; but its indirect effects in the way of justifying new generations of inquisitors and crusaders and in involving earnest seekers yet unborn in the toils of entangling verbal briars, may be considerable and grave.

Buddhas, I repeat, have no deliberate "wish to entice the blind"; but by the mere act of "letting words escape their golden mouth" they produce a situation which makes it almost seem *as if* they were playing a practical joke on humanity. They have no choice in the matter. For the principal difference between men and the animals consists precisely in the fact that men make use of conceptual language and the brutes do not. A human being who has never learned to speak, and who has therefore been unable to communicate with his fellows, is not fully human. (The authenticated cases of children brought up by animals make this abundantly clear.) The human world is in large measure a verbal world. That is why it is so full of "entangling briars"—briars which are nonexistent for beings on the animal level. But that is also why it is a world from which it is possible, as it is not for the inhabitants of the animal world, to go forward towards liberation and enlightenment.

"There is really nothing to argue about in this teaching," writes another Zen master; "any arguing is sure to go against the intent of it. Doctrines given up to dispute and argumentation lead by themselves to birth and death." This statement conveys a profound and important truth. But it is a truth of which we should know nothing unless it had been formulated in words, which are the raw materials of dispute and argument. Between man and man there can, normally, be no communication except in words; and since the duty of communicating the truth to all who may desire to know it is incumbent upon those who possess even an inkling of its nature, it follows that, in spite of the dangers inherent in making statements which can never be fully accurate or adequate, words must be used. The final chapter of the Tao Te King opens with the saying:

> *He who knows does not speak,*
> *He who speaks does not know.*

Taken quite literally, this is false. Most or all of those who knew have spoken, and some speakers at least have known. Nevertheless it remains true that most speakers do not know and that they speak for the wrong reasons—to make an effect, to earn praise, to win power, to force an opinion upon their hearers. Conversely, the knowers who spoke have always been well aware that their words were inadequate to the known reality about which they were trying to talk.

In "The Diamond Sutra" one may find some very interesting remarks on the relationship between experience and the words in which it is the duty of the knower to hand on his experience.

"The Lord Buddha addressed Subhuti, saying: What think you? Has the Lord Buddha attained to supreme spiritual wisdom? Or has he a system of doctrine which can be specifically formulated?

"Subhuti replied, saying: As I understand the meaning of the Lord Buddha's discourse, he has no system of doctrine which can be specifically formulated, nor can the Lord Buddha express, in explicit terms, a form of knowledge which can be described as supreme spiritual wisdom. And why? Because what the Lord Buddha adumbrated in terms of the law is transcendental and inexpressible. Being a purely spiritual concept, it is neither consonant with law, nor synonymous with anything apart from the law. Thus is exemplified the manner in which wise disciples and holy Buddhas, regarding intuition as the law of their minds, severally attained to different planes of spiritual wisdom."

On later pages we find two other passages relevant to the point under discussion. Here is the first. "The Lord Buddha again inquired of Subhuti, saying: What think you? May an Arhat thus meditate within himself, I have obtained the condition of an Arhat? Subhuti answered, saying: No, honoured of the worlds! And why? Because there is not in reality a condition synonymous with the term Arhat. Honoured of the worlds! if an Arhat thus meditates within himself, I have obtained the condition of an Arhat, there would be obvious recurrence of such arbitrary concepts as an entity, a being, a living being and a personality."

The second passage runs as follows: "The Lord Buddha addressed Subhuti, saying: If a disciple, having immeasurable spheres filled with the seven treasures, bestowed these in the exercise of charity; and if a disciple, whether man or woman, having aspired to supreme spiritual wisdom, selected from this scripture a stanza comprising four lines, then rigorously observed it, studied it and diligently explained it to others; the cumulative merit of such a disciple would be relatively greater than that of the other.

"In what attitude of mind should it be diligently explained to others? Not assuming the persistence or reality of earthly phenomena, but in the conscious blessedness of a mind at perfect rest."

These passages provide, by implication, the solution to the problem which was posed in the Zen paradox cited at the beginning of this paper. Let me try to state it as clearly as I can. In spiritual matters, knowledge is dependent upon being; as we are, so we know. Hence words have different meanings for people on different levels of being. The utterances of the enlightened are interpreted by the unenlightened in terms of their own character, and are used by them to rationalize and justify the wishes and actions of the Old Adam.

Another danger arises when the words, as words, are taken too seriously, when men devote their lives to analyzing, explaining and developing the utterances of the enlightened ones, imagining that this activity is in some Pickwickian way the equivalent of becoming enlightened. "As for the philosophers," we read in Yoka Daishi's "Song of Enlightenment," "they are intelligent enough, but wanting a Prajna (illumination). They take an empty fist as containing something real, and the pointing finger for the object pointed at." Taken too seriously, theology may lead men away from

the truth instead of towards it. At the same time it is one of
the most fascinating of studies, and as such, may easily become one of the most God-eclipsing of intellectual distractions. Nor is this all: being a theologian is commonly
regarded as a highly creditable occupation; consequently it
is fatally easy for those who make it their business to manipulate theological language to develop a deadly spiritual
pride. (The Arhat, who meditates on the fact that he is an
Arhat, thereby ceases to be an Arhat.)

Nevertheless, in spite of all these dangers inherent in talking about religious experience, it is the duty of anyone who
has had such experience "to explain it diligently to others"
—provided always that two conditions be fulfilled. First, he
must not imagine that he can do more than indirectly hint
at the nature of intuitively known reality; he must take care
not to be deceived into believing that he has a system of
doctrine which *is* the truth, or which completely expresses
the truth. Secondly, he must speak in the right spirit and
for the right reasons—with a mind at perfect rest and in
order that the truth may be known and glorified. Even so, it
is possible that his recorded words may sooner or later serve
to "entice the blind and fill the world with entangling
briars." But this risk must be taken; for unless it is taken,
those capable of forming a correct idea of the truth will
never have a chance of hearing about it and advancing towards enlightenment. Meanwhile, it is the business of the
theologian to try (avoiding as best he can the peculiar pitfalls
which beset his path) to work on the problem of finding the
most adequate words in which to adumbrate the transcendent and inexpressible. There have been periods in the history
of the various cultures, when the language of spirituality was
clear, accurate and exhaustive. At the present time it is muddled, inadequate to the facts and dangerously equivocal. Lacking a proper vocabulary, people find it hard, not only to
think about the most important issues of life, but even to
realize that these issues exist. Words may cause confusion
and create entanglements; but the absence of words begets a
total darkness.

# Some Aspects of Buddha's Thought

## SWAMI PRABHAVANANDA

### 1. RELIGION AS REALIZATION

WE READ in one of the Buddhistic Scriptures, "The Tathagata has no theories." If any one came to Buddha with the intent of merely satisfying an idle curiosity with respect to metaphysical problems, he was certain to be disappointed. We read in one of the Buddhistic records of an enquirer who came to discuss theories of the soul, the world, and the problem of knowledge. Buddha replied that if one has been wounded by a poisoned arrow and refuses to accept help from the physician until he has learned the exact nature of the man who wounded him, to what caste he belonged, his stature and his complexion, such a one would indeed be foolish. Some questions Buddha dismissed as useless and unnecessary, while others he said could not be answered in logical terms. Just so do the Upanishads admonish us "to give up vain talk, for it brings weariness to the tongue." And they further speak of the truth "which words cannot express." "The mind," they say, "comes away baffled, unable to reach it."

Moreover, Buddha, like the sages of the Upanishads, insisted that one should experience the truth for one's self. In the Upanishads we read: "I have known the self-luminous Being beyond all darkness. You also, knowing the truth, attain to your immortality. There is no other way." And Buddha says: "For Brahman I know, and the world of Brahman, and the path which leadeth unto it. Yea, I know it even as one who has entered the Brahman world, and has been born within it." And the truth of Brahman is to be known by one's own exertion in one's own soul. For we read in the teachings of Buddha: "Therefore, O Ananda, be ye lamps unto yourselves. Be ye a refuge to yourselves. Betake yourselves to no external refuge. Hold fast to the truth as a lamp. Hold fast as a refuge to the truth. And whosoever, Ananda, either now or after I am dead, shall be a lamp unto themselves, and a refuge unto themselves, shall betake themselves to no external refuge, but holding fast to the truth as their lamp, and holding fast as their refuge to the truth, shall look not for refuge to any one besides themselves—it is they, Ananda, among my bhikkhus, who shall reach the very topmost height! But they must be anxious to learn." [1]

"But they must be anxious to learn." One must experiment to know the truth—an attitude towards the personal life of the spirit held by all the great religious teachers of India. For them essential religion does not lie in dogma or creed, nor in doctrines or theories, but in experience alone. From the Vedic age to our own, every leader has declared this primary truth: that one must realize God in his own soul.

And Buddha, for all his apparent negation, belongs to the group of Indian teachers who have affirmed in this way the life of the soul. He undertakes to show the way to "quiescence, knowledge, supreme wisdom, and Nirvana"—not in another life but here and now. The late Professor Irving Babbitt of Harvard University, a deep student and strong admirer of the Hindu saint, remarks:

"One should add that the 'Nirvana here and now' (Samditthakam Nibbanam) of the Buddhist has much in common with the 'release in this life' (jivanmukti) of the Hindu philosopher. One may, however, affirm confidently that no religious teacher was ever more opposed than Buddha in his scheme of salvation to every form of postponement and procrastination. He would have his followers take the cash and let the credit go—though the cash in this case is not the immediate pleasure but the immediate peace."

Philosophically, the Buddhist nirvana is identical with the *moksha* of the Hindu philosophers, which is the release from bondage to karma and ignorance and the attainment of the kingdom of heaven within. I have purposely used the phrase

[1] *Maha-Parinivvana Sutta.*

"attainment of the kingdom of heaven within," in order to remind Western readers that in reality there is no difference in the ultimate goal between Hinduism, Buddhism, and Christianity. The moksha of the Hindus, the nirvana of the Buddhists, and the "kingdom of heaven within" of the Christians are really one and the same, though unfortunately the exponents of Christianity would have us believe otherwise. The late Mr. Chesterton, for example, attempts to show the superiority of Christian over Buddhist saints, declaring, "The Buddhist saint always has his eyes shut, while the Christian saint always has them very wide open. The Buddhist is looking with peculiar intentness inward. The Christian is staring with frantic intentness outward." Professor Babbitt has beautifully met Mr. Chesterton's effusion: "But a saint," he remarks, "whether Buddhist or Christian, who knows his business as a saint, is rightly meditative and in proportion to the rightness of his meditation is the depth of his peace. We have it on an authority which Mr. Chesterton is bound to respect that the kingdom of heaven is within us. It would be interesting to hear Mr. Chesterton explain how a saint can find that which is within by 'staring frantically outwards.' Failing like many others to discriminate between romanticism and religion, Mr. Chesterton has managed to misrepresent both Buddhism and Christianity. The truth is, that though Christianity from the start was more emotional in its temper than Buddhism, and though an element of nostalgia entered into it from an early period, it is at one in the final emphasis with the older religion. In both faiths this emphasis is on the peace that passeth understanding."

## 2. IS BUDDHISM PESSIMISTIC?

The Four Noble Truths which Buddha taught are these: (1) that there is suffering; (2) that there is a cause of suffering; (3) that suffering can be overcome; and (4) that there is a way to overcome it.

Because Buddha taught that the world is full of suffering, he has often been called pessimistic. But that is a mistake. If he drew attention to the misery in life, it was only in order to direct the soul toward Freedom. So long as we cling to sense experience, he knew, so long shall we fail to discover eternal truth; it is therefore well that we should realize as speedily and vividly as possible the sorrow which is at the core of such experience. Death, for example: let us face that. "Not in the sky"—so reads the Dhammapada—"nor in the depths of the ocean, nor in the caves of the mountain, nor in any place in the whole world may a man dwell without being overpowered by death." And again: "How is there laughter, how is there joy, as the world is always burning? Why do you not seek a light, ye who are surrounded by darkness? This body is wasted, full of sickness and pain; this heap of corruption breaks to pieces; life indeed ends in death."

In this recognition of suffering Buddhism but joins hands with all the religions of the world. Had the joys of the flesh proved entirely satisfactory, the need either of religious consolation or even of inquiry into spiritual truths would not have been apparent. Did not Jesus cry out to her who gave him water from the well: "Whosoever drinketh of this water shall thirst again?" Thus it is, he meant to say, with the pleasures of the world. And then he went on: "But whosoever drinketh of the water that I shall give him shall never thirst; but the water that I shall give him shall be in him a well of water springing up into everlasting life." In like manner the Upanishads declare, "There is no happiness in the finite. In the Infinite alone is happiness."

If by pessimism, therefore, be meant full acknowledgment of the obvious fact that the world bears a burden of sorrow, that joy is but a momentary experience, that mortal life ends inevitably in death, then Buddhism is clearly pessimistic. And if by pessimism is meant, further, that true, unalloyed happiness cannot be achieved in a finite world unless it be achieved by overcoming all worldliness, then is Buddhism clearly pessimistic. But likewise pessimistic, it must be added, are all other religions.

It all amounts to this. If we would steadfastly seek after eternal happiness and peace, we must necessarily look upon the momentary pleasures of the world with indifference, knowing that they end in suffering. Especially did Buddha look upon worldly pleasures as painful—so painful that the wise man must renounce them. His message was not essentially different from that of Christ when he said, "Except a man be born again he cannot enter the kingdom of heaven" —where to be born again means to overcome the world, and thus to find the peace that passeth understanding. The desire to overcome the world and attain perfect peace cannot arise in one who still clings to the lusts of the flesh. We read in the *Katha Upanishad* the story of Nachiketas, who went to the King of Death to learn of immortality. But before Nachiketas could be taught the truth, the King of Death wished by a test to discover if it was really a thirst for knowledge that filled the heart of the young boy. So he promised him all earthly wealth to make him happy. But Nachiketas replied, "Keep thou thy houses, keep dance and song for thyself. Shall we be happy with these things when we see thee, O Death!" "Blessed are they," said Jesus, "which do hunger and thirst after righteousness, for they shall be filled."

Buddha's doctrine, then, is not one of despair, since his insistence is upon rising above the world of the senses into a realm of eternal peace. The word *Buddha* itself means "enlightened," "awakened."

Psychologically, Buddha regards this world of sense experience as a dream world. If we compare our state with that of a Buddha, we are living in a world of dreams. The saying of Goethe, the wise man of the world, that "Error stands in the same relation to truth as sleeping to waking," finds its religious counterpart in the almost identical words of the Gita: "What is sleep to the ignorant, that, to the wise, is waking."

# Buddha and Bergson

## Swami Prabhavananda

With respect to the world of mind and matter, Buddha has very forcefully declared that all things are in a state of constant flux. Nothing in the universe is permanent. It is for this reason that Buddha makes his reiterated declaration that the world is full of suffering. In one of his dialogues he converses upon this subject with his disciples thus: "And that which is transient, O monks, is it painful or pleasant?" "Painful."

Because of the transitory and changing nature of the world, Buddha does not say that it is real nor does he say that it is unreal, but that it is somewhere between the real and the unreal.

"This world, O Kaccana, generally proceeds on a duality, on the 'it is' and the 'it is not.' But, O Kaccana, whoever perceives in truth and wisdom, how things originate in the world, in his eyes there is no 'it is not.' Whoever, Kaccana, perceives in truth and wisdom how things pass away in this world, in his eyes there is no 'it is' in this world——'Everything is'——this is one extreme, O Kaccana. 'Everything is not'——is another extreme. The truth is the middle." [1]

Buddhistic literature employs the figure of the torch whirled rapidly round so as to create an illusion of a perfect circle of fire in order to illustrate the truth that the identity or permanency of anything in our experience is not real, but that this appearance of identity or permanency is caused by succession and constant flux. That is to say, an object never remains the same from moment to moment, but there exists the appearance of reality because of a series of successive states. Furthermore, an unchanging law called by Buddha dharma, continues to operate—the law of causation which

[1] Samyutta Nikaya.

makes for the basis of continuity and the appearance of identity. "I will teach you the dharma," says Buddha, "that being present, this becomes: from the arising of that, this arises. That being absent, this does not become: from the cessation of that, this ceases." [2]

The operation of this dharma or law of causation upon one state changes it into a successive state, and thus is created the ceaseless pulsation or continuous flux. Sir S. Radhakrishnan makes this comment on the doctrine of dharma:

"The causal evolution is not to be viewed as a mechanical succession of movements, in which case the world process becomes a series of extinctions and fresh creations, but is one state working itself up to another state or informing it with a ceaseless pulsation. It is the determination of the present by the past. Buddhism believes in transitive causation, where one state transmits its paccayasatti, or causal energy, to some newly conceived germ. Causal relations are of the type of the seed growing into a tree, where the one is necessary for the other." [3]

Buddha is not concerned with the philosophical explanation of this law of dharma nor is he interested in explaining the doctrine of flux. He simply states the psychological experience one has of the universe of flux and proceeds to a scientific analysis of it. "All are impermanent, body, sensation, perception, sankharas, and consciousness, all these are sorrow. They are not self." Both the world outside and the world within are in a state of constant flux.

Does a "being," a reality, something permanent, exist behind this ever-changing flux? The meaning and purpose of all philosophy and all religion alike, and of life, are bound up in the effort to find, in the words of the Upanishads, "the eternal amongst the non-eternals, the abiding joy in the midst of the fleeting pleasures of life." And in the midst of change there is, in the words of Buddha, the escape from sorrow in the cessation of the eternal flux as one attains "tranquillity, knowledge, supreme wisdom, and Nirvana."

Before we come to explain the nature of this attainment, let us repeat that Buddha does not assert a mere philosophy

[2] Majjhima Nikaya.
[3] "Indian Philosophy," by S. Radhakrishnan.

of the flux but one that will enable one to escape the flux. And herein lies the fundamental difference between Buddha and Western philosophers of the flux.[4]

Buddha's teachings have in fact often been mistakenly identified with the philosophy of flux as expounded by Bergson, Croce, and, to a certain degree, William James. This identification is especially true with respect to Bergson. Superficially indeed the two appear much alike but on deeper analysis they prove to be poles apart. According to Bergson, "the ultimate reality is an incessant flux, a creative evolution, or real duration." Buddha admits, it is true, that the universe of experience is in constant flux; but he does not admit that this incessant flux is the ultimate reality. The universe of flux, to Buddha, is neither real nor unreal. Bergson, on the other hand, revels in this flux, and his intuition, in Professor Babbitt's phrase, "whirls forever on the wheel of change," or, in Hindu parlance, "within the bonds of Maya." To Bergson "time" or "duration" is real, and we should accordingly strive to see things not *sub specie aeternitatis* but *sub specie durationis*. Buddha perceives the flux and seeks a way of escape by rising above time, space, and causation.

In Plato's words, "Too many of our modern philosophers in their search after the nature of things are always getting dizzy from constantly going round and round; and then they think that there is nothing stable or permanent, but only

[4] Compare Plato's doctrine of the One and the many. Compare also Shelley's great lines from "Adonais":

> "The One remains, the many change and pass:
> Heaven's light forever shines, Earth's shadows fly:
> Life, like a dome of many-coloured glass,
> Stains the white radiance of Eternity,
> Until Death tramples it to fragments."

Compare also Wordsworth's:

> "Even such a shell the universe itself
> Is to the ear of Faith; and there are times,
> I doubt not, when to you it doth impart
> Authentic tidings of invisible things;
> Of ebb and flow, and ever-enduring power;
> And central peace, subsisting at the heart
> Of endless agitation."

flux and motion and that the world is full of every sort of motion and change." And these words uttered centuries ago by the wisest of the Greeks may be justly applied to the modern votaries of the god Whirl. Buddha, like Plato, sought to find the state beyond the flux; Bhava-nirodha-nibbanam . . . "To withdraw from the flux is to attain Nirvana."

These philosophers—James and Bergson and Croce—have done great service to Western philosophy by pointing out that the ultimate reality cannot be discovered by the intellect alone, but they have egregiously failed to discover a way whereby one may rise above the reason and arrive at the very source of knowledge itself. It is true that both Bergson and Croce speak much of intuition, but this intuition of theirs is confined to the realm where "time" is supreme and a sense of the "many" prevails. Theirs is essentially a naturalistic interpretation of reality, that is, it issues entirely from the senses and the faculty of cognition. The Bergsonian *élan vital* is merely vital expansion within the universe of relativity and plurality and flux or change; i.e., within the bonds of Maya. Frankly, the use, or abuse, of this word intuition by the modern philosophers of the flux can only mean a sinking below the reason and the conscious mind into the realm of instinct which we share with the lower animals.

But all of this pseudo-intuition of Bergson and Croce has no relation to the Nirvana of Buddha, the Samadhi of the Yogis, and the Turiya or transcendental consciousness of the Upanishad. Nirvana is in fact the "state in which both sensations and ideas have ceased to be," in which "the sage is delivered from time." [5] It is a state of Shunnyata, wrongly translated as "nothingness," but which really means "the absence of subject-object relation." The Mandukya Upanishad describes Turiya which is similar to Buddhistic Nirvana: "Turiya is not that which is conscious of the subjective world, nor that which is conscious of the objective world, nor that which is conscious of both, nor that which is a mass of all sentiency, nor that which is simple consciousness, nor that which is insentient. It is unseen by the senses, not related to anything, incomprehensible to the mind, uninferable, unthinkable, indescribable, essentially of the nature of

[5] Maha-Parinivvana Sutta, VI, 12.

consciousness constituting the Self alone, negation of all phenomena, the Peaceful, all-bliss, and the non-dual."

The Nirvana of the Buddhists and the Turiya of the Upanishads are not conceptual in that they are beyond the relation of subject and object or of the knower and the object of knowledge, beyond time, space, and causation. In sum, they refer to consciousness itself without the contents of consciousness—something from the relative point of view unthinkable and inconceivable but yet attainable. They are consciousness itself, beyond all awareness of flux and relativity, not attainable by any *élan vital* or by the submersion of the self below the level of consciousness; rather are they attained by a *frein vital* (inner check), a control of the conscious and the subconscious mind, and, by a supreme act of self-restraint and of meditation, a rising above and beyond reason. So long as we remain upon the level of the flux, and experience only the objects within the flux, we are asleep. "How many people," asks Buddha, "eat, drink, and get married; buy, sell, and build; make contracts and attend to their fortunes; have friends and enemies, pleasures and pains; are born, grow up, live, and die—but asleep?" To attain Nirvana is simply to break this sleep in which we experience only the flux and to wake to an intuition of the One.

Buddha, like all the philosophers of India, believed in the Law of Karma and in reincarnation as the working out of this Law, in that we are bound to the wheel of birth and death until we finally break our chains and attain illumination in Nirvana. Then no longer is there birth and death as we pass into a state of being that is indescribable and unthinkable in concrete terms. Buddha even refused to define in positive terms what he meant by the word Nirvana. To define is to limit, and definition is possible only of something within the limits of "time, space, and causation."

But though Nirvana must remain indefinable, yet we know the effects it produces in life.

Professor Babbitt in this connection remarks in substance as follows: " 'By their fruits ye shall know them,' said the Divine One of Galilee. And St. Paul has named these fruits as follows: 'Love, joy, peace, long-suffering, gentleness, goodness, faith, meekness, temperance' (Galatians 5:22-23). Asoka, the great Buddhist Emperor of India who was like St. Paul as a founder of a Buddhistic canon, carved in stone these fruits: 'Compassion, liberality, truth, purity, gentleness, peace, joyousness, saintliness, self-control.' "

Thus we may see that, however divergent the paths and however wide the approach, we may know experimentally that they all lead to the same ultimate goal, the release of the human spirit from the wheel of change and the refining of our individual lives through the development of similar qualities in our several natures. This central truth, then, lies at the heart of every religion, in the words of the Upanishads, final attainment of "infinite knowledge, infinite freedom, and infinite peace." "Come unto me, all ye that labour and are heavy-laden, and I will give you rest," and "My peace I give unto you," said Christ. And Buddha uttered these words: "His thought is quiet, quiet are his word and deed, when he has obtained freedom by true wisdom, then he has become a quiet man."

# The Philosophia Perennis

## GERALD HEARD

THOSE WHO ARE INTERESTED in Vedanta and the West are naturally always on the lookout for the rising of one more of those bridges which must, in this generation of birth-and-death, make possible a new understanding between men of good will in East and West. For, speaking as a Westerner—and it is a judgment with which an Oriental would doubtless agree—the state of our Occidental culture today much resembles that critical path into which the older West found itself precipitated in the second century of the Christian era. Then, an Oriental religion, the last of many Oriental competitors for the prize of the Roman Empire, had begun to win converts in a surprising way. The Imperial Court was interested, a possible heir to the throne was found to be involved: neither patrician nor slave was safe from the contagion of the new faith. But faith without a frame of reference is always a wine without a bottle. As we know, the frame of reference for Christianity, the form in which that faith became the philosophy and culture known as Christendom, was found in Greek thought. With that amalgam the world in the West remains content until today. Now in our generation that system has reached exhaustion, no longer answering the intellectual questions of men nor giving a sanction to their propriety. Hence our crisis. And, once again, at the moment of crisis, out of the East has come a light and a faith—or perhaps we should say that, though the light is one, it has come and is coming to us like a rainbow, a thing not only of hope but of many colors.

This brief note is to draw the attention of others similarly interested, who may not have come across this particular thinker, to the work of Dr. Coomaraswamy. For some time, thoughtful people have been gathering the articles of this writer. They reveal an immense scholarship which is not only thoroughly at home in our Western religious and philosophical thought but which shows its relevance and illumination through the Light from Asia. Dr. Coomaraswamy is the curator of Oriental art at the Boston Museum of Fine Art. He has, therefore, the entree to minds which would not otherwise listen to his words about religion—for culture can still command respect in our decadent West where cultus is despised. Dr. Coomaraswamy has used this approach to show us of the West that we cannot really understand art, still less hope to produce it, until we understand that it can only spring from a profoundly religious point of view. In his searching essay, "Am I My Brother's Keeper?" which appeared in the magazine *Asia,* he points out that when we collect works of art we kill what we would preserve, like uneducated children tearing up wild flowers. And he points out that we ourselves really know this, for, until the smash came, the demand of the tourist was to find a place which he called "unspoilt"— viz., a place where his own "culture" had not yet penetrated. He adds that the words "to spoil" mean not only to ruin but also to loot.

But it is to an essay which has lately appeared in book form that the rest of these remarks must be devoted. This small booklet is called "Hinduism and Buddhism." [1] The point of view is that of the Hinayana school of philosophy. But the author, by taking that position, does not wish to oppose it to the Mahayana form.

The greater and the lesser vehicle can both travel along the noble eightfold path. What he is concerned to show is that Buddhism and Hinduism are not in conflict: the one is a development out of the massive foundation of the other. Still further, Dr. Coomaraswamy wishes to show—and certainly his scholarship would seem to sustain it—that the essentials of Christianity, of Buddhism in its two forms, and of Hinduism are one. Here is the Philosophia Perennis, here the Eternal Gospel.

History does not repeat itself but it does recapitulate, and the themes sounded earlier are found in the vast orchestra-

[1] "Hinduism and Buddhism," Dr. A. Coomaraswamy. The Library of Philosophy. 15 East 40th St. New York City.

tion of life coming back time and again with new and fuller harmonization. So is it with East and West in this matter of religion. Today we shall not repeat in any detail the great syncretistic effort of the Second Century. But, on a larger scale, we shall see another blending of East and West. The original element in this new blending will be, as Dr. Coomaraswamy has pointed out, not a borrowing, indeed not a real syncretism, but a recognition of a common thought manifesting its power under different forms. As he says, the great religions do not so much borrow from each other as all draw from a basic philosophy, a way of life, an apprehension of reality which has been there all the while but which we have forgotten. This realization that ignorance is our greatest mistake and fault is of course a thought which the East has stressed more than the West, but, if it is true, then what the East can do for the West is not so much to convert it, still less to make it adopt its forms, as to remind it of the truth which it knows but has forgotten and let drop to the back of its mind.

It is here that we return to the thought of such perennial teaching—that it is in the life lived, in the fruit of the tree of religion that its power of propaganda resides. Religions may appeal because they are strange and subtle in their philosophy or rich and colorful in their rituals. They will only last if they can alter the quality of character. The practical man makes that his test. It is also the test given by Christ and by Buddha. Dr. Coomaraswamy points out how this Eternal Gospel has a stark simplicity and a total demand. He quotes repeatedly that telling statement of Eckhart, as summing up all the truth: "The Kingdom of God belongs only to the thoroughly dead." The doctrine of being born again by dying to the self—the teaching of the story of the pearl of great price: that everything must be given for it—this to him is the perennial philosophy. It is always being overlaid and mistaken. So, when we have let it be lost, the East comes to us again to remind us that there is a commandment greater even than the commandment to love your neighbor—which we have thought to be the last word of morality. The first commandment comes first not only because it is first by its very nature but because, unless it is practiced first, the second can never be fulfilled. Otherwise, our love for our neighbor will remain only a slogan and when we try to put it into practice we shall in fact start liquidating him—because, in the form in which he actually appears, we really detest him. The first commandment is, then, the guarantee, the only possible sanction for the second, the only possible power which can give "The Social Gospel" any virtue to redeem mankind. Some may say: "Why do we need yet another voice to tell us that, why do we require the same light thrown from another angle?" The fact remains that a new voice often awakes us when we are drowsing under the repetition of the truth spoken to us in familiar terms. Further, Hinduism is also teaching the West that, since "All roads lead to God" men have to find that road which suits best their nature. Catholicism helps some, hinders others: Vedanta likewise. Here in Dr. Coomaraswamy's rendering of Hinayana is still another way of reaching the same goal.

# Reflections on the Lord's Prayer—I

## ALDOUS HUXLEY

FAMILIARITY DOES NOT necessarily breed comprehension; indeed, it often interferes with comprehension. We take the familiar thing for granted, and do not even try to find out what it is. To millions of men and women the sentences of the Lord's Prayer are the most familiar of all forms of words. They are far from being the most completely understood. That is why, in the past, it has been the subject of so many commentaries; and that is why it has seemed worth while to add these brief reflections to the list.

The invocation defines the nature of the God to whom the prayer is addressed. The full significance of the phrase can best be grasped by emphasizing in turn the individual words of which it is composed.

"*Our* Father which art in heaven."

God is ours in the sense that He is the universal source and principle, the being of all beings, the life of all that lives, the spirit of every soul. He is present in all creatures; but all creatures are not equally aware of His presence. The degree of this awareness varies with the quality of that which is aware, for knowledge is always a function of being. God's nature is fully comprehensible only to God Himself. Among creatures, knowledge of God's nature expands and becomes more adequate in proportion as the knower becomes more God-like. As St. Bernard puts it, "God who, in His simple substance is all everywhere equally, nevertheless, in efficacy, is in rational creatures in another way than in irrational, and in good rational creatures in another way than in the bad. He is in irrational creatures in such a way as not to be comprehended by them; by all rational creatures, however, He can be comprehended by knowledge; but only by the good is He also comprehended by love" and, we might add, by contemplation, which is the highest expression of man's love of God.

The final end of man's existence is this: to make himself fit to realize God's presence in himself and in other beings. The value of all that he thinks and does is to be measured in terms of his capacity for God. Thoughts and actions are good, when they make us, morally and spiritually, more capable of realizing the God who is *ours,* immanently in every soul and transcendently as that universal principle in which we live and move and have our being. They are bad when they tend to reinforce the barriers which stand between God and our souls, or the souls of other beings.

"Our *Father* which art in heaven."

A father begets, supports and educates, loves and yet punishes.

All sentient beings are capable of disobedience to the Father's will, man pre-eminently so. Conversely, man is pre-eminently capable of obedience.

God as He is in Himself cannot be known except by those who are "perfect as their father in heaven is perfect." Consequently, the intrinsic nature of God's love for the world must remain, for the overwhelming majority of human beings, a mystery. But of God's love in relation to us, and from our point of view, we are able to form a sufficiently clear idea. And the same is true of what is called God's anger, or the stern and punishing aspect of the divine fatherhood. Any disobedience to God's will, any flouting of the nature of things, any departure from the norms governing the universes of matter, mind and spirit, results in more or less serious consequences for those directly or even indirectly involved in the transgression. Certain of these undesirable consequences of disobedience are physical, as when some flouting of the laws of nature or of human nature leads, for example, to disease in the individual or war in the body politic. Others are moral and spiritual, as when bad habits of thought and conduct lead to degeneration of character and the erection of insurmountable barriers between the soul and God. These fruits of human disobedience are commonly regarded as the expression of God's anger.

In the same way, we commonly regard as the expression of

God's love those desirable consequences, physical, moral or spiritual, which flow from obedience to the divine will and conformity to the nature of things. This is the sense in which, for the "natural man," God is our father, at once loving and stern. God's fatherhood as it is in itself cannot be known to us until we have fitted ourselves for the beatific vision of divine reality.

"Our Father which *art* in heaven."

This is the keyword of the invocation; for the ultimate fact about God is the fact of His being. "Who is He?" (I quote St. Bernard once again.) "I can think of no better answer than, He who is. No name is more appropriate to the eternity which God is. If you call God good, or great, or blessed, or wise, or anything of this sort, it is included in these words, namely, He is."

Philosophers have written interminably of Being, Essence, Entities. Much of this speculation is meaningless and would never have been undertaken, if the philosophers in question had troubled to analyze their medium of expression. In the Indo-European languages, the verb "to be" is used in a number of different ways and with meanings which are by no means always identical. Owing to this fact, much which used to pass as metaphysics has now come to reveal itself, with the advance of linguistic studies, as no more than misunderstood grammar. Does this apply to such statements as that God is He who is? The answer is, no. For the statement that God is He who is, is one that can be, in some measure, empirically verified by anyone who cares to fulfill the conditions upon which mystical insight into reality depends. For in contemplation the mystic has a direct intuition of a mode of being incomparably more real and substantial than the existences—his own and that of other things and persons—of which, by a similar direct intuition, he is aware at ordinary times. That God *is,* is a fact that men can actually experience, and is the most important of all the facts that can be experienced.

Everything that can be said about God, "is included in these words, namely, He is." Because He is, we apprehend Him as ours and as father. And also, because He is, we apprehend Him as being "in heaven."

"Our Father which art in *heaven*."

Throughout the prayer, heaven is contrasted with earth, as something different from it in kind. The terms have, of course, no spatial significance. The mind is its own place, and the Kingdom of Heaven is within. In other words, heaven is another and superior mode of consciousness. For the natural, unregenerate way of thinking, feeling and willing, must be substituted another way. The life of earth must be lost that the life of heaven may be gained. At first, as every mystic has taught, the mode of consciousness which we call "heaven" will be ours only fitfully, during moments of contemplation. But in the highest stages of proficiency *samsara* and *nirvana* are one; the world is seen *sub specie aeternitatis;* the mystic is able to live uninterruptedly in the presence of God. He will continue to work among his fellow men, here on earth; but his spirit will be "in heaven," because it is assimilated to God.

So much for the invocation; we have now to consider the prayer proper. This is couched in the imperative tense; but the full extent of its significance is best understood if we translate the clauses into the indicative and regard them as a series of statements about the end of human life and the means whereby that end is to be achieved.

Another point to remember is that, though the phrases are uttered successively, each one is relevant, as a statement simultaneously of cause and effect, to all the others. If we were making a diagrammatic representation of the prayer, it would not be correct to symbolize it under the image of a straight line or an open curve. The appropriate symbol would be a closed figure, in which there is no beginning or end and in which every section is the forerunner and successor of every other—a circle or, better, a spiral, where the repetitions are progressive and take place, as the conditions of advance are fulfilled, at ever higher points of achievement.

"Hallowed be Thy name."

Applied to human being, the word "holiness" signifies the voluntary service of, and self-abandonment to, the highest, most real good. Hallowing, or making holy, is the affirmation, in words and actions, that the thing hallowed partakes of the highest, most real good. That which alone ought to be hallowed (and we must pray for strength to hallow it un-

ceasingly) is the name of God—the God who *is,* and is therefore ours, the father and in heaven.

"The name of God" is a phrase which carries two principal
meanings. In so far as the Jews, like many other peoples of
antiquity, regarded the name of a thing as identical with its
inner principle or essence, the phrase means simply "God."
"Hallowed be Thy name" is equivalent to "hallowed be
Thou." The clause asserts that God is the highest, most real
good, and that it is to the service of this good alone that we
should dedicate our lives. What we pray for, when we repeat
this clause, is living, experiential knowledge of this fact, and
the strength unswervingly to act upon that knowledge.

So much for the first meaning of "Thy name." Its other
meaning accords with that view of language which has pre-
vailed in modern times. For us, the name of something is
essentially different from that which is named. Words are
not the things they stand for, but devices by means of which
we are enabled to think about things. To one who considers
the matter from the modern standpoint "the name of God"
is not the equivalent of "God." Rather, it stands for those
verbal concepts, in terms of which we think about God.
These concepts are to be hallowed, not of course in and for
themselves (for that would be mere magic), but inasmuch as
they contribute to the effective and continuous hallowing of
God in our lives. Knowledge is one of the conditions of love,
and words are one of the conditions of any form of rational
knowledge. Hence the importance, in the spiritual life, of a
working hypothesis regarding the highest, most real good.
Hallowing God's *name* is thinking verbalized thoughts about
God, as a means to passing from mere intellectual knowledge
to a living experience of reality. Discursive meditation precedes and is the preparation for contemplation; access to
God Himself can be had through a proper use of the name
of God. This is true, not only in the extended sense in which
the word has hitherto been used, but also in the most limited
and literal sense. Wherever spiritual religion has flourished,
it has been found that a constant repetition of sacred names
can serve a very useful purpose in keeping the mind one-
pointed and preparing it for contemplation.

The relationship between this first clause of the prayer and the succeeding clauses may be summed up in a few sentences. The hallowing of God and of His name is an indispensable condition of achieving the other aims mentioned in the prayer—namely, the realization of God's kingdom and the doing of His will, and the fitting of the soul to receive from God grace, forgiveness and liberation. Conversely, the better we succeed, through liberation, forgiveness and grace, in doing God's will and realizing His kingdom, the more adequately shall we be enabled to hallow God's name and God Himself.

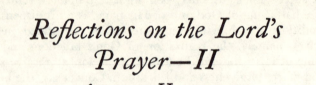

# Reflections on the Lord's Prayer—II

## Aldous Huxley

"Thy kingdom come . . . in earth as it is in heaven."

The end of man's existence is to use his opportunities in space-time in such a way that he may come to the knowledge of God's kingdom of timeless reality—or, to put it the other way round, that he may be fit for reality to come to manifestation in and through Him. The "is," in "as it is in heaven," was introduced into the English translation as a mere linguistic convenience. But if we choose to underline it, so as to make it carry, like the "art" of the invocation, a suggestion of real and substantial being, the word will help us to realize more clearly what it is we are praying for—the strength to pass through time to a realization here, in time, of eternity, for the power to give eternity a chance of possessing us, not merely virtually, but in realized actuality. For the contemplative saints who are "perfect as their Father in heaven is perfect," *samsara* and *nirvana* are one, God's kingdom comes on earth as it is in heaven. Nor is the change merely personal and subjective. The influence of these people has power to change the world in which they live.

The end of human life cannot be achieved by the efforts of the unaided individual. What the individual can and must do is to make himself fit for contact with reality and the reception of that grace by whose aid he will be enabled to achieve his true end. That we may make ourselves fit for God, we must fulfill certain conditions, which are set forth in the prayer. We must hallow God's name, do God's will and forgive those who have trespassed against us. If we do this, we shall be delivered from the evil of selfhood, forgiven the sin of separateness and blessed with the bread of grace, without which our contemplation will be illusory and our attempts at amendment vain.

"Thy will be done, in earth as it is in heaven."

This phrase carries two meanings. So far as ultimate reality is concerned, the will of God is identical with God's being or kingdom. To pray that the will of God may be done in earth as in heaven is to pray, in other words, for the coming into time of the kingdom of eternity. But the words do not apply only to ultimate reality; they also apply to human beings. So far as we are concerned, "doing the will of God" is doing what is necessary to fit ourselves for the grace of enlightenment.

Earth is incommensurable with heaven, time with eternity, the ego with the spirit. The kingdom of God can come only to the extent to which the kingdom of the natural man has been made to go. If we would gain the life of union, we must lose the life of passion, idle curiosity and distractions, which is the ordinary life of human selves. "Fight self," says St. Catherine of Siena, "and you need fear no other foe."

All this is very easy to read and write, but enormously difficult to put into practice. Purgation is laborious and painful; but purgation is the condition of illumination and union. Conversely, a certain measure of illumination is a condition of effective purgation. The stoic thinks to deny himself by making acts of the surface will. But the surface will is the will of the self, and his mortifications tend rather to strengthen the ego than eliminate it. He is apt to become, in the tremendous phrase coined by William Blake, "a fiend of righteousness." Having denied one aspect of his ego merely to strengthen another and more dangerous aspect, he ends up by being more impervious to God than he was before he started his process of self-discipline. To fight self exclusively with the self serves only to enhance our selfhood. In the psychological field there can be no displacing without replacing. For preoccupation with self must be gradually substituted preoccupation with reality. There can be no effective mortification for enlightenment without meditation or devotion, which direct the attention away from self to a higher reality. As I have remarked before, all spiritual processes are circular, or rather spiral. In order to fulfill the conditions of enlightenment we must have the glimmerings, if not of enlightenment itself, at least of an idea of what enlightenment consists in. God's will must be done by us, if God's kingdom is to come in us; and God's kingdom must begin to come, if we are effectively to do God's will.

"Give us this day our daily bread."

It is possible that the word translated as "daily" may really carry another meaning and that the phrase should read: "Give us this day our bread of the (eternal) day." This would emphasize the fact, already sufficiently obvious to anyone familiar with the language of the gospels, that the bread referred to is a divine and spiritual nourishment—the grace of God. In the traditional translation the spiritual nature of the bread is taken for granted and an additional emphasis is laid on the thought already expressed in the words "this day."

A man cannot be nourished by the anticipation of tomorrow's dinner, or the recollection of what he ate a week ago. Bread serves its purpose only when consumed "this day"—here and now. It is the same with spiritual food. Remorseful thoughts about the past, pious hopes and aspirations for a better future contain no nourishment for the soul, whose life is always now, in the present, and not at any other un-actual moment of time. In its passage from the vegetative and animal level to the spiritual, life passes from what may be called the physiological eternity of mindless existence, through the human world of memory and anticipation, past and future, into another and higher timelessness, the eternal kingdom of God. In the ascending spiral of being, the contemplative saint stands at a point exactly corresponding, on his higher level, to the position of a flower or a bird. Both inhabit eternity; but whereas the flower's or the bird's eternity is the everlasting present of mindlessness, of natural processes working themselves out with little or no accompanying consciousness, the saint's eternity is experienced in union with that pure consciousness, which is the ultimate reality. Between these two worlds lies the human universe of foresight and retrospect, of fear and craving and memory and conditioning, of hopes and plans and day-dreams and remorses. It is a rich world, full of beauty and goodness as well as of much evil and ugliness—but a world which is not the world of reality; for it is *our* world, man-made, the product of the thoughts and actions of beings who have forgotten their true end and have turned to things which are not their highest good. This is the truth proclaimed by all the great spiritual teachers of history—the truth that enlightenment, liberation, salvation, call it what you will, can come only for those who learn to live now in the contemplation of eternal reality, no longer in the past and future of human memories and habits, desires and anxieties.

Christ was especially emphatic on the urgent necessity of living in the spiritual present. He exhorted his disciples to model their life upon that of the flowers and the birds, and to take no thought for the morrow. They were to rely, not on their own anxious scheming, but upon the grace of God, which would be given in proportion as they gave up their own personal pretensions and self-will. The phrase of the Lord's Prayer, which we are now considering, sums up the whole gospel teaching on this head. We must ask God for grace *now*, for the good reason that the nature of grace is such that it can only come now, to those who are ready to live in the eternal present.

As usual, the practical problem for the individual is enormously difficult. Liberation cannot come unless we take no thought for tomorrow and live in the eternal present. But at the same time prudence is one of the cardinal virtues and it is wrong to tempt Providence by being rash and thoughtless.

> *Oh wearisome condition of humanity!*
> *Born under one law, to another bound;*
> *Vainly begot, and yet forbidden vanity;*
> *Created sick, commanded to be sound.*

For such a being (and Fulke Greville's description is eminently accurate) no problem can be anything but hard. This particular problem—the finding of a right relation between the world of eternal reality and the human world of time—is surely one of the hardest of all. We need grace in order to be able to live in such a way as to qualify ourselves to receive grace.

# Reflections on the Lord's Prayer—III

## ALDOUS HUXLEY

"FORGIVE US OUR TRESPASSES, as we forgive them that trespass against us."

"As we forgive them that trespass against us" is a phrase which must be thought of as qualifying all the classes of the prayer. Forgiving is merely a special case of giving, and the word may be taken to stand for the whole scheme of non-egotistic life, which is at once the condition and the result of enlightenment. As we forgive, or, in other words, as we change our "natural," egotistic attitude towards our fellow beings, we shall become progressively more capable of hallowing the name of God, of doing God's will and co-operating with God to make His kingdom come. Moreover, the daily bread of grace, without which nothing can be achieved, is given to the extent to which we ourselves give and forgive. If one is adequately to love God, one must love one's neighbors—and one's neighbors include even those who have trespassed against us. Conversely, one must love God, if one is adequately to love one's neighbors. In the spiritual life, every cause is also an effect, and every effect is at the same time a cause.

We have now to consider in what sense God forgives our trespasses or debts, as we forgive our debtors, or those who trespass against us.

On the human level, forgiveness is the waiving of an acknowledged right to payment or punishment. Some of these acknowledged rights are purely arbitrary and conventional. Others, on the contrary, seem to be more fundamental, more closely in accord with what we regard as just. But these fundamental notions of justice are the notions of the "natural," unregenerate man. All the great religious teachers of the world have insisted that these notions must be replaced by others—the thoughts and intuitions of the liberated and enlightened man. The Old Law is to be replaced by the New, which is the law of love, of *mahakarun*, of universal compassion. If men are not to enforce their "rights" for payment or punishment, then most certainly God does not enforce such rights. Indeed, it is absurd to say that such "rights" have any existence in relation to God. If they exist upon the human level, it is solely in virtue of the fact that we are either isolated selves or, at best, self-sacrificing members of groups which have the character of selves and whose selfish behavior vicariously satisfies the ego-feelings of those who have sacrificed themselves to these groups. The "natural" man is motivated either by selfishness or that social sublimation of selfishness which Philip Leon has aptly called "alter-egoism." But because God does not enforce any "rights" of the kind that unregenerate individuals and societies enforce, under the plea of justice, it does not follow that our acts are without their good or evil consequences. Here again the great religious teachers are unanimous. There is a law of *karma;* God is not mocked, and as a man sows, so shall he reap. Sometimes the reaping is extremely obvious, as when a habitual drunkard reaps bodily sickness and a failure of mental power. Very often, on the contrary, the reaping is of a nature which it is very difficult for any but enlightened eyes to detect. For example, Jesus was constantly inveighing against the Scribes and Pharisees. But the Scribes and Pharisees were models of austere respectability and good citizenship. The only trouble with them was that their virtues were only the virtues of unregenerate men—and such righteousness is as "filthy rags" in the sight of God; for even the virtues of the unregenerate are God-eclipsing and prevent those who have them from advancing towards that knowledge of ultimate reality, which is the end and purpose of life. That which the Scribes and Pharisees reap is the more or less total inability to know the God they fondly imagine they are serving. God does not punish them, any more than he punishes the man who inadvertently steps over the edge of a cliff. The nature of the world is such that, if anyone fails to conform to its laws, whether of matter or mind or spirit, he will have to take the consequences, which may be immediate and spectacular, as in the case of the man who steps over the edge of the cliff, or remote, subtle and very far from obvious, as in the case of the virtuous man who is virtuous only in the manner of the Scribes and Pharisees.

Now, since God has no "rights" to enforce, he can never be thought of as waiving such "rights." And since he is the principle of the world, he cannot suspend those laws or make exceptions to those uniformities, which are the manifestation of that principle. Does this mean, then, that God cannot forgive our debts and trespasses? In one sense it certainly does. But there is another sense in which the idea of divine forgiveness is valid and profoundly significant. Good actions and thoughts produce consequences which tend to neutralize, or put a stop to, the results of evil thoughts and actions. For as we give up the life of self (and note that, like forgiveness, repentance and humility are also special cases of giving), as we abandon what the German mystics called "the I, me, mine," we make ourselves progressively capable of receiving grace. By grace we are enabled to know reality more completely, and this knowledge of reality helps us to give up more of the life of selfhood—and so on, in a mounting spiral of illumination and regeneration. We become different from what we were and, being different, cease to be at the mercy of the destiny which, as "natural," unregenerate beings, we had forged for ourselves by our evil thoughts and actions. Thus the Pharisee who gives up his life of self-esteeming respectability and uncharitable righteousness, becomes capable thereby of receiving a measure of grace, ceases to be a Pharisee and, in virtue of that fact, ceases to be subject to the destiny forged by the man he once was and is no more. The making oneself fit to receive grace is effective repentance and atonement; and the bestowal of grace is the divine forgiveness of sins.

In a rather crude form, this truth is expressed in the doctrine which teaches that merits have the power to cancel out their opposites. Moreover, if divine forgiveness is the bestowal of grace, we can understand how vicarious sacrifices and the merits of others can benefit the soul. The enlightened person transforms not merely himself, but to some extent the world around him. The unregenerate individual is more or less completely without real freedom; only the enlightened are capable of genuinely free choices and creative acts. This being so, it is possible for them to modify for the better the destinies unfolding around them by inspiring the makers of these destinies with the wish and the power to give, so that they may become fit to receive the grace which will transform them and so deliver them from the fate they had been preparing for themselves.

"Lead us not into temptation, but deliver us from evil; for *thine* is the kingdom, and the power, and the glory."

The nature of the evil from which we pray to be delivered is defined by inference in the succeeding phrase. Evil consists in forgetting that kingdom, power and glory are God's and acting upon the insane and criminal belief that they are ours. So long as we remain average, sensual, unregenerate individuals, we shall constantly be tempted to think God-excluding thoughts and perform God-eclipsing actions. Nor do such temptations cease as soon as the path of enlightenment is entered. All that happens is that, with every advance achieved, the temptations become more subtle, less gross and obvious, more profoundly dangerous. Belial and Mammon have no power over the advanced; nor will they succumb when Lucifer offers them his more material baits, such as worldly power and dominion. But for souls of quality Lucifer also prepares more rarefied temptations and many are those, even far advanced along the road to enlightenment, who have succumbed to spiritual pride. It is only to the perfectly enlightened and the completely liberated that temptations do not present themselves at all.

The final phrases of the prayer re-affirm its central, dominant theme, which is that God is everything and that man, as man, is nothing. Indeed, man, as man, is less than nothing; for he is a nothing capable of evil, that is to say capable of claiming as his own the things that are God's and, by that act, cutting himself off from God. But though man, as man, is nothing and can make himself less than nothing by becoming evil, man as the knower and lover of God, man as the possessor of a latent, inalienable spark of godhead, is potentially everything. In the words of Cardinal Bérulle, "man is a nothing surrounded by God, indigent of God, capable of God and filled with God if he so desires." This is the central truth of all spiritual religion, the truth that is, so to say, the major premise of the Lord's Prayer. It is a truth which the ordinary unregenerate man or woman finds it hard to accept in theory and harder still to act upon. The great religious teachers have all thought and acted theocentrically; the mass of ordinary human beings think and act anthropocentrically. The prayer which comes naturally to such people is the prayer of petition, the prayer for concrete advantages and immediate help in trouble. How profoundly different this is from the prayer of an enlightened being! Such a being prays not at all for himself, but only that God may be worshipped, loved and known by him as God ought to be worshipped, loved and known—that the latent and potential seed of reality within his own soul may become fully actualized. There is even a kind of irony to be found in the fact that this prayer of Christ's—the theocentric prayer of a supremely enlightened being—should have become the prayer most frequently repeated by millions upon millions of men and women, who have only a very imperfect notion of what it means and who, if they fully realized its revolutionary significance, so immensely remote from the more or less kindly humanism by which they govern their own lives, might even feel rather shocked and indignant. But in the affairs of the spirit, it is foolish to think in terms of large numbers and "public opinion." It may be true that the Lord's Prayer is generally misunderstood, or not understood at all. Nevertheless it is a good thing that it should remain the most familiar formulary used by a religion which, particularly in the more "liberal" of its contemporary manifestations, has wandered so far from the theocentrism of its founder, into an entirely heretical anthropocentrism or, as we now prefer to call it, "humanism." It remains with us, a brief and enigmatic document of the most uncompromising spirituality. Those who are dissatisfied with the prevailing anthropocentrism have only to look into its all too familiar, and therefore uncomprehended depths, to discover the philosophy of life and the plan of conduct for which they have been looking hitherto in vain.

# The Sermon on the Mount—I
## SWAMI PRABHAVANANDA

EVERY GREAT TEACHER, no matter whether he is a Divine Incarnation or a prophet, or an illumined soul, has two sets of teachings—one for the multitude and the other for his disciples. The elephant has two sets of teeth: the tusks with which he defends himself from external difficulties, and the teeth with which he eats. The teacher of religion clears the path for his message, as it were, with his tusks; but he gives the inner truth of religion only to his intimate disciples. For religion is something which can actually be transmitted. A truly illumined teacher can transmit to us the energy and impulse which makes us unfold within ourselves. But the field must be fertile and the soil ready before the seed can be sown. The disciple must make himself ready and prepared.

In the Upanishads we read: "The teacher must be wonderful and the disciple must be wonderful: where this combination is found there grows the beautiful tree with flowers and fruits."

We read in the Gita: "Some have actually looked upon the Atman and comprehended all its wonders. Others can only speak of it as wonderful, beyond their comprehension. Others know its wonder only by hearsay. And still others, though they hear, do not understand it at all." It is not that these truths are kept secret. They are all recorded. We read them, we memorize them: but still they do not sink deep into our own consciousness. Very few of us try to live them.

When we study Christ's Sermon on the Mount, the first thing that strikes us is that He is not talking for the multitude. His disciples could grasp what He was teaching them not merely through His words, but also because He was personally transmitting something to them—something for which their hearts had already been prepared.

"Blessed are the poor in spirit, for theirs is the Kingdom of God." Christ's opening sentence speaks of this preparedness of the disciple, which should be his chief characteristic. Before the teaching can be given, before the consciousness of the disciple can be raised up, he must be poor in spirit. What does that really mean? In the Upanishads we read that the disciple must approach the teacher with a "straw in his mouth." This is to show that he is poor in spirit, open-hearted, ready to accept what the illumined soul has to offer him; and that he is free from the vanity of possessions, the vanity of learning, the vanity which makes an individual man say: "I am so-and-so." That vanity must be shaken off before we can learn. Sri Krishna says in the Gita: "Those illumined souls who have realized the Truth will instruct you in the knowledge of Brahman, if you will prostrate yourself before them, question them and serve them as a disciple."

As we study the Sermon on the Mount, we shall gradually discover what are the conditions of discipleship. Once upon a time—this is a true story—a man came to a teacher and said: "Make me a disciple!" The teacher had spiritual insight, and he knew that the man was not yet ready to become a disciple; so he told him: "Do you know what you have to do to become a disciple?" The man said that he didn't. Would the teacher please tell him? "Oh," said the teacher, "you have to fetch water, dig the garden, gather fuel, and do many hours daily of physical work. Then you have to study for so many hours. This is a hard life. Are you willing to do all that?" Then the man said: "Now I know what the disciple has to do. Tell me, please, what does the teacher do?" "Oh, the teacher sits and gives forth the truth in his quiet way." "Ah," said the man, "now I understand. I don't want to be a disciple. Please make me a teacher!" We all want to be teachers. But before we become teachers we must be disciples. We must humble ourselves. We must approach the teacher with the straw in our mouth.

Swami Brahmananda once said: "Who is there ready to accept the truth of God? We are willing to give, but they come to us to buy vegetables, potatoes, eggplants, onions. We have the treasure within us to give them, but they don't want that treasure."

In Hindu philosophy it is taught that certain conditions must be fulfilled before we can receive the truth of God. These are: Discrimination, shunning ephemeral pleasures, acquiring the six treasures of life, and the desire for freedom from the bondage of life.

First learn to discriminate between the eternal and the non-eternal. This discrimination is the most important thing of all. Why is it that we want to seek the truth of God? Because we find that everything in the Universe, everything that we sense, perceive, know, and enjoy, is transient. There is something in our hearts which cannot remain satisfied with the transient. Those in whom discrimination has developed, discriminate consciously. When desires and impulses arise, they ask themselves: "Is this really eternal? Is this something abiding?" As this discrimination grows in you, you lose your thirst for the pleasures of the objective world. Man wants happiness above everything. He will run after happiness wherever he can get it. But, if he has this spiritual discrimination, he will see that the pleasures of the external world are not really satisfactory because they are not abiding. And so he will shun them, and turn toward that abiding joy, that infinite happiness. Mere renunciation of desire does not help. In order to prevent the mind from running after objects, a man must cultivate certain qualities in himself.

These qualities are called in our Scriptures the Six Treasures. They are the true treasures of life. The first is tranquillity of the mind, interior calmness, peace. Then comes sense-control, mastery over your passions. As long as we remain slaves to the senses and the mind, with its passions and its restlessness, so long we cannot really desire God. The third treasure is patience and forbearance. The next is burning faith in the ideal. The heart must move toward its ideal with pleasure—the pleasure is very important. When we move toward the objects of sense-attraction, we feel great pleasure in our hearts. We must find just as much pleasure in the search for God. It is no good merely saying: "Oh, yes, I believe in God." That is not what is known as faith. But, if you really believe in God, then your heart will move toward the ideal of God-realization with great enthusiasm. We must cultivate that. It doesn't come all at once. We have to cultivate all these treasures.

Then comes self-surrender. And, finally, the desire for freedom from the bondage of life. That is the most important thing of all—that thirst, that longing for God and that desire for freedom from the things that hinder our approach to Him.

Christ, in His Sermon, as we shall see, speaks of these same conditions to be fulfilled in order that the purity of heart can be achieved and the truth of God may be revealed. But before we proceed on the subject, let me first try to explain the central note of the Sermon.

"Blessed are the pure in heart, for they shall see God." "Be ye therefore perfect, even as the Father which is in Heaven is perfect." These two verses give the central note of the Sermon on the Mount. Whatever Scriptures one reads, one finds this same note, this same theme. See God! Be ye therefore perfect! Know God! Realize Him! That is the one purpose and ideal of life.

Swami Turiyananda once told me that when he was a young boy he studied the Scriptures and philosophy, but nothing could satisfy him: he could not understand the purpose of life. Then one day in his study he came across a passage which says: "A man is born not to desire life in the world of senses, but to realize the bliss of an illumined soul who has attained his liberation." And he told me that, as he read that passage from the writings of Sankara: "It just took away a burden from my heart." Later, of course, he met Sri Rama-krishna, and did enjoy that bliss while living. In the Upanishads we read: "Blessed is he who realizes God in this life. If not, it is his greatest calamity."

My Master often used to repeat to us this one thing: "First seek and find that ocean of immortal bliss!" Theologians today may argue whether one can find God or whether perfection can be achieved or not, or what Christ meant by knowing the truth or seeing God: but this much I can say definitely —that when Christ spoke to His disciples He meant literally that God could be seen in their present lives. And the disciples were hungering just for that truth, to know God, to be perfect even as the Father in Heaven is perfect. How can a spiritual aspirant who is hungering for the truth be satisfied with theology, with philosophy, with doctrines and creeds? Christ was not teaching any creed, He was not teaching any doctrine, but He was teaching how to know and realize God. The disciples who were sitting at His feet knew that the first thing in spiritual life is to know God while living in this world, not after this body is left behind, but here and now! That is what is meant by religion. That is the central note of the Sermon on the Mount. And the chief method of knowing God is told in the verse: "Blessed are the pure in heart." The Beatitudes and the Sermon explain how that purity of heart is to be achieved. But we must remember that seeing God and attaining that perfection is not possible in what we call our normal life and consciousness. Nobody has seen God with these eyes. There is no perfection if we live in this life of the senses.

In the Gita we read how Sri Krishna was teaching his disciple Arjuna the way to realize God, and how Sri Krishna said: "But with these eyes you cannot see Him. I shall give you that divine sight." So that divine sight we have to acquire. The Hindu philosophers call it Turiya, the fourth state of consciousness. We have to go beyond this normal state of consciousness—from waking, dreaming, and dreamless sleep—and wake up to that fourth state, the transcendental, in which the divine sight opens.

If you go to the source, to the actual founders of the world's great religions, to Christ, to Buddha, to Krishna, or to Ramakrishna, you will find that one truth expressed: Realize God *in this life*. And in every religion you will find two principles: there is the ideal to be realized and there is the method of realization: there is the purity of heart which leads to the realization of God. These are the two principles which Christ and every other great teacher taught. All the rest of their teachings are just ways and means by which we can attain to that purification of our hearts, so that the Truth of God can be revealed within ourselves.

# The Sermon on the Mount—II

## Swami Prabhavananda

CHRIST HAS TAUGHT US THAT, in order to see God, we must be pure in heart. What is meant by this purity? We all know of individuals whom we would describe as pure, in an ethical sense: but these people have not seen God. What is the reason?

Try to think of God now, this very moment. What do you find? The thought of God passes through your mind, perhaps, like a flash; then all kinds of distractions begin. You find you are thinking of everything else in the universe *but* God. That is the test of true purity, as Christ understood the word: can a man, without any distraction whatever, keep his mind fixed upon love for God? Why are there these distractions? Because the mind remains impure from birth to birth —impure, because it has gathered so many impressions of so many kinds, good and bad.

These impressions have to be removed completely: to remove them, we have to know their cause. Yoga psychology defines five root causes of all our impressions.

First, is ignorance, in a universal sense: this is the chief of all causes of impurity of the mind. It is natural to all mankind: because of it, we do not see God. Ignorance is our normal state of consciousness. God is within us, and all around us: we are carrying Him with us all the time. But, instead of seeing God, we see this universe, and believe it to be the ultimate reality—just as a man who sees a rope lying on the ground in the dusk may believe it, in the twilight of his ignorance, to be a snake.

Then there is the sense of ego, which makes me think of myself as an individual being, and say: I must possess, I must enjoy, I must have this and that. This sense of ego separates us from one another, and from the reality of God.

From the sense of ego, we develop attachment and aversion: I want one thing, I hate another. That desire, and that hatred, are both obstacles in the path to God.

The final cause of our mental impurity is our clinging to life, our fear of death—and this is natural to all, good and bad alike. Buddha calls it *Tanha,* the thirst for life, and Christ refers to it in the saying: "He who loves his life shall lose it." Only the illumined saint has no sense of ego, no attachment, no hatred, and no fear of death; they have all vanished.

Even if we could have spiritual enlightenment instantly, this very moment, we shouldn't like it, we should draw back at the borderline. Even if we have been seeking God, we draw back at the moment when we feel we are about to have the vision of Him: we are afraid, because we cling to this life and this consciousness. We are so afraid of losing this everyday consciousness, even though it means passing into that wider infinite consciousness—in comparison with which our normal perceptions are, as the Gita says, "like a thick night and a sleep."

Swami Vivekananda himself, although he was a pure soul who was hungering for God, experienced that same fear. When he first came to Sri Ramakrishna, the Master gave him a touch, and his spiritual vision began to open. Then Vivekananda cried out: "What are you doing to me? I have my father and mother at home!" And Sri Ramakrishna said: "Oh, you too!" He saw that even this great soul was subject to this universal clinging to our normal consciousness.

Before we are ready to realize God, we must purify our hearts, we must prepare ourselves. Christ teaches us how to do this. First of all, we must free ourselves from the vanity of earthly ego and possession, and from the vanity of our learning. If an aspirant feels that he is rich in the world's goods, or that he knows a great deal, he cannot make spiritual progress: he has to feel, as it were, alone—that everything is in vain. "Blessed are they that mourn, for they shall be comforted." When we feel that we are poor in spirit, then we feel that real lack, that loss of God within ourselves. We feel the burden of our ignorance. Yes, we all mourn, no doubt—we mourn the loss of worldly pleasures and possessions—but that is not the kind of mourning that Christ speaks of. The mourning which Christ calls "blessed" is very rare—because very few people feel this spiritual loss, this loneliness. Most of us are quite satisfied with the surface-life of this world. In the back of our minds, perhaps, we feel the sense of something incomplete—but still we have the hope that this lack can be filled by our senses, our mind, and the sense-objects of the world.

Sri Ramakrishna used to say: "Men weep rivers of tears because a son is not born or because they cannot get riches. But who sheds even a single tear-drop because he has not been fortunate enough to see the Lord?" It is our ignorance which gives us this false sense of values. Sankaracharya, in explaining the nature of this ignorance, says that the True Self, the Spirit, is opposed to matter as light is opposed to darkness. Yet, such is the inexplicable power of ignorance, that even the wisest amongst us habitually identifies the spirit with matter, the True Self with the ego. It is very easy to understand, intellectually, that you are different from your body—just as the house you live in is different from you—and yet, when the body is diseased, we say: "I'm sick." Intellectually, we can understand that we are different from our minds; and yet, if a wave of happiness or suffering arises in the mind, we say: "I am happy. I am miserable." Also, we identify ourselves with our parents, children, relatives, friends: anything happening to them seems to be happening to us. We identify ourselves with our possessions: if we lose our wealth, we feel as if we had lost ourselves, there is nothing left to live for.

But when we begin to feel the lack within ourselves, when we begin to mourn as Christ wished us to mourn, when we shed even a few tears for God—then that comfort comes, then we know that God can be realized. Sri Ramakrishna passed many days longing for the moment when he would realize God in the form of Mother Kali. And every evening, when the temple bells rang for vespers, he would exclaim: "O Mother, another day has passed and I have not seen You!" That is true mourning!

"Blessed are the meek, for they shall inherit the earth." What is the cause of our delusion? Our sense of ego. This egotism in us must be overcome. Therefore—blessed are the meek. But why does Christ say that they shall inherit the earth? At first sight, this seems difficult to understand. Among the Yoga aphorisms, we find one which says: "The man who is confirmed in non-stealing becomes the master of all riches." What is meant by "non-stealing?" It means that we must give up this egotistic delusion that we can possess things, that anything can belong exclusively to us as individuals. We may say of ourselves: "But we don't steal anything! We are good people. Whatever we have, we have worked for and earned. It belongs to us by right." But the truth is that nothing belongs to us, nothing at all. As soon as we realize this, as soon as we give up our deluded, individual claims to this object or that—then we find that, in the truest sense, everything *does* belong to us, after all. We inherit the earth. Conquerors, who try to become masters of the world by force of arms, never inherit anything except worry and trouble and headaches; misers who accumulate huge wealth are only chained to their gold, they never really possess it. But the man who has given up his ego experiences the satisfaction without the misery of possession. Many people dislike this saying of Christ's because they think that the meek man can never achieve anything. They think that there is no pleasure to be had from life unless you are aggressive. When they are told to give up their ego, to be meek, they imagine that they will lose everything. Christ says no—by losing yourself, you will *gain* everything: you will inherit the earth.

"Blessed are they which do hunger and thirst after righteousness, for they shall be filled." That is the next stage, after the mourning. The longing for God becomes more intense, until it is a raging hunger and a burning thirst. That righteousness cannot mean what we ordinarily think of as moral virtues or good qualities; but that righteousness which is righteousness itself, the very essence. In Sanskrit, it is called "the-goodness-itself"—in other words, God. The word God is derived from that which is goodness itself—not relative good as opposed to evil, or relative virtue as opposed to vice. So the hunger and thirst after righteousness is a hunger and thirst after God Himself.

"Blessed are the merciful, for they shall obtain mercy."

There is an aphorism in the Yoga *sutras* which corresponds to this: "Friendship, mercy, gladness and indifference, when they are taught with regard to happy, unhappy, good, and evil subjects, respectively, calm the restlessness of the heart." So, to be merciful is one of the conditions necessary for the purification of our hearts. Jealousy and hatred exist in almost all of us, because they are linked up with our ego-sense, which is born of ignorance. How are we to overcome them? By thinking contrary thoughts. When somebody is happy, you should not feel jealous of him; you should try to be happy with him, by realizing your friendship, your unity. When somebody is unhappy we should not be glad; we should feel sympathy and be merciful. Be glad, not envious, when a man is good; when he is bad, do not hate him. You do not have to love the evil in him, but be indifferent to it. Any thought of hatred—even so-called "righteous hatred" of evil—will raise a wave of hatred and evil in our own minds, causing greater ignorance and greater restlessness, so that we cannot think of God, or love Him, until it has subsided.

"Blessed are the peacemakers, for they shall be called the Children of God." It is only when you have attained to the vision of God that you become a child of God and a peacemaker. Of course, we are children of God in ignorance, also; but, until we have known God, we can never make and bring peace. There is a passage in the Bhagavatam which says: "He in whose heart God has become manifested brings peace, and cheer, and delight everywhere he goes." I am reminded of a life that I have seen—the life of my Master, Swami Brahmananda. There was something peculiar in him which I have found nowhere else: whoever came into his presence would feel a joyous upliftment. You felt that you did not belong to this world, you belonged to God. We call it *Utsav*, a "celebration of joy": wherever he was, it was like a festival.

In one of the monasteries of our Order there were a number of young monks, not yet trained, fresh from schools and colleges. When they had been together a while, their old tendencies began to work, and they formed groups, and started to quarrel amongst themselves. So a senior Swami of our Order went to investigate the whole affair: he questioned everybody and soon found out who were the ringleaders.

Then he told Swami Brahmananda, who was then the head of our Order, that those boys were unfitted for monastic life, and that they must be expelled. My Master answered: "Do nothing about it. I am coming to see about it myself." And he did. When he arrived, he didn't question anybody: he simply started living in the monastery; and he only insisted on one thing—that all the boys should meditate regularly in his presence. Then he began to instruct them, without making any distinction between individuals, good or bad; and, gradually the whole atmosphere of the place was lifted. The boys forgot their quarrels, because they had no time for such things, any more. And when, after two or three months, he left, there was perfect harmony in the monastery. Nobody had to be expelled. They were transformed.

When I first joined the monastery, there were two young men who quarrelled and came to blows. One of the older Swamis saw this, and told Swami Brahmananda that it would be better to send them away. But Swami Brahmananda answered: "Brother, they have not come here as perfect souls. They have come to you to attain that perfection. Do something for them so that they will not fight and quarrel." Then this great Swami said: "You are right." So he gathered all of us boys together and came to Swami Brahmananda, and prostrated himself before him, and said: "Now, brother, I have brought them all. You must transform them." And, one by one, we went and prostrated ourselves at the feet of our Master. All he did was to raise his hand over our heads. And, in every one of us there came such a feeling of exaltation that we forgot any wish to quarrel or fight. That is the way a real peace-maker affects us. When men's hearts are uplifted by his presence, they cannot fight, because they are all engaged in the love of God.

"Blessed are they which are persecuted for righteousness' sake, for theirs is the kingdom of Heaven." Men of the world do not understand the value of the spiritual life. They mock at the spiritual aspirant, and sometimes revile him and try to do him an injury, but a truly spiritual soul does not react to that: he sees the unity, he sees the ignorance, he is merciful, but he does not choose to please the people of the world. There is the story of a young monk, who was on his travels.

He got tired, and lay down under a tree. He had no pillow, so he got some bricks and rested his head upon them. Some women were going along the road to the river, to fetch water, and they saw the young monk lying there, and they said to each other: "Look—that young man has become a monk, and yet he can't do without the idea of a pillow. He has to have bricks instead." They went on their way, and the monk said to himself: "They were quite right to criticize me." So he threw the bricks away, and lay down again with his head on the earth. Presently, the women returned, and saw that the bricks had gone; and they exclaimed contemptuously: "That's a fine sort of monk! He feels insulted because we said he had a pillow. Now, look—he has thrown his pillow away!" Then the monk said to himself: "If I have a pillow, they criticize me, and if I don't have a pillow, that doesn't suit them either—you can't please them." No really spiritual man will do any action with the idea of making a good impression upon others, or in order to create prestige for himself. He may sometimes feel just the opposite—that, if he has to go contrary to the whole world for the sake of truth he will do it, and do it alone; he does not care what others think of him. He tries only to please God, no one else. That must be the attitude of a spiritual aspirant—to maintain poise, tranquillity, patience and forbearance in the midst of the conflicts and contradictions of life.

# *The Sermon on the Mount—III*

## SWAMI PRABHAVANANDA

"YE ARE THE SALT OF THE EARTH: but if the salt have lost his savour, wherewith shall it be salted? It is thenceforth good for nothing, but to be cast out and to be trodden under foot of men."

In India, when a disciple comes to a teacher, the teacher tries first of all to give him a firm faith in himself, and a feeling that weakness and cowardice and failure have no part in his true nature. Almost the first words that Sri Krishna says to Arjuna, in the second book of the *Gita*, are: "Do not be so weak-spirited. It is unworthy of you."

But, at the same time, we must remember the beatitude: "Blessed are the meek." Meekness and faith in oneself must go together. This faith which the teacher tries to arouse in his disciple is not faith in the lower self, the ego, but faith in the higher Self, faith in God within. With that faith comes self-surrender, and the strength which is gained through freedom from ego.

Sri Ramakrishna brings out this truth. He used to tell how Radha, the chief of the shepherdesses, whom Krishna loved best, became apparently very egotistic. The other shepherd-esses came to Krishna and complained about her; so Krishna told them to go to Radha and ask her what kind of ego she had. And Radha replied: "Certainly, I have an ego. But whose is it? It is not mine, for everything I have belongs to Krishna." A man who has surrendered everything to God has no ego in the ordinary sense of the word, but he has strong faith in the true self within him.

This saying of Jesus: "Ye are the salt of the earth . . ." reminds me of a saying my Master, Swami Brahmananda, used to quote to us: "You have the grace of God, you have the grace of the guru, and you have the grace of God's devotees, but for the lack of one grace you may be cast out." What is that one grace? It is the grace of your own mind. If, in spite of all those graces which would otherwise make you "the salt of the earth," you lack the grace of your own mind, you may be cast out. So we must struggle hard to surrender ourselves completely and wholeheartedly to God—in order that the "salt," which is His grace, may not lose its savour.

An Avatar like Jesus gathers pure souls around him, and teaches them not only by word of mouth but by actual transmission of spiritual power. "Ye are the light of the world," he tells them. "A city that is set on an hill cannot be hid. Neither do men light a candle, and put it under a bushel, but on a candlestick; and it giveth light unto all that are in the house." Here we find that Christ was, as it were, transmitting this illumination to his disciples. We can only become that light of the world if we obtain illumination by uniting ourselves with the light which dwells in the hearts of all. Only such illumined ones are fitted to be true teachers of mankind: they alone can carry on the message of an Avatar. When Sri Ramakrishna met anyone who wished to teach the word of God, he would ask: "Have you the Divine Commission?" Only he whose heart is illumined can receive God's commission, His direct command to teach. Religion degenerates when it is taught by the ignorant. One may be learned in the scriptures like the scribes and pharisees, but unless one has known God one cannot teach. It is no good relying on your degree at a theological college: book-learning cannot give you illumination.

How, then, does one obtain illumination? By purification of the heart. When your heart has been truly purified, you will see God; and when you have seen God, your light shines forth and gives comfort to all. You do not have to go out and look for disciples, then. As Sri Ramakrishna used to say, when the lotus blossoms, the bees come from all around, of their own accord, to gather the honey. "Make that lotus blossom!" he used to tell his disciples. When such an illumined soul appears, and spiritual aspirants gather around him, they cannot do otherwise than glorify God, because in his presence, they feel the presence of the Father. This is very easy to understand: there is no mystery about it. When you go to see a lawyer, what kind of thoughts come into your mind? Thoughts about legal matters. With a doctor, you think about sickness and medicine. These thoughts come to us because the person we are with at that moment is living in that particular atmosphere. So, also, with a truly spiritual man: you may not know anything about him, but this is the test: when you come into his presence, the thought of God will come to you, because he has that light. That was what I experienced, in my own life, as a young boy. I did not know anything about God, until I had the blessed fortune to meet and associate with holy men who had seen that light of the world, and in their presence I felt joyful, and I could not help thinking of God and loving Him, even though they might be talking of something quite different. This is what Jesus was speaking of when he said: "Let your light so shine before men, that they may see your good works, and glorify your Father which is in Heaven."

Then he says: "Think not that I am come to destroy the law, or the prophets: I am not come to destroy, but to fulfil. For verily I say unto you, Till heaven and earth pass, one jot or one tittle shall in no wise pass from the law, till all be fulfilled. Whosoever therefore shall break one of these least commandments and shall teach men so, he shall be called the least in the kingdom of heaven: but whosoever shall *do* and *teach* them, the same shall be called great in the kingdom of heaven."

In the *Gita,* Sri Krishna tells Arjuna: "Whenever righteousness is forgotten, and unrighteousness prevails, then I body myself forth." And why? In order to teach men once more the eternal truths they have neglected and forgotten. That is why Jesus was bodied forth into this world. He tells us so, himself. Those who insist on regarding the life and teachings of Jesus as unique are bound to have great difficulty in understanding that life and those teachings. Christ's life can be truly understood only in the light of other great lives and teachings. No Divine Incarnation ever came to refute the religion taught by another, but to fulfil all religions. Because the truth of God is an eternal truth. If, in all the history of the world, Jesus had been the sole originator of the truth of God, then it would be no truth; for truth cannot be originated, it is an existing fact. But if Jesus simply unfolded and interpreted that truth, then it follows that many others must have done so before him, and that many will do so after him. And, in fact, as we read the teachings of Jesus, we find that he wishes *all* of us to unfold that truth. He has come, he declares, not to destroy the eternally existing truth, but to restate it, to give it new life by presenting it in a new way. Each successive age needs a new and characteristic presentation of the truths of religion. For these presentations, once they have been spoken or written down, are like cut flowers: they slowly begin to shrivel, they become dry and dead. Men often treasure dead flowers, for the memory which clings to them, and this is very natural: but one must not forget that they *are* dead. Those who cling too devotedly to the dead flowers, to the letter of the law, lose consciousness of its undying spirit. Those are the scribes and pharisees: the jealous guardians of tradition which has become obsolete. That is why Christ says: "Except your righteousness shall exceed the righteousness of the scribes and pharisees, ye shall in no case enter into the kingdom of heaven."

The pharisees are very ethical upright men in their own way, but they cling to forms and outward observances, and this makes them inclined to intolerance, narrowness and dogmatism. The righteousness which exceeds the righteousness of the scribes and pharisees is the very opposite of this. It is an ethic which is based, not on rules of conduct and lists of sins with their punishments, but upon the intuition of the heart, which cares little for commandments and texts and regulations, and knows only one thing: to love God is to love all men. "Whosoever," Christ tells us, "is angry with his brother without a cause shall be in danger of judgment." It's not enough just to obey the old commandment: "Thou shalt not kill." Even the mere thought of killing, the anger, is as deadly as the act. You cannot love God and hate your neighbour. It is not possible. If you really love God, you will find Him in everyone, so how can you hate another?

"Therefore if thou bring thy gift to the altar, and there rememberest that thy brother hath aught against thee; leave there thy gift before the altar, and go thy way; first be reconciled to thy brother, and then come and offer thy gift."

Until we actually reach oneness with God, it is, of course, quite natural that we should have misunderstandings and quarrels with each other. But we must not let that resentment stay with us, or it will eat into our hearts like cancer. We must be reconciled as soon as possible. There is only one way to feel sincerely reconciled, and that is to suppress our own ego. If you can do that, you will find that you immediately gain something spiritually. Try to see God in all beings, and love Him in all. Humble yourself—not before your adversary, but before God within him. Never humble yourself before anyone but God. That is how hatred is driven out, and love of God takes its place. If you keep that hatred in your own heart, it will hurt nobody except yourself.

"Ye have heard that it was said by them of old time, Thou shalt not commit adultery: But I say unto you, That whosoever looketh on a woman to lust after her hath committed adultery with her already in his heart. And if thy right eye offend thee, pluck it out and cast it from thee: for it is profitable for thee that one of thy members should perish, and not that thy whole body should be cast into hell."

Here Jesus is telling of the necessity for an inner check, an inner control of the passions. Without that control, it is impossible to reach spiritual illumination. Nowadays, everything has become externalized; all our thinking is outward; even our religion is taught entirely in terms of external action. Today, the great teaching of all churches is that we must serve Mankind: even those who do not believe in religion or in God believe in this. But nearly everybody seems to have forgotten what Christ himself taught. Yes, certainly, he taught service to our fellowmen—but in what spirit? In the spirit of love toward God. He taught that our action must be turned inward as well as outward. We forget that. Yet, without that inward regard, without that loving dedication of all our work to God, what does morality amount to? Just social behavior.

This is a fundamental principle of spiritual life: that you must control the mind. Merely refraining from evil actions is not enough: evil thoughts must be checked, as well. We may pretend to ourselves that it doesn't matter what we think, as long as we act rightly. But, when the test comes, we always betray ourselves, for it is the thought which really counts most. When the test comes, if our thoughts are full of hatred, that hatred will express itself in acts of violence and destruction and murder. Standing up in the pulpit and talking about love will not help us, it will not stop war and cruelty, when there is no love in our hearts. Love will not come to us because we just say we have it, or hypothetically try to impress other people with the seeming sweetness of our natures. Love comes only when we have controlled our inward passions and subdued our ego. Then love of God grows in us, and with it love of our fellowmen. But the love of God has to be won through self-discipline, and we have neglected to practise this discipline. We have forgotten the aim of life—to realise, know and see God. That is our whole difficulty. That is why, when Jesus says: "Love your enemies," we are unable to obey him, even if we wish to do so. We don't know how.

There are, of course, many teachers who would say: "Yes, indeed, we agree: an inner check on the passions is certainly necessary. Our young people must use self-control." But very few of those teachers could answer *why* self-control is needed. That is why the young people of today question them, and even begin to suspect that the teachers are jealous spoilsports, who hate pleasure for its own sake, because they are too old to take part in it themselves. "What does it matter," ask the young, "what we do, as long as we don't harm anybody else?" They are perfectly honest and sincere about this. How are we going to answer them?

It is no use telling them that their pleasures are wicked, or that it is wrong to be happy, because they will never believe you: their instincts tell them that you are lying. When you talk about Sin, they will disregard you; and they will continue to do so. But if you stop telling them that they are sinful, and begin to tell them that God is inside each one of them; if you hold up the ideal of Self-realization, God-realization, and show them that the struggle for self-discipline is hard but exciting, like training for athletics; if you show them that by dissipating themselves they are cutting themselves off from the greatest joy in life, a joy far greater than all their worldly pleasures—then you will be talking a language they can understand. They may be sceptical, but some of them, at least, will want to try it for themselves.

The ideal of continence has been so misrepresented in this country that nearly everybody thinks of it as something negative, as a "don't." Don't be incontinent, the churches tell us: it is a sin. And a famous athlete, in a magazine article, wrote that the men of the armed forces should stay continent, because otherwise they might catch some disease. In this way, for the great majority of people, who instinctively hate "dont's," the idea of continence has become unattractive, and associated with repression, gloom, and cowardice; while the idea of incontinence becomes more and more attractive, and is associated with freedom, fun and courage.

This is a terrible and destructive misunderstanding, which, if it is not corrected, will gradually poison the whole national life. Unless the boys and girls of this country can be taught the vital connection between continence and spiritual life, they will gradually waste all their powers, they will lose the possibility of spiritual growth, and with it all creativeness, all awareness, all the higher faculties. Continence is *not* repression, it is a storing up of energy and an application of that energy to better uses. Sex-energy controlled becomes spiritual energy. To one who is continent, spiritual growth comes quickly and easily. That is why every great religion has taught continence—not as a "don't," not as a negative commandment, but as a positive step towards a fuller, richer life.

You may think that, by being continent, you will lose the greatest pleasure this world has to offer: but the strange fact is that you will not really lose anything. As the sex-energy is conserved and as it becomes transformed, you will find a new and much more intense pleasure growing up inside you; and that is the joy of coming closer and closer to union with God.

# The Sermon on the Mount—IV

## SWAMI PRABHAVANANDA

"YE HAVE HEARD that it hath been said, 'An eye for an eye, and a tooth for a tooth.' But I say unto you, 'Resist not evil: but whosoever shall smite thee on thy right cheek, turn to him the other also. . . .' Ye have heard that it hath been said, 'Thou shalt love thy neighbor, and hate thine enemy.' But I say unto you, 'Love your enemies, bless them that curse you, do good to them that hate you, and pray for them which despitefully use you, and persecute you. . . .' "

Now this truth—that we should love our enemies and not resist evil—is the highest truth which has been taught by every religion. Nevertheless, it is a truth which is very unpopular, and one which most people find it nearly impossible to understand and practice. In fact, Christ himself, after teaching us this truth about non-resistance, goes on to say: "Be ye therefore perfect, even as your Father which is in Heaven is perfect." In other words, the practice of this truth in our own lives would make us perfect; and, indeed, only he who is perfect, he who has reached that Unity with God, who is able to see one Divine Existence everywhere, can practice non-resistance and Universal Love.

Once a young disciple of Sri Ramakrishna was crossing the Ganges in a ferry boat from Calcutta on his way to visit his Master. The other passengers in the boat were speaking against Sri Ramakrishna, saying that he was crazy, and a fake who misled young men. At first, when the disciple heard this, he argued with them mildly, saying: "If you knew Him you would not talk about Him like that. He is a very Holy man. Besides, he is my Master, so I must ask you not to speak ill of Him in my presence." But this mildness only encouraged the critics to further attack. They began to say the most sarcastic and unpleasant things they could think of. Then the young disciple got very angry. He jumped to his feet, and began to rock the boat, exclaiming: "If you don't stop, I'll upset this boat and drown you all!" The passengers were scared. They saw that the disciple was an athletic young man, well able to do what he threatened. Not another word was said against Sri Ramakrishna during the rest of the trip. Later, when the disciple told his Master about this incident, Sri Ramakrishna was displeased with him. "Why should you care," he asked, "whether people praise me or blame me?" And he taught him never to offer violence under any circumstances. However, on another occasion, another of Sri Ramakrishna's disciples was traveling by the same boat, and once again the passengers were talking against Sri Ramakrishna. The disciple begged them to stop, but they would not listen. So he kept quiet. Later, when he reported this to his Master, Sri Ramakrishna reproved him severely. "What!" he exclaimed: "You call yourself my disciple, and you let them slander me in your presence? Didn't you have the courage and the strength to force them to stop?"

Here we find Sri Ramakrishna giving what appears to be altogether contradictory advice. His reason for doing so was, of course, that he was dealing with two separate individuals. He wished to correct the over-aggressiveness of the one and the timidity of the other. Referring to this same problem, he told a parable. Once upon a time, there was a holy man who came to a village; and the villagers warned him that he must not go along a certain path because a venomous snake always lay there. "He won't hurt me," said the holy man, and went on his way. Sure enough, the snake presently reared its head, hissing and ready to strike, but when it saw the holy man it prostrated itself humbly at his feet and asked to become his disciple. Then the holy man taught it to give up the idea of hating and biting and killing others. The snake, having received initiation, went off blissfully to its hole to pray and meditate according to instructions. The holy man proceeded on his way. Soon, however, the boys of the village discovered this change in the character of the snake. Knowing that it was harmless, they would attack it with sticks and stones whenever it came out of its hole, but the snake would never strike back. After a while, the snake became so weak from its injuries that it could scarcely crawl, and retired in its hole altogether. When next the holy man came to that village, he was told that the snake was dead. "That's impossible," said the holy man. "It cannot die until it has attained the supreme realization of God." So he went to the snake's hole and called it, and the snake came squirming out, crippled from the blows it had received and terribly thin because it was not getting enough to eat. The holy man questioned it about the reason for its condition, and it said: "I did just as you told me, Master. The boys beat me, but I wouldn't bite them. I just lay there silent and suffered all their torments." The snake expected to be praised for its obedience. To its great surprise, however, the holy man got quite cross: "Idiot!" he cried: "I told you not to bite. Did I tell you not to hiss?"

Sri Ramakrishna's meaning in this parable is that householders who live in the world are still bound to love their neighbor and their enemy equally, and to abstain from violence; but this does not mean that they are to be so soft and simple as to invite violence from others. The goody-goody man who lets himself be cheated and tricked and pushed around, is not being saintly. Most often, he is merely giving way to weakness, laziness, and cowardice. If such a man arouses the aggressive instinct of another, then he shares the guilt in that aggression. Those who are perfect alone can practice non-violence in its absolute form. The rest of us have to hiss now and then.

Indian thought has always pointed out that there are gradations of duty. The duty of one kind of man is not the same as the duty of another. At both ends of the scale, we find apparent inaction; but a whole world lies between the stillness of the stone and the stillness of the saint. The way upward from inertia to illumination passes through the sphere of action, and we cannot miss out any of the steps if we are to have true spiritual growth. First gain the power to resist: then control and renounce that power. And remember always: non-resistance is the highest ideal of all. There must be no compromise with regard to that.

"Take heed that ye do not your alms before men, to be seen of them: otherwise ye have no reward of your father which is in Heaven. Therefore when thou doest thine alms, do not sound a trumpet before thee, as the hypocrites do in the Synagogues and in the streets, that they may have glory of men. Verily I say unto you, 'They have their reward.' But when thou doest alms, let not thy left hand know what thy right hand doeth: that thy alms may be in secret: and thy father which seeth these secrets himself shall reward thee openly."

This brings us to the law of Karma, and what the Gita calls "the fruits of action." I do some good deed for you and I get my reward. Whether you yourself give me that reward or not does not matter. If I do good, I shall receive good in return. If I do bad, bad will come back to me. That is the law. Those are "the fruits of action." But in order that we may reach perfection—which Christ called "purity of heart"—we must free ourselves from *all* the fruits of action, the good as well as the bad. We must purify our minds from every kind of impression and tendency—for good actions create tendencies also. Therefore the Gita teaches that we must learn to work for the work's sake only—for God's sake—without fixing our desire upon the results. We must turn all our work into worship of God. Then, and only then, shall we free ourselves from the wheel of cause and effect, deed and reward, and obtain the Infinite.

Next, Christ begins to teach us how to pray. He tells us to pray secretly. "And when thou prayest, enter into thy closet, and when thou hast shut the door, pray to thy Father which is in secret; and thy Father which seeth in secret shall reward thee openly." And what is this reward? It is God Himself. If you want anything less than God, you can have it. The good fruits of this world can be earned by observing the law of Karma. If you want a reputation for holiness, then go out into some public place and pray where everybody can see you. But if you truly worship God for Himself, wanting Him alone, then never mind the world, never mind whether it blames or admires you, go apart into a secret place, and ask for Him. You can be certain that He will give Himself to you.

And now, Christ gives us an actual prayer which we can use—The Lord's Prayer. "Our Father which art in Heaven," it begins: "Hallowed be Thy name."

Let us first try to understand what is meant by this word "Heaven." All the religions of the world teach us that heaven is within. Now, what does that really mean? If Heaven is within us, where is the earth? Is that within us too? The answer is Yes. You are in earth and you are also in Heaven. You do not know that you are in Heaven, but it is there nevertheless. What is the earth? In what sense are we "in it"? The earth-consciousness is our physical consciousness: our consciousness of time, space, and relativity, our consciousness of change. What is Heaven? That which abides forever. In Sanskrit, the word earth means that which is always moving, always changing. In the three states of consciousness—waking, dreaming, and deep sleep—we have a sense of identity and continuity. It is like a river, always changing, ever flowing. But, on either side of the river, there are as it were two banks: these may be thought of as the unchangeable consciousness which is the Atman, which is God, which is Heaven. So when we say that Heaven is within, this does not mean that Heaven has a spatial existence in or outside the body, but that it is Consciousness itself. And when we say that God is Immanent this does not mean that God is identical with the Cosmos, or that He is extra-cosmic; but that God is supra-cosmic. We have first to recognize Heaven within ourselves; then we can find it everywhere.

The experience of the saint teaches that, when God is realized, there is no consciousness of the body at all, neither of inside nor of outside. That is because the saint has gone beyond space and time and relativity. But because we cannot have this consciousness all in a moment we should begin by thinking of God as dwelling within our hearts, and praying to Him there. That is as near as we can go in a relative way, using words and ideas which belong to the relative plane of life. The absolute truth about God is beyond all language, all expression. We are like people living far from the ocean. One of us wishes to direct the other how to get there. He cannot say: "That is the ocean itself," but only: "If you follow that road and climb to the top of that hill over there, then you will get a view of the ocean."

Christ tells us that our Father *is* in Heaven. In every age, people ask for proof of the existence of God. But there is only one way to prove the existence of God, and that is to see Him. All attempts to arrive at a proof by means of reasoning are futile—because what you are trying to prove is only the existence of your *idea* of God; and so, even if you could possibly make such a proof, how could you guarantee that your idea and the Reality of God would correspond? Standing in our present position, far inland, we cannot prove the existence of the ocean, we cannot even be certain that our idea of that ocean corresponds in any way to the reality. We can only say: "Take that road, go to the top of that hill. Then you will see the ocean itself, and you will not need any further proof." During the course of the world's history, there have been many people, great teachers and saints and Illumined Souls, who have told us: "God exists. I know, because I have seen Him." The only question that remains for us is: do we or don't we believe them? If, after watching their lives, or learning all that can be known about them, we feel that these men were not deluded, were not insane—then a conviction begins to grow in our own hearts also. And, when once we have the beginning of that conviction, it will be our own fault if we do not try to obtain certainty, by starting to travel along the road which those men travelled, in order that we may reach the hilltop, like them, and see the ocean for ourselves.

The next idea we have to consider is contained in the words "Our Father." Christ is teaching us how to think of God when we pray to Him. We are to think of Him as a person, as our very own Father, whom we regard partly with awe and reverence but chiefly with trust, absolute confidence and love. We are under His protection. We are safe with Him.

Sri Ramakrishna said that God is personal, impersonal and beyond. In other words, there are two ways in which our human minds can try to think of Him—as a personal being and as an impersonal being. But, behind and beyond these two aspects is another—the absolute reality of God which no mind can grasp, even to the very slightest degree. That is the divine "beyond" which can be described only by means of negation, by saying "it is not this, it is not this." However, the religion which Christ taught is fundamentally what the

Hindus call Bhakti Yoga, the path of loving devotion. The devotee who follows this path finds that God's aspect as an impersonal being is too much of an abstraction to be loved. In order to be able to pray and meditate we have, as Sri Ramakrishna was always teaching, to enter into a relationship with God as a person. Various relationships with God are, of course, possible. We can think of Him as our Master, our Father or Mother, our Friend and Playmate, our Child or our Lover. What matters is that we learn to think of Him with devotion and love.

"Hallowed be Thy Name." In almost every religion and system of philosophy we find that emphasis is laid upon the Name, the Logos, the Word. In India, we find that same idea accepted which is expressed at the beginning of the Fourth Gospel, that the name of God is identical with God. In Vedanta, God's name is called the *Mantram:* a Mantram is given by the teacher to every devotee at the ceremony of his initiation. The idea is that by repeating this Mantram, by hallowing His name, over and over again, we let God take possession of our conscious mind; so that, finally, no matter what we are doing or saying or thinking, some part of our mind will be praising Him. The Mantram is like a rope which will draw us to God almost without our effort. All we have to do is to hold fast to it.

"Thy Kingdom Come. Thy Will be done in earth, as it is in Heaven." When a Hindu performs ritualistic worship, the first prayer he says is: "As with eyes wide open, a man sees the sky above him, so the Seer sees God continually, the Supreme Truth, the All-Pervading Existence." If only our Divine sight opens we shall see God's Kingdom come here. This is not a hope for the future. God's Kingdom has come already: it has always been with us. So Christ is teaching us to pray that we may transcend space and time while living here on earth, and may know God's Kingdom in our hearts and all around us.

How is a beginner in spiritual life to do the will of God? How can he possibly know if what he is doing is God's will or not? Throughout history, in every country, we find all sorts of people, from kings and dictators down to beggars, doing what *they* want to do and announcing confidently that it is God's will. Even those dismal people who habitually do the most unpleasant things, the things they least want to do, still cannot be sure that they are doing God's will: they may be just taking a delight in torturing themselves. No—until we become spiritually illumined, until God actually speaks to us, we cannot know, in any given situation, what His will may be. But we *can* say confidently, even in our present ignorance, that His will is whatever will lead us to Him. And when the day comes that brings us into perfect union with Him, so that we are literally filled with God, then we can become His instruments and actually do His will. So let us pray: "Lord, I do not know what Your will is, but do it through me. Let Your will, not my will, be done! Make me a tool in Your hand."

"Give us this day our daily bread." Nearly all Bible commentators agree that the bread which is spoken of here is the bread of Grace. We are praying that this Grace may be revealed to us. We are asking to have it "this day," not tomorrow, not in a year's time, but now, this very moment! As a child, I used to love the story of the girl who went out into the woods to wait for God. She was certain that, sooner or later, He would pass by. Year followed year, she became a woman and then an old woman, but always she waited with eager expectancy. She was ready for Him at every moment of every day. Whenever a leaf fell or a creature moved in the undergrowth, she would think: "Here He comes!" and at last, God did really come. He passed by her, and her whole life was blessed. That is the faith we need: we must know that God's Grace can be revealed to us at any moment, and at the same time we must be prepared to wait a whole life long, or many lives, if need be. Very few people have learned to live in that spirit of expectancy. Most of us feel that we have so many impurities, so many faults to overcome, so much discipline to work through, that we cannot possibly reach God until some distant point in the future. This apparent humility is really a form of vanity, because it presupposes that we can know God through our own efforts, our own will power. That is all nonsense! Your own struggles will never make you pure or bring you the sight of God. That can come only through His Grace. True, there must be self-effort. We must struggle desperately, with every ounce of our strength. But we must also know that, quite irrespective of our achievement, God's Grace may descend upon us at any moment. Always be ready.

# The Sermon on the Mount—V
## SWAMI PRABHAVANANDA

"AND FORGIVE US OUR DEBTS, as we forgive our debtors." A
Hindu or Buddhist who reads this passage will at once understand the word "debt" to mean the debt of Karma. When
we recognize this debt, when we realize that everything,
good or bad that comes to us has been previously earned by
ourselves alone, then we know that we must not hold anybody else responsible for anything that we suffer in our lives.
Ordinarily, we all have that tendency to put the blame on
the other fellow. At the very beginning of creation, we find
Adam putting the blame on to Eve. And Eve, in her turn,
put the blame on to the Serpent. If we are ready to assume
responsibility for our own debts, and not blame others, then
it will be easy for us to forgive our own debtors, those who
take something away from us or do us some harm. From that
point, we can go on to say: "If it is by my own doing that I
am what I am, then I can also become what I wish to be."
And so we struggle to improve ourselves, and finally transcend the law of Karma altogether.

"And lead us not into temptation, but deliver us from
evil." This part of the prayer is hard for exclusively Christian theologians to understand. But to a student of the Gita
it seems very natural. How is it possible, the Christian asks,
for God to tempt anybody? The Gita replies that this whole
universe is one gigantic temptation, and that this universe
is Maya, the Divine Illusion. It is God Himself, as seen from
our ignorant and degenerate viewpoint. As soon as we are
born, we are caught in the power of this Maya. In the story
of the Garden of Eden, Adam is warned not to eat the fruit
of the Tree. As soon as he has eaten it, his *Atman* becomes
identified with the sense of ego: he recognizes good and evil
and the whole universe which Maya created.

Ego is the root-cause of our ignorance. Our only way of escape from Maya is to surrender the ego, all our actions, and all our thoughts, completely to God. As Christ puts it, we must recognize that God's is "the kingdom, and the power, and the glory, for ever."

"When ye fast, be not, as the hypocrites, of a sad countenance: for they disfigure their faces, that they may appear unto men to fast. Verily I say unto you, 'They have their reward.' But thou, when thou fastest, anoint thine head, and wash thy face; that thou appear not unto men to fast, but unto thy Father which is in secret: and thy Father, which seeth in secret, shall reward thee openly."

Sri Ramakrishna often used to quote a traditional saying: "Beware of these: The man who wears the sacred leaf on his ear, one who is secretive and does not talk at all, one who cannot keep a secret and talks too much, a woman with a double veil, and the water of a pond which is covered with scum." In other words, beware of things which are other than they seem. A man who makes a show of religion has no religion at all. If a man finds religion inside, he will hate to show it outside: he keeps it sacred within himself. The truly illumined souls, for this reason, are very difficult to recognize. They do not advertise. But when they meet a seeker after truth who is sincere and earnest, and who is ready to hear their word, then they reveal themselves to him, and show him the way to God. We find that Jesus, also, asks his disciples not to preach to anybody and everybody, but only to those who are ready for it. "Give not that which is holy unto the dogs, neither cast ye your pearls before swine, lest they trample them under their feet, and turn again and rend you."

"Lay not up for yourselves treasures upon earth, where moth and rust doth corrupt, and where thieves break through and steal: But lay up for yourselves treasures in heaven." Here Jesus is repeating in a different way what we have heard already, that one of the conditions for successfully starting to live the spiritual life is to have right discrimination. We must be able to discriminate between the eternal and the non-eternal. We must know what it is that we are looking for. Once we are sure that it is the treasures in heaven we want, and not the treasures upon earth, then we shall not fail. No matter how often we may show weakness and make mistakes, we shall reach the goal in the end, as long as we can keep up the struggle. A little baby tries to walk: as one watches him falling down so often, it seems incredible that he will ever succeed. But he picks himself up, again and again, because the urge within him is so strong, and in the end he can walk upright without faltering. There is no failure in the spiritual life, as long as we do not give up the fight. And we shall never give it up, when once we can discriminate and know the true goal. So, whatever our weaknesses, let us be uncompromising about one thing, about our ideal, because "no man can serve two masters." The attempt to serve "God and Mammon" simultaneously is quite hopeless. Nobody can do it, and the sooner we stop trying, the better. "If thine eye be single, thy whole body shall be full of light. But if thine eye be evil, thy whole body shall be full of darkness." The "evil" spoken of here is the non-eternal, which can only lead us further and further into the night of spiritual confusion.

"Take no thought for your life," Jesus tells us. And he asks us to consider the fowls of the air, which neither sow nor reap, and yet are fed; and the lilies, which are so beautifully dressed, although they do not spin. "Seek ye first the kingdom of God and his righteousness, and all these things shall be added unto you."

In the West, people have known these words since their childhood, and thought them beautiful but quite unpractical. They prefer the worldly-wise motto: Trust in God, and keep your powder dry. And they are right, as long as they want to go on living by the values of this world. These teachings *are* unpractical for any individual who is not completely devoted to God. If he tries not to take thought for the morrow, it would be nonsense. But if you truly seek the Kingdom of God, then you will not care where you live, what you eat, or where you sleep. And there are actually hundreds and thousands of men and women living like this in the world today. Because this spirit has always kept alive to some extent in India, Indian culture has lived on and survived many other cultures which have been anxious for the conquests and triumphs of this earthly life, and have taken "thought for the morrow," and kept their powder dry. We have a story about a devotee who was being attacked by some robbers, so he prayed: "O God, come and help me!" Shiva, the God of Gods, and Mother Durga were sitting chatting together, when Shiva rose abruptly, without any explanation, and left her. However, after a moment, he reappeared again. So Durga asked Shiva where he had been. "You see," Shiva explained, "this devotee called me, so I had to go. But, when I reached him, I found that he was already chasing the robbers away with a stick. Although he called on me, he is trying to help himself. Let him try, then. I shall not go to his aid."

"Judge not, that ye be not judged. For with what judgment ye judge, ye shall be judged: and with what measure ye mete, it shall be measured to you again."

Everybody has that tendency, to gossip, criticize, and judge others. This gossip is a kind of relish—as we say in India, a chutney with your food. It may seem very innocent; yet it causes immense harm in human society, and particularly to those who indulge in it. Nobody can see a fault in another unless he has that fault in himself. Indeed, most often, this fault we seem to see exists only in our own impure imagination. How many of us can really look into the depths of another man, and see all the motives which are prompting him to act in a particular way? And yet we are so ready to judge, and to impute motives—the motives which *we* ourselves should have in similar circumstances. And these motives are always evil, because that gives the relish to the gossip. You will invariably find that if you criticize another person for a certain fault, and go on criticizing, that fault will grow in yourself. We relish finding fault with others because it swells our own ego-sense. Behind all such criticism, there is the same feeling: "*I* don't have this fault. I am greater than he is."

In India we have a saying that the fly sits on the filth as well as on the honey, but that the bee seeks only the honey and avoids the filth. And so the first vow which is given to the spiritual aspirant is: "May I follow the example of the bee, not that of the fly!" As we progress in the spiritual life, we learn to see the good in everyone. Real holy men have that attitude toward mankind: if you have the least drop of goodness in you they see an ocean of goodness within that drop. Not because they are foolishly optimistic, but because they see the possibility of future growth, and they emphasize that. The ideal is to see God in everybody. We must learn to see God looking out from behind the mask of so-called wickedness and worthlessness.

Does this mean that we should be blind to one another's faults, and never try to correct them? No—Jesus does not say that. But he says: "Thou hypocrite, first cast out the beam out of thine own eye; and then shalt thou see clearly to cast out the mote out of thy brother's eye." That is what makes the difference: not to be a hypocrite. If you really have that love for mankind, and are not just hypocritically finding fault in order to enlarge your own ego, then you can correct your brother's defects. Then you can tell him where he fails, not with malicious relish, but with love and sympathy. My master, Swami Brahmananda, like all such great souls, had moods in which he was unable to see any faults in anyone, because he was full of the divine consciousness. He saw God everywhere, and nothing but God. But at other times he scolded us, thundered at us, pounded at our faults. And then he would say: "Do you think you can run away from me, because I am apparently so cruel? The mother holds the child, and spanks it. The baby cries 'Mother!' And all the while it is in its mother's arms." But until we have that love, we have no right to criticize others. Let us rather see the fault in ourselves.

"Ask, and it shall be given you; seek, and ye shall find; knock, and it shall be opened unto you: for every one that asketh receiveth; and he that seeketh findeth; and to him that knocketh it shall be opened. Or what man is there of you, whom if his son ask bread, will give him a stone? Or if he ask a fish, will he give him a serpent? If ye then, being evil, know how to give good gifts unto your children, how much more shall your Father which is in heaven give good things to them that ask him?"

In this passage, Jesus sums up the whole truth of religion— and what is that? Two things: longing for God, and faith. What is faith? It is when we feel the presence of God, when we knock at the door *knowing* that it will be opened. This faith does not come until we have achieved purity of heart. The impurities in our minds, the lusts, passions, fleshly desires, prevent us from seeing God, who is nevertheless present all the time, everywhere. The more you knock, the more you ask and pray, the more this world will be seen to be a mere appearance, and the reality of God's presence will show through. Use all your power, all your strength, to open that door.

"Therefore all things whatsoever ye would that men should do to you, do ye even so to them: for this is the law and the prophets." Here Jesus is telling us how we must conduct ourselves in human society. In the Gita there is a parallel passage: "He who is aware of both the grief and the happiness within every being to the same degree as he feels them within himself—him, O Arjuna, I hold to be the highest yogi." Just previously to this, Sri Krishna has been telling Arjuna how to meditate, how to love God and how to become absorbed in the consciousness of God. And then he teaches him this truth. There are some who believe that the search for God is apt to make the searcher indifferent to the sufferings of human beings. But the very opposite is true. The more sensitive we become, the more we become aware of others, and the more we care for them. We begin to know that our own Self is the same Self in everyone else. Because we wish to be happy, we cannot cause unhappiness to others; and so we cannot hurt others in any way.

"Enter ye in at the strait gate: for wide is the gate, and broad is the way, that leadeth to destruction, and many there be which go in thereat: because strait is the gate, and narrow is the way, which leadeth unto life, and few there be that find it."

Here Jesus warns us that realization of God is not easy. Purity of heart can only be achieved after a great struggle. In the Katha-Upanishad, we read: "Like the sharp edge of a razor, the sages say, is the Path—hard it is, and difficult to walk." We are also told that the Lord created the senses "outgoing." The natural human tendency is to rush out through the broad ways of the senses and lose oneself in the world. The process of religious growth is to turn that whole current of life around, and make it flow inward, through "the strait gate." In this connection, it is interesting to remember the mystical teaching of the Yoga Aphorisms of Patanjali. Here, mention is made of three nerve-passages in the spine, which are called the *Ida,* the *Pingala* and the *Sushumna.* The *Ida* and the *Pingala* are the two outer passages of the spinal nerves, but modern anatomists have been unable to find any use for the *Sushumna,* the central passage. However, Yoga tells us that, if the nerve-current can be made to flow through that narrow channel, a man rises above space, time and causation, and sees the Reality. So this Sushumna would be literally a narrow gate leading to knowledge of God Himself.

"Beware of false prophets, which come to you in sheep's clothing, but inwardly they are ravening wolves." Jesus tells us to discriminate between true and false religion. True religion shows us how to overcome the world, but the teachers of false religion hold out the promise of success and wealth in the world. "Ye shall know them by their fruits. Do men gather grapes of thorns, or figs of thistles?" The fruits of false religion are worldly success; the fruits of true religion are illumination. Sri Ramakrishna followed the paths of many religions during his life on earth, and always applied the same test to each: "Will it give me the illumination of God?" If he got that, then he knew that that was a true religion. When told about some new sect, he would ask: "Do they teach love for God? Do they teach people how to realize God?" If not, he would have nothing to do with it.

"Not every one that saith unto me, 'Lord, Lord,' shall enter into the kingdom of heaven; but he that doeth the will of my Father which is in heaven."

Now this, and the verses which follow, have frequently been misinterpreted into a kind of humanistic religion. Matthew Arnold, for example, said that "religion is ethical life touched by emotion." The humanists interpret this phrase about doing "the will of my Father" to mean doing good works in the external world. They say: "Lord, Lord," to give the work a touch of emotion, and then go ahead with their social service. They use God as a scavenger to clean out the drains of human society.

But there is only one way of doing the will of God, and

that is, first, to realize Him. Until we have done that, we can never know what His will is. Does this mean that we must give up our humanitarian work? No, it does not mean that. But we are not to do the work simply as philanthropy, as service to mankind; but as service to God, and out of love for God. There is a very important distinction between these two attitudes. Among those who go to serve mankind, we find an egotism arising. They begin to think and say: "Without me, everything will go to pieces. I am vitally important. Nothing must stand in the way of this work. The world needs me." And then, it is not long before they are saying: "God needs me." When I first came to this country, I visited a Sunday-school class, and the teacher had written on the board: "God needs your help." And later on I heard a minister say: "We all know that God is not omnipotent. We must help Him to gain more power." That is the direct opposite of what Jesus taught. He came to tell us that God does *not* need us; we need Him.

When you do your social service as service to God, you may seemingly do the same work, but there is a vast difference. Swami Vivekananda said that when we help another we should kneel down before him and give thanks that God lets us have this opportunity of serving Him. Religion must not be either egocentric or altruistic, but theocentric. We have to center our whole thought and mind upon God, and then extend our arms to everyone, embracing them all in the love of God. That, and not humanistic social service, is what Jesus actually taught.

"Therefore whosoever heareth these sayings of mine, and doeth them, I will liken him unto a wise man, which built his house upon a rock: and the rain descended, and the floods came, and the winds blew, and beat upon that house; and it fell not: for it was founded upon a rock."

That rock is the rock of experience. When once you have been face to face with Reality, when you are founded upon that, then nothing can shake you. Until we have built upon that rock—no matter how strong our faith may seem to be, emotionally—we shall be shaken by these storms of doubt; and the house will fall, and have to be rebuilt, again and again. The faith which merely exclaims: "Oh, I believe in

Jesus, I accept him!" and does nothing further, is no true faith. It will give us no support when the storm begins to blow. And so we come back to that basic truth: religion is something practical, it is something you have to do, and be, and live, or else it is nothing.

"And it came to pass, when Jesus had ended these sayings, the people were astonished at his doctrine: for he taught them as one having authority, and not as the scribes." Jesus was not speaking from hearsay. He knew what he was saying was true, because it was his own experience; he spoke from the rock of personal knowledge. No second-hand report, no amount of study, no wealth of eloquence, can be compared to the absolute guarantee of first-hand witness which an illumined teacher brings us. The reports may be convincing, the arguments of the theologians may be sound, the eloquence may move us to tears—but always that little obstinate area of doubt must remain in our own minds. Yes, and even when a Christ, a Buddha, a Ramakrishna arises, and says: "I have seen Him"—even *that* is not enough. Actually to have been present, to listen to the Sermon on the Mount, must have been one of the most tremendous experiences a human being could have—yet even this was an experience at second-hand; and so we find that some of Christ's most intimate disciples were later troubled with doubts. Swami Vivekananda had doubts too, even after long intimacy with Sri Ramakrishna. And those doubts only vanished finally when the goal had been reached, the goal of all spiritual life; actual, personal realization of God.

# Maya and Mortal Mind

## John van Druten

In part five of his analysis of the Sermon on the Mount, Swami Prabhavananda raises a point which, he says, is hard for exclusively Christian theologians to understand, but very natural to a student of the Gita. It is also, oddly enough, comparatively natural to a student of that latter-day religion called Christian Science, or at any rate to one who has studied the more recent interpretations thereof.

And since this magazine avows its purpose as "promoting the work of spiritual and philosophical understanding between the East and the West," I feel I need not apologize for this attempt to show the coincidence of those two understandings on this question.

The point of which the Swami is speaking is the phrase: "Lead us not into temptation," and his explanation thereof, derived from the Gita, is that the whole universe is one gigantic temptation, being Maya, the Divine Illusion. The universe, he points out, is God Himself, as seen from our ignorant and degenerate viewpoint. Which is, when referring to the so-called material world, exactly what the Christian Scientist calls "Mortal Mind," defined, among other definitions, by Mary Baker Eddy, as "a belief that life, substance and intelligence are in and of matter; the opposite of Spirit, and therefore the opposite of God." Maya, or Mortal Mind, both are illusions, or false conceptions of reality.

"Ego," says the Swami, "is the root-cause of our ignorance." What is Ego but a belief in separation from God, a belief in a separate and individual existence—at best, a belief in duality, a duality of man and God, of matter and Spirit; at worst, a belief in finite and material existence as reality, and as the whole of reality? The holding of these beliefs, it has long seemed to me, must be the so-called sin against the

Holy Ghost, since they are the beliefs that prevent one from ever seeing, knowing or understanding the holy Spirit. I have used the phrases "at best" and "at worst" in classifying them as lesser and greater forms of the same error, but I am by no means sure that such a classification is justified, or that there is any fundamental difference between them as far as understanding God is concerned. It is surely no greater blasphemy, heresy or misconception of the divine nature to deny its whole existence, than to deny its omnipotence and omnipresence, since those qualities *are* its nature, and to attempt to limit them, to believe in a joint-partnership of Spirit and matter, is no different from denying Spirit in its entirety, for Spirit must be all or nothing.

The belief, then, in existence apart from God, is the major sin; ultimately, it is the only sin, error or misconception. Too many people, of whatever professed religious faith, including many Christian Scientists, adhere in their hearts to this conception of the universe; imagining, as a Christian Science teacher has recently put it, "that the spiritual universe has a kind of imperfect repetition in a material universe . . . a material world in which almost everything is wrong, while somewhere afar off is the spiritual universe, good and perfect, in fact, heaven itself." It is part of the teaching of Christian Science that "by constantly identifying yourself with the limited and the imperfect, you perpetuate these restrictions for yourself, and thereby for that which appears as your world."

In other words, by believing in the joint partnership, one makes oneself subject to it; by accepting the illusion as reality, one is bound to it, and to its illusory laws of pain, lack and limitation—just as though, having read or been told of some arbitrary and non-existent law of the country he was living in, the ordinary man would consider himself bound by it, and find his liberty considerably restricted; or as a man, not knowing he has crossed the frontier from a tyrannous to a free country, would continue to act as though still oppressed by the rigours of the former. Not until one knows and surrenders to the knowledge that one is a subject only of the Kingdom of God, owing obedience only to the laws thereof, is true freedom of living manifested.

How is this knowledge and this surrender to be arrived at? What is the way of escape from Maya? "Only," says the Swami, "to surrender the ego, all our actions, and all our thoughts completely to God. As Christ puts it, we must recognize that God's is 'the kingdom, and the power, and the glory, for ever.'"

Surrender of the ego means, surely, first of all, surrender of the illusion of an existence separate from God, of personal sense in all that it implies of any effort, power or achievement of one's own; or, even "with God's help." For God does not "help"; God *does,* or *is.* The very word "help" suggests duality; implies it, even, of necessity, since, in order that help can be possible, there must be two parties—the helped and the helper. And to accept the belief that one can need or receive help, even though it may be an abasement of the ego, a temporary admission of its limitations, still affirms its existence as an entity. For God to "help" means that He is not omnipotent, but lending His power as an adjunct to another power, a mortal one. The extreme of this belief can be seen in a remark reported to me once by a Church of England country clergyman, to whom one of his parishioners, recounting an experience of trial and fortitude, in which she found herself putting forth a physical strength she did not know she possessed, explained: "Of course, the Good Lord helped me all He could."

Ego, personality, a sense of human power and existence; these are the stumbling-blocks that perpetuate the Maya. And this is no exclusive tenet of Oriental philosophy. In speaking of the miracles of the New Testament, Dr. de Lange, one of the most absolute and advanced of Christian Science teachers, whom I have already quoted above, recently said: "Had the Master accepted as his habitual thought of himself the picture painted of him by his family and friends—a loving person going around performing miracles— he never could have accomplished a single one of his works. That which appears as a person can never attain his highest aspiration of divine good, unless the personal sense yields to the divine."

Personal sense, and Ego; Mortal Mind and Maya; the terms seem interchangeable. One is the cause, and the other the effect; and yet cause and effect are one, and both, in the absolute sense, non-existent. If God, or Spirit, is All, then Ego, a separate material being, has no reality, save as a misconception of what we truly are; and it is this misconception that produces Maya which, being illusion, is self-defined as non-existent. The temptation, then, from which we are to pray for deliverance, is the temptation to deny God as All-in-All. So long as we do deny Him, so long will other temptations, temptations of the world, products of our ignorance, beset us, and we will continue to whine, to complain, or to boast and congratulate ourselves. As another teacher of Christian Science has recently put it: "When we say to ourselves 'O Lord, how long?,' the answer will come back 'Just as long as you deny My omnipresence.'"

# Martha

## Amiya Corbin

"Come unto Me, . . . and I will give you rest. . . ." With the automatic persistence of a mantram these words of her Lord repeated themselves in Martha's brain as she laid herself down to rest one hot afternoon. She felt more tired than usual; there were so many extra things to be done whenever the Master came to visit them, and He was coming that very evening. Though physically tired, Martha felt none of the nervous exhaustion which had usually accompanied her former preparations, and as she lay there, she recalled again, as she so often did, that never-to-be-forgotten day when Jesus had taught her the great secret of service.

What a day that had been! It seemed that everything had gone wrong from the very moment she got up that morning. There was yet much to be done, and she still felt nervous and tired from the previous day's activities, and, to make matters worse, Mary was nowhere to be found. Not that she was ever much help now-a-days. Ever since their first meeting with the Master, she had changed. She had always been something of a dreamer, and, since the coming of Jesus, she would spend hours alone in her room or in the garden. Martha knew she was always thinking of Him, and the things He had taught her, and it was all right with her; she sometimes wished that she, too, had time to day-dream or "meditate" as Mary called it. But everybody couldn't be dreamers. There were things to be done; household duties didn't just drop away, that she knew only too well; but that she should go off completely at such a time was too much for Martha. She became furious, and it did nothing to lessen her annoyance when later Mary arrived with the Master and His friends, whom she had gone out to meet.

Martha recalled how curtly she had welcomed the guests,

and how angry she had felt toward Mary as she returned to the kitchen and the cooking. She had been sure that Mary would at least help her serve the meal. Looking back over the scene it was difficult for Martha now to understand how she could have allowed herself to get so upset. But upset she had been! She could have shaken her sister, but instead she had made that ghastly mistake! A chill ran over her as she recalled that most dreadful scene. Why could not Mary have used some initiative, why could she not have felt Martha's extremity, and at least have offered to help? How much pain it might have saved! Or so Martha thought. But when, instead, poor Martha lost her last ounce of control and burst in upon them, there was Mary sitting at the feet of Jesus, looking up into His face, and listening to His words with rapt attention! And then the reproach that followed her demand for help! "Martha, Martha, thou art careful and troubled about many things: but one thing is needful: and Mary hath chosen that good part. . . ." Poor Martha! Stunned and crushed, she returned to her kitchen. She wondered vaguely what Mary thought about it all. Did she understand what He meant by the "good part"? She did not blame her sister; rather she felt that somehow she herself was at fault, but how? In silence she served her guests, only waiting till she could steal away to the solitude of her own room.

All that afternoon the question haunted her: what was that one needful thing, what was that "good part"? In what way was Mary's part better than hers? In what way were they different? She tried to recall something Jesus might sometime have said which would answer the question for her, but in vain. She realized sadly that she had always been too busy to find much time to sit at His feet like Mary did, and listen to His teachings. She realized that she was with Him only at mealtimes, and these times were always occasions of festivity. Perhaps, after all, in her anxiety to serve Him, she had actually neglected Him! But He came so seldom, His life was so lonely, His comforts so few, that she had always felt that no effort was too great, no service too small, if only she could give Him even a little happiness and comfort. Didn't He *know* that? Didn't He know why she had been angry at

Mary? Surely He must know; and He must also know the agony of remorse that followed her outburst!

She did not see Him again that day until she went to bid Him goodnight as He sat in the garden. At first He did not see her as she approached, but, as the moon cast her shadow across the path He looked up and smiled. To Martha it seemed as if the very gates of heaven had opened! Never had she seen such a smile on any face, not even on His. She stood transfixed! Softly He spoke, "Come unto Me. . . ." Instantly Martha was at His feet, sobbing her weary heart out. And even as she wept she knew that He did know everything that was in her heart; she knew that all the doubts and perplexities that clouded her mind were clear to Him.

For some time they remained silent, and as she knelt at His feet, Martha felt that all her grief was dispelled, all her doubts were quieted, and a peace had descended upon her, such as she had never known. Then, as He spoke, she looked up into His face and listened as He explained to her how difficult the path of action was to follow. It was like walking a tight-rope—so easy to lose one's balance, because the moment any attachment to the action itself, or to the fruits of the action entered in, the balance was lost, one fell from the ideal, and by so falling, suffered. And, because attachment brought suffering, Jesus urged Martha to lay her yoke upon Him, and not upon her service to Him, for, as long as one laboured for the meat which perished, one would always be dissatisfied, disturbed, and harassed, just as she had been that very day.

How gently, yet how very clearly He had explained what the "good part" was which Mary had chosen. Fundamentally neither sister was superior to the other. Both were right, both were devoted, but each expressed her devotion according to her own temperament and capacity. By her very nature Mary was a contemplative, whereas Martha was active, and found her best expression in service to others. While Mary had united—or yoked—herself to the Christhood of Jesus, in contemplation of Him, Martha had attached herself to Jesus the man through service and devotion to the personality. The "good part" lay in the constant remembrance of God, whether through meditation or through action it did not matter.

As Martha learned all these things, she felt as if her whole life had been completely transformed, so much so, that, from the moment when she left Him, still sitting in the garden, never did she forget Him. She could not. She felt that her mind had become forever united with her Lord's. Everything she did, she did as an offering to Him, until gradually, even as her sister Mary, she too became a contemplative, while yet remaining active. She saw Him in all beings, and served Him in all.

And, now, as she lay resting, it seemed she could hear His voice saying once again: "Well done, thou good and faithful servant . . .", and she felt as if her whole being had been caught up into that peace which He had promised when He said: ". . . and you shall find rest unto your soul."

# *The Gita and War*
## CHRISTOPHER ISHERWOOD

IN THE COURSE of a year spent studying the Bhagavad-Gita, I have talked about its philosophy to a considerable number of people. Whatever else they had to say, I found them, almost without exception, agreed on one point: that the Gita "sanctions" War. Some were glad of this. Others were sorry. But all, I think, were puzzled. Educated in the Christian tradition, they were accustomed to a gospel which is uncompromisingly pacifist. However deeply they might be convinced of the justice or necessity of some particular conflict, they didn't like what they regarded as a general approval of the use of military force. They themselves, mere human beings struggling in the everyday world, might be driven to fight and kill one another, but they wanted Krishna, like Jesus, to stand for a higher ideal. That was their reaction.

I do not wish to sound superior or conceited when I say that I myself do not put this interpretation upon the teaching of the Gita. I will try to explain why I do not: not merely for the information of the few people who may be interested, but because I want to straighten out my own ideas. The question is of the greatest importance to me, because I am myself a pacifist, and because I believe the Gita to be one of the major religious documents of the world. If its teachings did not seem to me to agree with those of the other gospels and scriptures, then my own system of values would be thrown into confusion, and I should feel completely bewildered.

Briefly, the circumstances of the Gita dialogue can be described as follows:

Two factions, closely bound to each other by ties of blood and friendship, are about to engage in a civil war. Arjuna, one of the leading generals, has Krishna for his charioteer. Krishna has told Arjuna that he will not fight, but has promised to accompany him throughout the battle. Just before it begins, Arjuna asks Krishna to drive his chariot into the no-man's-land between the two armies. Krishna does so. Arjuna looks at the opposing army, and realizes that he is about to kill those whom he loves better than life itself. In his despair, he exclaims: "I will not fight!"

Krishna's reply to Arjuna occupies the rest of the book. It deals not only with Arjuna's immediate personal problem, but with the whole nature of action, the meaning of life, and the aims for which man must struggle, here on earth. At the end of their conversation, Arjuna has changed his mind. He is ready to fight. And the battle begins.

Before trying to analyze Krishna's arguments, I must mention two points which certain commentators have raised with regard to the battle itself. In the first place, it is sometimes said that the battle of Kurukshetra cannot possibly be compared to a battle in modern war. It was, in fact, a kind of tournament, governed by all the complex and humane rules of ancient Indian chivalry. A soldier mounted upon an elephant may not attack a foot-soldier. No man may be struck or shot at while running away. No one may be killed who has lost his weapons. And we are told, in the Mahabharata, that the opposing armies stopped fighting every evening, and even visited each other and fraternized during the night. In the second place, it is sometimes said that the whole battle is to be regarded allegorically. Arjuna is the individual man, Krishna is the indwelling Godhead, the enemies are man's evil tendencies, and so forth.

All this is interesting, of course. But it has nothing to do with our problem. If Krishna is only talking figuratively, or only about War under certain conditions, then the Gita is just a fable, an archaic curiosity: we need not discuss it. Personally, I prefer to forget Kurukshetra and ancient India altogether, and imagine a similar dialogue taking place today, in a plane over the European front or the Japanese positions on a Pacific island. If the Gita has any validity, its reference is equally to this war and this very year.

To understand the Gita, we must first consider what it is and what it is not. We must consider its setting. When Jesus spoke the words which are recorded as the Sermon on the

Mount, he was talking to a group of followers in the most peaceful atmosphere imaginable, far from the great city, far from all strife and confusion. He was expressing the highest truth of which man's mind is capable, in general terms, without reference to any immediate crisis or problem. And even in the Garden of Gethsemane, when he told Peter to sheathe his sword, he was addressing a dedicated disciple, a monk, a man who was being trained to preach and live the spiritual life. For Peter, there could be no compromise. He must learn to accept the highest and strictest ideal, the ideal of non-violence.

The Gita is very different. Krishna and Arjuna are on a battlefield. Arjuna is a warrior by birth and profession. He corresponds to the mediaeval knight of Christendom. His problem is considered in relation to the circumstances of the moment. The Gita fits into the narrative of an epic poem, the Mahabharata, and must be read in the light of previous happenings. It is not simply a sermon, a philosophical treatise.

This, I believe, is the cause of much misunderstanding. We all tend to remember most clearly the part of a book which we read first. The opening chapters of the Gita deal with a particular case: they are concerned with a soldier and the duties of a soldier. Later on, Krishna passes from the particular to the general, and utters those same truths which were afterwards taught by Jesus and the Buddha. But the first impression is apt to remain. The superficial reader closes the book and remembers only Arjuna and the battle. He says to himself: "Krishna tells us that we must fight."

Krishna, it must be repeated, is not talking to a monk. We ought to be glad of this, not sorry. The vast majority of mankind are not monks, but householders. What a great teacher has to say to a married man, a soldier, is of immediate interest to the world at large.

We must realize, also, that Krishna, in teaching Arjuna, employs two sets of values, the relative and the absolute. This duality is inherent in the circumstances of the story. For Krishna is both Arjuna's personal friend and his illumined teacher. He is a fellow-mortal and he is God. As God, he expresses the absolute truth, the highest ideal. As a fellow-man, he presents the relative values which apply to Arjuna's particular condition. Considered superficially, this duality of attitude may seem to produce contradictions. Carefully studied, it will be seen to compose into a complete and satis-fying philosophical picture. For life itself is double-faced; and any attempt at simplification will only bring us to ulti-mate confusion.

One circumstance renders Arjuna's compassion suspect: its occasion. Arjuna himself is dimly aware of this. "Is this real compassion I feel," he asks Krishna, "or only a delusion? My mind gropes about in darkness. I cannot see where my duty lies." Up to this moment, Arjuna has not hesitated. He has accepted the necessity of the war. He has assumed responsi-bility for its leadership. Then, suddenly, he sees the other side of the picture: the bloodshed, the horror. And he recoils.

In the years that followed the 1914–18 war, much pacifist propaganda was based on gruesome narratives of battle and books of photographs showing mutilated corpses. "This is what War is like," said the authors. "Isn't it horrible? Do you want to go through this again?" And nearly everybody agreed that they didn't. But this sort of revulsion is always short-lived, because it appeals, fundamentally, to our cowardice. When a new war-situation develops, most of us react in the opposite direction, and rightly. Men can never, ultimately be deterred from any course of action by cowardice alone. Otherwise we should never have evolved from the jellyfish. We have to go forward, and the path is always dangerous, in one way or another. Arjuna has to go forward. Krishna tells him so. Arjuna must accept the sum of his actions up to that moment—and the sum is this battle.

Krishna's reply begins by dealing with Arjuna's feelings of revulsion, on general grounds. Arjuna shrinks from the act itself, the act of killing. Krishna reminds him that, in the absolute sense, there is no such act. The Atman, the in-dwelling Godhead, is the only reality. This body is simply an appearance: its existence, its destruction, are alike illu-sory. In the absolute sense, all talk of killing or being killed is meaningless.

> *"Some say this Atman*
> *Is slain, and others*
> *Call It the slayer:*
> *They know nothing.*
> *How can It slay*
> *Or who shall slay It?"*

Therefore, if Arjuna is objecting to the act of killing, as such, he need have no scruples. For he only seems to kill.

Then, with one of those changes of viewpoint which may bewilder and shock a reader who opens the Gita for the first time and takes only its surface meaning, Krishna begins to talk to Arjuna as man to man:

"Even if you consider this from the standpoint of your own caste-duty, you ought not to hesitate; for, to a warrior, there is nothing nobler than a righteous war. . . .

"But if you refuse to fight this righteous war, you will be turning aside from your duty. You will be a sinner, and disgraced. People will speak ill of you throughout the ages. . . ."

For Arjuna, a member of the warrior caste, the fighting of this battle, in defense of his family and property, is undoubtedly "righteous." It is his duty. In the Gita, we find that the caste-system is presented as a kind of natural order. Men are divided into four groups, according to their capacities and characteristics. Each group has its peculiar duties, ethics and responsibilities; and these must be accepted. It is the way of spiritual growth. A man must go forward from where he stands. He cannot jump to the Absolute: he must evolve toward it. He cannot arbitrarily assume the duties which belong to another group. If he does so, his whole system of values will be upset, his conscience can no longer direct him, and he will stray into pride or doubt or mental confusion. "Prefer to die doing your own duty," Krishna teaches: "The duty of another will bring you into great spiritual danger."

Socially, the caste-system is graded. The merchants are above the servants. The leaders and warriors are above the merchants. The priestly Brahmins are highest of all. But, spiritually, there are no such distinctions. Krishna is very clear on this point. Everyone, he says, can attain the highest sainthood by following the prescribed path of his own caste-duty. In Southern India, we are told of seven saints who belonged to the lowest caste of all, the untouchables. And the same principle, of course, holds true if we apply the caste-classification to the social pattern of Europe. Men have grown into spiritual giants while carrying out their duties as merchants, peasants, doctors, popes, scullions or kings.

In the purely physical sphere of action, Arjuna is, indeed, no longer a free agent. The act of war is upon him: it has evolved out of his previous actions. He cannot choose. "If, in your vanity, you say 'I will not fight,' your resolve is vain. Your own nature will drive you to the act." At any given moment in time, we are what we are; and our actions express that condition. We cannot run away from our actions, because we carry the condition with us. On the highest mountain, in the darkest cave, we must turn at last and accept the consequences of being ourselves. Only through this accept-ance can we begin to evolve further. We may select the battleground. We cannot avoid the battle.

Arjuna is bound by the law of Karma, the law of cause and effect which has brought him face to face with this particular situation. Now he is compelled to act, but he is still free to make his choice between two different ways of performing the action. Krishna introduces this great theme—the prin-cipal theme of the Gita—in the passage which immediately follows. He proceeds to define the nature of action.

In general, mankind almost always acts with attachment: that is to say, with fear and desire. Desire for a certain result, and fear that this result will not be obtained. Attached ac-tion binds us to the world of appearance, to the continual doing of more action. We live in a delirium of doing, and the consequences of our past actions condition the actions we are about to perform. According to the Gita, it is attached action which compels us to revisit this world, to be reborn again and again.

But there is another way of performing action; and this is without fear and without desire. The Christians call it "holy indifference," and the Hindus "non-attachment." Both names are slightly misleading. They suggest coldness and lack of enthusiasm. That is why people often confuse non-attach-ment with fatalism, when, actually, they are opposites. The fatalist simply does not care. He will get what is coming to him. Why make any effort? Fatalists are apt to get drunk or spend most of the day in bed. The doer of non-attached action, on the other hand, is the most conscientious of men. He does not run away from life: he accepts it, much more completely than those whose pleasures are tinged with anxiety and whose defeats are embittered by regret. No matter whether he is sweeping out a room, or calculating the position of a star, or taking the chair at a meeting, he does it to the utmost limit of his powers—so carefully, so devotedly, so wholeheartedly, that the dividing-line between the chosen activity and the necessary chore disappears altogether. All work becomes equally and vitally important. It is only toward the results of work that he remains indifferent. Perhaps a dog runs across the clean floor with muddy paws. Perhaps his researches are recognized by Harvard University. Perhaps somebody throws a rotten egg at him. It doesn't matter. He goes right on with his job. We find something of this spirit in the lives of all truly great men and women, including the professed atheists and agnostics. Madame Curie refuses the Legion of Honor with the matter-of fact words: "I don't see the utility of it." Lenin, in 1921, with the White armies converging on Moscow, his regime apparently doomed, his work brought to nothing, calmly sits down and writes the order: "The peasants in the localities of Gorki and Ziianova are immediately to be supplied with electric light." This, in its highest development, is the attitude of the saint. When action is done in this spirit, Krishna teaches, it will lead us to true wisdom, to the knowledge of what is behind action, behind all life: the ultimate Reality. And, with the growth of this knowledge, the need for further action will gradually fall away from us. The law of Karma will cease to operate. We shall realize our true nature, which is God.

It follows, therefore, that every action, under certain circumstances and for certain people, may be a stepping-stone to spiritual growth—if it is done in the spirit of non-attachment. All good and all evil is relative to the individual point of growth. For each individual, certain acts are absolutely wrong. Indeed, there may well be acts which are absolutely wrong for every individual alive on earth today. But, in the highest sense, there can be neither good nor evil.

> *"The Lord is everywhere*
> *And always perfect:*
> *What does He care for man's sin*
> *Or the righteousness of man?"*

Because Krishna is speaking as God Himself, he can take this attitude, and advise Arjuna to fight. Because Arjuna has reached this particular stage in his development, he can kill his enemies and actually be doing his duty.

There is no question, here, of doing evil that good may come. The Gita does not countenance such opportunism. Arjuna is to do the best he knows, in order to pass beyond that best to better. Later, his fighting at Kurukshetra may seem evil to him, and it *will* be evil—then. Doing the evil you know to be evil will never bring good. It will lead only to more evil, more attachment, more ignorance.

How, in this complex world, are we to know what our own duty is? There is no greater problem. Yet, somehow, we have to find our position and make our stand. For the majority, much self-analysis, much trial and error, would seem to be the only way. But, having found that position, we must accept it in its entirety. The soldier has many responsibilities and duties besides fighting. The pacifist has much else to do besides refusing to fight. These duties and responsibilities extend equally over wartime and peace: they cover our whole life. But, in every case, the final ideal is the same.

The Gita neither sanctions War nor condemns it. Regarding no action as of absolute value, either for good or evil, it cannot possibly do either. Its teaching should warn us not to dare to judge others. How can we prescribe our neighbor's duty when it is so hard for us to know our own? The pacifist must respect Arjuna. Arjuna must respect the pacifist. Both are going toward the same goal. There is an underlying solidarity between them which can be expressed, if each one follows, without compromise, the path upon which he finds himself. For we can only help others to do their duty by doing what we ourselves believe to be right. It is the one supremely social act.

# Action and Contemplation
## ALDOUS HUXLEY

THE VOCABULARY of even intelligent and well educated people is full of words and phrases which they glibly use without ever having troubled to analyze them or exactly determine their meaning. One could fill an entire volume with a discussion of such commonly used, but undefined and unanalyzed phrases. Here, however, I propose to deal with only one of them, the phrase "life of action," so frequently used, in discussions of spiritual religion, in contradistinction to the "life of contemplation." What exactly does this phrase mean? And, passing from the sphere of words to the spheres of facts and values, how is action related to contemplation, and how ought the two to be related?

In ordinary language, "life of action" connotes the sort of life led by film heroes, war correspondents, business executives, politicians and so forth. Not so in the vocabulary of the religious life. To the religious psychologist the "active life" of common speech is merely worldly life, lived more or less unregenerately by people who have done little or nothing to rid themselves of the "Old Adam" and to establish contact with ultimate reality. What the religious psychologist or theologian calls "active life" is the life of good works. To be active is to follow the way of Martha, who ministered to the needs of the master, while Mary (the personification, in the West, of the contemplative life) sat and listened to his words. So far as the contemplative is concerned, the "active life" is not the life of worldly affairs; it is the life of consistent and strenuous virtue.

Pragmatism regards action as the end and thought as the means to that end; and contemporary popular philosophy accepts the pragmatist position. In the philosophy underlying Eastern and Western spiritual religion this position is reversed. Here, contemplation is the end, action (in which is included discursive thought) is valuable only as a means to the beatific vision of reality. "Action," wrote St. Thomas Aquinas, "should be something added to the life of prayer, not something taken away from it." This is the fundamental principle of the life of spiritual religion. Starting from it, practical mystics have critically examined the whole idea of action, and have laid down rules for the guidance of those whose concern is with ultimate reality rather than the world of selves. In the following paragraphs I shall summarize the Western mystical tradition in regard to the life of action.

In undertaking any action, those whose concern is with spiritual religion should model themselves upon God himself; for God created the world without in any way modifying his essential nature, and it is to this kind of action without attachment or involvement that the mystic should aspire. But to act in this way is impossible except for those who devote a certain amount of time to formal contemplation and who are able in the intervals constantly to "practice the presence of God." Both tasks are difficult, especially the latter, which is possible only to those far advanced along the road of spiritual perfection. So far as beginners are concerned, the doing even of good works may distract the soul from God. Action is safe only for proficients in the art of mental prayer. "If we have gone far in orison," says one Western authority, "we shall give much to action; if we are but middlingly advanced in the inward life, we shall give ourselves only moderately to outward life; if we have only a very little inwardness, we shall give nothing at all to what is external." To the reasons for this injunction already given, we may add others of a strictly utilitarian nature. It is a matter of experience and observation that well-intentioned actions performed by ordinary, unregenerate people, sunk in their selfhood and without spiritual insight, seldom do much good. St. John of the Cross put the whole matter in a single question and answer. Those who rush headlong into good works without having acquired through contemplation the power to act well—what do they accomplish? *"Poco mas que nada, y a veces nada, y aun a veces dano."* Little more than nothing, and sometimes nothing whatever, and sometimes even harm.

One reason for hell being paved with good intentions is to be found in the intrinsically unsatisfactory nature of actions performed by ordinary unregenerate men and women. That is why spiritual directors advise beginners to give as little as possible to external action until such time as they are fit to act profitably. It is a noteworthy fact that, in the biographies of the great Christian mystics, the period of activity has always been preceded by a preliminary stage of retirement from the world—a period during which these contemplatives learned to practice the presence of God so continuously and unwaveringly that the distractions of outward activity were powerless any longer to draw the mind away from reality. Indeed, for those who have reached a certain degree of proficiency in "active annihilation," action assumes a sacramental character and becomes a means for bringing them nearer to reality. Those for whom it is not such a means should refrain as far as possible from action—all the more so since, in all that concerns the saving of souls and the improving of the quality of people's thoughts and behavior, "a man of orison will accomplish more in one year than another man in all his life."

What is true of good works is true, *a fortiori*, of merely worldly activity, particularly when it is activity on a large scale, involving the cooperation of large numbers of individuals in every stage of unenlightenment. Good is a product of the ethical and spiritual artistry of individuals; it cannot be mass-produced. This brings us to the heart of that great paradox of politics—the fact that political action is necessary and at the same time incapable of satisfying the needs which called it into existence. Even when it is well-intentioned (which it very often is not), political action is foredoomed to a partial, sometimes even a complete self-stultification. The intrinsic nature of the human instruments with which, and the human materials upon which political action must be carried out, is a positive guarantee against the possibility of such action yielding the good results expected of it.

For several thousands of years now men have been experimenting with different methods of improving the quality of human instruments and materials. It has been found that something can be done by strictly humanistic methods, such as the improvement of the social and economic environment and the various techniques of character training. With certain individuals, too, startling results are obtainable through conversion and catharsis. All these methods are good so far as they go; but they do not go far enough. For the radical and permanent transformation of personality, only one effective method has been discovered—that of the mystic. The great religious teachers of East and West have been unanimous in asserting that all human beings are called to achieve enlightenment. They have also unanimously asserted that the achievement of enlightenment is so difficult, and demands a degree of self-abnegation so horrifying to the average unregenerate human being, that, at any given moment of history, very few men and women will be ready even to attempt the labor. This being so, we must expect that large-scale political action will continue to yield the profoundly unsatisfactory results it has always yielded in the past.

The contemplative does not work exclusively for his own salvation. On the contrary, he has an important social function. At any given moment, as we have seen, only a few mystical, theocentric saints exist in the world. But few as they are, they can do an appreciable amount to mitigate the poisons which society generates within itself by its political and economic activities. They are the "salt of the earth," the antiseptic which prevents society from breaking down into irremediable decay.

This antiseptic and antidotal function of the theocentric saint is performed in a variety of ways. First of all, the mere fact that he exists is extremely salutary and important. The advanced contemplative is one who is no longer opaque to the immanent reality within, and as such he is profoundly impressive to the average unregenerate person, who is awed by his presence and even by the mere report of his existence into behaving appreciably better than he otherwise would do.

The theocentric saint is generally not content merely to be. He is almost always a teacher and often a man of action. Through teaching, he benefits surrounding society by multiplying the number of those who undertake the radical transformation of their character and thus increases the amount of antiseptics and antidotes in the chronically diseased body

politic. As for the action into which so many advanced contemplatives have plunged, after achieving "active annihilation"—this is never political, but always concerned with small
groups or individuals; never exercised at the center of society, but always on the margin; never makes use of the
organized force of the State or Church, but only of the non-
coercive, spiritual authority which belongs to the contemplative in virtue of his contact with reality. It is a matter of
plain historical fact that the greatest of the world's spiritual
leaders have always refused to make use of political power.
No less significant is the fact that, whenever well-intentioned
contemplatives have turned from the marginal activities appropriate to spiritual leaders and have tried to use large-scale
action to force an entire society, along some political short
cut, into the Kingdom of Heaven, they have always failed.
The business of a seer is to see; and if he involves himself in
the kind of God-eclipsing activities which make seeing impossible, he betrays not only his better self, but also his fellow
men, who have a right to his vision. Mystics and theocentric
saints are not always loved or invariably listened to: far
from it. Prejudice and the dislike of what is unusual may
blind their contemporaries to the virtues of these men and
women of the margin, may cause them to be persecuted as
enemies of society. But should they leave their margin,
should they take to competing for place and power within
the main body of society, they are certain to be generally
hated and despised as traitors to their seership. Only the
greatest spirituals are fully consistent. The average, unregenerate person loves the thoughts, feelings and actions that
poison society, but also, and at the same time, loves the spiritual antidotes to the poison. It is as a poison-lover that he
persecutes and kills the seers who tell him how to make himself whole; and it is as one who nostalgically yearns for vision
that he despises the potential seer who forfeits his vision by
wrong activity and the pursuit of power.

# Unknown Indian Influences

## GERALD HEARD

NOTHING IS MORE INTERESTING, to those who believe that all religions have one source and one goal, than to trace the same ideas and expressions appearing in religious writings separated in time by thousands of years and in space by continents.

The thirteenth-century hymn of German origin I quoted in another of these articles [1] might have been sung by any student of the Vedas in India any time in the last five thousand years. As Ramakrishna said, all religions lead to God. It is interesting however to inquire in this place, where the contribution of India to forming the world's thought in religion is constantly illustrated, how far these parallelisms which we note in all lofty developments of religion are by direct borrowing or by convergence of all spiritual minds on the same goal, so that toward the end their courses lie side by side. This is of course one of the liveliest controversies in the subject of physical evolution and in that field will probably never be settled. Does the highest form of bodily life—man—spring from a single stock or have several blended to produce this astounding creature? Are the great apes like men because they are his cousins—common descendents from a single ancestral type or are they as they are because every animal species and genus must, if it continues and can keep for long enough unspecialized, become humanoid—that is, develop a body which best permits the expression of a rational and exploratory mind? This very same problem appears again in this subject under discussion in these paragraphs: Does the spiritual inheritance of man flow down one river bed from which irrigation channels spread to left and right across the earth or are there many separate streams rising from different

[1] See "Is there Progress?" p. 432.

springs—though all fed from the same underlying water-table and all flowing to mingle in the same sea? Many authorities have felt that in India there is a source-land rich and constant enough in its yield of the Water of Life to have fed all mankind's ecclesiastical channels. Others feel there is no evidence that India directly influenced, for instance, that stream of lofty devotion which arose in the Rhineland in the spring of the Middle Ages and flowed down until it died away (as an uncontaminated source) when late XVIIIth-century pietism found itself between a materialistic rationalism claiming to have all the facts and a rationalistic mysticism claiming to have all the immediate contemporary inspiration. Yet if India's influence on this peculiar Germanic thought (which combines metaphysical subtlety with intense devotionalism) is not direct there is no doubt that it is indirect. There is no sign of the complete transcendence of anthropomorphism as a goal, and thought and word as a medium, in Christian religion until the introduction into the West of the thought of Bar Sudali—the Syrian monk who calls himself by the "ghost name" Dionysius the Areopagite. This profoundly influences Scotus Erigena, the strange Irishman who in the ninth century is teaching at the court of Charlemagne's descendant Charles the Fat.

Bar Sudali's work is not condemned by the church because in his book he praises the ecclesiastical hierarchy saying it is a mirror of the orders of angelic powers in heaven. This made a church council specifically praise the treatise which thereafter naturally becomes sacrosanct. Erigena however wrote under his own name and was very unguarded in his theological statements. Hence his work was condemned. Nevertheless this strain of advanced thought continues to fascinate religious explorers and we can trace quite clearly the teaching of the Syrian monk of the fifth century shaping the thought of men on the upper Rhine in the fourteenth. Considering how little there is in the pseudo Dionysius of traditional Christianity it is hardly possible to avoid the conclusion that here we have a strain of Indian thought entering the Levant and so spreading to western Europe. It is a fascinating sideline of research to try and discover how lofty a mysticism the Roman Church will accept and where and why it draws the line, calling one mystic anathema and another blessed. As a matter of fact condemnations seem to alternate with approvals, curses with benedictions. Bar Sudali is almost canonised: his student Erigena cut off from the church: Erigena's student Richard and other Victorines are treated as little short of being inspired. Their successor Eckhart is condemned: his spiritual sons Tauler and Suso are approved manuals for the devout. Up in Belgium, Ruysbroeck, using extremes of language which were sufficient to make Eckhart an outcast, is, on the contrary, named Doctor Ecstaticus, while in the south at Ulm in the Danubian basin Albert called the Great not only teaches a thought, Protestant in its severity towards symbols and Indian in its refusal to state the ultimate nature of God, Indian also in its equal statement of God's transcendence of thought and immanence in the mind of man, but is the revered teacher of Thomas Aquinas, the Doctor Angelicus of the Roman Church, the master inter-preter of orthodox theology. As this remarkable man, Albert, was teacher, administrator, Bishop of Ulm, a re-starter of natural science and some three years ago was canonised by the late Pope (perhaps more to vex the Nazis than to guide the orthodox) , we may take his work as a good example of that Western mysticism which has such strange parallels with the East; or, it may be, is a far away "runner" of Indian thought—a root planted by the Ganges sprouting, a millen-nium after, on the Danube. At the end of his life, during which he had found time to write a whole library of books on an encyclopaedic range of subjects, the old man, who had out-lived his spectacular pupil Aquinas, decides that he must leave on record one more small volume. It is the most im-portant thing he can say. It is the secret of his life and living. He calls it simply De Adherendo Deo. In spite of all his multifarious activities he had had one interest and desire— how he might cling to God. Such a type, it might be thought, so combining work with devotion, must surely be following the path of Karma Yoga by offering all its incessant activities to God and so aiming at union. And so in a way this saintly Bishop must have been. Yet when we read in his remarkable little book—surely here is a spirit which has another path for entering into the Presence, a path which seems closest to

Raja Yoga. Consider the following words, remembering that they were written by a Catholic Bishop now a Saint of the Roman Church, whose intercession may therefore be sought by all the faithful when they pray. "Happy," he exclaims, "is the man who by continually effacing of all images and who by introversion and the lifting up of his mind to God, at last forgets and leaves behind all images. By this means he works inwardly with a naked, simple, pure intellect and affection about that most pure and simple object, God. See then that your whole exercise about God within you depend wholly and only on your naked intellect, affection and will. For indeed this exercise cannot be discharged by any corporeal organs or the external senses but by that which constitutes (essentially) a man—understanding and love. If so then you desire a safe stair and sure path to God, to arrive at the end of true bliss then with an intent mind earnestly desire and aspire after continual cleanness of heart and purity of mind with a constant calm and tranquility of the senses and recollecting of the affections of the heart, continually fixing them above. Work to simplify the heart that being immovable and at peace from any invading vain fantasms you may always stand fast in the Lord within, to that degree as if your soul had already entered into that always present Now of eternity, that is, of the Deity. To mount to God is to enter into oneself. For he who so mounting and entering goes above and beyond himself, truly mounts up to God. The mind must then raise itself above itself and say, He whom above all I need is above all I know. And so, carried into the darkness of the mind, gathering itself into that all sufficient good the mind learns to stay so at home and with whole affection cleave and become habitually fixed in the supreme good within. So do until you become immutable and arrive at that true life which is God himself: perpetually, without any vicissitude of space or time reposing in that inward quiet and secret mansion of the Deity." Here is a pathway of such austere simplicity and directness that it would be hard to attribute it to any specific religion. One can but say this is the essence of all living religion. The austerity of the approach may seem forbidding but, as the Saint remarks after a lifetime of practice and achievement, it is a "sure path and safe stair," as direct as a ladder, as clearly marked—and as steep. And the goal can be seen so clearly even by those on the lower rungs that no one who has glimpsed it would choose to take any route more gently graded but more circuitous. All the direct guides tell us then the same thing. The way is always open for those who wish to climb. About the less direct approaches—approaches which permit us to postpone the time when we shall reach the clear air and the intense light, spiritual advisers differ and vary their directions. But about the straight way to God for those who want him only, though the advice may be hard to follow, the path is lit by all the enlightened ones who have found him, it leads without deviation to him and every soul who cares to give all its energy to scale that path may in this life achieve the only end which makes meaning of life, the **Eternal Presence.**

# Readings in Mysticism

## ALDOUS HUXLEY

I AM OFTEN ASKED by friends or unknown correspondents to suggest a course of reading in the literature of mysticism. My own knowledge of that literature is very far from being exhaustive; but I have read enough to be able to give what I think may be useful advice to those who have had fewer opportunities for study than myself. In the paragraphs that follow I shall name and, where necessary; briefly describe certain books, from the reading of which one may derive a good working knowledge of the nature and historical development of mysticism. It should be noted that most of the books mentioned belong to the literature of Western spirituality. This is due, not to deliberate choice, but to the limitations imposed by ignorance and the inaccessibility of the relevant books. The compilation of even an elementary bibliography of Oriental mysticism is entirely beyond my powers, and I shall therefore mention only a few books which I personally have found illuminating and helpful.

Before embarking on my task, I feel impelled to utter a few words of warning in regard to mystical literature in general. There have been published, in recent years, vast numbers of books dealing with meditation and contemplation, yoga and mystical experience, higher consciousness and intuitive knowledge of Reality. Many of these books were written by people with excellent intentions, but lamentably ignorant of the history and science of mysticism, and lacking any genuine spiritual experience. In other cases the authors did not even have good intentions, but were concerned, not in the least with the knowledge of God, but with the exploitation of certain yogic and mystical practices for the purpose of getting wealth, success and physical well-being. Such books, whether merely silly, ill-informed and "phony," or downright bad and pernicious, should be avoided at all cost. When choosing books on mysticism a good rule is to confine yourself to the writings either of acknowledged saints and persons whom you have good reason to believe are on the road to sanctity, or else of reputable scholars. Outside these two categories of writers, the reader whose concern is with enlightenment cannot hope to find the smallest profit.

The first-hand experiences of those who are not saints—not even better-than-average human beings—may be startling and exciting enough on their own psychic level; but they will certainly not be genuine experiences of ultimate Reality, or God. For such genuine spiritual experiences happen, as a general rule, only to those who have gone some way along the road of purgation, and themselves lead to an improvement in the quality of the experiencer's living—an improvement amounting in exceptional cases to that total transformation of character, manifesting itself in sanctity. Psychic experiences, which do not contribute to sanctification, are not experiences of God, but merely of certain unfamiliar aspects of our psycho-physical universe. The validity of a supposed experience of God is in some sort guaranteed by the sanctification of the person who has the experience. Where there is no evidence of sanctification, there is no reason to suppose that the experience had anything to do with God. It is a significant fact that occultism and spiritualism have produced no saints.

In view of all this, the serious student should pay no attention to any descriptions of first-hand experiences, except those written by saints and by persons who show evidence of advancing towards saintliness, and to no second-hand documents except those written by sound scholars, who may be relied upon to give an accurate account of saints and their teachings.

Spirituality is the art of achieving union with God, and consists of two branches—asceticism and mysticism, the mortification of the self and that contemplation by means of which the soul makes contact with ultimate Reality. Mortification without contemplation, and contemplation without mortification are both useless, and may even be positively harmful. That is why all genuine mystical literature is also ascetical literature, while all good ascetical literature (such as "The Imitation of Christ") treats also, explicitly or by implication, of mystical prayer. The combination of asceticism and mysticism is very clearly seen in Buddhist and Hindu writings. Thus, in the Buddhist eightfold path, the first seven steps prescribe a complete course of mortification of the ego, while the eighth inculcates the duty of mystical contemplation. The ascetical teaching of the Buddha is found in the best known of the sermons attributed to him. Selections from these may be read in the recently published "Bible of the World" (a valuable anthology from the canonical books of the principal religions of the East and West), and in Warren's "Buddhism in Translation," a more extended anthology. Edward Thompson's historical novel, "The Youngest Disciple," treats the later life and teachings of the Buddha in fictional form, but with strict fidelity to the original texts.

For detailed descriptions of the techniques employed by the Buddhists in contemplation, one may consult "The Path of Purity," published by the Pali Text Society and, for what concerns the Northern school, the three volumes of translations from the Tibetan, edited by Evans Wentz and published by the Oxford University Press. The volume on Tibetan yoga contains a valuable collection of techniques of concentration, meditation and contemplation. The biography of Milarepa graphically describes the life of a Buddhist saint. And the Bardo Thodol, or Tibetan Book of the Dead (one of the world's religious masterpieces), sets forth the significance of contemplation in relation to the after-life of man.

Those who wish to read brief, but scholarly, summaries of Buddhist thought and practices will find what they want in "What is Buddhism?", compiled and published by the Buddhist Lodge, London; "Mahayana Buddhism," by Mrs. Suzuki, and "Buddhism," by Professor Rhys Davids. Particular aspects of Buddhist spirituality are treated under numerous headings in Hastings' Encyclopaedia of Religion and Ethics, a valuable work of reference covering the entire field of religion.

The spiritual literature of Hinduism is so enormous that the unprofessional Western student must, in mere self-preservation, confine himself to a minute selection. Here are a few of the indispensable books. The Bhagavad Gita, with some good commentary, such as that by Aurobindo Ghose; the Yoga Sutras of Patanjali, with the commentaries of Vivekananda; the Upanishads, translated in the Sacred Books of the East series; Sankara, in Jacob's translation, or at second hand, in some brief history of Indian philosophy, such as Max Muller's or Deussen's; the life of Ramakrishna, and the writings of Vivekananda on the various kinds of yoga. From these books one may derive, not indeed a comprehensive view of Hindu spirituality, but at least a pretty accurate synthetic picture of its fundamental character. The knowledge so gained will be a fair and characteristic sample of the total knowledge which can only be acquired by years of intensive study.

Spirituality in the Far East is mainly Buddhist or Taoist. In the sphere of Buddhism, China was content to follow in the footsteps of the Mahayana teachers of northern India and Tibet. From sources derived from China, Japan developed that strange and not entirely satisfactory kind of spirituality, Zen mysticism. This is most conveniently studied in the writings of Professor Suzuki, who has published many volumes, dealing with Zen in all its aspects.

Taoist spirituality is best represented by the first and greatest of its canonical books, the Tao Te King of Lao-Tzu. To this most wonderful scripture one may return again and again, certain of finding, with every enrichment of one's own experience of life, ever deeper and subtler significances in its allusive, strangely abbreviated and enigmatical utterances.

In compiling my elementary bibliography of Western spirituality, I shall begin with a list of sound scholarly volumes dealing with its historical development, its philosophy and its practical procedures, and go on to enumerate a few of the most valuable of its original, first-hand documents.

Perhaps the most comprehensive general history of Christian asceticism and mysticism is the "Christian Spirituality" of Father Pourrat. Three volumes of this work, covering the period from gospel times to the middle of the seventeenth century, have been translated into English.

Other sound and well documented works are Evelyn

Underhill's "Mysticism," Dean Inge's "Christian Mysticism," Saudreau's "Life of Union with God" and Poulain's "The Graces of Interior Prayer." This last book is probably the most elaborate, subtle and exhaustive analysis of the psychology of mystical states ever attempted and, despite a certain rather forbidding dryness of style, deserves to be carefully read by any serious student of the subject.

Another great monument of French scholarship in this field is Henri Brémond's "Histoire Littéraire du Sentiment Religieux en France," a work in eight volumes, of which, so far as I know, not all have yet been translated into English. Brémond's book treats exhaustively of the revival of mysticism in France during the seventeenth century, and is a treasure house of the most fascinating biographical material, copiously illustrated by citations, often of great literary beauty, from the works of the spiritual writers of the period.

Many Catholic writers have written volumes of detailed instruction on the art of mental prayer and contemplation. Among the best of these (and still, fortunately, accessible in a reprint) is the "Holy Wisdom" of Augustine Baker, an English Benedictine monk of the seventeenth century. Baker was himself an advanced mystic, and the book in which he embodies his teachings is wonderfully complete, lucid and practical.

For those who wish to know something about other Catholic methods of meditation and contemplation "The Art of Mental Prayer," by Bede Frost, may be recommended. This is a brief, but thoroughly scholarly, modern work, summarizing the spiritual teachings of a number of mystical and ascetic writers from the sixteenth century onwards. A good contemporary manual on the same subject is Father Leen's "Progress through Mental Prayer." "Spiritual Exercises," by A. Tillyard, includes in a single volume a number of the best-known Christian methods and of analogous methods employed by Hindu, Buddhist and Sufi mystics.

Valuable modern studies of individual mystics include Bede Frost's monumental volume on St. John of the Cross, Von Hügel's monograph on St. Catherine of Genoa and Wautier d'Aygalliers' "Ruysbroeck, the Admirable." Slighter sketches of mediaeval and early-modern mystics may be found in Miss Underhill's "Mystics of the Church" and in "The Flowering of Mysticism," by Rufus Jones.

We have now to consider the first-hand documents of mysticism—the autobiographies, the journals, the spiritual letters, the descriptive and speculative treatises left by the great masters of Western spirituality. Here are a few of the most significant. The Confessions of St. Augustine; the Life of St. Teresa, written by herself; the Journal of John Woolman; the spiritual letters of St. François de Sales, of St. Jeanne Chantal, of Fénelon; the "Mystical Theology" and "Divine Names" of Dionysius the Areopagite (interesting in themselves and historically significant as the bridge connecting Christian mysticism with neo-platonic and Oriental thought); the sermons and other writings of Meister Eckhart, the Western mystic who approaches most nearly to the Vedantic position; the short but incomparably profound and beautiful "Cloud of Unknowing," by an anonymous English mystic of the fourteenth century; the Theologia Germanica; the various writings of Tauler; the "Imitation of Christ" and the "Following of Christ"—the latter once attributed to Tauler, but now given to another unknown author and regarded as somewhat heretical; the writings of St. John of the Cross; the "Introduction to the Devout Life" and "Treatise of the Love of God," by St. François de Sales; the "Spiritual Doctrine" of Lallemant and the little treatise by Surin, called "Abandonment." All these are not only admirable in themselves, but possess the further merit of being reasonably accessible. Anyone who reads even some of them, together with one or two of the scholarly volumes previously cited, will possess a very fair knowledge of Western mysticism, its character, its psychology, its practices and its philosophy.

In conclusion, let me cite a paragraph on the reading of spiritual books from the pen of Augustine Baker. "But as for spiritual books, the intention of an internal liver ought not to be such as is that of those who live extroverted lives, who read them out of a vain curiosity, so as to be thereby enabled to discourse of such sublime matters without any particular choice or consideration whether they be suitable to their spirit for practice or not. A contemplative soul in reading such books must not say, this is a good book or passage, but, moreover, this is useful and proper for me, and by God's grace I will endeavor to put in execution, in due time and place, the good instructions contained in it, so far as they are good for me."

# Mysticism in the "Theologia Germanica"

## GERALD HEARD

IT IS OF CONSIDERABLE INTEREST to those who today are attempting to put into current practice the teaching of Religion as it has been most profoundly expressed by India, to see how far the mystics of the West following the Christian tradition succeeded in rendering in Western terms thoughts which we today would mainly classify as Oriental. For that purpose this short essay is taking one specific book. This book, however, though it is short and anonymous, nevertheless had a great influence on European religion at the critical time when the papacy was losing its ascendency and men were daring—not seldom with unhappy results, but inevitably—to attempt to think for themselves and to experience religion "on their own." The book in question is the famous Theologia Germanica. Of course it is no theology in the usual sense of the word but rather a brief manual for instruction in living the inner spiritual life. Nevertheless it is seldom possible—and certainly at that time and place was definitely not—to give people instruction in actual spiritual living and the necessary exercises without introducing a certain amount of actual theology. If you are to teach a man to sail you need not at once teach him to read oceanic maps but quite soon he will have to master the meaning of charts if he is to handle his ship in any actual seas. The author's name is unknown, probably at his own wish, for these associates who banded themselves together under the name of the Friends of God cultivated anonymity, dreading that spiritual pretentiousness which is a greater obstacle to enlightenment than physical indulgence or than possessions. We know, however, his associates and the scene in which he lived his life.

The Friends of God made a loose association, of layfolk, monks, and priests, all of whom were bonded by the practice of spiritual exercises and by the tie of secrecy. This author probably lived at that terrible time when man and nature, nature with the great plague called the Black Death and man by a furious, protracted and unstinted feud between the Pope and the Emperor, were doing their best to make ordinary kindly human living impossible. The reaction of the ordinary man was despair or hideous brutality: the reaction to the same stimuli by these other few, the men who loved God, was for their lives to be raised to an ever more constant and deeper communion with him. This book found an immediate answer from such seekers. The author, one may say "of course," is strictly orthodox. Yet the reader today feels that though he is constantly careful to bring his teaching in line with tradition and the Church's rulings, he does not depend on these, and moreover sometimes his actual findings do not square very well with the tradition. No doubt the author was quite honest in his attempt to combine what may not in fact have been the same conclusions—those of his own soul and those of the Church. He had very good and right reasons for wanting to find that the Church was or should be teaching the loftiest spirituality. The Church was the only channel of grace for the ordinary man. Cut off from that source, muddied though it was, he would die of spiritual thirst. Nor was that all. The world was already full of people who had so cut themselves off, declared the Church to be hopeless— which was all too easy to believe—and that they themselves were the true and full channels of illumination, which was pleasant for themselves to believe but certainly far from easy for anyone who watched their lives to take as true or wise. Against these types—common enough today—the author turns with sound austerity. If he has to choose between the Church and these vain indulgents who see God everywhere and preach the free spirit so that they can live loosely then he chooses the Church with all its mistakes. That in brief is the setting of this important book—a world sick to death, most men despairing, a few using the breakdown of morality as an excuse for grotesque license, and far fewer turning all the more earnestly to find Reality.

Yet the teaching has certain apparent inconsistencies which do not seem to be accounted for by what is said above—the need to back a dying authority against a worse, far worse, anarchy. In the writer's own spiritual thinking there seem two strains which he himself in his own heart never quite reconciled. One strain is that familiar in the near East and the Eastern orthodox Church and taken over from those centres by the Western Church. That is mortificatory. The body is "this sack of worms"—a phrase from Luther's last sermon, for Luther never settled accounts with his body either as a monk or after his breaking his vows and marrying. The teaching of the Fathers of the Egyptian deserts is here dominant—a sick body is the greatest health for the soul. They denied Paul's teaching that the body is "the Temple of the Holy Ghost." All life is to be an agony. The author tells us that Christ from the moment he was born till he died on the Cross never had anything but moment after moment of acute pain—a picture certainly not sustained by the Gospels. As Christ always suffered so must we. We must never attempt to attain to that calm which is above all pain. That is not for this life. That is for heaven after death. The thought of illumination here, after which, in a way, this world is heaven, a doctrine which Eckhart actually states (saying he has no wish to die and go to heaven for heaven will only be more in quantity, not more in quality, from what he has now been given by God's grace). Yet the author, when he has said these things and given the clear picture of the man who torments himself body and mind so that after death he may have earned a life of endless joy, says a number of other things which show that, though that was the orthodox picture for those who wished to live the higher life, he and his saintly friends had found something different, something which really did not fit into that picture. He speaks of a man he knows who has attained to what we may all attain, and it is the constant power of going into the presence of God. He speaks of any man as long as he is here "passing from heaven to hell," from banishment from the presence of God to full knowledge of that presence. In this statement there are two things which refuse to fit into the mortificatory, after-death-heaven design. The first is the obvious fact that when you

are in the presence of God you are, as the author allows, in
Heaven, and you cannot be said to be in utter wretchedness
simply awaiting the release of death. Secondly, he notes that
when you are in "hell" even then you would rather be there
than "with creatures," for though no man may comfort you
nor would you take comfort of any, yet this state is both safe
and blessed. It seems clear that if this means anything, and
with an author as honest and as acute as this it must, it means
that the soul is then filled with such an intense longing for
God that it knows it is separate from Him and so suffers, but
the fact which makes this suffering better than any pleasure
is that in it is such a vivid conviction of God's Being that
one's own loss and damnation matter nothing. HE IS and in
that fact everything else, oneself of course included, is well
lost. It seems rather misguiding to apply to such a state,
which most earnest seekers have tasted, if not drunk of, the
name Hell. Hell is self-centred despair, if it is anything. In fact
a classic description of hell is given by this same great author.
Nothing, he tells us with that assurance which we know in
ourselves is true the moment we read it—nothing burns in
hell save the self and its self-will. The author, then, it seems
would have done better had he been able to make use of a
freer phraseology and a more exact metaphysic than the
rigid theology of his day permitted. Another point of confusion seems to appear, not when he is trying to describe the
state of alert austerity in which the soul must live if it is to
travel toward union with God, a union which does not depend on death but upon the degree to which the soul can
lose itself in God, but when he is speaking of those upper
states of wonderful result into which the soul, by God's grace
working on its dedicated will, may enter. He describes the
steps of purgation, illumination and union. But the illumination is not the intense quality we now recognize in the
records of the great Oriental saints, and in one or two of the
West, while the union seems to fall far short of any Samadhi.
Is this due to the fact that the author has made a ruling
which he often repeats, that perfect calm is not and must not
be attained in this life? He seems to feel that it would be
wrong to attempt to know God in this life. And yet when one
has said that, on ample evidence, one comes on other passages

where he says roundly that a man may "look into eternity" and receive clear foretastes of the eternal blessedness. In fact it does not seem possible to reconcile this great devotee's findings. We are faced, it would seem, not with a finished treatise of the spiritual life by a master proficient but the notes of a great seeker and finder who puts down all that he knows and does not try to make it consistent. His picture of Christ's suffering throws a little light on these antinomies which he feels he must somehow preserve and set down in all their self-contradictoriness. He tells us that though Christ suffered horribly all his life and his Passion was more terrible than human suffering can ever be, nevertheless Christ "had two eyes" and though the one eye looked on the world and suffered in it all the time prodigiously, the other looked upon his Father and never suffered at all. That picture of the Avatar, "perfect God in touching His Godhead and perfect Man in touching His Manhood" is of course the picture the so-called Athanasian Creed gives of Jesus of Nazareth and it is a picture which Aurobindo Ghose says the Gita renders as Krishna's interpretation of Avatarhood. We in the West are now swinging away from the picture of the suffering God-man to the picture and ideal of the serene Buddha, who though of course he has suffered and still can feel yet those feelings never disturb his expression, still less the serenity of his mind. He does not weep for a dead friend whom he is about to raise to life nor over a doomed capital of his race because it will not get rid of its overtaking karma. Yet of course it is possible to see that a Son of God could take on humanity so closely that he would share their sorrows with a sympathy which they could understand—when they could not grasp his serenity—while all the time his soul in itself and in its full consciousness looked on; the eye fixed on God translating all the tragedy which came in through the eye fixed on man.

Probably even an authority—which the writer of this note certainly is not—could not make a consistent picture of the spiritual life from the Theologia Germanica but because the spiritual life can probably never be at our level consistent but always somewhat of a paradox and abounding in antinomies, this book is a help to all seekers, with its manifest sincerity, its flashing insights, its deep unbroken devotion. It is also a great challenge to us today showing how adversity made these men able to become under the terrible pressure of their days more and more fit for the great title they took for themselves—the Friends of God.

# The Spiritual Message of Dante

## Guido Ferrando

DANTE, AS A MAN, belongs to the middle ages; his life stretches from the last part of the XIII century, probably the most glorious century in the Christian era, to the first two decades of the XIV century, which marks the beginning of the transition from the feudal age to the modern age, from scholasticism to humanism. He was educated in the liberal arts as they were taught in his times; he studied scholastic philosophy, following with equal interest the teaching of the two great rival religious orders of that period, the Dominicans and the Franciscans; he took part in the political life of his native city, Florence, and also in the many feuds and quarrels of the powerful families which caused so much harm and such tragic confusion in the Italy of that century; he accepted without discussion the dogmas of the Christian Church, and he shared many of the superstitions and fears of his contemporaries. In short, in his intellectual formation he was typically medieval; in his philosophical writings he used the language of the Schools and the syllogistic or deductive method, and never questioned the authority of Aristotle: "the master of those that know." But all this is only the transient element of his nature and of his work; it is the frame, and not the picture. If we really want to understand Dante and his wonderful vision, we must not stop at the outer intellectual form in which he presents his message, but go deeper until we grasp its spiritual meaning which transcends the limits of our mind and is the revelation of the Eternal. We must also remember that Dante is essentially a poet, though he is also a profound thinker, and that he reaches certain universal truths using his intuitive powers rather than his reason; he is not a systematic, constructive philosopher like his master St. Thomas Aquinas, but an artist endowed with an insight that has rarely been equalled and never surpassed in the field of literature.

I said that Dante is essentially a poet, but a poet who is also a prophet; a "vates," to use the Latin term. There are two fundamentally different types of poets, taking the word in its etymological meaning of a maker, a creator: the pure artist and the prophet. The poet who is a pure artist has no special message to give us; he looks at the world, at nature, at man, with eyes full of wonder, and listens to mysterious sounds and voices not heard by the common man; and he tries to express what he sees and what he hears, in beautiful words in which we may still find a faint echo of the sweet melodies that gladdened or saddened his heart. He interprets life as beauty, just as a scientist interprets it as order, or law. He is not a visionary, because he sees more deeply and more clearly than the psychologist and the philosopher into the soul of man and gives voice to the infinite variety of human emotions. He is a dreamer, no doubt, as we all are, more or less; but with this great difference, that while our dreams are inconsistent and meaningless, his dream has an eternal value, is the revelation of beauty. He is the poet that Shelley describes to us in those magic lines:

> *Nor seeks nor finds he mortal blisses*
> *But feeds on the aerial kisses*
> *Of shapes that haunt thought's wildernesses.*
> *He will watch from dawn to gloom*
> *The lake-reflected sun illume*
> *The yellow bees in the ivy bloom*
> *Nor heed, nor see what things they be;*
> *But from these create he can*
> *Forms more real than mortal man,*
> *Nurslings of immortality!*

He seldom asks himself what is the meaning of life and whether it has a goal or not: he accepts it, not passively, but actively, and makes it more bearable by adding beauty to it. Shakespeare is undoubtedly the supreme representative of this type of poet; he is the pure artist; he has no ideology, no special philosophy or creed to impart to us; he interprets life as he sees it, without trying to explain the why, the

whence or the whereto: . . . "Men must endure Their going hence even as their coming hither; Ripeness is all." For
him life is a dream, a shadow of a dream; but, like Prospero
in "The Tempest," by a simple touch of his magic wand he
can transform the world of dream into a world of reality
whose dwellers are more real than mortal man.

Dante belongs to the other class of poets, the prophets, the
seers, the religious teachers. He has a message to convey to
us; he has a mission, that of showing us the true path to God,
the way to salvation. He firmly believes that our human existence has a goal, not in this world, but in a world beyond,
and so he does not accept life as it is, but teaches us what it
should be. This earthly existence of ours is not a dream, but
a trial, a preparation for an eternal life; death is not the end,
"ultima linea rerum," but the beginning. In sharp contrast
with Shakespeare, who is so impersonal, who loses himself in
that infinitely various world of man which he creates with
his wonderful imagination, Dante is intensely personal,
though he manages to attain the highest form of impersonal-
ity when, through his extraordinary imaginative power, he
makes us feel and realize that he is the personification of all
humanity; and his personality is so strong, so overpowering,
that we are fascinated by it almost as much as by the marvelous beauty of his poetry. Moreover Dante is very much interested in all that is going on around him; he takes an active
part in the political, social, religious, artistic and even scientific life of his time; he is a fighter, first for his party, later on
for an ideal of peace and justice, and at the end for a spiritual
truth of which he is the prophet, and in the name of which
he feels justified to judge his contemporaries. It is evident,
therefore, that to look upon Dante simply as a supreme poet
and to read his Divine Comedy only as a work of art, is to
renounce the possibility of understanding his great spiritual
message.

It would be folly to try and condense into a short article
the great vision of Dante. He presents it to us in an allegorical
form, because allegory was for him the best means of expressing the deeper, mystic meaning of his teaching. We must
remember that, for the medieval artist and religious teacher,
symbolism was the natural way of communication, as it ren-

dered in a realistic, immediate form the meaning of an abstract idea which common people were unable to understand otherwise. For instance, the idea of sacrifice and of salvation was, and still is, concretely expressed in the symbol of the Cross; and the Holy Virgin, whom Dante worshiped almost as a feminine personification of God, not only expressed womanhood in its essential attributes; mother, spouse and daughter, but also the idea of compassion, and at the same time symbolized the eternal link between the divine and the human.

Dante in his poem imagines that on the night before Good Friday of 1300, the year of the great papal jubilee which marked an intense religious revival and was thus peculiarly appropriate for a moral awakening, he comes to himself in a dark wood, wild and entangled, having gone astray from the straight path. This frightful, dreary forest is the symbol of the errors, confusion and vices of mankind. He tries hard to escape from it, and manages to do so after a painful struggle. Then he looks upward and sees a little hill whose top is illumined by the rays of the rising sun: the hill of righteousness, lit by spiritual truth. He moves toward it, but his path is obstructed by three fierce looking beasts, a lion, a leopard and a she-wolf, symbolizing the three fundamental human sins: incontinence, violence and fraud. He is slowly driven backwards toward darkness and destruction, when suddenly a man, or rather a shadow, appears before him; it is Virgil, the great Latin poet of the Roman empire, who personifies reason, human understanding. Virgil tells him that the only way to escape spiritual death and to attain salvation is to visit with him the realm of the dead, to descend into the black pit of Hell and after to ascend again to light and climb the steep slopes of the mountain of Purgatory. Then, having reached the top of the mountain, where the Terrestrial Paradise is, he will be ready to fly up to Heaven under the guidance of Beatrix, the lady he had loved in his youth and who is now the symbol of Revelation, divine intelligence.

Literally interpreted, the Divine Comedy is the narrative of this journey through the three realms of the other world, a journey described so vividly, with such an intense realism, that the reader is apt to forget it is only a vision. Allegorically the narrative symbolizes the regeneration of the individual soul that, under the guidance of reason personified by Virgil, becomes aware of the true nature of sin, a process typified by the journey through Hell; and then is ready to undertake its purification by discipline, which is typified by the laborious ascent of Purgatory. Finally, having regained its purity, the soul, guided no longer by reason but by revelation represented by Beatrix, can mount upwards to the ultimate vision.

But the allegory in Dante is not purely poetical; it is the expression of a profound mystical experience. If we follow the poet on his mystic journey through Hell, Purgatory and Paradise to its ultimate consummation in the vision of God, not merely with the wish to enjoy the beauties of the poem, but also with the hope of sharing a great experience, then, and then only, we will be in a position to grasp its real meaning. Then we will realize that the Divine Comedy, though a marvelous work of art, is first of all and above all, an act of faith; the creation of a great soul struggling to find its way to God and yearning to help other souls to their spiritual salvation. But, since the poem is an act of faith, in order to understand its true message, one must have faith, one must share with the poet at least the fundamental belief that man's life has a meaning and a goal which transcend the limits of our intellect and cannot be perceived and explained by our self-conscious mind. Dante, being a Christian and a man of the middle ages, accepts the tenets and the dogmas of his Church; but, as a true mystic, he sees beyond the veil that hides the spiritual truth, and gazes at the light coming "from that Serene which is untroubled ever." It is this spiritual truth that interests us today, not the theological frame in which he presents it; and this truth may be summed up in a single sentence: "God has created the world through love, and it is through love, which is the highest form of understanding, that man can realize the unity of life and return to God." Unfortunately today many people, owing to a mistaken scientific training, refuse to accept the idea of God; they believe only in facts, in intellectual evidence, and God's existence cannot be proved by logic. And yet, as another great Italian has so beautifully said in a little book which he wrote for the working class and entitled "The Duties of Man," "God exists, because we exist; to try and prove His existence is blasphemy, as to deny it is folly. Everyone consciously or unconsciously worships God whenever he *feels* life, because God is life; he cannot be understood, he can be felt and loved." The God that Dante worships, "the Love that moves the Sun and all the Stars," is the same Creative Energy of which contemporary science speaks as the only source of life, immanent and transcendent at the same time. But even those who are agnostic, who do not believe in God, and they are more to be pitied than condemned, can not only appreciate the beauty of Dante's poetry but also accept part of his vision if interpreted as a personal experience and a psychological document. Dante tells us in the first two "Cantiche" that man, being imperfect, sins; and if the sin becomes a habit, he becomes a slave to it, he is no longer able to use his reason and his power of will to get rid of it; then his moral and intellectual disintegration begins, and he is, to use the theological term, damned. The terrible consequences of this degradation of man to the level of a brute are vividly presented to us in the allegory of Hell; it is Virgil, the human reason, that shows them to us. But evidently, if reason is capable of analyzing evil, it is powerful enough to avoid it, to turn its back to darkness, to ascend again toward light, and then, with an effort of will, to climb the mountain of purgation. It is a stiff climb, as a very severe discipline is needed in order to eliminate all that is selfish, wicked and irrational in our being; it is a hard and painful struggle to conquer that moral freedom which is latent in every human soul. Once the purification is completed, man becomes free in the sense that he is guided only by reason which controls all his feelings and emotions. This moral freedom is the final goal for the agnostic who, I suppose, will be prepared to follow Dante up to this point; but for Dante, as for all religious teachers, this is the beginning of a new life, the awakening of a higher form of consciousness. Reason, that distinguishes man from the brute, gives us the clear knowledge of the unity of life, but the realization of this unity can only be obtained through love and faith. For Dante, moral wisdom is only the preparation for a spiritual wisdom that leads us to the vision of God; and this is the theme of his Paradise. It might be easier for the rationalist to accept Dante's creed if he realized that all great geniuses, without exception, have not only believed in this spiritual power, but made use of it in the creation of their work. The intuition of a scientist like Newton or Galileo, the inspiration of a poet or an artist like Shakespeare, Michelangelo or Beethoven, the illumination of a saint or a leader like St. Francis or Lincoln, are different expressions of the same Eternal Creative Force. Dante, being at the same time a poet and a mystic, had both the inspiration and the illumination which lifted him up to the vision of God; and he was able to convey to us at least an idea of his wonderful experience in his marvelous work of art.

# Some Notes
## on Brother Lawrence's Practice of the Presence of God—I
### GERALD HEARD

As THE SWAMI drew attention last year to the fact that Brother Lawrence was one of the modern Western devotees who attained to a definite level of enlightenment, it may be of interest to readers to consider in some detail Brother Lawrence's actual account of his method. As the following lines suggest, that method, though the description of it has been popular, has owed its popularity not to the fact that it is really simple or rudimentary but because we have felt sentimental about a pretty title and a charming old man.

This book has had uncommon success, awakening trust and response in Catholics and Protestants alike. That is because it is so simple, direct, sincere, and good that no one can doubt the author's *bona fides* nor fail to wish to imitate his life. The method he suggests is so plain that there are no theological terms over which dispute and confusion could arise nor procedures with which people of different practices might find it difficult to comply. A system which requires only a minimum theology—that God is all-powerful, all-wise, and all-loving—and which dispenses with all method save the constant reminding of ourself of that one fact—that God is always present and only asks for our attention—certainly we can understand its appeal, especially when we learn the results yielded by its practice. And yet if that is so why, though the book has been so popular and is so simple, have the results not been more striking? Long before God ceased to be believed in as Catholic and Protestant believed three generations ago, this little book was being studied, and its practice not practiced. Indeed had its practice been practiced God would still be believed in as Lawrence believed in Him. People who studied it must have wished to adopt its method; but somehow they failed. They read, admired, they wished to follow: they did not arrive; they did not become such as Lawrence. He and those like him say the way is simple and cannot fail. *They* arrived: there is no doubt. Why have we, using their instructions, fallen so far short in result?

The usual answer is that they were inherently gifted. With any method or none they would have done remarkably well. It is true that many people seem incapable of understanding what the spiritual life is about—they are like color-blind people taken to look at pictures, or the tone-deaf at a concert. But those who care to study such books as Lawrence's, they are not in such a category. You are not color-blind if you delight in looking at masterpieces of painting. If, after that, you proceed to produce daubs in which your attempts at color harmonies are clumsy smears or hideous discordances there is something wrong with you other than the lack of direct apprehension. In painting it has been found that the fault was the lack of teaching or wrong teaching leading to wrong method and discouragement. In painting that matters—but not much—a few thousands of people denied a pleasant hobby and fine outlet: a few hundreds of pleasant pictures not painted and bad pictures done in their stead. In the spiritual life that matters incalculably—matters for the spiritual who are stranded or sunken—matters for the world with these their pioneer light-ships lost and the whole convoy of civilization guideless on a dark sea. We cannot then discuss this problem by saying that the world is divided into Saints who can attain God's Presence and into the rest of us who can't, and that the books the Saints write and we read are as little use to us, and indeed as little for the Saints themselves, as color charts to help the color-seeing or the color-blind to see colors. We need teaching: we who study the Saints and study our conditions individual and social: we who realize how only by such characters, and by our being able to produce such characters, can we salvage ourselves and our civilization. The Saints do not start perfect, very far from it, and they did work very hard constantly and pertinaciously as they rose from level to level.

So we can return to Brother Lawrence and his popular booklet. The answer does not lie in "inborn genius": that is not the reason why his method does not make us into characters like him. It may then be worth while examining in some detail this brief book to see if we can discover, as it is a text book, a book for practical working, why it so seldom works or perhaps one should say, why it has so many failures. There are of course hundreds, perhaps thousands, of spiritual guide books and of each of them this same pressing question might be asked. But there are very few so simple, so brief, so well-known, so commended, so free of all particular provincialisms of the ecclesiastical or religious world, so directly concerned with the one main issue, so clearly pointing out the essentials of method and the desirability of the End as this particular book. It is a book which not only every and any Christian can understand and put into practice but it is one with which most Buddhists and Vedantists could do the same. We may then say that it would be hard to find any other spiritual guide better suited to act as the subject of this pressing inquiry. If we can with its aid and through careful study of it understand why spiritual guide books fail to bring interested readers to their goal we shall have found something which will help us not only to use "The Practice of the Presence" but also these other books, and to use them so as to produce those essential alterations and mutations in our lives which, with these rules, the authors first produced in their own.

The first thing that a careful study of these four conversations and fourteen letters discloses is that though the language is so simple, often even conventional, yet they contain far more specific information than the easy rapid reading suggests. The second thing arises from considering and ordering this information: for, that done, we find that this is not at all a beginner's book. Its simplicity of diction, the directness with which the process and the End are described, disguise from us, until we have worked at it, that the system is simple because it is advanced. This is not a spiritual child speaking with unreflective simplicity. This is a man at the end of an intense, never-remitted struggle of a dedicated life-time, having won to that consummate ease, that master's power to extemporise in any mode, which comes only to those who, at the top and climax of their form, having achieved all particular controls, now have such perfect command of expression and apprehension that every event becomes precisely that opportunity which allows fresh, unexhaustible creativeness to be exhibited. This opinion is so contrary to that commonly held by readers of Brother Lawrence that it will probably be well to support this analysis not merely by quotations from his well-worn words; but, by comparison with other such advisers, to show that, though they are considered advanced and difficult, and he for babes, the reverse is true. The two who closely resemble his approach, but both of them scholars and stylists, are St. Albertus Magnus in his "De Adherendo Deo," and the anonymous Master who wrote "The Cloud of Unknowing." Their books, comparison seems to show unmistakably, are complex because they deal with an earlier stage of the dedicated life, of spiritual evolution, than does the Practice of the Presence: they are showing how the masterful simplicity, the apparent spontaneity and easy freedom of Lawrence may be attained and must be purchased.

The first and simplest thing to note is the actual age of the workers to whom these three books refer. We know the "Cloud" was specifically written for a man of twenty-four just having completed a novice training and on his choosing to adopt the life of a pure contemplative. Albert is looking back across his immense life; he was a patriarch and an encyclopaedist and resolved as a parting gift to leave the actual instructions whereby anyone who cares to follow the path may find the goal. Lawrence is an old man speaking only and wholly of his own experience without reference to earlier mystics and even doubting whether other people have so found. The second thing is that Lawrence himself shows that he was singularly gifted in spiritual character, being converted at eighteen not by concern for himself but by sheer wonder at God's creative power (Plato's "redeeming amazement"). This early, favorable, and unrevoked start did not excuse him from most arduous efforts and mortifying experi-

ences. He went through the severe discipline of an austere
Carmelite training but his real novitiate was the four years
in which, in spite of his manifest simple goodness and in
spite also of kind and wise encouragement, he remained
convinced that he must be damned. The Lawrence of twenty-
four, yes even of forty-four would no doubt, if he could have
been persuaded to speak, have said things far more wrought
with effort and checkered with reflections than did he of old
age. Even in the letters we have a hint of a still-growing freedom and ease. Not only does he tell us in a sort of aside that
he has had spiritual sufferings and raptures which both were
keen enough to outweigh any physical pleasures and pains he
had ever endured, but we can note the last flush of self-con-
sciousness dying away when in the first letter he implores his
correspondent not to show to anyone this letter giving his
method. So deep are his self-misgivings still, that after prefac-
ing his remarks by telling of the difficulty it gave him to tell,
even under importunity, anything of his spiritual way, he
adds that if he thought what he had written should be seen
by a third party even his wish for his friend's spiritual ad-
vancement could not persuade him to help. This is strong
language for one who believed firmly that to miss your way
in this life was to miss it for good and come to a state of endless misery beside which any earthly misfortune was a baga-
telle. Nor were the four years of intense self-despair all his
purgation, though surely that was a heavy initiation and
should dispel from our minds the picture of a charming old
innocent who all his life had played alongside his accompanying fancy a God as sunny and as unrealistic as himself.
He tells us that the four years were followed by a decade during which he was on tenter-hooks and unable to find rest in
his vision because he could not reconcile such a marvelous
grace—the constant sense of God's Presence—with the inescapable awareness of his own poor despicable nature. Why
should he have the supreme comfort and solace when better
Christians were denied it? This problem of the acute sense
of the self being rendered agonizing just because the sense of
God's Presence is perfectly real—that the supreme desire and
its satisfaction is accompanied by supreme bafflement and
hopelessness, this purgatorial paradox of the spiritual life is

of course dealt with in "The Cloud." There the able author has much to say on this stage and how it is to be endured: but he does not speak, save as a distant goal, of the resultant condition and state from which the Lawrence of the letters and the conversations speaks. Lawrence, it is true, is sometimes considered simple, and even as one comfortably arrested at an early and childlike stage of the mystic ascent, because he uses language in describing his method which uses, with an indifference to detail, anthropomorphic imagery. He declares, in the first letter, that he regards God as his Father, as his King, as his God: that he carries on conversation with Him and goes through an "imaginary" scene of judgment and generous forgiveness. Both Albert and "The Cloud's" author are careful in this sort of description. They both urge their readers to clear their minds of imagery and they give good psychological reasons for this procedure in obtaining contact with the Eternal. Is not, then, Lawrence more rudimentary in this respect? I believe his carelessness or conventionality in phraseology and imagery—though no doubt all the more natural in a man of his intellectual simplicity and his time— when the Church was stricter in exacting verbal conformity than in the earlier centuries—also comes from his spiritual maturity and is a sign of his attainment. His achievement is so complete that under what seems looseness of phrase he is, in fact and as a matter of actual living, combining these antinomian aspects of ultimate Reality, which all thinkers have to face but which few, very few, can blend into a single concept yielding both the power to face things as they actually fall out and also the ability to act, in the face of such experience, with dynamic sanity and constant initiative. When Lawrence calls God his Father and his King, his God and his judge, he meant as a fact of conduct that he could both love the supreme Reality and yet also face the realization that such Reality could permit him to be tortured and destroyed. The advanced theological thought of India calls this the confronting of the soul with God as Creator, Sustainer, and Destroyer. It also with intellectual subtlety indicates how sanity is to be persevered in and indeed creativeness enhanced by such a revelation, and its solution is Lawrence's: to persevere in facing the fact not with stoical despair but with sublime self-

forgetfulness. Then, as Lawrence tells and the Gita proph-
esies, suddenly what has seemed a hideous paradox is in a
flash reconciled as a supreme revelation. Under the focal
strain, under the blinding jet of the oxygen flame of the
divine love and the acetylene blaze of the divine reality the
one seeking the sinner: the other hopelessly desired, incomparably self-sufficient and unattainable—under this fusing
heat the ego melts, for the only thing which burns in hell is
self—and the individual by perishing and in the act of voluntary immolation knows himself to be God. Without any
metaphysical aid Lawrence by a prodigious love, knew that
God was Love when He destroyed, and, by that acceptance,
what was destroyed was his separation—intellectual and
moral—from God and God became for him the never-inter-
mitted Presence. Lawrence was possessed because Nicholas
Hermann of Lorraine had been annihilated. He tells us of
this possession in some detail so we can have no doubt about
it. The years when as he says he had to work constantly to
keep the sense of the Presence may, it seems, most probably
be correlated with the four years of purgation. There is a
large consensus of spiritual opinion both in the East and the
West that the period of purgation usually takes from three
to four years, during which unremitting and often exhaust-
ing and almost hopeless effort is required, and also that during that time the soul must desire God ceaselessly and it will
be battered between the two rocks, the rock of despair which
echoes with the cries "You will never find Him: He will
never reveal Himself" and the rock of despair which counter-
cries "There He is and now do you, hopeless flotsam of the
seas, think you are going to climb out of the wave troughs up
and beyond the unattainable stars?" Then the habit becomes
fixed, the weary toiling to raise water from the deep well—to
use Teresa's simile—is changed, because now the well has
become an overflowing fountain. Lawrence was possessed by
the spirit he had dared to go on seeking when he was sure it
had damned him. He had not waited. He had thrown all that
could burn into hell and as the Divine is all save that which
is able to say I am I, when the I was gone Lawrence was filled
for good and all with God.

Besides also telling us of several stages in his spiritual evolution, stages which correspond with that *scala perfectionis* which the systematizing mystics have outlined, Lawrence also refers to his studies in such literature. In the first letter he notes that he began his intense search to attain union with Reality by reading "many books" on "different methods of going to God and divers practices of the spiritual life." No doubt these did not come his way when he was a foot soldier or while he was breaking crockery in the Treasurer's house as footman. We can assume he was given such works to study as a Carmelite novice and we may also feel fairly certain that with the works came adequate verbal instruction. We know from Brémond (Sentiment Religieux en France) that the Carmelites had only that decade been introduced into Paris and that their sponsors were men and women of the most remarkable and indeed advanced religious life. Brother Lawrence's instructors must themselves have been saintly men anxious to advance and help others advance in spirituality. This fact probably also accounts for the freedom to follow his bent, permitted him when he was seeking, and the wide respect shown him when it was recognized that he had found. An unlettered lay brother, a domestic servant of a poor monastery who can say to the inspecting Vicar General of one of the most powerful Cardinals that the great visitor could only come and see him if the Vicar General's one desire was sincerely to serve God, such a cookman, it is clear, is a recognized authority in the aliment of the soul. It was then, after having studied and been instructed, that Lawrence perfected his own simple, masterly, exacting method. Technically it is the attainment of uninterrupted monodeism. He tells us that he raised the threshold of attention until he could maintain it constantly at the same height which devout worship at the Sacrament keeps, for that time, the faithful sacramentalist. He adds the illuminative particular that the rush and noise of the kitchen when at full tide did not lower in any degree this intensity of other awareness. Nor, he makes it clear, was the concentration attained by a simple rudimentary disassociation through routine, muscular automatism. He could, he says, be continually asked for various things, his mental attention could be constantly summoned by practical demands and could give the right responses. Nor, again, was this state, the combination of surface practical awareness and deep attention fixed continually on God, dependent for its right working on familiar surroundings and customary stimuli. When he was sent on journeys to buy wine, though he dreaded the discomforts of travel—being crippled—he found his sense of the Eternal undisturbed. It is worth noting all he tells us of this state for, because of its simplicity, its profundity may escape us: because of its achieved facility we may fail to realize the extraordinariness of the condition. He remarks in one place that the business which he had to effect went well, as he had commended himself and it to God, for he found at the conclusion that it had all been managed as it should, though—and this is the phrase worth reflection—he himself recalled no particulars as to how it had been done. From these passages it is hard to escape the conclusion that this remarkable proficient of the will had so mastered his attention and set it upon the one object of its unceasing desire that he had produced a peculiar and most effective dissociation. By this means he was rid of all anxiety and strain, all haste and all fatigue. The attention he gave to the task which he was offering momentarily to God, was that quality of intense attention which can only be compared with that attention which the hypnotic subject gives to anything to which his controller tells him to attend. Such attention is so intense that it is without memory or foreboding, as much without boredom as it is free of possessive adhesion, for the ego, with its vibrant self-involvement, continually asking "Do I like: do I dislike this?" is absent. But whereas the hypnotized subject is dependent on the will of his controller and on that, even, to a limited degree, Lawrence was dependent on a will which he felt to be both infinitely powerful and kind. Nor, though this control was transcendent, did Lawrence feel it to be alien. He tells us he often felt as though God were in him and had he belonged to a spiritually more outspoken age, no doubt he would have said precisely that, feeling that such a phrase alone was adequate to describe in one term the abolition of his own will and the simultaneous discovery that he was more alive, more conscious, more tirelessly volitional, and full of initiative, response, and uncalculated effectiveness than ever he had been when he was concerned, careful, scrupulous, and self-conscious.

This condition, it is obvious, is very advanced. He who has it, has already entered Eternity, for time is gone. Time is a tension between some regret for the past and apprehension for the future, time is a state of mind created by the ego's characteristics, greed and fear. Albertus Magnus in his precise scholarly instruction makes this clear. He tells the student as "a sure path to Bliss"—that state of liberation as far beyond pleasure as it is above pain—to "mount up into the dark" or limit "of the mind," there to accustom himself to "stand fast in the Lord within you" when, after some practice "in recollecting the emotions and fixing them above," he will find that he has entered the Eternal Now. Brother Lawrence realized that he had entered Eternity while still in the body. He says, as clearly as Eckhart, the great thinker of mysticism, had said earlier, that "I now see God in such a manner as might make me sometimes say I believe no more but I see. In short I am assured beyond all doubt that my soul has been with God above these thirty years." The actual step which brings about this union ends time and passes the soul into Eternity. Lawrence himself describes it in a single sentence which for its depth might come from Plotinus. It is a classic description of the act of creative will, the mutation of consciousness. Having said his sole objective had become one thing—"nothing but how to become wholly God's"—he strikes to the heart in the phrase "This made me resolve to give the all for the All." Having seen that the One must be attained by yielding and exchanging for the One the manifold, he let the many go that he might be seized of the One. He succeeded in acting on Eckhart's great cry of prayer "O Lord God we beseech Thee to help us escape from the life which is divided into the life which is united." Only those who have completely misapprehended the "Practice of the Presence" can, in face of such a phrase, continue to think of Lawrence's method as a gentle, sentimental reverie, a method whereby a wandering-minded monk filled in with a theological daydream the longeurs of the conventual day. So much for Lawrence's own development and systematization, for the deeply cut steps he hewed to scale the purgatorial mountain and the firm platform he won on its lofty summit. His letters illustrate in still further detail how conscious and defined he had made his specific trail, how little he left to happy chance, how well he remembered and understood the intense effort needed at the start and for a long while, and how shrewd and calculating he was—what a sound practical psychologist in judging every difficulty and in suggesting ingenious and subtle ways of negotiating successive obstacles. There is no suggestion that he imagined any but proficients would find the way anything but a constant remedying of faults, repairing of slips and mistakes and indefatigable returning to the climb after bruise, stumble and fall—in fact a life of continual restarting after check and arrest. He advises beginners not to trust the stream of their feeling: on the contrary he specifically tells them "to do themselves violence" in setting themselves at this task of remembering God when it will actually seem "repugnant"— there will be a distinct emotional disgust for the work—and, alternately it will seem "time lost"—the whole task will seem an illusion, a silly bore. Then the beginner is to tie himself to the task as a steersman lashes himself to the wheel when facing contrary seas. He is to bind himself by the express resolve that, whether he makes harbor or no, the ship, even if it sink, shall be found facing toward port. He is to resolve till death to hold his course. Then when the will is set—that naked intent of the will—that blind beholding which is the whole teaching of the "Cloud"—then, with that, sure and based, can come a number of subtle devices and advices. Once the will is really purified in the fire of love and is true metal without alloy it can be tempered. There is a finer, surer strength than rigidity and that is suppleness. To revert to voyaging similes: the ship must hold its course, but it must also know, if it is to climb the oncoming waves, how to rise and swing to them. The forces which meet him who would move ahead along an intentional progress are waves as surely as the sea's. There must be give and then go. No one can advance unremittingly until they are reborn and leave the sea for the air. The beginner will find the true criterion of his strength—or rather of the strength given him— not in swift progress which almost inevitably would lead to pride—but in his humble power of immediate recovery. True, a perfect ship keeps a wonderfully steady keel in all weathers but for a middlingly-built craft its safety lies in its power to roll to the waves: the thoroughly dangerous boat is that which will not roll at all. Suddenly hit by a heavy sea it reels clean over, never recovers and founders at one plunge. So are the rigid, self-assured, self-upheld stoics. So Lawrence warns strongly against all rolling in the wave trough of remorse. As Fénelon, the holy Marquis, was pointing out at the same time as this holy scullion, remorse and disgust at the self may be not repentance at all but actually wounded self-importance, mortified, not at having fallen from God but in being lowered in its own self-esteem. As soon as the dip is over the ship must rise. The ship will labor and stagger, rock and sway as we try to keep its masthead steady on the pilot star. The skilled steersman with ready hold does not expect absolute rigidity or throw up his hands when time and again the ship gives and reels: indefatigably he brings her head back again to the course. And as he ceases to worry and wrench at the helm, not only does his strength hold; the ship also reels less. Lawrence also notes for his beginners how much the actual impact of the wave may be modified by foresight. That is our peculiar power of mind which gives mind its one but, if employed, decisive supremacy over emotion. We can see the wave bearing down on us and we can handle our craft so that she takes the flood skilfully with her prow well set to it. Lawrence warns that the disturbances in prayer bear a close relation to the thought indulged in when out of prayer. And here we drop the simile of boat, steersman, and waves for all are one—we are ocean as well as ship and mariner and so we can decide if the sea is to be rough—it will be as rough as we care to stir it. We stir it with our constant daily preoccupation with other drives and urges, quite other than the urge to reach and abide in the unchanging eternal dynamic coordinative calm of the Presence and Peace of God.

# Notes on Brother Lawrence's Practice of the Presence of God—II

## GERALD HEARD

LAWRENCE HAD RIGHT to think his system the simplest, best, most thorough and swiftest. Extend the Kingdom of intention and control until there is no province, no quarter of an hour, in which its writ does not run. Then there will be no backwoods where outlaws may gather to attack and pester the camp and the city. Clean out every focus of infection, leave no pocket for flies to breed on its garbage of worry and private concern, the house of the Soul will not need all this screening and spraying nor its householder always be dashing from his lens and retort to swot the intruding insects. No more than flies can be present if breeding grounds are absent can distracting thoughts, still less worry, disturb the mind which has no concern but God. The Eternal Light sterilizes all these pests.

Again we must remind ourselves that Lawrence did not think this course anything but fatiguing for beginners. If we are seeking immediate comfort we shall not clean the garbage pit nor drain the puddles. Nearly all of us are seeking something short of the Eternal dynamic peace: we are, all save the Saints, beachcombers in soul: though we should feel disgust if we beachcombed in the flesh. Lawrence's recommendation that we should all the time be conscious, or strive to be, every minute, is a short sharp cure. Sharp because we are alternating creatures; short, because if we stick to it and succeed in switching over into continuous, intentional consciousness—the practice of the Presence—we have done at a stroke and for good what anyhow we must sooner or later do, what is easier done now than when, as must be at any later time, there must be more to undo, and what, if we stop and start again, we shall take many bites at the one cherry. Our many false starts will amount to a mileage equal to the mileage of the actual crossing if we went ahead and crossed straight away. Lawrence is too good a psychologist, has too much of actual spiritual experience to expect that one resolve, however keen, will see us through and over. He has warned us of the waves, of the opposing tides we stir up by our forward thrust. He does not expect us to make an unruffled drive and dive to our goal but he does expect and plan for an ever quicker recovery after each deflection, until what began as a zigzag advance, with pausing and panting at each hooking and crooking, shows less and less fluctuation, ripples forward with a quicker, smoother, straighter flow, till at last, like a streak and a flash, it strikes straight for its goal. Nothing distracts or delays it now. To change the simile, the perforations in the band of time become incessant, until, instead of a series of punctures, a continuous aperture is pierced through the Temporal into the Eternal. Then the Soul has attained: the fog and web of the Temporal never has a chance to form. The Light shines uninterruptedly. The hard-working and often fatigued and flustered servant is raised, hears the almost-too-good-to-be-true summons, "Friend, come up higher." He finds himself in the light, by the source and fount of all energy. Striving is over: the rough water left. With a prodigy of effort, beating and being beaten by waves and water, the swan strikes and batters itself along the sea surface. But suddenly the pounding pinions no longer buffet the stinging water. They strike, hold and mount upon the air and in a moment the agony is over, the huge bird is free in its element, the waves sink down impotently under, the last drops sweep from its feathers, falling to the sea, whose sound even now is waning as the wind currents bear the exultant creature racing upward into the sky. Yes, there are helpful wind currents to step us up from the sea surface. Lawrence warns us of this also. Be always ready, be alert to mount, but know also that you do not mount solely by that act of will. "You must raise your sail," said Ramakrishna. "The wind of Grace will fill it." Assuredly it will, but we have to learn patience. We must remember we have all of us missed many a tide, many a favorable wind. We cannot expect everything to be ready the moment we decide, at long last, that we are. But the waiting, too, has its purpose. *There are no accidents in the spiritual life.* The waiting shows us whether we are in earnest. We are, as a matter of fact, never kept waiting long: never as long as we ourselves have delayed. Lawrence, then, warns against that beginner's fever which would be immediately at its goal and is peremptory in its demand for instantaneous enlightenment. He uses the interesting phrase that the young hot-head he was indirectly counselling was wishing to go "faster than Grace." The wise gardener works indefatigably: he knows that though he must wait on Nature's time for fruits, yet there is always something he can be doing to help and that on the incessancy of his labor will depend, when the fruits appear, their abundance and their quality.

Such then was Brother Lawrence and such his method. As for its results on him we may say that it raised him past all the conflict of purgation to the effortless achievement and unvarying imperturbable happiness which is an authentic manifestation of the Eternal Peace. Circumstances of time and place; conditions of body; limitations of mind; the faults of the particular church to which he belonged; of the social system in which he lived; the distresses and diseases of an old crippled body ill-tended; the inadequacy of an intelligence long uneducated, of moderate endowment at best and given in the end but little actual instruction: all these handicaps were severe and might have proved arresting. With his single-hearted devotion toward God, to God in His inexpressible perfection, with his magnificent integrity of will Lawrence surmounted all. Through a system heavily encrusted and opalescent with dogma, with rigid and elaborate ordering, ritual and particularized symbolism, he made the pure eternal light shine as purely and certainly as intensely as any Sufi or Quaker. In a society where religion had been amalgamated into the State so that when the State collapsed his Church was completely involved in the ruin, he not only kept the witness of the Spirit alive in his heart: the Paraclete shone so brightly in this temple cleaned of all but the Supreme Presence that the worldly wise, as wearily awake to the hysteria of sham religion as they were to the simpler

more ruthless hypocrisy of ecclesiastical careerism nevertheless came to talk with and be roused from their sophisticated
despair by this man, who by the simple audacity of simply
"giving the all for the All" had found what they with all their
endowments had missed. These shrewd observers, used to
watching as well as listening, these inspectors well equipped
with critical power to expose even the eloquent pretentiousness of a Pascal (the lovely, seemingly sincere master style
and the queer life lived behind it), these official advisers of
Government, investigating the strange powers of defiant
Jansenism and finding, as they suspected and half wished to
find, behind the power of the appeal, the pride of the self
will, back of the inflexible martyr the persecuting bigot,
recessive to the wilful fidelity to a narrow vision an implac-
able uncharitability: such observers came to study Lawrence.
The Jesuits were in the saddle managing the King and his
gross sins in order, "A.M. D.G.," to manage the State. They
had denounced the Quietists and imposed a worship which
was filled with the images the mystic believes to prove obstacles. They had driven out the gentle saintly Fénelon ac-
cusing him of Quietism. Had Lawrence been even at Fene-
lon's level he might have been crushed. After all, he was no
Marquis, stylist, scholar, tutor of the heir to the throne, and
he could have been silenced by the mere hint of authoritative
disapproval. Less exertion, less reflection, than we take to
brush aside an ant would have swept him into oblivion. For
not only was he personally of complete insignificance, a lay
brother of a poor house, he was also of complete humbleness
and obedience possibly unattainable by one who has merited
the doom to be born to a marquisate and, even when he
chooses the church, to preach with eulogized eloquence; to
manage affairs and men of affairs with mastery; to conduct
a life of shining spectacular virtue against the terribly effective background of a court clever, pretentious and squalid.
Fénelon banished—banished to his archbishopric—banished
from such a court to his rightful flock which he was vowed
to feed spiritually and who did (however frugally he ate)
actually feed him—Fénelon submitted with dignity, with
true grace but not with cheerfulness. True he was leaving
his beloved pupil whom he had tamed from savagery and

trained to affection, a pupil dear to himself as a spiritual son and precious to himself as a loyal son of France, for this child—whom he had broken and reset—was it seemed to be France's sole master. But Lawrence, to whom the Presence of God made for him a light in which all and any conditions were radiant with God's will, love and marvelous design, Lawrence surely would not have written from the galleys, even still less from the archepiscopal palace of Cambrai, "I am enduring a dry and bitter peace." This is not to underrate the noble Archbishop: it is to elevate or show the true station of the ex-cook.

Lawrence was not silenced. That is the fact, more important than any speculation, however certain, as to how his radiance would have shone unabated had he been exiled, Lawrence might have been accused, when, passions were running high, of certain expressed carelessness about forms when forms were again being advocated as essential by the dominant party and that party, with the despot behind them, was striking successfully at figures great in rank and station, worthily high in prestige and consummate in expression and defense. Lawrence is inspected—it was the time when anyone of low rank in the Church and showing influence had to be inspected. Surely it may be doubted whether the first visit of the Vicar General of the Cardinal de Noailles was made solely that the busy, and probably harassed, official might talk about his own soul. Yet it is certainly clear that this hardworking man, at work which was probably hardening, this filterer of claims for preferment, this sanitary inspector of moral scandals, this server of tables none too clean besieged by the hungry, whose hunger had made them none too scrupulous, still found time to come once and again to get spiritual food for himself from the simpleton whom he inspected: he found time to write out for others what he had found, to enter that passage about his being forbidden to come again unless he would give up his life to God, and to urge on the Cardinal his master the publication of this pure and lofty Gospel, a request which was granted. The point disclosed here seems important. Recall that at that precise moment Lawrence's teaching could so easily, almost inevitably have been regarded as inexpedient. The Church, especially in France, had decided this was of all times the least auspicious in which to teach the laying aside of systems and the Quakerly doctrine that as all life is sacramental picking up a straw may and should be done as much for the love of God and in the clear conviction of His Presence as kneeling in adoration before the sacrament. This was what Lawrence taught and the teaching, advanced though it is, easily misunderstood as it certainly can be, was not only approved but promulgated by the ultra-cautious authorities, hardened with suspicion and hypersensitively nervous over any latitude or tolerance. Is there not in the fact a further and perhaps most important piece of evidence as to the spiritual height Lawrence had attained? Those who spoke with him noted not only his words, they were held by his appearance. Like all those few who have become the constant friends of God, he radiated, without the need of expression, the triple charisma, the love, joy and peace which fills those natures who have lost their egos. They do not have to think and say and act; they are, and their still silences bless us more than their arguments, their eloquence or their good deeds. Lawrence's words and reasoning could well have been misapprehended and suppressed. They were given a currency which would have astonished him, not by sectarians anxious by any secession to liberate the Spirit, when free, pure worship seemed deliberately attacked, but by the highest church authorities, men charged to err on the side of caution and repression. That denouement seems to have a moral for us today. It is clear that precisely the same words as Lawrence used would be used by a Quaker, by any devout schismatic or heretic. The book's success as wide as Christendom has established that. The words themselves therefore would not have assured themselves a welcome: on the contrary we should expect them to have been repressed kindly, maybe, but firmly. What made their issue seem safe and natural was Lawrence himself, or, to be precise, his lack of self. Something of an authenticity both so awe-inspiring and so gentle, irresistible in the dread strength of its open tenderness and unsuspecting love came out from the old man that those in his presence knew that he was only an open door. Through the incessant beauty of his soul shone the awful meekness of the Paraclete. To doubt that his words could do harm, to feel suspicion that such a spirit might be unsafe and endanger social security or ecclesiastical arrangements, such doubts and suspicions, in a presence instant with the authenticity of the Eternal, filled the enquirer with shame. He knew, below all argument of caution and reasons of State and Church, that nothing but good can flow from the Source of Good.

The question must rise in our minds—when we consider this man, his peculiar time of anxious, authoritative repression and his letters and conversations both so free and innocent of the passports of detailed dogmatic compliance, so emphatic that one thing alone matters above sins and sacraments, the constant communion with God—the question must be asked, "How often have the martyrs, by failing in profound incessant charity for those who opposed them, in their desire to throw at their persecutor's feet the challenge of their lives, failed to see that they were themselves debarring the spread of their message?" "The blood of the martyrs is the Seed of the Church." What Church? Certainly the implicit violence and hostility of not a few such witnesses were seed from which sprang a church as ruthlessly cruel in persecution as ever its persecutors. The message of the Sermon on the Mount was never carried by such martyrs. Today the world is in a desperate pass. Men of great courage and devotion and with a great cause to serve are resolved that the other side must be crushed beyond recovery and they themselves are ready to die and wreck the world if only their enemy may be totally destroyed. Each side maintains that there is not the slightest use expecting any decent or lasting settlement as long as the other is free to live. The enemy is one who is incapable of understanding the right. We have to go back to the wars of religion to find such a fatal implacability. And it is there, on the shore of that deadly sea of the mutual blind hatred of two intense devoted convictions, of the death duel of the champions of the Spirit of Freedom and the Spirit of Authority, that we find Brother Lawrence. He spoke, in the camp of Authority, for freedom and because of the love he felt for men, through the love he had won to and from God, the authoritarians listened and published his message. He succeeded in speaking of real religious liberty, that incessant service which is the only perfect freedom, to those obsessed with the need of order, because he never felt these men to be at heart different from himself. He knew that we all need God. That is our one peremptory overwhelming need but in spite of our awful thirst we cannot stoop and drink because we are masked in our prejudices and prides. Because he spoke with absolute simplicity and with living proof of what he had found, he knew he had nothing to fear from men whose need was as great as his. However fanatical, when we are dying of thirst we do not strike or silence one whom we see is coming to lead us to a well from which he has drunk and lived. His examiners, therefore, also knew they had nothing to fear from him. That is the one foundation of all peace-making: the assurance that from this man, at least, I have nothing to fear. Suspicion and its dim father, recoiling caution, could find no purchase in this man's innocent humility. Because, in a deeper sense than we say it, Lawrence never stood in his own light. In the light which streamed over him he strove to be perfectly transparent. He gave no personal or temporal tinge to his profoundly simple message. For that reason his anxious authorities passed it and published it and precisely for that reason those who have most loved God and cared least for anything else, even for the forms in which men have spoken of God, these saints of every race and sect, as well as those particular executives of his day, have loved and prized his words.

Here is a true bridge-builder, a *pontifex maximus,* spanning the gulf between the devotees of freedom and those of authority and his power to span and embrace and hold these two extremes, who else must destroy each other, is not ingenuity of compromising phrase or eloquence or appeal to reason. No, it is that gigantic gentleness, that irresistible authenticity which sees in all the same vast universal need it has felt in itself, that sees that need can only be satisfied by the same simple solution. Because Lawrence really did give the all for the All he received back from the All, all his fellows, now seen as part of that All and only needing to recognize their part in that All, by giving all themselves to it, to become one with the All. This and this only is the faith which overcomes the world, for it reunites all mankind by making it one communion with the Eternal. Those only, but they infallibly, who are so filled with the Presence of God may and must draw all men, none of whom they can think of as alien, into that incessantly practised communion. This is Lawrence's particular message to our day and hour—be filled until you are nothing but the All and then you will discover that because He is indeed the All you do indeed embrace and draw out of the ignorance and illusion of separateness every other human soul. For there can be no boundaries, no limitations, no exclusions toward any. However much any may feel that they are separate, the higher Knowledge, the true gnosis of charity won in the Presence of God, knows that this is illusion which must vanish when it meets the challenge of Truth in Love. This gnosis also knows that God's presence waits to descend fully to recreate man, until the last man shall consent to wish for that presence and, so attaining the power to see it in his neighbor, will be united with God in man. Finally the gnosis in the power of its endless life knows that, as each individual becomes aware of his real nature in God, his enlightenment gives him the power to kindle the same illumination in others.

# Self-Surrender

## SWAMI PRABHAVANANDA

I WILL BEGIN by quoting two famous passages from the Mundaka Upanishad: "Like two birds of beautiful golden plumage—inseparable companions—the individual self and the immortal Atman are perched on the branches of the self-same tree. The former tastes the sweet and bitter fruits of the tree. The latter remains motionless, calmly watching."

"The individual self, deluded by forgetfulness of its identity with the Divine Atman, grieves, bewildered by its own helplessness. When it recognizes the Lord—who alone is worthy of our worship—as its own Atman, and beholds its own glory, it becomes free from all grief."

These are revealed truths. They have been directly and immediately experienced by the seers and sages, within the depths of their own souls. Such truths are, of course, universal; and can be realized by every one of us who is ready to make the effort to do so.

The fable of the two birds is intended to teach us the truth about Man's real and apparent nature. It teaches that Man suffers only because he is ignorant of his true Being. God *is*. He is the absolute Reality, "ever-present in the hearts of all." He is the blissful Atman which sits, calmly watching the restlessness of its companion. And the fable goes on to tell us that, at last, the two birds merge into one. The Atman is all that exists.

Therefore, our suffering has no real cause, no necessity. This external life, this tasting of the sweet and bitter fruits of the tree of experience, is a dream, from which, at any moment, we may awake. Sometimes our dream is pleasant, sometimes unpleasant. There are philosophers who tell us that the unpleasant and evil things of Life are an illusion, and that only the pleasant and good things are real. But this cannot be true. Pleasure and pain, good and evil, belong inseparably together—they are what Vedanta calls "the pairs of opposites." They are like the two sides of a coin. Their nature cannot differ. Either both are real or both are unreal.

Theologians have argued for centuries over the problem of Evil. Why does this ignorance exist? Why is Man unaware of his Divine Nature? But this question could only be answered by those who have transcended our human consciousness, with its belief in good and evil. Why do we dream? We can only find the answer to that problem after we have awakened. The seers who have attained transcendental consciousness tell us that the so-called Problem of Evil is no problem at all, because Evil does not exist and has never existed. But for us who still live in the consciousness of the relative world, the problem of how our ignorance arose is merely academic. We need only to ask how we shall remove our ignorance.

What is the nature of this ignorance? It resides in our sense of ego, our belief that we are individual beings. The ego veils our eyes, as it were, and causes us to dwell in ignorance. Man is the Atman, the Spirit. He has a mind, senses and a body. When he forgets that he is the Atman, and identifies himself with body, mind and senses, then the sense of ego originates. With the birth of this ego-sense, the transcendental nature is forgotten. Man lives on the sense-plane and becomes subject to the law of Karma and rebirth.

In our ignorance, we are no longer aware of the Lord within us, and yet, nevertheless, because our true nature is divine, we feel a lack, an emptiness. We want to find something, although we do not know exactly what it is. We want some kind of happiness which will be lasting. And so desire rises in us, a craving for everything which seems to promise happiness and seems pleasant; a shrinking back from everything which seems unpleasant. Behind all our desires—even the very lowest and basest—there is the urge to find real, unalloyed happiness and freedom, to find immortality. This strong craving, which does not know what is its real object, involves us in all sorts of action. We try everything, in order to find what it is that we are seeking. And our actions, in their turn, involve us in the limitations and bondages of

Karma: as we sow, we reap. We begin to taste the fruits of the tree of experience. We wish to taste only the sweet fruits, but this is impossible, for the bitter fruit grows on the same tree, and we cannot have the one without the other.

Out of this attachment to what is pleasant and this aversion to what is unpleasant there grows a clinging to life. The ego clings to its ego-life, its sense of individuality: it does not want to die. Yet this "life" which the ego clings to is really death, because it is separation from our true nature, from God. That is why Jesus said: "He who loves this life shall lose it."

To find real life, the life of our true nature, we must transcend the ego. We shall never know happiness until we realize Brahman, the Ground, in which we are rooted. The ego is the only barrier to this knowledge. Sri Ramakrishna used to say that when the ego dies all troubles cease. And Jesus tells us: "Except a man be born again, he cannot enter the Kingdom of God." This rebirth, this birth in spirit, is the death of the ego. The Hindus have a saying: "Die while living." Die the death of the ego and be reborn spiritually, even in this life.

So the problem of all spiritual life, no matter whether you are a Christian, a Buddhist or a Hindu, simply amounts to this: How can I kill the ego? And the answer given by every one of these religions is the same: Surrender yourself. Give yourself up to God, completely and wholeheartedly. Love God with all your heart, all your soul and all your mind. Become absorbed, and forget yourself in the consciousness of God. The ego is the only obstacle to God-consciousness. The great yogi, Patanjali, compares it to the bank of a reservoir. You want to irrigate your fields. In the reservoir there is plenty of water—the living water of the Atman. All you have to do is to break down the bank, and the water will flow over the fields. Each one of us has that reservoir inside him, ready to flood his life with joy, wisdom and immortality, if only he will break down the ego, the barrier.

It sounds so simple: to love God, to surrender ourselves to Him, to kill this ego. But it is the hardest thing one can possibly do. It involves great spiritual disciplines; and the practice of these disciplines with the utmost patience and perseverance. The mind is always straining to go outward, toward everything that seems pleasant in the external world. And the ego reasserts itself perpetually. However we may try to banish it, it keeps reappearing, as it were, in different disguises. So we have to keep on trying.

What are these disciplines we have to practice? They are discrimination and dispassion. We have to discriminate, perpetually, throughout our lives, between what is real and what is unreal. God, the infinite, the unchanging, is the only reality. Everything else, all these appearances and forms of the external world, are unreal. As you practice this discrimination, you become convinced that God is, that He really exists. And, further, you begin to realize that, if there is a God, He must be attainable. Most people think that they believe in God, and there it ends. They imagine that mere belief in God is enough. It is sufficient to be what they call "a God-fearing man." But the great spiritual teachers have told us that religion means something far more than mere faith, a mere opinion that God exists. You have to believe that God is actually attainable. Otherwise, the practice of dispassion and discrimination does not mean anything at all. Simply by saying that we believe in God we cannot free ourselves from these experiences of life and death, pleasure and pain. These are the direct, immediate experiences of the dream which we call life. We have to wake from this dream, and know the Reality, which is also a direct, immediate experience. We have to break this dream while living on earth. We have to die while living, in order to enter the Kingdom of God. The proof of God's existence is not to be found in theological arguments, or even in the revealed scriptures. Yes, Jesus saw God; Ramakrishna saw God; but that is no proof for us. We must see God for ourselves: that is the only real proof.

Again, the practice of dispassion and discrimination does not mean that we are to give up the activities of life. It does not mean running away from the world. It is the mind which has to be trained. We have to cultivate yearning for God. We have to train our minds in such a way that we are surrendering our ego to God, every moment of our life.

How shall we cultivate this yearning, this love for God? It

cannot be done simply by sitting down, closing our eyes and fixing our hearts on God. That is only possible at a very advanced stage. What shall be our method of training? The Gita teaches Karma Yoga. In Karma Yoga we learn to surrender ourselves to God through our actions, through every breath we breathe. There are different ways of doing this. For instance, you can regard yourself simply as a machine. Who is the operator? The Atman within you. You have to try to forget the ego: for a machine has no will of its own. Or you can think of the fable of the two birds. You are the Atman, motionless, actionless, calmly observing. The senses move amongst the sense-objects, but you remain free from all action. You are actionless in the midst of action. Or again, you can make every action into a sort of ritual, an offering to God. As Sri Krishna says to Arjuna, in the Gita:

> *"Whatever your action,*
> *Food or worship;*
> *Whatever the gift*
> *That you give to another;*
> *Whatever you vow*
> *To the work of the Spirit;*
> *O son of Kunti,*
> *Lay these also*
> *As offerings before me."*

And he continues: "Thus you will free yourself from both the good and the evil effects of your actions. Offer up everything to me. If your heart is united with me, you will be set free from Karma even in this life, and come to me at the last."

When you fall in love with someone, your mind dwells on that person, no matter what you may be doing, all day long. That is how we should love God. Every day, we must fall in love with Him afresh, in a new way. Human love wears out and ceases; but love of God grows. You do not get tired of it. It is always a new thing. It gains in intensity. To cultivate this love, we must try to be conscious of God continually; and this is only possible if we practice regular meditation. Without meditation, Karma Yoga is impracticable. Just by being a good person, by living an ethical life, by trying to be selfless in your service, you cannot reach the transcendental Reality. By meditation, you have to awake the power that is within you. Then you begin to see the play of God in the outside world. Ethical life and service are an aid, but they are not an end in themselves. The end is to be one with God. Set aside some time each day to devote yourself completely and wholeheartedly to the contemplation of God. Think of nothing else but Him, and so the practice will become easy.

Where should we think of God? We are not to pray to some external Being, who hangs in the sky. God is omnipresent. He is nearer than anything we know. He is within us. We have to feel that living Presence within the chamber of our own hearts. Go into your own heart and surrender yourself, there, to the Ruler of the universe, without whom you could not breathe or act, without whom there is no consciousness, no reality. Surrender yourself completely and wholeheartedly to Him.

# The Churches, Humanism and Spirituality

## Gerald Heard

THIS IS AN AGE of growing discouragement for all Humanists. The belief that mankind can by amelioration of its circumstances attain to permanent happiness in this world, has been given blow after blow in the last twenty-five years until it is hardly tenable by the least intelligent. The last hope of such:—that though in the rest of the world this faith had failed, yet in one place, Russia, the light had dawned and was growing, that hope has been dimmed and darkened by a series of "successes" which have been more terrible than failure. The deliberate starving of some two million peasants, the ruthless executions of all who differed with the man at the top, and now the imperialistic lunges against a series of small neighbors—such acts can only be held as proofs of an approaching millennium by people who have ceased to attach any meaning to words or any value to human life.

This failure of Humanism is also reflected in a keen discouragement among many of the Churches. A large number of Protestant communions have increasingly during the last thirty years—especially in this country—come to identify their aims and their methods with those of Humanism. This is historically an interesting development. Ever since the Reformation, when Authority was denied to the Pope or the Councils of the Bishops of the Catholic Church, the basis of authority was shifted from the discussions and decisions of men (who might or not be inspired) to a Book. Authority had to be somewhere and as, to quote the Old Testament, there was no longer "Open Vision," the power of contemporary men to have the experience of God, the accounts of vision in the past had to take the place of vision in the present. But once authority is confined to a Book that Book is bound to be examined critically. If a small arch is to carry such a weight it must be clear that its bricks and stones are strong enough to do so. As we all know, the examination showed that what the Jews had claimed to be inspired and of unparalleled spiritual majesty showed itself to be of very mixed authority and doubtful strength. The Churches would not, however, have the courage, as the great Heresiarch Marcion pleaded, to throw over the "bronze age religion of the backward Semites" and cling only to the New Testament. This led to a first falling away of followers. But even had the Churches abandoned the Old Testament the difficulty would not have been surmounted. For a Church which attaches all its weight to the authenticity of certain accounts of a single life, a Church which tries to sanction the spiritual life and prove the reality of God and Heaven by the records made two thousand years ago of a small series of none-too-well-witnessed events, has to abide by the judgment of the textual critic and his verdict can hardly fail to be one of "Not Proven." This was the position in which the Protestant Churches found themselves a generation ago. They had no authority for maintaining that a spiritual or even a moral life could be established against all doubt on the evidence that they could produce. They, therefore, began a retreat from that untenable position, a retreat all the more serious because it was no longer the open desertion by individuals of the Churches they could no longer honestly support but was a steady lapse of the Churches themselves from their own formularies and creeds. Without changing the letter, gradually all spirit was taken out of it. Miracles were dropped first, then the key miracles of Virgin Birth and Resurrection (the latter had been nodal to the first great Western missionary, St. Paul), and finally it was taken for granted that the future life should not be mentioned or the spiritual world but that the whole energy of the Churches should be shifted over to "social duties" to the improvement of physical conditions in the vague belief that when everyone was comfortable they would then either be able to find heaven for themselves or would find that they did not need it. Heaven would have become unnecessary to people who

had such a good time on earth. So the Protestant Churches
have found themselves aligned with Humanism and as Humanism
has suffered a slump, the bottom of which no one
can yet see, the Churches too are having a fall which may
shake them severely. Yet this shaking may in the end prove
to be a very sensible blessing in disguise. The Churches have
no real alliance with Humanism. They only took up this line
of activity because they were privately or subconsciously convinced
by the Humanists' argument that there was nothing
in religion save its possible social value and that if they
would drop their "other-worldliness" the practical social
workers, the socialists and communists would see whether
they could find some side-line use for the older organizations
in the modern world. Now that these so-called realists are lost
in a fog of disappointment and acrimonious recrimination,
the Churches, who, after all, were never very much at home
with their new allies, can draw off and think their position
out. That charge of "other-worldliness," was it after all so
shameful an accusation? What in the name of earth and
heaven are Churches doing if they are not concerned with
some other world than that which the man-of-the-world calls
the world of common sense and which even he is suspiciously
aware is not the whole of the cosmos? The Churches should
be other-worldly as long as this world means materialism, for
materialism is such a lifeless abstraction of even present
reality that no society can hold together which tries to make
its picture of things in such a perspectiveless fashion. Yet the
difficulty remains: granted that materialism is unworkable
as a philosophy of life, at least of any social life, granted that
even to attain the goal of Humanism there has to be a metaphysic
and a way of life which outreaches and underspans
the Humanities, just to know that is not enough. I may
realize, I may accurately calculate the charge necessary to
disrupt the nucleus of the atom and so to bring about transmutation.
But, unless I can command that charge, the calculations
on paper, accurate to a volt though they may be, will
bring me no nearer to my practical goal than the recipe for
baking bread will feed a starving man. The first step, no
doubt, for the Protestant Churches is to realize that Humanism
is both in itself stalling and is anyhow none of their busi-

ness. If it is going to have its funeral it need not be theirs. But the second step is quite as important. The Churches have not merely to remedy a mistake, to dissolve a partnership. They have to take their own initiative, find their own line and invite men to a new, constructive and really progressive fellowship. To do that they have to begin by remaking their philosophy. That is not to say that what they used to teach is not true. All the working parts of it, undoubtedly, are. What they have to do is, as one of the most active minds in the English Church has said, the late Dean Inge, to change from the religion of authority, authority based on far too narrow an evidential basis, to the religion of experience. Of course many doubt whether this may be done with any intellectual integrity. Poor as is the quality of the historical evidence on which they base their faith their fastidious knowledge of the kind of emotionalism which they fear is all that can be called the religion of experience, makes them prefer a withered and crumbling archaeological fact, to a warm and coarse-smelling gust of conviction. Yet the religion of experience can be scientific, exact and even cool. If we leave it to the emotional it will naturally be "enthusiastic" but if the intellectual will explore this avenue, taking all their critical faculties with them, they will find that it is not they who will return empty-handed. On the contrary their finds will have about them a clarity and even hardness, and a detailed complexity—in short just those characteristics of true discoveries, those characteristics which the intellectual rightly demands and the emotional can hardly ever supply. This line of advance calls however for skill. An accurate technique is needed if accurate results are to follow. It is here that the Christian Churches will have to learn from India. It should not be too great an effort of condescension on their part. After all, in order to be up to date they, prematurely, jettisoned miracles, theology, and finally the whole essence of religion, the conviction that the spiritual world is the ultimate real and this only a significant shadow. Now in order to get back on the rails and to have a true faith, praxis, life and message they should not shrink from accepting the assistance of the wide and subtle metaphysic and the practical psychophysiological technique which Vedanta provides.

# *Idolatry*

## Aldous Huxley

EDUCATED PERSONS do not run much risk of succumbing to the more primitive forms of idolatry. They find it fairly easy to resist the temptation to believe that lumps of matter are charged with magical power, or that certain symbols and images are the very forms of spiritual entities and, as such, must be worshipped or propitiated. True, a great deal of fetishistic superstition survives even in these days of universal compulsory education. But though it survives, it is not regarded as respectable; it is not accorded any kind of official recognition or philosophical sanction. Like alcohol and prostitution, the primitive forms of idolatry are tolerated, but not approved. Their place in the accredited hierarchy of spiritual values is extremely low.

Very different is the case with the developed and civilized forms of idolatry. These have achieved, not merely survival, but the highest respectability. The pastors and masters of the contemporary world are never tired of recommending these forms of idolatry. And not content with recommending the higher idolatry, many philosophers and many even of the modern world's religious leaders go out of their way to identify it with true belief and the worship of God.

This is a deplorable state of affairs, but not at all a surprising one. For, while it diminishes the risk of succumbing to primitive idolatry, education (at any rate of the kind now generally current) has a tendency to make the higher idolatry seem more attractive. The higher idolatry may be defined as the belief in, and worship of, human creation as though it were God. On its moral no less than on its intellectual side, current education is strictly humanistic and anti-transcendental. It discourages fetishism and primitive idolatry; but equally it discourages any preoccupation with spiritual

427

Reality. Consequently, it is only to be expected that those who have been most thoroughly subjected to the educational process should be the most ardent exponents of the theory and practice of the higher idolatry. In academic circles, mystics are almost as rare as fetishists; but the enthusiastic devotees of some form of political or social idealism are as common as blackberries. Significantly enough, I have observed, when making use of university libraries, that books on spiritual religion were taken out much less frequently than in public libraries, frequented by persons who had not had the advantages, and the disadvantages, of advanced education.

The many kinds of higher idolatry may be classified under three main headings, technological, political and moral. Technological idolatry is the most ingenuous and primitive of the three; for its devotees, like those of the lower idolatry, believe that their redemption and liberation depend upon material objects, namely machines and gadgets. Technological idolatry is the religion whose doctrines are explicitly or implicitly promulgated in the advertising pages of newspapers and magazines—the source from which millions of men, women and children in the capitalist countries now derive their philosophy of life. In Soviet Russia, during the years of its industrialization, technological idolatry was promoted almost to the rank of a state religion. More recently, the coming of war has greatly stimulated the cult in all the belligerent countries. Military success depends very largely on machines. Because this is so, machines tend to be credited with the power of bringing success in every sphere of activity, of solving all problems, social and personal as well as military and technical. So whole-hearted is the faith in technological idols that it is very hard to discover, in the popular thought of our time, any trace of the ancient and profoundly realistic doctrine of Hubris and Nemesis. To the Greeks, Hubris meant any kind of overweening and excess. When men or societies went too far, either in dominating other men and societies, or in exploiting the resources of nature to their own advantage, this overweening exhibition of pride had to be paid for. In a word, Hubris invited Nemesis. The idea is expressed very clearly and beautifully in "The Persians" of

Aeschylus. Xerxes is represented as displaying inordinate Hubris, not only by trying to conquer his neighbors by force of arms, but also by trying to bend nature to his will more than it is right for mortal man to do. For Aeschylus, Xerxes' bridging of the Hellespont is an act as full of Hubris as the invasion of Greece, and no less deserving of punishment at the hand of Nemesis. Today, our simple-hearted technological idolaters seem to imagine that they can have all the advantages of an immensely elaborate industrial civilization without having to pay for them.

Only a little less ingenuous are the political idolaters. For the worship of tangible material objects, these have substituted the worship of social and economic organizations. Impose the right kind of organizations on human beings, and all their problems, from sin and unhappiness to sewage disposal and war, will be automatically solved. Once more we look almost in vain for a trace of that ancient wisdom which finds so memorable an expression in the "Tao Te Ching"— the wisdom which recognizes (how realistically!) that organizations and laws are likely to do very little good where the organizers and law-makers on the one hand, the organized and law-obeyers on the other, are personally out of touch with Tao, the Way, the ultimate Reality behind phenomena.

It is the great merit of the moral idolaters that they clearly recognize the need of individual reformation as a necessary prerequisite and condition of social reformation. They know that machines and organizations are instruments which may be used well or badly according as the users are personally better or worse. For the technological and political idolaters, the question of personal morality is secondary. In some not too distant future—so runs their creed—machines and organizations will be so perfect that human beings will also be perfect, because it will be impossible for them to be otherwise. Meanwhile, it is not necessary to bother too much about personal morality. All that is required is enough industry, patience and ingenuity to go on producing more and better gadgets, and enough of these same virtues, along with a sufficiency of courage and ruthlessness, to work out suitable social and economic organizations and to impose them, by means of war or revolution, on the rest of the human race—

entirely, of course, for the human race's benefit. The moral idolaters know very well that things are not quite so simple as this, and that, among the conditions of social reform, personal reform must take one of the first places. Their mistake is to worship their own ethical ideals instead of worshipping God, to treat the acquisition of virtue as an end in itself and not as a means—the necessary and indispensable condition of the unitive knowledge of God.

"Fanaticism is idolatry." (I am quoting from a most remarkable letter written by Thomas Arnold in 1836 to his old pupil and biographer-to-be, A. P. Stanley.) "Fanaticism is idolatry; and it has the moral evil of idolatry in it; that is, a fanatic worships something which is the creation of his own desires, and thus even his self-devotion in support of it is only an apparent self-devotion; for in fact it is making the parts of his nature or his mind, which he least values, offer sacrifice to that which he most values. The moral fault, as it appears to me, is the idolatry—the setting up of some idea which is most kindred to our own minds, and the putting it in the place of Christ, who alone cannot be made an idol and inspire idolatry, because He combines all ideas of perfection, and exhibits them in their just harmony and combination. Now, in my own mind, by its natural tendency—that is, taking my mind at its best—truth and justice would be the idols I should follow; and they would be idols, for they would not supply *all* the food which the mind wants, and whilst worshipping them, reverence and humility and tenderness might very likely be forgotten. But Christ Himself includes at once truth and justice and all these other qualities too. . . . Narrowmindedness tends to wickedness, because it does not extend its watchfulness to every part of our moral nature and the neglect fosters the growth of wickedness in the parts so neglected."

As a piece of psychological analysis this is admirable, so far as it goes. But it does not go quite far enough; for it omits all consideration of what has been called grace. Grace is that which is given when, and to the extent to which, a human being gives up his own self-will and abandons himself, moment by moment, to the will of God. By grace our emptiness is fulfilled, our weakness reinforced, our depravity transformed. There are, of course, pseudo-graces as well as real graces—the accessions of strength, for example, that follow self-devotion to some form of political or moral idolatry. To distinguish between the true grace and the false is often difficult; but as time and circumstances reveal the full extent of their consequences on the personality as a whole, discrimination becomes possible even to observers having no special gifts of insight. Where the grace is genuinely "supernatural," an amelioration in one aspect of personality is not paid for by atrophy or deterioration in another. Virtue is achieved without having to be paid for by the hardness, fanaticism, uncharitableness and spiritual pride, which are the ordinary consequences of a course of stoical self-improvement by means of personal effort, either unassisted or reinforced by the pseudo-graces which are given when the individual devotes himself to a cause, which is not God, but only a projection of one of his own favourite ideas. The idolatrous worship of ethical values in and for themselves defeats its own object—and defeats it not only because, as Arnold rightly insists, there is a lack of all-round watchfulness, but also and above all because even the highest form of moral idolatry is God-eclipsing, a positive guarantee that the idolater shall fail to achieve unitive knowledge of Reality.

# *Is There Progress?*

## GERALD HEARD

*Werd als ein Kind, werd taub und blind*
*Dein eignes Icht muss werden Nicht*
*All Icht, all Nicht treib ferne nur*
*Lass Statt, Lass Zeit, auch Bild lass weit*
*Geh ohne Weg den Schmalen Steg*
*So Kommst du auf der Wueste Spur.*
*O Seele mein, aus Gott geh ein*
*Sink als ein Icht in Goddes Nicht*
*Sink in die ungegrundete Fluth*
*Flieh ich von Dir, Du Kommst zu mir.*
*Verlass ich mich, So find ich Dich*
*O ueberwesentliches Gut!*

A child become, be deaf, blind, dumb
Thy inmost I must wholly die
All Aye All Nay but drive away
Leave Time, leave Place, e'en Thought efface
Thy way pursue with ne'er a clue
So coms't thou on the Trackless Trace.
O Soul of mine, through God untwine
Sink as "I so" in Godhead's "No,"
Sink in the never-sounded Flood!
Fly I from Thee, Thou coms't to me:
Forsake I me so find I Thee,
O inconceivable Good!

THE ABOVE VERSE, here transliterated into English, was written probably in the thirteenth century somewhere in Western Germany. Perhaps today the consideration of these lines,
of their date and place of origin (Statt and Zeit) is as striking
a refutation as we could find of our still stubborn illusion of

Progress. It dies hard, this mistaken belief that just by living we become wise, that "The Thoughts of men are widened by the circling of the suns." True, we have all been taught

> "*It is not growing like a tree*
> *In bulk doth make man better be,*"

but during the nineteenth century Western man increasingly felt that if only he had more goods he himself would become better. That men who lacked machines could be really moral began to be doubted. That rapid advances in Physics and Economics might actually render people proportionately more ignorant of Psychology, of their own natures and vital values, such a notion was considered too absurd, too reactionary, too defeatist to need refutation. Yet such is the conclusion which the history of the last twenty-five years has forced on us. The first part of the demonstration was purely shocking. We have had rubbed into us the fact that knowledge of means without an equal knowledge of ends leads simply to destruction accelerated by mechanism. If our possible experience stopped there we should indeed feel rightly hopeless. Here is our age which has patiently and ingeniously built up this vast tower, higher and stronger than that of Babel, to raise us forever above the flood and storm of material accident. Here are we, more cursed and stupid than Babel's builders, not merely, in a panic of hopeless misunderstanding, abandoning our prodigious labour, but turning on each other with all our gear and instruments in a frenzy of mutual homicide. There is however a second part to this demonstration. It is not as spectacular, but it is as hopeful as the first part is despairing. The essence of this discovery lies in the fact that in the past there have been epochs when men may have been physically ignorant but were psychically highly informed. Although (perhaps, indeed, because) they were without a distracting knowledge of means, they could see clearly their Ends. A few years ago a couple of Italian archaeologists, anxious to return with artistic spoil from Thibet, entered that land of fossilized mahayana Buddhism. One of them had taken the trouble to learn some Sanskrit. He notes in his diary with naif surprise that the first lama on whom he tried his knowledge, although the old man had seemed stupid and was obviously dirty and poor, suddenly dropped the mask and talked to him "the subtlest metaphysics."

Those who have suggested that in a return to a simpler, more intentional, less distracted way of living we might rebalance our life have failed to find general support for two reasons. In the first place until the present international breakdown it was impossible for the ordinary man to believe that mere increase of technical skills would not cure his discontents. On this were agreed capitalist and communist, materialist and social service Christian. In the second place until the psychological knowledge which the Past possessed came to light, there could be no assurance that even if we did simplify our life and copy an earlier model we should acquire a new insight and power. We can face the truth about our own condition because we know there is a way out. Instead of the crude idea of inevitable material progress leading us to a worldly Utopia we are coming to a true view of human history. We are now beginning to see that whenever men wish, with sufficient singleness of heart, they can come upon the "wuste spur"; when they seek, with a determination to give everything, they find.

No doubt the Rhineland, seven centuries ago, would have seemed technically backward compared with all the skills and machines which proliferated there until yesterday—when those trees of crooked knowledge bore their true fruit. Yet in the thirteenth century those Germans knew more about man's nature and its needs than any who speak in Germany today. So though we must take a grave view of our present pass we need not be hopeless. For the ruin of our strength may mean the recovery of our sanity, the self-destruction of our means permit the re-emergence into the vision of mankind of Ends worthy of a free man's service and worship and the disappearance of false knowledge lead to the rediscovery of the true. Whatever the outcome two facts are clear. The Germany which the world dreads is a phase: underneath, like a spring in the desert, flows that universal song of unity with the whole—a stanza of which heads these paragraphs. And whether it rise again to the surface in our time or no, here under our own feet, the same current of life Eternal flows. Whatever the nations do, however mankind may choose, each one of us can in himself dig down, find the living stream and know it "springing in himself to Life Eternal."

# God in Everything

## SWAMI PRABHAVANANDA

*"Through many a long life*
*His discrimination ripens:*
*He makes Me his refuge,*
*Knows that Brahman is all.*
*How rare are such great ones."*

So SAYS Sri Krishna in the Bhagavad Gita. To know that
"Brahman is all" is the last word of religion. After many
struggles, "through many a long life," when a man takes his
utter refuge in God, when he is completely freed from ego,
he realizes this ultimate truth and sees God in everything.

*"His heart is with Brahman,*
*His eye in all things*
*Sees only Brahman*
*Equally present,*
*Knows his own Atman*
*In every creature,*
*And all creation*
*Within that Atman."*

How does a man become illumined? Where does he realize
God and His presence? First he must learn to look within,
and learn to see the Infinite Presence within his own Atman; for only when he learns to see God and the whole of
creation within himself is he able to see that one Infinite
God equally and infinitely present everywhere in all creatures and in the whole of creation.

*"That Yogi sees me in all things,*
*And all things within me."*

> *"Absorbed in Brahman*
> *He overcomes the world even here,*
> *Alive in the world."*

This is the point we should note. An illumined soul who is absorbed in the consciousness of God and sees His Infinite Presence in everything "overcomes the world." What is our experience of the world? We experience birth and death, happiness and misery. We experience the shifting, changing world. The illumined soul, on the other hand, overcomes the world of our experience, by realizing behind the appearances of life and death, of happiness and misery, the one Unchangeable Reality, the Immortal God, the Blissful Atman.

"His mind is dead to the touch of the external." Just as the dream experience becomes dead to us as we wake up, and no longer affects us, similarly as we become illumined and see the Unchangeable Reality behind the appearances, the appearances no longer affect us. We experience the immortal, blissful consciousness.

"God in everything" is the transcendental experience of an illumined seer. To say merely, "God is all," and continue living in the world attached to the shadows and appearances, remaining subject to birth and death, to happiness and misery, does not help us to attain God. It is a matter of experience when the world-appearance no longer has the power to throw a man off his balance. He becomes established in the consciousness of God, and finds satisfaction and delight in Him.

And that is the ideal to be realized. In our present state of so-called normal consciousness, God remains hidden behind the world-appearance. The basis, the background of this appearance, however, is God. To quote Shankara: "No matter what a deluded man may think he is perceiving, he is really seeing Brahman and nothing else but Brahman. He sees mother-of-pearl and imagines that it is silver. He sees Brahman and imagines that It is the universe."

Philosophers and theologians have argued for ages about the creation of the universe. They have tried to prove the existence of a Creator, an extra-cosmic, intelligent Being who is the cause of this universe. But before we do this we should first inquire into the nature of the universe. For example, a man sees a rope lying on the ground before him, and thinks it is a snake. Furthermore, he even tries to find out who created the snake. Should he not first find out whether it really is a snake and not something else?

In the same way, before we try to find out the cause of this universe of our perception we should first inquire into its nature and our own perception of it. Though in all our practical behavior we take for granted the empirical reality of the universe, there is, in every intelligent human being, always a sense that things are not what they seem, that there is something more, something deeper, something behind the appearance which our senses cannot grasp.

The scientist who inquires into the nature of this universe does not rely solely upon his observations of sense. He invents instruments, the telescope, microscope, etc., in order that he may see behind and beyond the vision of the naked eye. And the seer, who inquires after the Ultimate Reality, sees It behind the appearance of things. To the scientist as well as to the seer the world-appearance becomes unreal in the sense that it is not what it appears to be. Although the scientist realizes that the appearance of matter is not really matter but energy, intelligence—this energy, this intelligence, remains unknown to him, whereas to the seer the universe of mind and matter becomes dissolved in Brahman. To him God becomes a fact, known and knowable, through transcendental experience.

What then is the cause of this world-appearance? What causes a man to see a snake instead of a rope? Faulty vision. This world-appearance is caused by ignorance. Therefore, the questions why and how God created this world, why there is evil in God's creation, cannot arise.

In order that we may arrive at any truth we must base our reasoning upon experience; we must take into account all the facts of our experience. We know that there are many varied experiences with lesser or greater degrees of reality. For instance, I have the dream experience. As long as I am dreaming, I cannot deny the experience as unreal. Yet we cannot base any philosophy or science solely upon the basis of dream-experiences. We have varied experiences in different states of consciousness. As we wake from the dream, the experience which seemed so real, vanishes; the dream-experience no longer touches our life.

The waking consciousness is a greater reality to us. In that state we see and experience this universe. We experience the pairs of opposites—pleasure and pain, birth and death, etc. If, however, we try to base our philosophy or science solely upon the reality of this experience, we shall never arrive at the whole truth. Beyond all these there is the transcendental experience which contains the greatest reality, inasmuch as it is abiding. It remains forever in our consciousness and when once we are awakened to the Reality, all sorrow and misery melt away into the everlasting peace of God.

As in relation to the waking consciousness the dream-experience becomes unreal, so in relation to the transcendental experience of the illumined seers, the experience of our waking consciousness becomes unreal. The seer, the prophet, the incarnate God, tell us to wake up from this long dream of ignorance, and not to remain forever subject to the woes and tribulations of the world. But to most people the call goes unheeded.

In Hindu mythology there is a story of Indra, king of the gods, who once became a pig and lived very happily in his sty with his family. Missing their king, the gods came down from heaven and said: "O Indra, you are king of all the gods, why do you wallow in this mire?" And Indra replied: "Leave me alone. I am quite happy here. Why should I care for gods and heaven when I have my family?" Being at their wits' end, the gods finally slew Indra's sow and all the little pigs; seeing them all lying dead, Indra began to wail and mourn. Whereupon the gods ripped open the pig-body of their king and Indra came out, and laughed at the hideous dream he had had. He wondered how he ever could have been happy in that pig-life, even to the point of wanting the whole world to share in it!

Man in his ignorance clings to his limited consciousness and the surface life of his wakeful state. Yet he is not exactly satisfied, for there is always a sense of lack and of unfulfilled desires as long as he remains within the boundary of his limited consciousness. When his discrimination ripens he begins to realize the vanity and emptiness of this prolonged dream—the so-called normal consciousness—and there arises in him a longing for God, for the abiding Reality behind the changing phenomena of life. This longing has to be intensified. Sri Ramakrishna used to give the illustration: a disciple went to a teacher and asked to be taught the knowledge of God. The teacher remained silent. When the disciple had repeated his request many times, the teacher took him to a river, and suddenly taking hold of him, held his head under water for a long time. When he let go he asked him how he had felt while under the water. As soon as the disciple could speak he said, "O for a breath of air!" Then the teacher said, "When you can long for God as intensely as you longed for air, you will find Him."

Intense longing for God is one of the fundamental conditions for the vision of the Reality, and when God becomes revealed, the world-appearance disappears. God alone is. You may dream that a tiger is chasing you, but as soon as the dream breaks, where is the tiger? Both it and your fear have disappeared. To the illumined seer the dream has broken, and with his inner awakening the world also has disappeared. There remains the Blissful Immortal Consciousness. He has overcome the world and its relative existence. He is established in Brahman. True, he comes back and again experiences this manifold universe, but his vision has changed, his consciousness has expanded. He never loses sight of the Reality.

Where lies the difference between the lower animals and man? The main difference is in the degree of consciousness. A dog, for instance, lives in the same world, but because of his limited consciousness is cut off from the world of man. A dog cannot enjoy the beauty and fragrance of a flower as a man does, because his consciousness is limited. In man there is an expansion of consciousness, and in an illumined soul the consciousness has expanded to the infinite consciousness of God. He lives in the same world as other beings, but his experience of the world is totally different from others. He sees the manifold universe and at the same time experiences the presence of God in every being and thing in the universe.

There is a saying in India, "Make the end the means also." That is to say, learn to see God existing behind the veil of appearances. Even while we are living in ignorance we must learn to see, or at least try to see the Reality. It is like being in a dark room; you know your beloved is there also, but you don't see him. You seem to imagine he is there because you cannot see him, and yet it is more than imagination. In the same way we are told by the Illumined seers who have seen God that He is present everywhere, and then you try to *imagine* His presence, or rather you *seem to imagine* His presence. To quote Swami Vivekananda's words: "Seek not God but see Him."

Religion is a de-hypnotising process. We are hypnotised into the belief and imagination that this world-appearance is real, that we are limited, finite beings. We have to de-hypnotise ourselves, and wake up to the Reality and know that God dwells in the hearts of all beings and things.

The spiritual disciplines for this de-hypnotisation are to cultivate the thought that God is real, and to constantly and consciously live and move and have our being in Him.

We must try to realize the vanity of this world by shutting ourselves off from all its appearances, and become absorbed in the consciousness of God. In other words, we must first close our eyes and realize God within our own self, then shall we open our eyes and see Him in everything.

# The Future of Mankind's Religion

## GERALD HEARD

IF ONE THING can be discerned through the smoke of the present conflagration it is that the world order, which set the mechanic convictions of the West in the forefront of civilization, will have to be scrapped. Even if fragments survive, the condition of the house of Western man's spirit will be such that even those parts which endure will have to be pulled down. What the flames will not have devoured will be calcined. This disaster may then be the way in which the Divine Power clears the stage for another and more modern structure. Western man was long warned that he was building a house which was not fireproof. He would not attend. What was even more serious was that the East and the Near East—as Europeans call that Slavic and Turanian belt of peoples that lies between Asia and Europe proper—though they should have known that this structure was only outwardly impressive, was indeed a fire-trap should it ever become ignited, became so impressed with its size that they were willing to imitate it and, to do so, to throw aside all their traditional wisdoms.

It is therefore of more than academic interest to inquire what will be the main lines of the practical philosophy which will make the new system in which mankind may find a shelter and a workshop. The first thing that is obvious is that the Indian contribution will be fundamental. . . . Scholarship has now proved as a fact of literature that the specific concepts which gave to Western religion its deepest insights and its most effective techniques were all imported from the Indian areas. In his latest book, "The Flowering of Mysticism," Dr. Rufus Jones has traced quite clearly the sources, coming through from Persia via Baghdad, Alexandria, Cordova, Padua and thence by Paris onto the Rhine, which influenced and formed the thought and practice of the first great schools of Western mysticism. Even before then it is clear that the Arabian monk, perhaps called Bar Sudali, using the pseudonym Dionysius the Areopagite, had spread a doctrine which was far more Vedantic than "Synoptic." The writer of this note was suddenly surprised the other day in reading "The Mystical Theology" of that author to find it stated: "For we must be in this work as it were men making an image of his naked unbegun nature, the which though it be within all creatures is congealed as it were in a cumbrous clog . . . we must pare (it) away." Here in quaint language is the doctrine of the Atman which is Brahman residing, hidden at the center of every man and to be realized by discarding of the obvious and the outer, the expressed and the expressible until the Dark Silence is reached. Further this author adds that this is to be done "in a manner that is unknown how unto all, but only to those who do it, and even to those who have learnt to do it they only know of the result, of the full nature of the experience at the moment that they experience it." In other words the high and pure state of consciousness and of union cannot be described by even those who have had it, in the words and the thoughts which are all they can use when they come back to us from that tremendous experience.

But apart from the establishment of the literary debt which the East owes to the West there is the deeper issue as to the form which a world religion might now take and the part that India might play in that new system to embrace mankind. The differences that it is common to say must exist between East and West are not geographical, we now know. They are partly temporal or chronological and partly psychological or temperamental. A medieval scholar would not have found Indian religion, in any of its forms, ridiculous. What he would have said against a number of them was that they were heretical. Indeed it seems that if there had been no Inquisition and the enforcement of a "party-line" in religion, Europe at the close of the middle ages would have been very like India, a land of many cults, theories, practices and hypostasies of the Godhead. If all the Christian heresies alone had been allowed to grow—as Christ evidently recommended —"till the harvest," Western religion would have been as rich and complex as India's, showing the full gamut of religious feeling from the austerity of Pali Buddhism to the luxuriousness of the Cult of the Mother in its least restrained developments. Times, however, change and with the change in time comes the change in expression. A child can be unself-conscious as an adult cannot be and the direct child mind does not find certain expressions and devotions yielding the impression which such things give to the adult, especially if the adult has been brought up in a way of life and morals much influenced by the effects of the puritan revolution. Nietzsche divided religion into the Apollonian and the Dionysian—the religion of repressed and the religion of expressed feeling. The West is convinced that the latter is the lower and the earlier. The West may not be right. Much of the non-committal attitude that we find common in the West toward the Holy may be accounted for by two things, neither of which are very superior conditions of soul. The one is that the ordinary man feels so little that he has nothing to express and as he feels little he believes, in his ignorance, that no one can feel more than he can. He does not believe very much in any spiritual reality and so when he finds someone taking the fact of God with the seriousness and the interest that such a fact, were it true, would surely deserve, he feels that so to behave is to be unbalanced or hypocritical. The other cause of the ordinary man's lack of expression in religion is what has been called the Tabu on Tenderness. Men are ashamed to say what they feel. Such a suppression is not we now believe very good for them, and of course it is a form of hypocrisy. Yet though we are likely to see a religion of much fuller expression appear when once more religion as a fact of life is brought back into our conduct, yet it is not necessary that the new forms should preserve exactly the old patterns. If, as there is more than a hope, there is about to arise a religion for mankind, there seems reason to suppose that it will follow the course of development taken by religion when the cult of the small nation of the Jews combined with the thought of the widely ranging Greeks and gave rise to the philosophy and practice, the ritual and ethics which we call the Christian religion. The religion of mankind will be syncretistic. Some Sankara of our age or of the oncoming generations will rear a philosophy and deduce a practice which drawing upon the past will give a contemporary answer and conduct to the present, for its needs and its activities. It is interesting to speculate what in broadest outline that cosmology or theology would be and what its deduced ethic. The most basic thing (at least so it seems to one inquirer) would be the working into a world-embracing picture of the doctrine of the Avatar—the line of Incarnations which eon by eon appear and dipping into the Time-process make it possible for mankind to "mutate," to take a step further up the ramp of ascent, from ignorance to enlightenment. So the witness of the various higher religions would be brought not into competing rivalry but into harmony. The next great postulate would, it seems, be the doctrine of God Personal-and-Impersonal, that only in such a polar concept can the fullness of man's spiritual experience be expressed. The third would be perhaps the doctrine of the evolution of the soul, that this life is only a cross-section in a far larger experience. The ethic which such a doctrine of Godhead, of Incarnation and of the nature of the soul would yield would seem to be one which by the fact that it stressed the *potential* divinity of all men would teach a respect for life and a reverence for the soul which would be one of the firmest sanctions for good living. It is increasingly clear that no sanction can be found for things of time unless the fulcrum of that sanction is placed outside time, in the timeless, the eternal. We may even speculate and ask whether such a doctrine and practice would not give us a form of society which might be called organic in distinction from the form which we have today and which may be called atomistic. For if men recover this deep reverence for life then they need not overlook the matter of inequality. Because a dog is not my equal—he is my superior in power of scent—that does not mean that I wish to exploit him or that he cannot trust me. When we see all mankind as parts of the divine body then and then only will all, even the humblest, have the one true guaranty of their rights, the right to be protected and to be helped develop to the highest. Where there is that hope shared by all there is no hardship in even the lowliest office, there is no pride in the highest. Whatever be the form this religion of the future takes, some such foundation, it seems clear, will underlie it.

# The Yellow Mustard

## ALDOUS HUXLEY

CABINED beneath low vaults of cloud,
　　Sultry and still, the fields do lie,
Like one wrapt living in his shroud,
　　Who stifles silently.

Stripped of all beauty not their own—
　　The gulfs of shade, the golden bloom—
Grey mountain-heaps of slag and stone
　　Wall in the silent tomb.

I, through this emblem of a mind
　　Dark with repinings, slowly went,
Its captive, and myself confined
　　In like discouragement.

When, at a winding of the way,
　　A sudden glory met my eye,
As though a single, conquering ray
　　Had rent the cloudy sky

And touched, transfiguringly bright
　　In that dull plain, one luminous field;
And there the miracle of light
　　Lay goldenly revealed.

And yet the reasons for despair
　　Hung dark, without one rift of blue;
No loophole to the living air
　　Had let the glory through.

In their own soil those acres found
　　The sunlight of a flowering weed;
For still there sleeps in every ground
　　Some grain of mustard seed.

# The Wishing Tree

## CHRISTOPHER ISHERWOOD

ONE AFTERNOON, when the children are tired of running around the garden and have gathered for a moment on the lawn, their uncle tells them the story of the Kalpataru Tree.

The Kalpataru, he explains, is a magic tree. If you speak to it and tell it a wish; or if you lie down under it and think, or even dream, a wish; then that wish will be granted. The children are half skeptical, half impressed. Truly—it'll give you anything you ask for? *Anything?* Yes, the uncle assures them solemnly: anything in the world. The audience grins and whistles with amazement. Then someone wants to know: what does it look like?

The uncle, pleased at the success of his story-telling, casts his eye around the garden and points, almost at random: "That's one of them, over there."

But this is too much of a good thing. The children are mistrustful, now. They look quickly around at their uncle's face, and see in it that all-too-familiar expression which children learn to detect in the faces of grown-ups. "He's just fooling us!" they exclaim, indignantly. And they scatter again to their play.

However, children do not forget so easily. Each single one of them, down to the youngest, has privately resolved to talk to the Kalpataru Tree at the first opportunity. They have been trained by their parents to believe in wishing. They wish when they see the new moon; or when they get the wish-bone of a chicken. They wish at Christmas, and just before their birthdays. They know, by experience, that some of these wishes come true. Maybe the tree is a magic tree, maybe it isn't—but, anyhow, what can you lose?

The tree which the uncle pointed out to his nephews and nieces is tall and beautiful, with big feathery branches like the wings of huge birds. It looks somehow queer and exotic among the sturdy familiar trees of that northern climate. There is a vague family tradition that it was planted years ago by a grandfather who had travelled in the Orient. What nobody, including the uncle, suspects is that this tree really *is* a Kalpataru Tree—one of the very few in the whole country.

The Kalpataru listens attentively to the children's wishes— its leaves can catch even the faintest whisper—and, in due time, it grants them all. Most of the wishes are very unwise— many of them end in indigestion or tears—but the wishing-tree fulfills them, just the same: it is not interested in giving good advice.

Years pass. The children are all men and women, now. They have long since forgotten the Kalpataru Tree, and the wishes they told it—indeed, it is part of the tree's magic to make them forget. Only—and this is the terrible thing about the Kalpataru magic—the gifts which it gave the children were not really gifts, but only like the links of a chain—each wish was linked to another wish, and so on, and on. The older the children grow, the more they wish: it seems as if they could never wish enough. At first, the aim of their lives was to get their wishes granted: but, later on, it is just the opposite—their whole effort is to find wishes which will be very hard, or even impossible, to fulfill. Of course, the Kalpataru Tree can grant any wish in the world—but they have forgotten it, and the garden where it stands. All that remains is the fever it has kindled in them by the granting of that first, childish wish.

You might suppose that these unlucky children, as they became adults, would be regarded as lunatics, with horror or pity, by their fellow human beings. But more people have, in their childhood, wished at the Kalpataru Tree than is generally supposed. The kind of madness from which the children are suffering is so common that nearly everybody has a streak of it in his or her nature—so it is regarded as perfectly right and proper. "You want to watch those kids," older people say of them, approvingly: "They've got plenty of ambition. Yes, sir—they're going places." And these elders, in their friendly desire to see this ambition rewarded, are always suggesting to the children new things to wish for. The children listen to them attentively and respectfully, believing that here must be the best guides to the right conduct of one's life.

Thanks to these helpful elders, they know exactly what are the things one must wish for in this world. They no longer have to ask themselves such childish questions as: "Do I honestly want this?" "Do I really desire that?" For the wisdom of past generations has forever decided what is, and what is not, desirable, and enjoyable, and worthwhile. Just obey the rules of the world's wishing-game, and you need never bother about your feelings. As long as you wish for the right things, you may be quite sure you really want them, no matter what disturbing doubts may trouble you from time to time. Above all, you must wish continually for money and power—more and more money, and more and more power—because, without these two basic wishes, the whole game of wishing becomes impossible—not only for yourself, but for others as well. By not wishing, you are actually spoiling their game—and that, everybody agrees, is not merely selfish, but dangerous and criminal too.

And so the men and women who were shown the Kalpataru Tree in the garden of their childhood, grow old and sick, and come near to their end. Then, perhaps, at last, very dimly, they begin to remember something about the Kalpataru, and the garden, and how all this madness of wishing began. But this remembering is very confused. The furthest that most of them go is to say to themselves: "Perhaps I ought to have asked it for something different." Then they rack their poor old brains to think what that wish, which would have solved every problem and satisfied every innermost need, could possibly have been. And there are many who imagine they have found the answer when they exclaim: "All my other wishes were mistaken. Now I wish the wish to end all wishes. I wish for death."

But, in that garden, long ago, there was one child whose experience was different from that of all the others. For, when he had crept out of the house at night, and stood alone, looking up into the branches of the tree, the real nature of the Kalpataru was suddenly revealed to him. For him, the

Kalpataru was not the pretty magic tree of his uncle's story—
it did not exist to grant the stupid wishes of children—it was
unspeakably terrible and grand. It was his father and his
mother. Its roots held the world together, and its branches
reached behind the stars. Before the beginning, it had been—
and it would be, always.

Wherever that child went, as a boy, as a youth, and as a
man, he never forgot the Kalpataru Tree. He carried the
secret knowledge of it in his heart. He was wise in its wisdom
and strong in its strength: its magic never harmed him. Nobody ever heard him say, "I wish," or "I want"—and, for this
reason, he was not very highly thought of in the world. As
for his brothers and sisters, they sometimes referred to him,
rather apologetically, as "a bit of a saint," by which they
meant that he was a trifle crazy.

But the boy himself did not feel that he had to apologize,
or explain anything. He knew the secret of the Kalpataru,
and that was all he needed to know. For, even as an old man,
his heart was still the heart of that little child who stood
breathless in the moonlight beneath the great tree, and
thrilled with such wonder and awe and love that he utterly
forgot to speak his wish.

# *Lines*

## ALDOUS HUXLEY

SURE, there are groves, there are gardens; but the cactus
Is never far, the sands are never far,
Even from the cedars and the nightingales,
Even from the marble fauns, the little gazebos,
Where, all in breathing silence, a girl's breasts
Are captive doves, and a ripeness as of grapes
Her nipples—never far; for suddenly
A hot wind blows and, frantic on the wind,
Dust and more dust, swarm on swarm of dust,
Peoples your summer night with the illusion
Of living wings and joy. But all the dance
Is only of powdered flint; and, feel! the doves
Are dead within your hands, and those small grapes
Withered up to oak galls, and the nightingales
Choked in mid song, the cedars brown, the lawns
Savage with stones and aloes, while the wind
Rattles among the leaves, and the June darkness
Creeps, as it were, with the horny stealth of lice.

But always, through the frenzy of the dust,
Always, above that roaring mindlessness,
That headlong absence of a goal, eclipsed
But still unfailing, the familiar Wain
Circles around a point of steady fire.

# THE CONTRIBUTORS

*Adbhutananda, Swami:* direct disciple of Sri Ramakrishna, known as Latu.

*Chaitanya, Sri:* fifteenth-century Indian saint.

*Corbin, Amiya:* former church secretary of the Vedanta Society of Southern California and since 1952 the Countess of Sandwich.

*Ferrando, Guido:* professor of Italian literature and authority on Dante.

*Fitts, George:* since 1958, Swami Krishnananda of the Ramakrishna Order of India.

*Heard, Gerald:* writer and lecturer.

*Hunter, Allan:* pastor of the Mount Hollywood Congregational Church.

*Huxley, Aldous:* novelist and essayist on the perennial philosophy.

*Isherwood, Christopher:* novelist and co-translator of Vedantic classics.

*Manchester, Frederick:* professor of English literature, formerly at the University of Wisconsin.

*Prabhavananda, Swami:* head of the Vedanta Society of Southern California.

*Shivananda, Swami:* direct disciple of Sri Ramakrishna and second president of the Ramakrishna Order.

*van Druten, John:* playwright and novelist, died in 1957.

*Vivekananda, Swami:* leader with Swami Brahmananda of Sri Ramakrishna's direct disciples and first preacher of Vedanta in America.

*Wood, Christopher:* English writer living in Los Angeles.

*Yatiswarananda, Swami:* senior swami of the Ramakrishna Order, who spent some fifteen years teaching Vedanta in Europe and America.